W9-BLU-961

RULES
FOR
WRITERS
A Brief Handbook

Process

Design

Clarity

Grammar

Punctuation

Mechanics

Argument

Research

Basics

RULES FOR WRITERS
A Brief Handbook

FOURTH EDITION

Diana Hacker

Bedford/St. Martin's
Boston • New York

For Bedford/St. Martin's
Developmental Editor: Michelle McSweeney
Production Editor: Anne Noonan
Production Supervisor: Cheryl Mamaril
Marketing Manager: Karen Melton
Assistant Production Editor: Coleen O'Hanley
Editorial Assistant: Jeannine Thibodeau
Copyeditor: Barbara G. Flanagan
Text Design: Claire Seng-Niemoeller
Cover Design: Hannus Design Associates
Composition: York Graphic Services, Inc.
Printing and Binding: RR Donnelley & Sons Company

President: Charles H. Christensen
Editorial Director: Joan E. Feinberg
Director of Editing, Design, and Production: Marcia Cohen
Managing Editor: Elizabeth M. Schaaf

Library of Congress Catalog Card Number: 99–61996

Manufactured in the United States of America.

4   3   2   1   0
f   e   d   c

For information, write: Bedford/St. Martin's, 75 Arlington Street, Boston, MA 02116 (617) 399-4000

ISBN: 0–312–24142–9

Acknowledgments

Nelson W. Aldrich, Jr., from *Old Money: The Mythology of America's Upper Class.* Copyright © 1988 by Nelson W. Aldrich, Jr. Reprinted by permission of Alfred A. Knopf, Inc.

Acknowledgments and copyrights are continued at the back of the book on page 530, which constitutes an extension of the copyright page.

Preface for Instructors

Fifteen years ago, Bedford Books published the first edition of *Rules for Writers*, a brief handbook that later evolved into the longer *Bedford Handbook*. When Chuck Christensen and Joan Feinberg proposed four years ago that we revive *Rules for Writers*, I was delighted, for the book is an old favorite of mine. It grew directly out of my classroom experience at Prince George's Community College. The brevity of *Rules for Writers* appeals to my students, and so does its price.

To keep the book brief, I have limited myself within each section to the essentials: straightforward rules backed up by concise explanations, realistic examples, and short comments on examples. In its coverage, however, the book is complete. It is a guide to the full range of conventions of grammar, punctuation, mechanics, and usage as well as to the writing process, paragraphs, document design, style, argument, and the research paper.

The fourth edition of *Rules for Writers* reflects changes—mainly technological—that have occurred in the teaching of composition in the past four years. Here are the principal features, both old and new, of this fourth edition.

Designed for quick reference

Rules for Writers is a quick reference that students can consult on their own. Several reference features help students find quick answers to their questions.

Graphic access through icons. To help today's visually oriented students find the information they need, icons, like those on the toolbars of computer programs, are keyed to each part of *Rules for Writers*. The icons appear in six places: on the cover, in the brief menu inside the front cover, in the detailed menu inside the back cover, in the table of contents, on the part openers, and on the tabs on all left-hand pages.

In most circumstances, the brief menu inside the front cover is the fastest way into the book. Designed for student use, it is as simple as possible, containing just the nine icons and sixty sections, with no subsections listed. By consulting this menu, students can usually locate the icon and the section number for the information they need. Then they can simply flip pages in search of the appropriate tab. The tabs on the left-hand pages display the icons, and those on the right-hand pages give the section numbers.

At times students may want to use other reference features of *Rules for Writers*: the detailed menu inside the back cover, the index, the Glossary of Usage, or one of the book's directories to documentation models. "How to Use This Book" (pp. xv–xx) describes these reference features and includes several tutorials that give students hands-on experience using the book.

Clear, uncluttered page design.   Because the two-color page design highlights rules and hand-edited examples, *Rules for Writers* is easy to skim for quick answers to questions. Readers who want more help will find it in concise explanations following rules and in brief comments pegged to examples.

A user-friendly index.   The index of *Rules for Writers* helps students find what they are looking for even if they don't know grammatical terminology. When facing a choice between *was* and *were*, for example, some students may not know to look up "Subject-verb agreement." To help such students, *Rules for Writers* includes index entries for "*was* versus *were*" and "*were* versus *was*." Similar user-friendly entries appear throughout the index.

Updated for the electronic age

In the four years since publication of the third edition of *Rules for Writers*, technology has had a pronounced effect — often for good, sometimes for ill — on what happens in our classrooms. The fourth edition assumes that students will be working on-line; when necessary, it cautions them about dangers lurking in the electronic world.

More coverage of online sources. Technology has transformed the entire process of research both in the library and on the rapidly changing Internet. The research section now reflects those changes, offering advice on conducting searches, previewing and evaluating both print and electronic sources, managing information (without plagiarizing), and documenting sources in the electronic age.

Fifty grammar checker boxes. New to this edition are fifty boxes that show students just what current grammar checkers can do — and what they can't do. To discover the capabilities and limits of grammar checkers, I have run a large bank of exercise sentences (many containing errors), along with some student drafts, through four grammar checker programs. The results, summarized in shaded boxes with computer icons throughout the book, show that grammar checkers can help with some but by no means all of the typical problems in a draft.

Advice on e-mail and Web pages. The section on document design now provides advice on the rhetoric and etiquette of e-mail and gives tips on designing effective Web pages.

A companion Web site. On the *Rules for Writers* Web site < http://www.bedfordstmartins.com/hacker/rules > , students and instructors will find interactive exercises, writing assignments and student essays, and links to some of the best research and writing sites on the Web. A related site by Diana Hacker, *Research and Documentation Online* < http://www.bedfordstmartins.com/hacker/resdoc > , has links to online resources in more than twenty-five disciplines, a glossary of research terms, and updated documentation guidelines for MLA, APA, *Chicago,* and CBE styles. The *Rules for Writers* Web site also links directly to *The Bedford/ St Martin's English Research Room,* which provides interactive, step-by-step tutorials on key research techniques.

Written for a variety of instructional needs

Though it is brief, *Rules for Writers* is comprehensive enough to be used in a variety of writing courses.

Expanded array of writing assignments.   *Rules for Writers* now contains seven writing assignments, each illustrated with at least one model essay. The first three assignments are based on personal experience or observation. The last four, new to this edition, are based on reading: summarizing two readings, analyzing a reading, arguing a point, and researching an issue.

These writing assignments and model essays also appear on the *Rules for Writers* Web site < http://www.bedfordstmartins .com/hacker/rules >.

Extensive help for culturally diverse students.   Not all of our students speak standard English or English as a first language. For speakers of nonstandard English, section 27 gives special help on such matters as omitted *-s* and *-ed* endings and omitted verbs; in addition, section 21 on subject-verb agreement includes charts of standard verb forms. Section 17d, on non-standard English, contains cross-references to practical advice that appears elsewhere in the book.

Three sections focus exclusively on common problems facing speakers of English as a second language. Section 29 discusses ESL problems with verbs; section 30 explains when to use the articles *a*, *an*, and *the*; and section 31 alerts ESL students to a variety of other potential trouble spots. ESL boxes throughout the book point out possible ESL problems; a quick-reference chart of these boxes appears at the back of the book.

Nine short sections on the research paper.   For easy reference, the Research Guide is broken up into nine short sections. The section on finding sources emphasizes computerized library resources and the Internet. The MLA and APA sections are up-to-date, and each documentation style is illustrated with a model research paper. The MLA paper topic is new to this edition.

Other sections focus on matters most troublesome to students: choosing and narrowing a topic, crafting a thesis, citing sources, integrating quotations, and avoiding plagiarism at both the note-taking and the drafting stages. At the end of the Research Guide are two new checklists for revision, one for global matters and the other for proper handling of sources.

Two sections on argument. Using a process approach, section 46 shows students how to construct an argument that will have some hope of persuading readers who do not already agree with their views. The logical fallacies and common mistakes in inductive and deductive reasoning are covered in section 47.

Extensive exercises, some with answers. At least one exercise set accompanies nearly every section of the book. Most sets begin with five lettered sentences that have answers in the back of the book so students can test their understanding independently. The sets then continue with five or ten numbered sentences, the answers for which appear only in the instructor's edition so instructors may use the exercises in class or assign them as homework.

Supported by a wide array of ancillaries

In addition to the instructor's edition, *Rules for Writers* is available with the following ancillaries:

> *Developmental Exercises to Accompany Rules for Writers*, by Wanda Van Goor and Diana Hacker
> *Rules for Writers* Web site < http://www.bedfordstmartins.com/hacker/rules >

The publisher is also making available most of the resources accompanying *The Bedford Handbook*. These supplements can easily be used with *Rules for Writers* because its central section numbers (8–45) correspond with those in *The Bedford Handbook*. All of the ancillaries are free of charge to instructors, and some are available for student purchase as well.

PRACTICAL RESOURCES FOR INSTRUCTORS

> *Quizzes and Diagnostic Tests to Accompany The Bedford Handbook,* with ESL versions (available on disk)
> *Transparencies to Accompany The Bedford Handbook*

PROFESSIONAL RESOURCES FOR INSTRUCTORS

> *Background Readings for Instructors Using The Bedford Handbook*
> *The Bedford Guide to Teaching Writing in the Disciplines*

The Bedford Guide for Writing Tutors
The Bedford Bibliography for Teachers of Writing, Fifth Edi-
    tion, available online < http://www.bedfordstmartins.com/
    bb > and in print.

RESOURCES FOR STUDENTS

Supplemental Exercises for The Bedford Handbook (with
    Answer Key)
Research and Documentation in the Electronic Age, available
    online < http://www.bedfordstmartins.com/hacker/resdoc >
    and in print.
Preparing for the CLAST with The Bedford Handbook
Preparing for the TASP with The Bedford Handbook

SOFTWARE

The Electronic Bedford Handbook (Windows® and Macintosh)

Acknowledgments

I would like to thank the following reviewers for contributing
useful insights based on their varied experiences in the classroom: John Bagge, Landmark College; Geneva H. Baxter, Spel-
man College; Robin A. Boyle, St. John's University School of Law;
Linda Chown, Grand Valley State University; Sandra Carey, Lex-
ington Community College; Stanley Coberly, West Virginia University at Parkersburg; Tom DeMarchi, Florida International University; Susan Injejikian Henry, Glendale Community College;
Kathleen Johnson, Colorado University at The Springs; Mary
Little, San Joaquin Delta College; Susan Noguera, Madonna University; Barry R. Nowlin, University of South Alabama; Richard
Pepp, Massasoit Community College; Patricia Schade, Merced
College; Andrew L. Smith, Holyoke Community College; Lynn
Steiner, Cuesta College; Kathryn Zipperian, Cuesta College.

Writing a handbook is truly a collaborative effort. Barbara
Flanagan, Lloyd Shaw, William Peirce, and Ruth Thomas helped
me update the research paper chapters; William Peirce assisted
with the chapter on argument.

I am indebted to the students whose essays appear in this
edition—Gary Cohen, Michelle Fitzpatrick, John Garcia, Mary
Kenny, Andrew Knutson, Lauren Pent, Karen Shaw, Claire Tarvin,
Marie Visosky, Tom Weitzel, and Diane Williford—not only for
permission to use their work but for permission to adapt it for
pedagogical purposes as well. My thanks also go to the follow-

ing students for permission to use their paragraphs: Diana Crawford, Connie Hailey, William Hill, Linda Lavelle, Kathleen Lewis, Chris Mileski, Julie Reardon, Margaret Smith, Margaret Stack, John Thatcher, and David Warren.

Several talented editors contributed to the book. Michelle McSweeney has been a first-rate developmental editor: tactful, savvy, and good-humored. Her knowledge of computers and the Internet proved invaluable as we worked to bring the fourth edition into the electronic age. Copyeditor Barbara Flanagan has once again brought grace and consistency to the final manuscript; her keen eye has saved me from many a blunder. Jeannine Thibodeau coordinated the review program and fielded a variety of problems too numerous to mention.

Book editor Anne Noonan expertly steered the book through production with the help of Coleen O'Hanley; Cheryl Mamaril ably guided the book through the manufacturing process; and managing editor Elizabeth Schaaf orchestrated the production of the book with her usual attention to detail. I continue to be indebted to award-winning designer Claire Seng-Niemoeller for designing clean, uncluttered pages that highlight the book's hand-edited sentences.

Special thanks are due to Bedford/St. Martin's president Chuck Christensen and editorial director Joan Feinberg. Fifteen years ago Chuck took a chance on an unknown community college instructor with an inexplicable urge to write a handbook. I am deeply grateful to him for giving me this opportunity. In retrospect, I suppose Chuck knew that almost anyone could learn to write a handbook under the guidance of Joan Feinberg. Certainly a better teacher-editor could not have been found. Joan has consistently set a standard of excellence, and over the years she has nudged me toward it, always with intelligence, grace, and good humor. It would be impossible to overstate my gratitude.

Finally, a note of thanks goes to my mother, Georgiana Tarvin, and to Joseph and Marian Hacker, Robert Hacker, Greg Tarvin, Betty Renshaw, Bill Fry, Bill Mullinix, Joyce Neff, Christine McMahon, Anne King, Wanda Van Goor, Melinda Kramer, Tom Henderson, the Dougherty family, Robbie Wallin, and Austin Nichols for their support and encouragement; and to the many students over the years who have taught me that errors, a natural by-product of the writing process, are simply problems waiting to be solved.

Diana Hacker
Prince George's Community College

How to Use This Book

Though it is small enough to hold in your hand, *Rules for Writers* will answer most of the questions you are likely to ask as you plan, draft, and revise a piece of writing: How do I choose and narrow a topic? What can I do if I get stuck? How do I know when to begin a new paragraph? Should I write *none was* or *none were*? When does a comma belong before *and*? What is the difference between *accept* and *except*? How do I cite a source with two authors?

How to find information with an instructor's help

When you are revising an essay that has been marked by your instructor, tracking down information is simple. If your instructor marks problems with a number such as *16* or a number and letter such as *12e*, you can turn directly to the appropriate section of the handbook. Just flip through the colored tabs on the upper right-hand corners of the pages until you find the number in question. The number *16*, for example, leads you to the rule "Tighten wordy sentences," and *12e* takes you to the subrule "Repair dangling modifiers." If your instructor uses an abbreviation such as *w* or *dm* instead of a number, consult the list of abbreviations and symbols on the page right before the back endpapers. There you will find the name of the problem *(wordy; dangling modifier)* and the number of the section to consult.

How to find information on your own

With a little practice, you will be able to find information in this book without an instructor's help — usually by tracking the icons that appear on the cover and inside the front cover. At times, you may want to consult the detailed menu inside the back cover, the index, the Glossary of Usage, or one of the directories to the documentation models.

The icons. Because the icons are right on the cover, it won't take you long to become familiar with the organization of *Rules for Writers*. These icons also appear on a brief menu inside the front cover. Usually this menu is the fastest way into the book.

Let's say that you are having problems with run-on sentences. Your first step is to find the appropriate icon on the menu inside the front cover—in this case the check mark for "Grammar." Next, find the appropriate numbered topic "20. Run-on sentences." Finally, use the tabs on the right-hand corners of the pages to find section 20. The running head next to the tab ("Run-on sentences") will tell you that you are just where you want to be.

At times you can work straight from the icons on the cover. These icons appear on every left-hand page of the book and on the solid-color part openers. To look up correct uses of the semicolon, for example, you can find the traffic light icon (for "Punctuation") on the left-hand pages, and then, just by flipping, you can locate the appropriate running head ("The semicolon") on the right-hand pages.

The back endpapers. The detailed menu appears inside the back cover. When the numbered section you're looking for is broken up into quite a few lettered subsections, try consulting this menu. For instance, if you have a question about the proper use of commas for items in a series, this menu will lead you quickly to section 32c.

The index. If you aren't sure which topic to choose from one of the menus, consult the index at the back of the book. For example, you may not realize that the issue of *is* versus *are* is a matter of subject-verb agreement (section 21). In that case, simply look up "*is* versus *are*" in the index and you will be directed to the exact pages you need.

The Glossary of Usage. When in doubt about the correct use of a particular word (such as *affect* and *effect*, *among* and *between*, or *hopefully*), consult the Glossary of Usage at the back of the book. This glossary explains the difference between commonly confused words; it also lists colloquialisms and jargon that are inappropriate in formal written English.

Directories to documentation models. When you are documenting a research paper with either the MLA or the APA style, you can find appropriate documentation models by consulting the MLA or APA directory. The MLA directory is easy to find. Just look for the first of the pages marked with a vertical band of teal. The APA directory appears on the first of the pages marked with a vertical band of gray.

How to use this book for self-study

In a composition class, most of your time should be spent writing. Therefore, it is unlikely that you will want to study all of the chapters in this book in detail. Instead you should focus on the problems that tend to crop up in your own writing. Your instructor (or your college's writing center) will be glad to help you design an individual program of self-study.

Rules for Writers has been designed so that you can learn from it on your own. By providing answers to some exercise sentences, it allows you to test your understanding of the material. Most exercise sets begin with five sentences lettered a–e and conclude with five or ten numbered sentences. Answers to the lettered sentences appear in an appendix at the end of the book.

Diana Hacker

Tutorials

The following tutorials will give you practice using the book's menus, index, Glossary of Usage, and MLA directory. Answers to the tutorials begin on page 517.

TUTORIAL 1 Using the menus

Each of the following "rules" violates the principle it expresses. Using the brief menu inside the front cover or the more detailed menu inside the back cover, find the section in *Rules for Writers* that explains the principle. Then fix the problem. Examples:

Tutors in
~~In~~ the writing center, ~~they~~ say that vague pronoun reference
^
is unacceptable. 23

Be alert for irregular verbs that have ~~came~~ to you in the
$$\overset{come}{\wedge}$$
wrong form. *27a*

1. A verb have to agree with its subject.
2. Each pronoun should agree with their antecedent.
3. About sentence fragments. You should avoid them.
4. Its important to use apostrophe's correctly.
5. Check for *-ed* verb endings that have been drop.
6. Discriminate careful between adjectives and adverbs.
7. If your sentence begins with a long introductory word group use a comma to separate the word group from the rest of the sentence.
8. Don't write a run-on sentence. you must connect independent clauses with a comma and a coordinating conjunction or with a semicolon.
9. For clarity, a writer must be careful not to shift your point of view.
10. Do not capitalize a word just to make it look Important.

TUTORIAL 2   Using the index

Assume that you have written the following sentences and want to know the answers to the questions in brackets. Use the index at the back of the book to locate the information you need, and edit the sentences if necessary.

1. Each of the candidates have agreed to participate in tonight's debate. [Should the verb be *have* or *has* to agree with *Each*?]
2. We had intended to go surfing but spent most of our vacation lying on the beach [Should I use *lying* or *laying*?]
3. We only looked at two houses before buying the house of our dreams. [Is *only* in the right place?]
4. In Saudi Arabia it is considered ill-mannered for you to accept a gift. [Is it okay to use *you* to mean "anyone in general"?]
5. In Canada, Joanne picked up several bottles of maple syrup for her sister and me. [Should I write *me* or *I*?]

TUTORIAL 3   Using the menus or the index

Imagine that you are in the following situations. Using either the menus or the index, find the information you need.

1. You are Ray Farley, a community college student who has been out of high school for ten years. You recall learning to punctuate items in a series by putting a comma between all items except the last two. In your college readings, however, you have noticed that most writers use a comma between all items. You're curious about the current rule. Which section of *Rules for Writers* will you consult?

2. You are Maria Sanchez, an honors student working in your university's writing center. Mike Lee, who speaks English as a second language, has come to you for help. He is working on a rough draft that contains a number of problems involving the use of articles (*a, an,* and *the*). You know how to use articles, but you aren't able to explain the rather complicated rules on their correct use. Which section of *Rules for Writers* will you and Mike Lee consult?

3. You are John Pell, engaged to marry Jane Dalton. In a note to Jane's parents, you have written "Thank you for giving Jane and myself such a generous contribution toward our honeymoon trip to Hawaii." You wonder if you should write "Jane and I" or "Jane and me" instead. Upon consulting *Rules for Writers*, what do you learn?

4. You are Selena Young, an intern supervisor at a housing agency. Two of your interns, Jake Gilliam and Susan Green, have writing problems involving *-s* endings on verbs. Jake tends to drop *-s* endings; Susan tends to add them where they don't belong. You suspect that both problems stem from nonstandard dialects spoken at home.

   Susan and Jake are in danger of losing their jobs because your boss thinks that anyone who writes "the tenant refuse" or "the landlords agrees" is beyond hope. You disagree. Susan and Jake are more intelligent than your boss supposes, and they have asked for your help. Where in *Rules for Writers* can they find the rules they need?

5. You are Joe Thompson, a first-year college student. Your friend Samantha, who has completed two years of college, seems to enjoy correcting your English. Just yesterday she corrected your sentence "I felt badly about her death" to "I felt bad about her death." You're sure you've heard many educated persons, including professors, say "I felt badly." Upon consulting *Rules for Writers,* what do you discover?

TUTORIAL 4   Using the Glossary of Usage

Consult the Glossary of Usage to see if the italicized words are used correctly. Then edit any sentences containing incorrect usage. Example:

> *an*
> The pediatrician gave my daughter a̶ injection for her allergy.

1. Changing attitudes *toward* alcohol have *effected* the beer industry.
2. It is *mankind's* nature to think wisely and act foolishly.
3. This afternoon I plan to *lie* out in the sun and work on my tan.
4. Everyone in our office is *enthused* about this project.
5. Most sleds are pulled by no *less* than two dogs and no more than ten.

TUTORIAL 5   Using the directory to MLA works cited models

Assume that you have written a short research paper on the growth of gambling operations on Indian reservations. You have cited the following sources in your paper, using MLA documentation, and you are ready to type your list of works cited. Turn to page 411 and use the MLA directory to locate the appropriate works cited models. Then write a correct entry for each source and arrange the entries in a properly formatted list of works cited. *Note:* Do not number the entries in a list of works cited.

> A book by Bruce E. Johansen entitled *Life and Death in Mohawk Country.* The book was published in Golden, Colorado, in 1993 by North American Press.

> An e-mail about casinos on reservations in the Northeast, sent to you by Helen Codoga on April 10, 1999. The subject line reads "Gambling on Reservations."

> An article by Eric Schine entitled "First Gambling, Then a Bank: California Has Reservations," from the weekly magazine *Business Week.* The article appears on page 47 of the September 9, 1996, issue of the magazine.

> An article by Sam Ridgebear entitled "Guilty Hands: Traditionalism and the Indian Gaming Industry" from the online journal *Many Voices: American Indian Students Journal.* The article appears in volume 1, issue 1, of this journal in 1995, and there is no pagination. You accessed the article through the Internet on April 2, 1999, at the following address: http://thecity.sfsu.edu/users/BANN/journal/guiltyhands.html >.

> A journal article by Mary H. Cooper entitled "Native Americans' Future: Do U.S. Policies Block Opportunities for Progress?" The article appears on pages 603 to 619 of *CQ Researcher,* which is paginated by volume. The volume number is 6 and the year is 1996.

> An article by James Dao entitled "Gambling Proponents See Indian Casinos as Alternative." The article was published on January 30, 1997, and it appears on page B2 of the late edition of the *New York Times.*

> An article by Kenan Pollack entitled "Mashantucket Pequots: A Tribe That's Raking It In," available on *U.S. News Online* at the address < http://www.usnews.com/usnews/issue/gamble8.htm >. No page numbers are given, and there is no information available about the print version of the article, but the online version of the article was last updated on February 17, 1998. You accessed the article on May 1, 1999.

Contents

Grammar   167

Punctuation 271

Mechanics   319

Argument 347

Research Guide 365

The Basics   **473**

The Writing Process

Since it's not possible to think about everything all at once, most experienced writers handle a piece of writing in stages. Roughly speaking, those stages are planning, drafting, and revising. You should generally move from planning to drafting to revising, but be prepared to circle back to earlier stages whenever the need arises.

1

Generate ideas and sketch a plan.

Before attempting a first draft, spend some time generating ideas. Mull over your subject while listening to music or driving to work, jot down inspirations on scratch paper, and explore your insights with anyone willing to listen. At this stage you should be collecting information and experimenting with ways of focusing and organizing it to best reach your readers.

1a Assess the writing situation.

Begin by taking a look at the writing situation in which you find yourself. The key elements of the writing situation include your subject, the sources of information available to you, your purpose, your audience, and constraints such as length, document design, review sessions, and deadlines.

It is unlikely that you will make final decisions about all of these matters until later in the writing process—after a first draft, for example. Nevertheless, you can save yourself time by thinking about as many of them as possible in advance. For a quick checklist, see pages 10–11.

Subject

Frequently your subject will be given to you. In a psychology class, for example, you might be asked to explain Bruno Bettelheim's Freudian analysis of fairy tales. Or in a course on the history of filmmaking, you might be assigned an essay on the political impact of D. W. Griffith's silent film *The Birth of a Nation*. In the business world, your assignment might be to draft a quarterly sales report or craft a diplomatic letter to a customer who has complained about your firm's computer software.

Sometimes you will be free to choose your own subject. Then you will be wise to select a subject that you already know something about or one that you can reasonably investigate in the time you have. Students in composition classes have written successfully on all of the subjects listed here, most of which were later narrowed into topics suitable for essays of 500–750 words. By browsing through the lists, perhaps you can pick up some ideas of your own.

Education: computers in the classroom, an inspiring teacher, sex education in junior high school, magnet schools, a learning disability such as dyslexia, programmed instruction, parochial schools, teacher certification, a local program to combat adult illiteracy, creative means of funding a college education

Careers and the workplace: working in an emergency room, the image versus the reality of a job such as lifeguarding, a police officer's workday, advantages of flextime for workers and employers, company-sponsored day care, mandatory drug testing by employers, sex or racial discrimination on the job, the psychological effects of unemployment, the rewards of a part-time job such as camp counseling, e-mail privacy issues

Families: an experience with adoption, a portrait of a family member who has aged well, the challenges facing single parents, living with an alcoholic, a portrait of an ideal parent, growing up in a large family, the problems of split custody, an experience with child abuse, the depiction of parent-child relationships in a popular TV series, expectations versus the reality of marriage, overcoming sibling rivalry, the advantages or disadvantages of being a twin, overseeing a child's access to the World Wide Web

Health: a vegetarian diet, weight loss through hypnotism, a fitness program for the elderly, reasons not to smoke, the rights of smokers or nonsmokers, overcoming an addiction, Prozac as a treatment for depression, the side effects of a particular treatment for cancer, life as a diabetic, the benefits of an aerobic exercise such as swimming, caring for a person with AIDS

Sports and hobbies: an unusual sport such as free-fall parachuting or bungee jumping, surviving a wilderness program, bodybuilding, a sport from another culture, the philosophy of karate, the language of sports announcers, pros and cons of banning boxing, coaching a Little League team, cutting the costs of an expensive sport such as skiing, a portrait of a favorite sports figure, sports for the handicapped, the discipline required for a sport such as gymnastics, the rewards of a hobby such as woodworking, salary caps for professional athletes

The arts: working behind the scenes at a theater, censorship of rock and roll lyrics, photography as an art form, the Japanese tea ceremony, the influence of African art on Picasso, the appeal of a local art museum, a portrait of a favorite musician or artist, performing as a musician, a high school for the arts, the colorization of black-and-white films, science fiction as a serious form of literature, a humorous description of romance novels or hard-boiled detective thrillers

Social justice: an experience with racism or sexism, affirmative action, reverse discrimination, making public transportation accessible for the physically handicapped, an experience as a juror, a local program to aid the homeless, discrimination against homosexuals, pros and cons of a national drinking age of twenty-one

Death and dying: working on a suicide hotline, the death of a loved one, a brush with death, caring for terminally ill patients, assisted suicide, the Buddhist view of death, explaining death to a child, passive euthanasia, death with dignity, an out-of-body experience

Violence and crime: an experience with a gun, a wartime experience, violence on television news programs, visiting a friend in prison, alternative sentencing for first offenders, victims' rights, a successful program to eliminate violence in a public high school, Internet fraud, capital punishment, preventing terrorist attacks, domestic violence and the courts

Nature and ecology: safety of nuclear power plants, solar energy, wind energy, air pollution in the national parks, forest fires on the California coast, grizzly bears in Yellowstone, communication among dolphins, organic gardening, backpacking in the Rockies, marine ecology, cleaning up Boston Harbor, the preservation of beaches in Delaware

Science and technology: pros and cons of writing on a computer, genetic engineering, an experimental farming technique, a medical breakthrough, free speech and the Internet

Many of these subjects are too broad. Part of your challenge as a writer will be whittling broad subjects down to manageable topics. If you are limited to a few pages, for example, you could not possibly do justice to a subject as broad as "sports for the handicapped." You would be wise to restrict your paper to a topic more manageable in the space allowed—perhaps a description of the Saturday morning athletic program your college offers for handicapped children.

Sources of information

Where will your facts, details, and examples come from? Can your topic be illustrated by personal experience, or will you need to search out relevant information through direct observation, interviews, questionnaires, reading, or the Internet?

PERSONAL EXPERIENCE   You can develop many topics wholly through personal experience, depending of course on your own life experiences. The students who wrote about lifeguarding, learning disabilities, weight loss through hypnotism, and free-fall parachuting all spoke with the voice of experience, as did those who wrote about flextime, coaching a Little League team, and company-sponsored day care. When narrowing their subjects, those students chose to limit themselves to information they had at hand. For example, instead of writing about company-sponsored day care in general—a subject that would have required a great deal of research—one student limited her discussion to the successful day care center at the company for which she worked.

DIRECT OBSERVATION   Direct observation is an excellent means of collecting information about a wide range of subjects, such as male-female relationships on the television program *Friends*, the clichéd language of sports announcers, or the appeal of a local art museum. For such subjects, do not rely on your memory alone; your information will be fresher and more detailed if you actively collect it, with a notebook or tape recorder in hand. As writer Stuart Chase advises young journalists assigned to report on their city's water system, "You will write a better article if you heave yourself out of a comfortable chair and go down in tunnel 3 and get soaked."

INTERVIEWS AND QUESTIONNAIRES   Interviews and questionnaires can supply you with detailed and interesting information on a variety of subjects. A nursing student interested in the care of terminally ill patients might interview nurses at a hospice; a

The Writing Process

political science major might speak with a local judge to learn about alternative sentencing for first offenders; a future teacher might conduct a survey on the classroom use of computers in local elementary schools. It is a good idea to tape interviews to preserve any lively quotations that you might want to weave into your essay. Keep questionnaires simple and specify a deadline to ensure that you get a reasonable number of responses.

READING Reading will be your primary source of information for many college assignments, which will generally be of two kinds: analytical assignments that call for a close reading of one book, essay, or literary work and research assignments that send you to the library to consult a variety of sources on a particular topic. For analytical essays, you can usually assume that your reader is familiar with the work and has a copy of it at hand. You select details from the work not to inform readers but to support an interpretation. When you quote from the work, page references are often sufficient. For research papers, however, you cannot assume that your reader is familiar with your sources or has them close at hand. This means that you must formally document all quoted and summarized or paraphrased material (see section 50). When in doubt about the need for formal documentation, consult your instructor.

THE INTERNET If you have access to the Internet, take advantage of its many resources. To generate ideas, you might surf the Web, join chat groups and online discussion groups, or browse through online periodicals. Be aware, however, that the wealth of information available through the Internet can be overwhelming and that Internet sources are not always reliable. For advice on using the Internet to explore your subject, see page 18. For advice on evaluating and documenting online sources, see pages 384–88, 417–30, and 456–57.

Purpose

Your purpose will often be dictated by the specific writing situation that faces you. Perhaps you have been asked to take minutes for a club meeting, to draft a letter requesting payment from a client, or to describe the results of a biology experiment. Even though your overall purpose is fairly obvious in such situations, a close look at that purpose can help you make a variety of necessary decisions. How detailed should the minutes be? Is your purpose to summarize the meeting or to establish a careful record of discussion in case future controversies arise? How firmly should your letter request payment? Do you need the money at all costs, or do you hope to get it without risking loss of the client's business? How technical does your biology professor want your report to be?

In many writing situations, part of your challenge will be discovering a purpose. Consider, for example, the topic of magnet schools—schools that draw students from different neighborhoods because of features such as advanced science classes or late-afternoon day care. Your purpose could be to inform parents of the options available in your county. Or you might argue that the county's magnet schools are not promoting racial integration as had been planned. Or you might propose that the board of education create a magnet high school for the arts on your college campus.

Although no precise guidelines will lead you to a purpose, you can begin by asking yourself which one or more of the following aims you hope to accomplish.

PURPOSES FOR WRITING

to inform	to evaluate
to persuade	to recommend
to call readers to action	to request
to change attitudes	to propose
to analyze	to provoke thought
to argue	to express feelings
to theorize	to entertain
to summarize	to give aesthetic pleasure

It is surprising how often writers misjudge their own purposes: informing, for example, when they should be recommending; summarizing when they should be analyzing; or expressing feelings about problems instead of proposing solutions. Before beginning any writing task, therefore, pause to ask, "Why am I communicating with my readers?" And this question will lead you to another important question: "Just who are those readers?"

Audience

Audience analysis can often lead you to an effective strategy for reaching your readers. One writer, whose purpose was to persuade teenagers not to smoke, jotted down the following observations about her audience:

dislike lectures, especially from older people

have little sense of their own mortality

are concerned about physical appearance and image

want to be socially accepted

have limited budgets

This analysis led the writer to focus more on the social aspects of smoking (she pointed out, for instance, that kissing a smoker is like licking an ashtray) than on the health risks. Her audience analysis also warned her against adopting a preachy tone that her readers might find offensive. Instead of lecturing to her audience, she decided to draw examples from her own experience as a hooked smoker: burning holes in her best sweater, driving in zero-degree weather late at night in search of an open tavern to buy cigarettes, rummaging through ashtrays for stale butts, and so on. The result was an essay that reached its readers instead of alienating them.

The following checklist will help you decide how to approach your audience.

AUDIENCE CHECKLIST

—How well informed are your readers about the subject?

—What do you want them to learn about the subject?

—How interested and attentive are they likely to be?

—Will they resist any of your ideas?

—What is your relationship to them: Employee to supervisor? Citizen to citizen? Expert to novice? Scholar to scholar?

—How much time are they willing to spend reading?

—How sophisticated are they as readers? Do they have large vocabularies? Can they follow long and complex sentences?

Of course, in some writing situations the audience will not be neatly defined for you. Nevertheless, many of the choices that you make as you write will tell readers who you think they are (novices or experts, for example), so it is best to be consistent—even if this means creating an audience that is in some sense a fiction.

BUSINESS AUDIENCES Writers in the business world often find themselves writing for multiple audiences. A letter to a client, for instance, might be distributed to sales representatives as well. Readers of a report may include persons with and without technical expertise or readers who want details and those who prefer a quick overview. To satisfy the demands of multiple audiences, business writers have developed a variety of strategies: attaching cover letters to more detailed reports, adding boldface headings, placing summaries in the left margin, and so on.

ACADEMIC AUDIENCES In the academic world, considerations of audience can be more complex than they seem at first. Your professor will read your essay, of course, but most professors play multiple roles while reading. Their first and most obvious roles are as coach and judge; less obvious is their role as an intelligent and objective reader, the kind of person who might reasonably be informed, convinced, entertained, or called to action by what you have to say.

Some professors create writing assignments that specify an audience, such as a hypothetical supervisor, readers of a local newspaper, or fellow academics in a particular field of study. Other professors expect you to imagine an audience appropriate to your purpose and your subject. Still others prefer that you write for a general audience of educated readers—nonspecialists who can be expected to read with an intelligent, critical eye. When in doubt about an appropriate audience for a particular assignment, check with your professor.

Length and document design

Writers seldom have complete control over length and document design. Journalists usually write within strict word limits set by their editors, businesspeople routinely aim for conciseness, and most college assignments specify an approximate length.

Certain document designs may also be required by your writing situation. Specific formats are used in the business world for documents such as letters, memos, reports, budget analyses, and personnel records. In the academic world, you may need to learn precise conventions for lab reports, critiques, research papers, and so on. For most undergraduate essays, a standard format is acceptable (see 6a).

Checklist for assessing the writing situation

At the beginning of the writing process, you may not be able to answer all of the questions on this checklist. That's fine. Just be prepared to think about them later.

NOTE: It is not necessary to think about the elements of a writing situation in the exact order listed in this chart.

SUBJECT

- Has a subject (or a range of possible subjects) been given to you, or are you free to choose your own?
- Is your subject worth writing about? Can you think of any readers who might be interested in reading about it?
- How broadly can you cover the subject? Do you need to narrow it to a more specific topic (because of length restrictions, for instance)?
- How detailed should your coverage be?

SOURCES OF INFORMATION

- Where will your information come from: Personal experience? Direct observation? Interviews? Questionnaires? Reading? The Internet?
- If your information comes from reading or the Internet, what sort of documentation is required?

PURPOSE

- Why are you writing: To inform readers? To persuade them? To entertain them? To call them to action? Some combination of these?

In some writing situations, you will be free to create your own document design, complete with headings, displayed lists, and perhaps even visuals, such as charts and graphs. Quite sophisticated results are now possible on computers, and both writers and readers are becoming increasingly interested in designs that improve readability. For a discussion of the principles of document design, see section 5.

Assessing the writing situation (*continued*)

AUDIENCE

- How well informed are your readers about the subject? What do you want them to learn about the subject?
- How interested and attentive are they likely to be? Will they resist any of your ideas?
- What is your relationship to them: Employee to supervisor? Citizen to citizen? Expert to novice? Scholar to scholar?
- How much time are they willing to spend reading?
- How sophisticated are they as readers? Do they have large vocabularies? Can they follow long and complex sentences?

LENGTH AND DOCUMENT DESIGN

- Are you working within any length specifications? If not, what length seems appropriate, given your subject, your purpose, and your audience?
- Must you use a particular design for your document? If so, do you have guidelines or examples that you can consult?

REVIEWERS AND DEADLINES

- Who will be reviewing your draft in progress—your instructor, a writing center tutor, your classmates, a friend, someone in your family?
- What are your deadlines? How much time will you need to allow for the various stages of writing, including typing and proofreading the final draft?

Reviewers and deadlines

Professional and business writers rarely work alone. They work with reviewers, often called editors, who offer advice throughout the writing process. In the academic world, too, the use of reviewers is increasingly common. Some instructors will play the role of reviewer for you; others may ask you to visit your college's writing center. Still others schedule peer review sessions in class (sometimes conducted online, in a networked classroom). Such sessions give you a chance to hear what other students think about your draft in progress—and to play the role of reviewer yourself.

Deadlines are a key element of any writing situation. They tell you what is possible and help you plan your time. For complex writing projects, such as research papers, you'll need to plan your time quite carefully. By working backward from the final deadline, you can create a schedule of target dates for completing various parts of the process. (See p. 366 for an example.)

EXERCISE 1–1

Choose one of the subject areas mentioned on pages 3–4 and add at least five subjects to those already on the list. If other members of your class have also done this exercise, pool the results.

EXERCISE 1–2

Narrow five of the following subjects into topics that would be manageable for an essay of two to five pages.

1. Working behind the scenes at a theater
2. A sport from another culture
3. Domestic violence and the courts
4. The advantages or disadvantages of being a twin
5. An experience with adoption
6. The side effects of a particular treatment for cancer
7. Computers in the classroom
8. Parochial schools
9. Performing as a musician
10. An experience with racism or sexism

EXERCISE 1–3

Which of the following subjects might be illustrated wholly by personal experience? For the others, suggest possible sources of information: direct observation, interviews, questionnaires, reading, or the Internet.

1. The problems of split custody
2. Working in an emergency room
3. Backpacking in the Rockies
4. The influence of African art on Picasso
5. Violence on television news programs

6. The discipline required for a sport such as gymnastics
7. Photography as an art form
8. Online marketing techniques
9. A local program to aid the homeless
10. Visiting a friend in prison

EXERCISE 1–4

Suggest a purpose and an audience for five of the following subjects.

1. A vegetarian diet
2. Cutting the costs of an expensive sport such as skiing
3. The challenges facing single parents
4. Advantages of flextime for workers and employers
5. Growing up in a large family
6. Pros and cons of a national speed limit of sixty-five
7. Science fiction as a serious form of literature
8. An unusual sport such as bungee jumping
9. A police officer's workday
10. Working on a suicide hotline

1b Experiment with ways to explore your subject.

Instead of just plunging into a first draft, experiment with one or more techniques for exploring your subject, perhaps one of these:

listing	keeping a journal
clustering	talking and listening
asking questions	surfing the Web
freewriting	using invention software
annotating texts and taking notes	

You can use most of these techniques whether you are working with pencil and paper or entering ideas into a computer.

Whatever technique you turn to, the goal is the same: to generate a wealth of ideas. At this early stage of the writing process, you should aim for quantity, not necessarily quality, of ideas. If an idea proves to be off the point, trivial, or too far-fetched, you can always throw it out later.

Listing

You might begin by simply listing ideas, putting them down in the order in which they occur to you—a technique sometimes known as "brainstorming." Here, for example, is a list one student writer jotted down:

The Phillips Collection

Washington, D.C.

1612 21st Street, close to Mass. Ave.

near Dupont Circle, in an interesting neighborhood

hard to find a parking space; better to take subway

elegant red brick townhouse, once home of Duncan and Marjorie Phillips (art collectors)

turned into a museum in 1918

facade reminds me of a bygone era—teas and debutante balls

free concerts on Sundays

mostly Impressionists, Postimpressionists, and modern masters

Renoir's *Luncheon of the Boating Party*—warm and joyful—you can almost smell the breeze off the Seine and hear the hum of conversation

you can wander through small rooms filled with paintings by Van Gogh, Degas, Cézanne, Bonnard, and Klee

the Rothko room, with huge color paintings—pulsating, sensuous reds, yellows, blues, greens

the new wing—no more bygone era—clean and uncluttered lines appropriate for modern masters like Picasso, Pollock, Dalí, Braque

a walled garden

The ideas appear here in the order in which they first occurred to the writer. Later she felt free to rearrange them, to cluster them under general categories, to delete some, and to add others. In other words, she treated her initial list as a source of ideas and a springboard to new ideas, not as an outline.

Clustering

Unlike listing, the technique of clustering highlights relationships among ideas. To cluster ideas, write your topic in the center of a sheet of paper, draw a circle around it, and surround that with related ideas connected to it with lines. If some of the satellite ideas lead to more specific clusters, write them down as well. The writer of the following diagram was exploring ideas for an essay on home uses for computers.

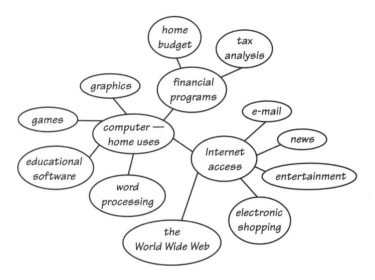

Asking questions

By asking relevant questions, you can generate many ideas—and you can make sure that you have adequately surveyed your subject. When gathering material for a story, journalists routinely ask themselves Who? What? When? Where? Why? and How? In addition to helping journalists get started, these questions ensure that they will not overlook an important fact: the date of a prospective summit meeting, for example, or the exact location of a neighborhood burglary.

Whenever you are writing about events, whether current or historical, the journalist's questions are one way to get started. One student, whose subject was the negative reaction in 1915 to D. W. Griffith's silent film *The Birth of a Nation*, began exploring her topic with this set of questions:

> *Who* objected to the film?
> *What* were the objections?
> *When* were protests first voiced?
> *Where* were protests most strongly expressed?
> *Why* did protesters object to the film?
> *How* did protesters make their views known?

In the academic world, scholars often generate ideas with questions related to a specific discipline: one set of questions for analyzing short stories, another for evaluating experiments in social psychology, still another for reporting field experiences in anthropology. If you are writing in a particular discipline, try to discover the questions that scholars typically explore. These are frequently presented in textbooks and software as checklists.

Freewriting

In its purest form, freewriting is simply nonstop writing. You set aside ten minutes or so and write whatever comes to you, without pausing to think about word choice, spelling, or even meaning. If you get stuck, you can write about being stuck, but you should keep your pencil moving. The point is to loosen up, relax, and see what happens. Even if nothing much happens, you have lost only ten minutes. It's more likely, though, that something interesting will emerge on paper—perhaps an eloquent sentence, an honest expression of feeling, or a line of thought worth exploring.

Annotating texts and taking notes

When you write about reading, one of the best ways to explore ideas is to mark up the text—on the pages themselves if you own the work, on photocopies if you don't. Here, for example, are two paragraphs from an essay by philosopher Michael Tooley as one student annotated them.

> Why is the American policy debate not focused more intensely on the relative merits or demerits of our current approach to drugs and of possible alternatives to it? The lack of discussion of this issue is rather striking, given that America has the most serious drug problem in the world, that alternatives to a prohibitionist approach are under serious consideration in other countries, and that the grounds for reconsidering our current approach are, I shall argue, so weighty. . . .
>
> I want to turn in detail to perhaps the two most important reasons for

But the subject has been discussed.

I guess he's for legalizing drugs. Why doesn't he say so?

True? How is he defining "drug problem"?

reconsidering our current drug policy: first, the difficulty of providing any adequate justification for the restrictions that prohibitive laws place on people's liberty; and second, the enormous social and personal costs associated with a <u>prohibitionist</u> approach.

Biased language?

The first reason seems off the point. Is it really worth half of our attention?

Aren't there important aspects of the subject that he's ignoring?

In addition to annotating texts, you may want to take notes on your reading (see section 50c).

Keeping a journal

A journal is a collection of personal, exploratory writings. An entry in a journal can be any length—from a single sentence to several pages—and it is likely to be informal and experimental.

In a journal, meant for your eyes only, you can take risks. In one entry, for example, you might do some freewriting or focused freewriting. In another, you might pose a series of interesting questions, whether or not you have the answers. In still another, you might play around with language for the sheer fun of it: writing "purple prose," for instance, or parodying the style of a favorite author or songwriter.

Keeping a journal can be an enriching experience in its own right, since it allows you to explore issues of concern to you without worrying about what someone else thinks. A journal can also serve as a sourcebook of ideas to draw on in future essays; on rare occasions, in fact, a journal entry may emerge as a polished essay of interest to readers other than yourself. Some writers find that they do their best work when writing for themselves, deliberately ignoring the constraints of a formal writing situation.

Talking and listening

The early stages of the writing process need not be lonely. Many writers begin a writing project by brainstorming ideas in a group, debating a point with friends, or engaging in conversation with a professor. Others turn to themselves for company— by talking nonstop into a tape recorder.

If your computer is equipped with a modem, you can "virtually converse" by exchanging ideas through e-mail, by joining an Internet chat group, or by following a listserv discussion. If you are part of a networked classroom, you may be encouraged to exchange ideas with your classmates and instructor in an electronic workshop.

Talking can be a good way to get to know your audience. If you're planning to write a narrative, for instance, you can test its dramatic effect on a group of friends. Or if you hope to advance a certain argument, you can try it out on listeners who hold a different view.

As you have no doubt discovered, conversation can deepen and refine your ideas before you even begin to set them down on paper. Our first thoughts are not necessarily our wisest thoughts; by talking and listening to others we can all stretch our potential as thinkers and as writers.

Surfing the Web

The Internet is a rich source of information that is fast and convenient to use, although its sheer magnitude can be overwhelming. A good way to begin exploring your subject on the Internet is through a search engine such as *Yahoo!* or *Excite*. A student looking for trends in teenage smoking, for example, might start by entering *teenage and smoking* in *Excite*'s search box. Even a fairly focused subject such as this can unleash thousands of sites, however, so always be prepared to narrow your search to make it more manageable. In the smoking example, the student might modify the search to read *teenage and smoking and advertising*, which would cut the number of sites listed in half. For more detailed advice on using the Internet to research a subject, see 46d. For advice on evaluating and documenting Internet sources, see 47c and 53.

Using invention software

You may have access to invention software in a networked classroom, in your school's writing center, or even on your own computer. Invention software prompts you to think about your subject by raising a series of exploratory questions and sometimes by generating group discussion. To make the most of invention software, be sure to keep an open mind and allow yourself to explore the subject freely. For invention programs tailored to specific disciplines, check with your instructors.

EXERCISE 1–5

Generate a list of at least fifteen items for one of the subjects listed on pages 3–4.

EXERCISE 1–6

Using the technique of clustering or freewriting, explore one of the subjects listed on pages 3–4.

1c Settle on a tentative focus.

As you explore your subject, you will begin to see possible ways to focus your material. At this point, try to settle on a tentative central idea. The more complex your subject, the more your initial central idea will change as your drafts evolve.

For many types of writing, your central idea can be asserted in one sentence, a generalization preparing readers for the supporting details that will follow. Such a sentence, which will ordinarily appear in the opening paragraph of your finished essay, is called a *thesis*. A successful thesis—like the following, all taken from articles in *Smithsonian*—points both the writer and the reader in a definite direction.

> Much maligned and the subject of unwarranted fears, most bats are harmless and highly beneficial.

> Geometric forms known as fractals may have a profound effect on how we view the world, not only in art and film but in many branches of science and technology, from astronomy to economics to predicting the weather.

> Aside from his more famous identities as colonel of the Rough Riders and president of the United States, Theodore Roosevelt was a lifelong professional man of letters.

The thesis sentence usually contains a key word or controlling idea that limits its focus. The preceding sentences, for example, prepare for essays that focus on the *beneficial* aspects of bats, the *effect* of fractals on how we view the world, and Roosevelt's identity as a writer, or *man of letters*.

It's a good idea to formulate a thesis early in the writing process, perhaps by jotting it on scratch paper, by putting it at the head of a rough outline, or by attempting to write an introductory paragraph that includes the thesis. Your tentative thesis will probably be less graceful than the thesis you include in the final version of your essay. Here, for example, is one student's early effort:

> Although they both play percussion instruments, drummers and percussionists are very different.

The thesis that appeared in the final draft of the student's paper was more polished:

> Two types of musicians play percussion instruments—drummers and percussionists—and they are as different as Quiet Riot and the New York Philharmonic.

Don't worry too soon about the exact wording of your thesis, however, because your main point may change as you refine your ideas.

For a more detailed discussion of the thesis, see 2a.

1d Sketch a tentative plan.

Once you have generated some ideas and formulated a tentative thesis, you may want to sketch an informal outline. Informal outlines can take many forms. Perhaps the most common is simply the thesis followed by a list of major supporting ideas.

> Hawaii is losing its cultural identity.
>
> —pure-blooded Hawaiians increasingly rare
> —native language diluted
> —natives forced off ancestral lands
> —little emphasis on native culture in schools
> —customs exaggerated and distorted by tourism

Clustering diagrams, often used to generate ideas, can also serve as rough outlines (see p. 15). And if you began by jotting down a list of ideas (see p. 13), you may be able to turn the list into a rough outline by crossing out some ideas, adding others, and numbering the ideas to create a logical order.

Planning with headings

When writing a relatively long college paper or business document, consider using headings to guide readers. In addition to helping readers follow the organization of your final draft, headings can be a powerful planning tool, especially if you are working on a computer. You can type in your tentative thesis and then experiment with possible headings; once you have settled on the headings that work best, you can begin typing in chunks of text beneath each heading. Here, for example, is what one student typed into his laptop computer when planning a long history paper. The headings, written in the form of questions, are centered.

```
Although we will never know whether Nathan Bedford
Forrest directly ordered the massacre of Union
troops at Fort Pillow, evidence strongly suggests
that he was responsible for it.

            What happened at Fort Pillow?
      Why do the killings qualify as a massacre?
           Did Forrest order the massacre?
        Did the men have reason to think Forrest
                   wanted a massacre?
```

For more detailed advice about using headings, see 5b. For examples of papers that use headings, see pages 71–75, 438, and 461.

When to use a formal outline

Early in the writing process, rough outlines have certain advantages over their more formal counterparts: They can be produced more quickly, they are more obviously tentative, and they can be revised more easily should the need arise. However, a formal outline may be useful later in the writing process, after you have written a rough draft, especially if your subject matter is complex.

The following formal outline brought order to a complex subject, methods for limiting and disposing of nuclear waste. Notice that the student's thesis is an important part of the outline. Everything else in the outline supports it, either directly or indirectly.

Thesis: Although various methods for limiting or disposing of nuclear wastes have been proposed, each has serious drawbacks.

I. The process of limiting nuclear waste through partitioning and transmutation has serious drawbacks.
   A. The process is complex and costly.
   B. Nuclear workers' exposure to radiation would increase.

II. Antarctic ice sheet disposal is problematic for scientific and legal reasons.
   A. Our understanding of the behavior of ice sheets is too limited.
   B. An international treaty prohibits disposal in Antarctica.

III. Space disposal is unthinkable.
   A. The risk of an accident and resulting worldwide disaster is great.
   B. The cost is prohibitive.
   C. The method would be unpopular at home and abroad.

IV. Seabed disposal is unwise because we do not know enough about the procedure or its impact.
   A. Scientists have not yet solved technical difficulties.
   B. We do not fully understand the impact of such disposal on the ocean's ecology.

V. Deep underground disposal endangers public safety and creates political problems.
   A. Geologists disagree about the safest disposal sites, and no sites are completely safe.
   B. There is much political pressure against the plan from citizens who do not want their states to become nuclear dumps.

In constructing a formal outline, keep the following guidelines in mind.

1. Put the thesis at the top.
2. Make items at the same level of generality as parallel as possible (see section 9).
3. Use sentences unless phrases are clear.

4. Use the conventional system of numbers and letters for the levels of generality.

I.
    A.
    B.
        1.
        2.
            a.
            b.
                (1)
                (2)
                    (a)
                    (b)
II.

5. Always use at least two subdivisions for a category, since nothing can be divided into fewer than two parts.
6. Limit the number of major sections in the outline; if the list of roman numerals begins to look like a laundry list, find some way of clustering the items into a few major categories with more subcategories.
7. Be flexible; in other words, be prepared to change your outline as your drafts evolve.

2

Rough out an initial draft.

As you rough out an initial draft, keep your planning materials — lists, diagrams, outlines, and so on — close at hand. In addition to helping you get started, such notes and blueprints will encourage you to keep moving. Writing tends to flow better when it is drafted relatively quickly, without many starts and stops.

For most kinds of writing, an introduction announces a main idea, several body paragraphs develop it, and a conclusion drives it home. You can begin drafting, however, at any point. For example, if you find it difficult to introduce a paper that you have not yet written, you can draft the body first and save the introduction for later.

2a For most types of writing, draft an introduction that includes a thesis.

For most writing tasks, your introduction will be a paragraph of 50 to 150 words. Perhaps the most common strategy is to open the paragraph with a few sentences that engage the reader and to conclude it with a statement of the essay's main point. The sentence stating the main point is called a *thesis*. (See 1c.) In the following examples, the thesis has been italicized.

> To the Australian aborigines, the Dreamtime was the time of creation. It was then that the creatures of the earth, including man, came into being. There are many legends about that mystical period, but unfortunately, the koala does not fare too well in any of them. *Slow-witted though it is in life, the koala is generally depicted in myth and folklore as a trickster and a thief.*
> —Roger Caras, "What's a Koala?"

> When I was sixteen, I married and moved to a small town to live. My new husband nervously showed me the house he had rented. It was after dark when we arrived there, and I remember wondering why he seemed so apprehensive about my reaction to the house. I thought the place seemed shabby but potentially cozy and quite livable inside. The morning sun revealed the reason for his anxiety by exposing the squalor outdoors. Up to that point, my contact with any reality but that of my own middle-class childhood had come from books. *The next four years in a small Iowa town taught me that reading about poverty is a lot different from living with it.* —Julie Reardon, student

Ideally, the sentences leading to the thesis should hook the reader, perhaps with one of the following:

a startling statistic or unusual fact
a vivid example
a description
a paradoxical statement
a quotation or bit of dialogue
a question
an analogy
a joke or an anecdote

Such hooks are particularly important when you cannot assume your reader's interest in the subject. Hooks are less necessary in scholarly essays and other writing aimed at readers with a professional interest in the subject.

Although the thesis frequently appears at the end of the introduction, it can just as easily appear at the beginning. Much work-related writing, in which a straightforward approach is most effective, commonly begins with the thesis.

> *Flextime scheduling, which has proved its effectiveness at the Library of Congress, should be introduced on a trial basis at the main branch of the Montgomery County Public Library.* By offering flexible work hours, the library can boost employee morale, cut down on absenteeism, and expand its hours of operation.
> —David Warren, student

For some types of writing, it may be difficult or impossible to express the central idea in a thesis sentence; or it may be unwise or unnecessary to put a thesis sentence in the essay itself. A personal narrative, for example, may have a focus too subtle to be distilled in a single sentence, and such a sentence might ruin the story. Strictly informative writing, like that found in many business memos, may be difficult to summarize in a thesis. In such instances, do not try to force the central idea into a thesis sentence. Instead, think in terms of an overriding purpose, which may or may not be stated directly.

Characteristics of an effective thesis

An effective thesis should be a generalization, not a fact; it should be limited, not too broad; and it should be sharply focused, not too vague.

Because a thesis must prepare readers for facts and details, it cannot itself be a fact. It must always be a generalization demanding proof or further development.

TOO FACTUAL   The first polygraph was developed by Dr. John A. Larson in 1921.

REVISED   Because the polygraph has not been proved reliable, even under the most controlled conditions, its use by private employers should be banned.

Although a thesis must be a generalization, it must not be *too* general. You will need to narrow the focus of any thesis that you cannot adequately develop in the space allowed. Unless you were writing a book or a very long research paper, the following thesis would be too broad.

TOO BROAD   Many drugs are now being used successfully to treat mental illnesses.

You would need to restrict the thesis, perhaps like this:

REVISED   Despite its risks and side effects, Prozac is an effective treatment for depression.

Finally, a thesis should be sharply focused, not too vague. Beware of any thesis containing a fuzzy, hard-to-define word such as *interesting*, *good*, or *disgusting*.

TOO VAGUE   Many of the songs played on station WXQP are disgusting.

The word *disgusting* is needlessly vague. To sharpen the focus of this thesis, the writer should be more specific.

REVISED   Of the songs played on station WXQP, all too many depict sex crudely, sanction the beating or rape of women, or foster gang violence.

In the process of making a too-vague thesis more precise, you may find yourself outlining the major sections of your paper, as in the preceding example. This technique, known as *blueprinting*, helps readers know exactly what to expect as they read on. It also helps you, the writer, control the shape of your essay.

EXERCISE 2–1

In each of the following pairs, which sentence might work well as a thesis for a paper based on personal experience (not on reading)? What is the problem with the other one? Is it too factual? Too broad? Too vague?

1a. Of the many challenges facing single parents, the most difficult is learning to maintain a balance among work, school, a social life, and, most important, family.
 b. Single parents face many challenges, so they need to be well organized.

2a. From the time I was a young child, I have always had at least three cats.
 b. In addition to being the perfect size to be kept indoors, cats are clean, loving, graceful, and surprisingly intelligent animals.

3a. At the Special Olympics, disabled athletes are taught that with hard work and support from others they can accomplish anything: that they can indeed be winners.
  b. Working with the Special Olympics program is rewarding.

4a. Immigrants from many lands have made major contributions to American culture.
  b. When Uncle Jacob stepped onto Ellis Island with only a small suitcase and the clothes on his back, no one could have predicted that one day his stone carvings would grace many buildings and monuments in our nation's capital.

5a. History 201, taught by Professor Brown, is offered at 10 A.M. on Tuesdays and Thursdays.
  b. Whoever said that history is nothing but polishing tombstones must have missed History 201, because in Professor Brown's class history is very much alive.

EXERCISE 2–2

In each of the following pairs, which sentence might work well as a thesis for a paper based on reading? What is the problem with the other one? Is it too factual? Too broad? Too vague?

1a. So far, research suggests that zero-emissions vehicles are not a sensible solution to the problem of steadily increasing air pollution.
  b. Because air pollution is of serious concern to many people in the world today, several government agencies in the United States have implemented plans to begin solving the problem.

2a. Anorexia nervosa is a dangerous, sometimes deadly eating disorder found mainly in young, upper-middle-class teenagers.
  b. The eating disorder anorexia nervosa is rarely cured by one treatment alone; only by combining drug therapy with psychotherapy and family therapy can the patient begin the long, torturous journey to wellness.

3a. Although we cannot fully harness the powers that nature wields, we can manage most naturally occurring forest fires to benefit our national parks.
  b. The Yellowstone fires of 1988 taught many lessons to many people.

4a. Marijuana is classified by the Drug Enforcement Agency as a Schedule I drug.
  b. If marijuana was legalized for medical purposes, we could relieve some of the suffering associated with AIDS, cancer, and glaucoma.

5a. Was the man killed on July 22, 1934, in the alley next to the Biograph Theater in Chicago John Dillinger?
  b. Sweeping across the Midwest in the early 1930s, the Dillinger gang's crime wave epitomized the lawlessness of the era.

2b As you draft the body, keep your thesis in mind.

Before drafting the body of an essay, take a careful look at your introduction, focusing especially on your thesis sentence. What does the thesis promise readers? Try to keep this focus in mind.

It's a good idea to have a plan in mind as well. If your thesis sentence outlines a plan (see 2a) or if you have sketched a preliminary outline, try to block out your paragraphs accordingly. If you do not have a plan, you would be wise to pause for a moment and sketch one (see 1d). Of course it is also possible to begin without a plan—assuming you are prepared to treat your first attempt as a "discovery draft" that will almost certainly be tossed (or radically rewritten) once you discover what you really want to say.

For more detailed advice about paragraphs in the body of an essay, see section 4.

2c Attempt a conclusion.

The conclusion should echo the main idea, without dully repeating it. Often the concluding paragraph can be relatively short. By the end of the essay, readers should already understand your main point; your conclusion simply drives it home and perhaps suggests its significance.

In addition to echoing your main idea, a conclusion might summarize the essay's key points, pose a question for future study, offer advice, or propose a course of action. To end an essay detailing the social skills required of a bartender, one writer concludes with some advice:

> If someone were to approach me one day looking for the secret to running a good bar, I suppose I would offer the following advice: Get your customers to pour out their ideas at a greater rate than you pour out the liquor. You will both win in the end.   — Kathleen Lewis, student

To make the conclusion memorable, consider including a detail, example, or image from the introduction to bring readers full circle; a quotation or bit of dialogue; an anecdote; or a humorous, witty, or ironic comment. To end a narrative describing a cash register holdup, one student uses an anecdote that includes some dialogue:

> It took me a long time to get over that incident. Countless times I found myself gasping as someone "pointed" a dollar bill at me. On one such occasion, a jovial little man buying a toy gun for his son came up to me and said in a Humphrey Bogart impression, "Give me all your money, Sweetheart." I didn't laugh. Instead, my heart skipped a beat, for I had heard those words before. — Diana Crawford, student

Whatever concluding strategy you choose, avoid introducing wholly new ideas at the end of an essay. Also avoid apologies and other limp, indeterminate endings. The essay should end crisply, preferably on a positive note.

3

Make global revisions; then revise sentences.

For experienced writers, revising is rarely a one-step process. Global matters generally receive attention first—the focus, organization, content, and overall strategy. Improvements in sentence structure, word choice, grammar, punctuation, and mechanics come later. (See pp. 34–35 for examples of global and sentence-level revisions.)

3a Make global revisions: Think big.

Global revisions address the larger elements of writing. Usually they affect chunks of text longer than a sentence, and frequently they can be quite dramatic. Whole paragraphs might be dropped, others added. Material once stretched over two or three paragraphs might be condensed into one. Entire sections might be rearranged. Even the content may change dramatically, for the process of revising stimulates thought.

Many of us resist global revisions because we find it difficult to distance ourselves from a draft. We tend to review our work from our own, not from our audience's, perspective.

To distance yourself from a draft, put it aside for a while, preferably overnight or even longer. When you return to it, try to play the role of your audience as you read. If possible, enlist the help of reviewers—persons willing to play the role of audience for you. Ask your reviewers to focus on the larger issues of writing, not on the fine points. The following checklist may help them get started.

Checklist for global revision

PURPOSE AND AUDIENCE

- Does the draft accomplish its purpose—to inform readers, to persuade them, to entertain them, to call them to action (or some combination of these)?
- Is the draft appropriate for its audience? Does it take into consideration the audience's knowledge of the subject, level of interest in the subject, and possible attitudes toward the subject? Is the reading level appropriate?

FOCUS

- Do the introduction and conclusion focus clearly on the main point? Is the thesis clear enough? (If there is no thesis, is there a good reason for omitting one?)
- Are any ideas obviously off the point?

ORGANIZATION AND PARAGRAPHING

- Does the writer give readers enough organizational cues (such as topic sentences or headings)?
- Are ideas ordered effectively?
- Does the paragraphing make sense?
- Are any paragraphs too long or too short for easy reading?

CONTENT

- Is the supporting material persuasive?
- Which ideas need further development?
- Are the parts proportioned sensibly? Do major ideas receive enough attention?
- Where might material be deleted?

NOTE: When working on a computer, print out a hard copy so that you can read the draft as a whole rather than screen by screen. A computer screen focuses your attention on small chunks of text rather than the whole; a printout allows you to look at the entire paper when thinking about what global revisions to make.

Once you have decided what global revisions may be needed, the computer, of course, is an excellent tool. In fact, because the computer saves time, it encourages you to experiment with global revisions. Should you combine two paragraphs? Would your conclusion make a good introduction? Might several paragraphs be rearranged for greater impact? Will the addition of boldface headings improve readabilty? With little risk, you can explore the possibilities. When a revision misfires, it is easy to restore your original draft.

3b Revise and edit sentences.

Most of the rest of this book offers advice on revising sentences for clarity and on editing them for grammar, punctuation, and mechanics.

Some writers handle most sentence-level revisions directly at the computer, experimenting on screen with a variety of possible improvements. Other writers prefer to print out a hard copy of the draft, mark it up, and then return to the computer. Here, for example, is a rough-draft paragraph as one student edited it for a variety of sentence-level problems:

> Finally ~~we decided~~ *deciding* that perhaps our dream
>
> needed ~~some~~ prompting, ~~and~~ we visited a fertility
>
> doctor and began the expensive, time‑consuming
>
> round of procedures that held out ~~the~~ *some* promise of
> *our dream's fulfillment. Our efforts, however, were*
> ~~fulfilling our dream. All this was~~ to no avail. ~~and~~ *As*
>
> ~~as~~ we approached the sixth year of our marriage,
> *could no longer*
> we ~~had reached the point where we couldn't~~ even
>
> discuss our childlessness without becoming very

```
depressed. We questioned why this had happened to
                                      such a
us?. Why had we been singled out for this major
   ^
disappointment?
```

The original paragraph was flawed by wordiness and an excessive reliance on structures connected with *and*. Such problems can be addressed through any number of acceptable revisions. The first sentence, for example, could have been changed like this:

```
     Finally we decided that perhaps our dream
                            After visiting
needed some prompting/. and we visited a fertility
                      ^
         we
doctor, and began the expensive, time-consuming
   ^                                            ^
                          promised hope
round of procedures that held out the promise of
                                  ^
fulfilling our dream.
```

Though some writers might argue about the effectiveness of these improvements compared with the previous revision, most would agree that both versions are better than the original.

Some of the paragraph's improvements involve less choice and are not so open to debate. The hyphen in *time-consuming* is necessary; a noun must be substituted for the pronoun *this* in the second sentence, which was being used more loosely than grammar allows; and the question mark in the next to last sentence must be changed to a period.

Software tools

Software can provide help with some sentence-level revisions. Word processors have spell checkers that will catch many but not all spelling errors, and some have thesauruses to help with word choice.

Some word processing programs are equipped with grammar checkers (sometimes called "style checkers" or "text analyzers"). When using a grammar checker, you need to be aware of what this tool can—and cannot—do. Grammar checkers are fairly good at flagging wordy sentences, jargon, slang, clichés, and passive verbs. But such problems represent only a small fraction of the sentence-level problems in a typical draft. Because so many problems—such as faulty parallelism, mixed constructions, and misplaced modifiers—lack mathematical precision, they slip right past the grammar checker. You should not assume, therefore, that once you have run your draft through a grammar checker, your grammar problems are over.

Throughout this book, you will find grammar checker advice linked to specific problems. For example, in section 14 you will learn that grammar checkers can flag most but not all passive verbs and that they flag passive constructions whether or not they are appropriate. In section 20 you will learn that grammar checkers flag some run-ons, miss others, and tell you that some sentences may be run-ons when in fact they are not.

The grammar checker advice is based on a large sample of correct and incorrect sentences that were run through two widely used grammar checker programs. For more details, see page ix of the preface.

3c Proofread the final manuscript.

After revising and editing, you are ready to prepare the final manuscript. (See 6a for guidelines.) At this point, make sure to allow yourself enough time for proofreading—the final step in manuscript preparation.

Proofreading is a special kind of reading: a slow and methodical search for misspellings, typographical mistakes, and omitted words or word endings. Such errors can be difficult to spot in your own work because you may read what you intended to write, not what is actually on the page. To fight this tendency, try proofreading out loud, articulating each word as it is actually written. You might also try proofreading your sentences in reverse order, a strategy that takes your attention away from the meanings you intended and forces you to think about small surface features instead.

Although proofreading may be tedious, it is crucial. Errors strewn throughout an essay are distracting and annoying. If the writer doesn't care about this piece of writing, thinks the reader, why should I? A carefully proofread essay, however, sends a positive message: It shows that you value your writing and respect your readers.

EXAMPLE OF GLOBAL REVISIONS

Sports on TV--A Win or a Loss?

Team sports are as much a part of Americain life as Mom and apple pie, and they have a good ~~tendency~~ to bring people together. They encourage team members to cooperate with one another, they also create shared enthusiasm among fans. Thanks to television, this togetherness now seems available to nearly all of us at the flick of a switch. We do not have to buy tickets, and travel to a stadium, to see the World Series or the Super Bowl, these games are on television. We can enjoy the game in the comfort of our own living rooms. ~~After Thanksgiving or Christmas dinner, the whole family may gather around the TV set to watch football together.~~ It would appear that television has done us a great service. But is this really the case?

Although television does make sports more accessible, it also creates a distance between the sport and the fans and between athletes and the teams they play for.

The advantage of television is that it provides sports fans with greater convenience.

[insert] ←

We can see more games than if we had to attend each one in person, and we can follow greater varieties of sports.

EXAMPLE OF SENTENCE-LEVEL REVISIONS

> *Televised*
> Sports ~~on TV~~--A Win or a Loss?
> ⌄

Team sports~~,~~ ~~are~~ as much a part of America*n*
⌄   *tend*
life as Mom and apple pie, ~~and they have a good~~
             us   ⌄
~~tendency~~ to bring ~~people~~ together. They encourage team
                   ⌄   *and*
members to cooperate with one another, they ~~also~~ create
                                    ⌄ *Because of*
shared enthusiasm among fans. ~~Thanks to~~ television,
                                        ⌄
this togetherness now seems available ~~to nearly all~~

of us at the flick of a switch. ~~It would appear that~~

~~television has done us a great service.~~ But is this
                                       makes
really the case? Although television ~~does make~~
                                        ⌄
sports more accessible, it also creates a distance

between the sport and the fans and between athletes
       their
and ~~the~~ teams~~. they play for.~~
     ⌄   ⌄

The advantage of television is that it provides

sports fans with greater convenience. We do not

have to buy tickets/ and travel to a stadium/
                                        but
to see the World Series or the Super Bowl/ ~~these~~
                                            any ⌄
~~games are on television. We~~ can enjoy ~~the~~ game in
                               rooms. ⌄
the comfort of our own living ~~room.~~ We can see˙
                                 ⌄
more games than if we had to attend each one in
                a   *variety*
person, and we can follow greater ~~varieties~~ of
                              ⌄   ⌄
sports.

4

Build effective paragraphs.

Except for special-purpose paragraphs, such as introductions and conclusions (see 2a and 2c), paragraphs are clusters of information supporting an essay's main point (or advancing a story's action). Aim for paragraphs that are clearly focused, well developed, organized, coherent, and neither too long nor too short for easy reading.

4a Focus on a main point.

A paragraph should be unified around a main point. The point should be clear to readers, and all sentences in the paragraph must relate to it.

Stating the main point in a topic sentence

As readers move into a paragraph, they need to know where they are—in relation to the whole essay—and what to expect in the sentences to come. A good topic sentence, a one-sentence summary of the paragraph's main point, acts as a signpost pointing in two directions: backward toward the thesis of the essay and forward toward the body of the paragraph.

Like a thesis statement (see 2a), a topic sentence is more general than the material supporting it. Usually the topic sentence comes first.

> *Nearly all living creatures manage some form of communication.* The dance patterns of bees in their hive help to point the way to distant flower fields or announce successful foraging. Male stickleback fish regularly swim upside-down to indicate outrage in a courtship contest. Male deer and lemurs mark territorial ownership by rubbing their own body secretions on boundary stones or trees. Everyone has seen a frightened dog put his tail between his legs and run in panic. We, too, use gestures, expressions, postures, and movement to give our words point. [Italics added.]   —Olivia Vlahos, *Human Beginnings*

Sometimes the topic sentence is introduced by a transitional sentence linking it to earlier material. In the following paragraph, the topic sentence (italicized) has been delayed to allow for a transition.

> But flowers are not the only source of spectacle in the wilderness. *An opportunity for late color is provided by the berries of wildflowers, shrubs, and trees.* Baneberry presents its tiny white flowers in spring but in late summer bursts forth with clusters of red berries. Bunchberry, a ground-cover plant, puts out red berries in the fall, and the red berries of wintergreen last from autumn well into winter. In California, the bright red, fist-sized clusters of Christmas berries can be seen growing beside highways for up to six months of the year. [Italics added.]
> —James Crockett et al., *Wildflower Gardening*

Occasionally the topic sentence may be withheld until the end of the paragraph—but only if the earlier sentences hang together so well that the reader perceives their direction, if not their exact point. The opening sentences of the following paragraph state facts, so they are supporting material rather than topic sentences, but they strongly suggest a central idea. The topic sentence at the end is hardly a surprise.

> Tobacco chewing starts as soon as people begin stirring. Those who have fresh supplies soak the new leaves in water and add ashes from the hearth to the wad. Men, women, and children chew tobacco and all are addicted to it. Once there was a shortage of tobacco in Kaobawa's village and I was plagued for a week by early morning visitors who requested permission to collect my cigarette butts in order to make a wad of chewing tobacco. Normally, if anyone is short of tobacco, he can request a share of someone else's already chewed wad, or simply borrow the entire wad when its owner puts it down somewhere. *Tobacco is so important to them that their word for "poverty" translates as "being without tobacco."* [Italics added.]
> —Napoleon A. Chagnon, *Yanomamo: The Fierce People*

Although it is generally wise to use topic sentences, at times they are unnecessary. A topic sentence may not be needed if a paragraph continues developing an idea clearly introduced in a previous paragraph, if the details of the paragraph unmistakably suggest its main point, or if the paragraph appears in a narrative of events where generalizations might interrupt the flow of the story.

Sticking to the point

Sentences that do not support the topic sentence destroy the unity of a paragraph. If the paragraph is otherwise well focused, such offending sentences can simply be deleted or perhaps moved elsewhere. In the following paragraph describing the inadequate facilities in a high school, the information about the word processing instructor (in italics) is clearly off the point.

> As the result of tax cuts, the educational facilities of Lincoln High School have reached an all-time low. Some of the books date back to 1985 and have long since shed their covers. The lack of lab equipment makes it necessary for four to five students to work at one table, with most watching rather than performing experiments. The few computers in working order must share one dot matrix printer. *Also, the word processing instructor left to have a baby at the beginning of the semester, and most of the students don't like the substitute.* As for the furniture, many of the upright chairs have become recliners, and the desk legs are so unbalanced that they play seesaw on the floor.

Sometimes the cure for a disunified paragraph is not as simple as deleting or moving material. Writers often wander into uncharted territory because they cannot think of enough evidence to support a topic sentence. Feeling that it is too soon to break into a new paragraph, they move on to new ideas for which they have not prepared the reader. When this happens, the writer is faced with a choice: Either find more evidence to support the topic sentence or adjust the topic sentence to mesh with the evidence that is available.

EXERCISE 4–1

Underline the topic sentence in the following paragraph and eliminate any material that does not clarify or develop the central idea.

> Historically, quilt making has served as an important means of social, political, and artistic expression for women. In the nineteenth century, especially, quilting circles provided one of the few opportunities for the women of a community to forge social bonds outside of their families. Once a week or more, they came together to sew as well as trade small talk, advice, and news. They used dyed cotton fabrics much like the fabrics quilters use today; surprisingly, quilters' basic materials haven't

changed that much over the years. Sometimes the women joined their efforts in the support of a political cause, making quilts that would be raffled to raise money for temperance societies, hospitals for sick and wounded soldiers, and the fight against slavery. The abolitionist movement, in particular, led one activist, Sarah Grimké, to memorably express her hopes for herself and fellow quilters: "May the points of our needles prick the slave owner's conscience." Quilt making also afforded women a means of artistic expression at a time when they had few other creative outlets. Within their socially acceptable roles as homemakers, many quilters subtly—and perhaps subconsciously—pushed back at the restrictions placed on them by experimenting with color, design, and technique.

4b Develop the main point.

Though an occasional short paragraph is fine, particularly if it functions as a transition or emphasizes a point, a series of brief paragraphs suggests inadequate development. How much development is enough? That varies, depending on the writer's purpose and audience.

For example, when she wrote a paragraph attempting to convince readers that it is impossible to lose fat quickly, health columnist Jane Brody knew that she would have to present a great deal of evidence because many dieters want to believe the opposite. She did *not* write:

> When you think about it, it's impossible to lose—as many diets suggest—10 pounds of *fat* in ten days, even on a total fast. Even a moderately active person cannot lose so much weight so fast. A less active person hasn't a prayer.

This three-sentence paragraph is too skimpy to be convincing. But the paragraph that Brody wrote contains enough evidence to convince even skeptical readers.

> When you think about it, it's impossible to lose—as many diets suggest—10 pounds of *fat* in ten days, even on a total fast. A pound of body fat represents 3,500 calories. To lose 1 pound of fat, you must expend 3,500 more calories than you consume. Let's say you weigh 170 pounds and, as a moderately active person, you burn 2,500 calories a day. If your diet contains only 1,500 calories, you'd have an energy deficit of 1,000 calories a day. In a week's time that would add up to a 7,000-calorie

deficit, or 2 pounds of real fat. In ten days, the accumulated deficit would represent nearly 3 pounds of lost body fat. Even if you ate nothing at all for ten days and maintained your usual level of activity, your caloric deficit would add up to 25,000 calories. . . . At 3,500 calories per pound of fat, that's still only 7 pounds of lost fat.   —Jane Brody, *Jane Brody's Nutrition Book*

4c Choose a suitable pattern of organization.

Although paragraphs (and indeed whole essays) may be patterned in any number of ways, certain patterns of organization occur frequently, either alone or in combination: examples and illustrations, narration, description, process, comparison and contrast, analogy, cause and effect, classification and division, and definition. There is nothing particularly magical about these patterns (sometimes called *methods of development*). They simply reflect some of the ways in which we think.

Examples and illustrations

Examples, perhaps the most common pattern of development, are appropriate whenever the reader might be tempted to ask, "For example?" Though examples are just selected instances, not a complete catalog, they are enough to suggest the truth of many topic sentences, as in the following paragraph.

> Normally my parents abided scrupulously by "The Budget," but several times a year Dad would dip into his battered, black strongbox and splurge on some irrational, totally satisfying luxury. Once he bought over a hundred comic books at a flea market, doled out to us thereafter at the tantalizing rate of two a week. He always got a whole flat of pansies, Mom's favorite flower, for us to give her on Mother's Day. One day a boy stopped at our house selling fifty-cent raffle tickets on a sailboat and Dad bought every ticket the boy had left—three books' worth.   —Connie Hailey, student

Illustrations are extended examples, frequently presented in story form. Because they require several sentences apiece, they are used more sparingly than examples. When well selected, however, they can be a vivid and effective means of developing a point. The writer of the following paragraph uses illustrations to demonstrate that Harriet Tubman, famous conductor on the underground railroad for escaping slaves, was a genius at knowing how and when to retreat.

Part of Harriet Tubman's strategy of conducting was, as in all battle-field operations, the knowledge of how and when to retreat. Numerous allusions have been made to her moves when she suspected that she was in danger. When she feared the party was closely pursued, she would take it for a time on a train southward bound. No one seeing Negroes going in this direction would for an instant suppose them to be fugitives. Once on her return she was at a railway station. She saw some men reading a poster and she heard one of them reading it aloud. It was a description of her, offering a reward for her capture. She took a southbound train to avert suspicion. At another time when Harriet heard men talking about her, she pretended to read a book which she carried. One man remarked, "This cannot be the woman. The one we want can't read or write." Harriet devoutly hoped the book was right side up.   —Earl Conrad, *Harriet Tubman*

Narration

A paragraph of narration tells a story or part of a story. Narrative paragraphs are usually arranged in chronological order, but they may also contain flashbacks, interruptions that take the story back to an earlier time. The following paragraph, from Jane Goodall's *In the Shadow of Man,* recounts one of the author's experiences in the African wild.

One evening when I was wading in the shallows of the lake to pass a rocky outcrop, I suddenly stopped dead as I saw the sinuous black body of a snake in the water. It was all of six feet long, and from the slight hood and the dark stripes at the back of the neck I knew it to be a Storm's water cobra—a deadly reptile for the bite of which there was, at that time, no serum. As I stared at it an incoming wave gently deposited part of its body on one of my feet. I remained motionless, not even breathing, until the wave rolled back into the lake, drawing the snake with it. Then I leaped out of the water as fast as I could, my heart hammering.   —Jane Goodall, *In the Shadow of Man*

Description

A descriptive paragraph sketches a portrait of a person, place, or thing by using concrete and specific details that appeal to one or more of our senses—sight, sound, smell, taste, and touch. Consider, for example, the following description of the grasshopper invasions that devastated the midwestern landscape in the late 1860s.

The Writing Process

They came like dive bombers out of the west. They came by the millions with the rustle of their wings roaring overhead. They came in waves, like the rolls of the sea, descending with a terrifying speed, breaking now and again like a mighty surf. They came with the force of a williwaw and they formed a huge, ominous, dark brown cloud that eclipsed the sun. They dipped and touched earth, hitting objects and people like hailstones. But they were not hail. These were live demons. They popped, snapped, crackled, and roared. They were dark brown, an inch or longer in length, plump in the middle and tapered at the ends. They had transparent wings, slender legs, and two black eyes that flashed with a fierce intelligence.

—Eugene Boe, "Pioneers to Eternity"

Process

A process paragraph is patterned in time order, usually chronologically. A writer may choose this pattern either to describe a process or to show readers how to perform a process. The following paragraph describes what happens when water freezes.

In school we learned that with few exceptions the solid phase of matter is more dense than the liquid phase. Water, alone among common substances, violates this rule. As water begins to cool, it contracts and becomes more dense, in a perfectly typical way. But about four degrees above the freezing point, something remarkable happens. It ceases to contract and begins expanding, becoming less dense. At the freezing point the expansion is abrupt and drastic. As water turns to ice, it adds about one-eleventh to its liquid volume.

—Chet Raymo, "Curious Stuff, Water and Ice"

Here is a paragraph explaining how to perform a "roll cast," a popular fly fishing technique:

Begin by taking up a suitable stance, with one foot slightly in front of the other and the rod pointing down the line. Then begin a smooth, steady draw, raising your rod hand to just above shoulder height and lifting the rod to the 10:30 or 11:00 position. This steady draw allows a loop of line to form between the rod top and the water. While the line is still moving, raise the rod slightly, then punch it rapidly forward and down. The rod is now flexed and under maximum compression, and the line follows its path, bellying out slightly behind you and coming off the water close to your feet. As you power the rod down through the 3:00 position, the belly of the line will roll forward. Follow through smoothly so that the line unfolds and straightens above the water. — *The Dorling Kindersley Encyclopedia of Fishing*

Comparison and contrast

To compare two subjects is to draw attention to their similarities, although the word *compare* also has a broader meaning that includes a consideration of differences. To contrast is to focus only on differences.

Whether a comparison-and-contrast paragraph stresses similarities or differences, it may be patterned in one of two ways. The two subjects may be presented one at a time, block style, as in the following paragraph of contrast.

> So Grant and Lee were in complete contrast, representing two diametrically opposed elements in American life. Grant was the modern man emerging; beyond him, ready to come on the stage, was the great age of steel and machinery, of crowded cities and a restless burgeoning vitality. Lee might have ridden down from the old age of chivalry, lance in hand, silken banner fluttering over his head. Each man was the perfect champion of his cause, drawing both his strengths and weaknesses from the people he led.
> —Bruce Catton, "Grant and Lee: A Study in Contrasts"

Or a paragraph may proceed point by point, treating the two subjects together, one aspect at a time. The following paragraph uses the point-by-point method to contrast the writer's academic experiences in an American high school with those in an Irish convent.

> Strangely enough, instead of being academically inferior to my American high school, the Irish convent was superior. In my class at home, *Love Story* was considered pretty heavy reading, so imagine my surprise at finding Irish students who could recite passages from *War and Peace.* In high school we complained about having to study *Romeo and Juliet* in one semester, whereas in Ireland we simultaneously studied *Macbeth* and Dickens's *Hard Times,* in addition to writing a composition a day in English class. In high school, I didn't even begin algebra until the ninth grade, while at the convent seventh graders (or their Irish equivalent) were doing calculus and trigonometry.
> —Margaret Stack, student

Analogy

Analogies draw comparisons between items that appear to have little in common. Writers turn to analogies for a variety of reasons: to make the unfamiliar seem familiar, to provide a concrete understanding of an abstract topic, to argue a point, or to provoke fresh thoughts or changed feelings about a subject. In the following paragraph, physician Lewis Thomas draws an analogy between the behavior of ants and that of humans. Thomas's analogy helps us to understand the social behavior of ants and forces us to question the superiority of our own human societies.

> Ants are so much like human beings as to be an embarrassment. They farm fungi, raise aphids as livestock, launch armies into wars, use chemical sprays to alarm and confuse enemies, capture slaves. The families of weaver ants engage in child labor, holding their larvae like shuttles to spin out the thread that sews the leaves together for their fungus gardens. They exchange information ceaselessly. They do everything but watch television.
> —Lewis Thomas, "On Societies as Organisms"

Although analogies can be a powerful tool for illuminating a subject, they should be used with caution in arguments. Just because two things may be alike in one respect, we cannot conclude that they are alike in all respects. (See *false analogy,* p. 359.)

Cause and effect

When causes and effects are a matter of argument, they are too complex to be reduced to a simple pattern (see p. 359). However, if a writer wishes merely to describe a cause-and-effect relationship that is generally accepted, then the effect may be stated in the topic sentence, with the causes listed in the body of the paragraph.

> The fantastic water clarity of the Mount Gambier sink-holes results from several factors. The holes are fed from aquifers holding rainwater that fell decades—even centuries—ago, and that has been filtered through miles of limestone. The high level of calcium that limestone adds causes the silty detritus from dead plants and animals to cling together and settle quickly to the bottom. Abundant bottom vegetation in the shallow sinkholes also helps bind the silt. And the rapid turnover of water prohibits stagnation. —Hillary Hauser,
> "Exploring a Sunken Realm in Australia"

Or the paragraph may move from cause to effects, as in this paragraph from a student paper on the effects of the industrial revolution on American farms.

The rise of rail transport in the nineteenth century forever changed American farming—for better and for worse. Farmers who once raised crops and livestock to sustain just their own families could now make a profit by selling their goods in towns and cities miles away. These new markets improved the living standard of struggling farm families and encouraged them to seek out innovations that would increase their profits. On the downside, the competition fostered by the new markets sometimes created hostility among neighboring farm families where there had once been a spirit of cooperation. Those farmers who couldn't compete with their neighbors left farming forever, facing poverty worse than they had ever known.

—Chris Mileski, student

Classification and division

Classification is the grouping of items into categories according to some consistent principle. Philosopher Francis Bacon was using classification when he wrote that "some books are to be tasted, others to be swallowed, and some few to be chewed and digested." Bacon's principle for classifying books is the degree to which they are worthy of our attention, but books of course can be classified according to other principles. For example, an elementary school teacher might classify children's books according to their level of difficulty, or a librarian might group them by subject matter. The principle of classification that a writer chooses ultimately depends on the purpose of the classification.

The following paragraph classifies species of electric fish.

Scientists sort electric fishes into three categories. The first comprises the strongly electric species like the marine electric rays or the freshwater African electric catfish and South American electric eel. Known since the dawn of history, these deliver a punch strong enough to stun a human. In recent years, biologists have focused on a second category: weakly electric fish in the South American and African rivers that use tiny voltages for communication and navigation. The third group contains sharks, nonelectric rays, and catfish, which do not emit a field but possess sensors that enable them to detect the minute amounts of electricity that leak out of other organisms.

—Anne Rudloe and Jack Rudloe, "Electric Warfare: The Fish That Kill with Thunderbolts"

Division takes one item and divides it into parts. As with classification, division should be made according to some consistent principle. Dividing a tree into roots, trunk, branches, and leaves makes sense; listing its components as branches, wood, water, and sap does not, for the categories overlap.

The following passage describes the components that make up a baseball:

> Like the game itself, a baseball is composed of many layers. One of the delicious joys of childhood is to take apart a baseball and examine the wonders within. You begin by removing the red cotton thread and peeling off the leather cover—which comes from the hide of a Holstein cow and has been tanned, cut, printed, and punched with holes. Beneath the cover is a thin layer of cotton string, followed by several hundred yards of woolen yarn, which make up the bulk of the ball. Slice into the rubber and you'll find the ball's heart—a cork core. The cork is from Portugal, the rubber from southeast Asia, the covers are American, and the balls are assembled in Costa Rica.
> —Dan Gutman, *The Way Baseball Works*

Definition

A definition puts a word or concept into a general class and then provides enough details to distinguish it from others in the same class. For example, in one of its senses the term *grit* names the class of things that birds eat, but it is restricted to those items—such as small pebbles, eggshell, and ashes—that help the bird grind food.

Many definitions may be presented in a sentence or two, but abstract or difficult concepts may require a paragraph or even a full essay of definition. In the following paragraph, the writer defines envy as a special kind of desire.

> Envy is so integral and so painful a part of what animates human behavior in market societies that many people have forgotten the full meaning of the word, simplifying it into one of the synonyms of desire. It is that, which may be why it flourishes in market societies: democracies of desire, they might be called, with money for ballots, stuffing permitted. But envy is more or less than desire. It begins with the almost frantic sense of emptiness inside oneself, as if the pump of one's heart were sucking on air. One has to be blind to perceive the emptiness, of course, but that's just what envy is, a selective blindness. *Invidia,* Latin for envy, translates as "nonsight," and Dante had the envious plodding along under cloaks of lead, their eyes sewn shut with leaden wire. What they are blind to is what they have, God-given and humanly nurtured, in themselves.
> —Nelson W. Aldrich, Jr., *Old Money*

EXERCISE 4–2

Write a paragraph modeled on one of the patterns discussed in this section. Some possible topics—most of which you'll need to restrict—are listed here.

Examples or illustrations: sexism in a comic strip, ways to include protein in a vegetarian diet, the benefits of a particular summer job, community services provided by your college, violence on the six o'clock news, educational software for children

Narration: the active lifestyle of a grandparent, life with an alcoholic, working in an emergency room, the benefits (or problems) of intercultural dating, growing up in a large family, the rewards of working in a nursing home, an experience that taught you a lesson, a turning point in your life

Description: your childhood home, an ethnic neighborhood, a rock concert, a favorite painting in an art gallery, a garden, a classic car, a hideous building or monument, a style of dress, a family heirloom (such as a crazy quilt or a collection of Christmas tree ornaments), a favorite park or retreat

Process: how to repair something, how to develop a successful job interview style, how to ask someone out on a date, how to practice safe scuba diving, how to build a set for a play, how to survive in the wilderness, how to train a dog, how to quit smoking, how to make bread

Comparison and contrast: two neighborhoods, teachers, political candidates, colleges, products; country living versus city living; the stereotype of a job versus the reality; a change in attitude toward your family's religion or ethnic background

Analogy: between a family reunion and a circus, between training for a rigorous sport and boot camp, between settling an argument and being a courtroom judge, between a dogfight and a boxing match, between raising a child and tending a garden

Cause and effect: the effects of water pollution on a particular area, the effects of divorce on a child, the effects of an illegal drug, why a particular film or television show is popular, why an area of the country has high unemployment, why early training is essential for success as a ballet dancer, violinist, or athlete

Classification: types of clothing worn on your college campus, types of people who join online chat groups, types of dieters, types of television weather reports, types of rock bands, types of teachers

Definition: an Internet addict, an ideal parent or teacher, an authoritarian personality, an intellectual, a sexist, anorexia nervosa, a typical heroine in a Harlequin romance, a typical blind date

4d Consider possible ways of arranging information.

In addition to choosing a pattern of development (or a combination of patterns), you may need to make decisions about arrangement. If you are developing a paragraph with examples, for instance, you'll need to decide how to order the examples. Or if you are contrasting two items point by point, you'll need to decide which points to discuss first, second, and so on. Often considerations of purpose and audience will help you make these choices.

Three of the most common ways of arranging information are treated in this section: time order, spatial order, and order of climax. Other possible arrangements include order of complexity (from simple to complex), order of familiarity (from most familiar to least familiar), and order of audience appeal (from "safe" ideas to those that may challenge the audience's views).

Order of time

Time order, usually chronological, is appropriate for a variety of purposes such as narrating a personal experience, telling an anecdote, describing an experiment, or explaining a process. The following paragraph, arranged in chronological order, is from an account of the author's travels on the back roads of America.

> Orion Saddle Road, after I was committed to it, narrowed to a single rutted lane affording no place to turn around; if I met somebody, one of us would have to back down. The higher I went, the more that idea unnerved me—the road was bad enough driving forward. The compass swung from point to point, and within five minutes it had touched each of the three hundred sixty degrees. The clutch started pushing back, and ruts and craters and rocks threw the steering wheel into nasty jerks that wrenched to the spine. I understood why, the day before, I'd thought there could be no road over the Chiricahuas; there wasn't. No wonder desperadoes hid in this inaccessibility.
> —William Least Heat Moon, *Blue Highways*

Time order need not be chronological. For example, you might decide to arrange events in the order in which they were revealed to you, not in the order in which they happened. Or you might choose to begin with a dramatic moment and then flash back to the events that led up to it.

Order of space

For descriptions of a location or a scene, a spatial arrangement will seem natural. Imagine yourself holding a video camera and you'll begin to see the possibilities. Might you pan the scene from afar and then zoom to a close-up? Would you rather sweep the camera from side to side—or from top to bottom? Or should you try for a more impressionistic effect, focusing the camera on first one and then another significant feature of the scene?

The writer of the following paragraph describes the contents of a long, narrow pool hall by taking us from the front to the back.

> The pool tables were in a line side by side from the front to the back of the long, narrow building. The first one was the biggest, and the best snooker players used it. Beyond it were the other tables used by lesser players, except for the last one. This was the bank's pool table, used only by the best players in the county.   —William G. Hill, student

Order of climax

When ideas are presented in the order of climax, they build toward a conclusion. Consider the following paragraph describing the effects on workers of long-term blue-collar employment. All of the examples have an emotional impact, but the final one —even though it might at first seem trivial—is the most powerful. It shows us just how degrading blue-collar work can become.

> I met people who taught me about human behavior. I saw people take amphetamines to keep up with ever-rising production rates. I saw good friends, and even relatives, physically attack each other over job assignments that would mean a few cents' difference. I observed women cheating on their husbands and men cheating on their wives. I watched women hand over their entire paycheck to a bookie. I saw pregnant women, their feet too swollen for shoes, come to work in slippers. I saw

women with colds stuff pieces of tissue up their nostrils so they wouldn't have to keep stopping to blow their noses.

—Linda Lavelle, student

Because the order of climax saves the most dramatic examples for the end, it is appropriate only when readers are likely to persist until the end. In much business writing, for example, you cannot assume that readers will read more than the first couple of sentences of a paragraph. In such cases, you will be wise to open with your most powerful examples, even at the risk of allowing the paragraph to fizzle at the end.

4e Make paragraphs coherent.

When sentences and paragraphs flow from one to another without discernible bumps, gaps, or shifts, they are said to be coherent. Coherence can be improved by strengthening the various ties between old information and new. A number of techniques for strengthening those ties are detailed in this section.

Linking ideas clearly

Readers expect to learn a paragraph's main point in a topic sentence early in the paragraph. Then, as they move into the body of the paragraph, they expect to encounter specific facts, details, or examples that support the topic sentence—either directly or indirectly. Consider the following paragraph, in which all of the sentences following the topic sentence directly support it.

> A passenger list of the early years of the Orient Express would read like a *Who's Who of the World,* from art to politics. Sarah Bernhardt and her Italian counterpart Eleonora Duse used the train to thrill the stages of Europe. For musicians there were Toscanini and Mahler. Dancers Nijinsky and Pavlova were there, while lesser performers like Harry Houdini and the girls of the Ziegfeld Follies also rode the rails. Violinists were allowed to practice on the train, and occasionally one might see trapeze artists hanging like bats from the baggage racks.
>
> — Barnaby Conrad III, "Train of Kings"

If a sentence does not support the topic sentence directly, readers expect it to support another sentence in the paragraph and therefore to support the topic sentence indirectly. The following paragraph begins with a topic sentence. The italicized sentences are direct supports, and the rest of the sentences are indirect supports.

> Though the open-space classroom works for many children, it is not practical for my son, David. *First, David is hyperactive.* When he was placed in an open-space classroom, he became distracted and confused. He was tempted to watch the movement going on around him instead of concentrating on his own work. *Second, David has a tendency to transpose letters and numbers, a tendency that can be overcome only by individual attention from the instructor.* In the open classroom he was moved from teacher to teacher, with each one responsible for a different subject. No single teacher worked with David long enough to diagnose the problem, let alone help him with it. *Finally, David is not a highly motivated learner.* In the open classroom, he was graded "at his own level," not by criteria for a certain grade. He could receive a B in reading and still be a grade level behind, because he was doing satisfactory work "at his own level."
>
> — Margaret Smith, student

Repeating key words

Repetition of key words is an important technique for gaining coherence. To prevent repetitions from becoming dull, you can use variations of a key word (*hike, hiker, hiking*), pronouns referring to the word (*gamblers . . . they*), and synonyms (*run, spring, race, dash*). In the following paragraph describing plots among indentured servants in the seventeenth century, historian Richard Hofstadter binds sentences together by repeating the key word *plots* and echoing it with a variety of synonyms (which are italicized).

> *Plots* hatched by several servants to run away together occurred mostly in the plantation colonies, and the few recorded servant *uprisings* were entirely limited to those colonies. Virginia had been forced from its very earliest years to take stringent steps against *mutinous plots,* and severe punishments for *such behavior* were recorded. Most servant *plots* occurred in the seventeenth century: a contemplated *uprising* was nipped in the bud in York County in 1661; apparently led by some left-wing offshoots of the *Great Rebellion,* servants *plotted* an *insurrection* in Gloucester County in 1663, and four leaders were condemned and executed; some discontented servants apparently

joined *Bacon's Rebellion* in the 1670s. In the 1680s the planters became newly apprehensive of discontent among the servants "owing to their great necessities and want of clothes," and it was feared that they would *rise up* and *plunder* the storehouses and ships; in 1682 there were plant-cutting *riots* in which servants and laborers, as well as some planters, took part. [Italics added.]
— Richard Hofstadter, *America at 1750*

Using parallel structures

Parallel structures are frequently used within sentences to underscore the similarity of ideas (see 9). They may also be used to bind together a series of sentences expressing similar information. In the following passage describing folk beliefs, anthropologist Margaret Mead presents similar information in parallel grammatical form.

Actually, almost every day, even in the most sophisticated home, something is likely to happen that evokes the memory of some old folk belief. The salt spills. A knife falls to the floor. Your nose tickles. Then perhaps, with a slightly embarrassed smile, the person who spilled the salt tosses a pinch over his left shoulder. Or someone recites the old rhyme, "Knife falls, gentleman calls." Or as you rub your nose you think, That means a letter. I wonder who's writing?
—Margaret Mead, "New Superstitions for Old"

A less skilled writer might have varied the structure, perhaps like this: *The salt gets spilled. Mother drops a knife on the floor. Your nose begins to tickle.* But these sentences are less effective; Mead's parallel structures help tie the passage together.

Maintaining consistency

Coherence suffers whenever a draft shifts confusingly from one point of view to another or from one verb tense to another. (See 13.) In addition, coherence can suffer when new information is introduced with the subject of each sentence. As a rule, a sentence's subject should echo a subject or object in the previous sentence.

The following rough-draft paragraph is needlessly hard to read because so few of the sentences' subjects are tied to earlier subjects or objects. The subjects appear in italics.

> *One* goes about trapping in this manner. At the very outset *one* acquires a "trapping" state of mind. A *library* of books must be read, and preferably *someone* with experience should educate the novice. *Preparing* for the first expedition takes several steps. The *purchase* of traps is first. A *pair* of rubber gloves, waterproof *boots*, and the grubbiest *clothes* capable of withstanding human use come next to outfit the trapper for his adventure. Finally, the *decision* has to be made on just what kind of animals to seek, what sort of bait to use, and where to place the traps.

Although the writer repeats a number of key words, such as *trapping*, the paragraph seems disconnected because new information is introduced with the subject of each sentence.

To improve the paragraph, the writer used the first-person pronoun as the subject of every sentence. The revision is much easier to read.

> *I* went about trapping in this manner. To acquire a "trapping" state of mind, *I* read a library of books and talked at length with an experienced trapper, my father. Then *I* purchased the traps and outfitted myself by collecting a pair of rubber gloves, waterproof boots, and the grubbiest clothes capable of withstanding human use. Finally, *I* decided just what kinds of animals to seek, what sort of bait to use, and where to place my traps.   —John Clyde Thatcher, student

Notice that Thatcher combined some of his original sentences. By doing so, he was able to avoid excessive repetitions of the pronoun *I*. Notice, too, that he varied his sentence openings (most sentences do not begin with *I*) so that readers are not likely to find the repetitions tiresome.

Providing transitions

Transitions are bridges between what has been read and what is about to be read. Transitions help readers move from sentence to sentence; they also alert readers to more global connections of ideas—those between paragraphs or even larger blocks of text.

SENTENCE-LEVEL TRANSITIONS   Certain words and phrases signal connections between (or within) sentences. Frequently used transitions are included in the following list.

TO SHOW ADDITION
and, also, besides, further, furthermore, in addition, moreover,
next, too, first, second

TO GIVE EXAMPLES
for example, for instance, to illustrate, in fact, specifically

TO COMPARE
also, in the same manner, similarly, likewise

TO CONTRAST
but, however, on the other hand, in contrast, nevertheless, still,
even though, on the contrary, yet, although

TO SUMMARIZE OR CONCLUDE
in other words, in short, in summary, in conclusion, to sum up,
that is, therefore

TO SHOW TIME
after, as, before, next, during, later, finally, meanwhile, then,
when, while, immediately

TO SHOW PLACE OR DIRECTION
above, below, beyond, farther on, nearby, opposite, close,
to the left

TO INDICATE LOGICAL RELATIONSHIP
if, so, therefore, consequently, thus, as a result, for this reason,
since

Skilled writers use transitional expressions with care, making sure, for example, not to use *consequently* when an *also* would be more precise. They are also careful to select transitions with an appropriate tone, perhaps preferring *so* to *thus* in an informal piece, *in summary* to *in short* for a scholarly essay. In the following paragraph, taken from an argument that dinosaurs had the " 'right-sized' brains for reptiles of their body size," biologist Stephen Jay Gould uses transitions (italicized) with skill.

I don't wish to deny that the flattened, minuscule head of
the large bodied "Stegosaurus" houses little brain from our subjective, top-heavy perspective, *but* I do wish to assert that we
should not expect more of the beast. *First of all,* large animals
have relatively smaller brains than related, small animals. The
correlation of brain size with body size among kindred animals
(all reptiles, all mammals, *for example*) is remarkably regular. *As*
we move from small to large animals, from mice to elephants *or*

small lizards to Komodo dragons, brain size increases, *but* not so fast as body size. *In other words,* bodies grow faster than brains, *and* large animals have low ratios of brain weight to body weight. *In fact,* brains grow only about two-thirds as fast as bodies. *Since* we have no reason to believe that large animals are consistently stupider than their smaller relatives, we must conclude that large animals require relatively less brain to do as well as smaller animals. *If* we do not recognize this relationship, we are likely to underestimate the mental power of very large animals, dinosaurs in particular. [Italics added.]

—Stephen Jay Gould, "Were Dinosaurs Dumb?"

CAUTION: Do not be too self-conscious about plugging in transition words while you are drafting sentences; overuse of these signals can seem heavy-handed. Usually, you will use transitions quite naturally, just where readers need them. If you (or your reviewers) discover places where readers cannot easily move from sentence to sentence in your rough draft, you can always add transition words as you revise.

PARAGRAPH-LEVEL TRANSITIONS   Paragraph-level transitions usually link the *first* sentence of a new paragraph with the *first* sentence of the previous paragraph. In other words, the topic sentences signal global connections.

Look for opportunities to allude to the subject of a previous paragraph (as summed up in its topic sentence) in the topic sentence of the next one. In his essay "Little Green Lies," Jonathan H. Alder uses this strategy in the following topic sentences, which appear in a passage describing the benefits of plastic packaging.

> Consider aseptic packaging, the synthetic packaging for the "juice boxes" so many children bring to school with their lunch. [*Rest of paragraph omitted.*]

> What is true for juice boxes is also true for other forms of synthetic packaging. [*Rest of paragraph omitted.*]

TRANSITIONS BETWEEN BLOCKS OF TEXT   In long essays, you will need to alert readers to connections between blocks of text more than one paragraph long. You can do this by inserting transitional sentences or short paragraphs at key points in the essay. Here, for example, is a transitional paragraph from a student research paper by Karen Shaw. It announces that the first part of her paper has come to a close and the second part is about to begin.

Although the great apes have demonstrated significant language skills, one central question remains: Can they be taught to use that uniquely human language tool we call grammar, to learn the difference, for instance, between "ape bite human" and "human bite ape"? In other words, can an ape create a sentence?

Another strategy to help readers move from one block of text to another is to insert headings in your essay. Headings, which usually sit above blocks of text, allow you to announce a new topic boldly, without the need for subtle transitions. (See 5b.)

4f If necessary, adjust paragraph length.

Most readers feel comfortable reading paragraphs that range between 100 and 200 words. Shorter paragraphs force too much starting and stopping, and longer ones strain the reader's attention span. There are exceptions to this guideline, however. Paragraphs longer than 200 words frequently appear in scholarly writing, where they suggest seriousness and depth. Paragraphs shorter than 100 words occur in newspapers because of narrow columns; in informal essays to quicken the pace; and in business letters, where readers routinely skim for main ideas.

In an essay, the first and last paragraphs will ordinarily be the introduction and conclusion. These special-purpose paragraphs are likely to be shorter than the paragraphs in the body of the essay. Typically, the body paragraphs will follow the essay's outline: one paragraph per point in short essays, a group of paragraphs per point in longer ones. Some ideas require more development than others, however, so it is best to be flexible. If an idea stretches to a length unreasonable for a paragraph, you should divide the paragraph, even if you have presented comparable points in the essay in single paragraphs.

Paragraph breaks are not always made for strictly logical reasons. Writers use them for the following reasons as well.

REASONS FOR BEGINNING A NEW PARAGRAPH

—to mark off the introduction and conclusion
—to signal a shift to a new idea
—to indicate an important shift in time or place
—to emphasize a point (by placing it at the beginning or the end, not in the middle, of a paragraph)

—to highlight a contrast
—to signal a change of speakers (in dialogue)
—to provide readers with a needed pause
—to break up text that looks too dense

Beware of using too many short, choppy paragraphs, however. Readers want to see how your ideas connect, and they become irritated when you break their momentum by forcing them to pause every few sentences. Here are some reasons you might have for combining some of the paragraphs in a rough draft.

REASONS FOR COMBINING PARAGRAPHS

—to clarify the essay's organization
—to connect closely related ideas
—to bind together text that looks too choppy

WRITING ASSIGNMENTS AND STUDENT ESSAYS

This section contains seven writing assignments, each illustrated with a student essay. The first three assignments are based on personal experience, and the last four are based on reading.

—Profiling a person or a place
—Explaining an insight
—Narrating an event
—Summarizing two readings
—Analyzing a reading
—Arguing a point
—Writing a research paper

Your instructor may decide to modify these assignments—or choose not to use them at all. You should of course follow the exact assignments that your instructor provides.

Even if you are not asked to do the assignments in this book, you may want to browse through the student essays. Don't be surprised if you pick up some writing ideas along the way: You can learn much about writing by seeing what has worked for others.

NOTE TO INSTRUCTORS: These writing assignments and sample student essays appear on the Hacker Handbook Web site: < http://www.bedfordstmartins.com/hacker/assignments >. Feel free to adapt the assignments for your own purposes. You may want to provide your students with other models, perhaps including a professional essay in addition to a student one.

Profiling a person or a place

THE ASSIGNMENT

A profile describes a person or a place—not just in general, but with a particular focus. You might focus on a person's interesting job, hobby, or lifestyle. You might write about someone who has made a major contribution to his or her community, church, place of employment, or organization; someone who has overcome a problem such as anorexia or a learning disability; or someone who played a significant role in your growing up. You could profile someone you do not admire: an abusive parent, for example, or a childhood friend who joined a violent gang.

If you'd rather profile a place, consider taking readers into an unfamiliar or exotic world—a scuba diving expedition, a spelunking adventure, a boat trip through the Everglades. Encourage readers to visit a favorite museum, historic district, or park (or discourage them from visiting a place you found disappointing). Introduce readers to a foreign country or an ethnic neighborhood with which you are familiar.

Unless you have a good reason for omitting it, include a thesis sentence in your introductory paragraph, probably at its end (see section 2a). For this assignment, your information should come from personal knowledge, interviews, or direct observation. Aim for an essay from 500 to 1,000 words long—two to four typed pages, double-spaced.

STUDENT PAPER: PROFILING A PERSON

Grandpa

I don't have a lot of fantastic memories of childhood. There were no spectacular family adventures, no unique family projects that taught some sort of moral lesson, no out-of-the-ordinary holidays. We ate family meals together, but most of the time the children and adults lived in different worlds. The kids went to school, did homework, and played; the adults worked. I was lucky, though. When I wanted a little of both worlds, I could always turn to Grandpa.

Thesis, at end of introduction, announces focus of paper.

I remember vividly the weekends at his house. Sitting on his lap, going to wrestling matches, walking down the street or through a park--these were things I did with Grandpa. I wasn't just a kid to him: I was his granddaughter, and I was special. He was special too.

Thomas D. Williford was a giant of a man. He stood six feet two inches and weighed over 250 pounds. He moved with purpose and carried himself with respect. Tom was a proud man, a good man, and all who knew him said so. Even if you didn't know him, you would notice his inner strength, his patience, his self-esteem.

Grandpa wasn't a scholar. In fact, he didn't even make it through grade school. He was born at the turn of the century, and educating black men wasn't a necessity then. He went to work when he was sixteen, and for the next forty years he worked in a coal factory. Then he worked in a steel mill for another twenty years. He stopped working only because the steel mill closed and he was too old to find another job.

When I was with Grandpa, I could be a child and yet see things through grown-up eyes. "You see that tree, Cookie," he would say. "That tree was here before those houses. God put that tree there; man put the houses. Which is more beautiful?" If I climbed a tree, he didn't say, "Get down." He said, "Climb it right so you won't fall."

"You appreciate what you work for," he used to say. He taught that lesson well. He never let me win any game; he taught me to win by learning to lose. If he couldn't answer a question, he was honest about it, but he would also say, "Why don't you find out and let me know too." He listened to me and he heard my feelings, not just my words.

There was a tougher side to Grandpa, and I suppose this, too, made him special. There was the black man who fled with his near-white wife and

Physical details help reader visualize subject.

Dialogue helps to develop the character.

Background
information
adds to reader's
understanding
of the character.

children from North Carolina to avoid harassment and
threats from the Ku Klux Klan. There was the quiet
man whose home was robbed three times by the same
drunk, who reported it three times to the police
with no results, and who finally waited for the man
to do it a fourth time--and shot him dead as he
climbed through the bedroom window in the middle of
the night. And there was the man who fractured his
leg at work, never reported it because he couldn't
afford not to work, and years later still endures
the pain of the ill-mended fracture.

Grandpa is almost ninety-five and now resides in
a nursing home in Windsor, North Carolina. The leg
he fractured forty years ago is too weak to carry

Paper ends by
summing up
tribute to the
character.

his weight. His eyes are going bad. But to me he's
still the big, strong man who used to take his
grandchild in his arms and rock her, the man who
taught a small child to see all the things around
her with open eyes, the man who taught a child to
try until she wins and becomes the best. He's still
special and, thanks to him, so am I.

— Diane Williford

STUDENT PAPER: PROFILING A PLACE

The Phillips Collection

Washington is a unique city for art lovers.
There is something for everyone, and it is all free.
On the Mall, the Freer offers its oriental treasures, the pristine marble of the National Gallery
houses the old masters of the Kress and Mellon collections, and the dynamic new Hirshhorn contains the
work of artists of this century. Not far away, one
can browse in the National Portrait Gallery or experience the Corcoran, where something new is always
happening. Georgetown and Capitol Hill boast clusters of small commercial galleries abounding with
contemporary efforts for those of more adventurous
tastes. My favorite Washington gallery, however, is

located in the once elegant and still interesting neighborhood surrounding Dupont Circle. There, on 21st Street, just above Massachusetts Avenue, you will find the Phillips Collection.

Duncan Phillips was an art collector extraordinaire. He and his wife, Marjorie, loved the Impressionists, Postimpressionists, and modern masters. Fortunately for us, they acquired their works by the score and hung them with care and pride in their red brick townhouse on 21st Street. When in 1918 Duncan Phillips decided to turn his hobby into a public institution, the house was included. To me, this is the great charm of the Phillips Collection. Many of the paintings still hang in that original residence.

As you stroll up 21st Street, the townhouse facades conjure up a feeling of a bygone era--an era of teas and debutante parties and glittering balls. Enter the door at 1612, and you find yourself not in a museum but in a gracious home whose owners have been kind enough to ask you in to view their treasures.

Wander at will through the rooms. Bask in the beauty of the Van Goghs, the Degas, the Cézannes. On a quiet day--and it usually is quiet and uncrowded there--you will swear you can hear the tinkle of crystal and the music and laughter of an elegant, long-ago party.

Suddenly, in the midst of your musings, you find yourself in a room ablaze with light, color, and life. There on the wall is Renoir's <u>Luncheon of the Boating Party</u>. Take a seat and treat yourself to a longer look. Settle back and feel the joy and warmth of the painting. Smell the early summer breeze off the Seine. Hear the rustle of the leaves and the hum of the conversation. Stay as long as you like, but remember, there is more.

As the collection grew, it became evident that the Georgian townhouse could not adequately display the new acquisitions. So in 1960 a new wing was opened adjoining the Phillips home. It too is beau-

Thesis, at end of the opening paragraph, announces focus of paper.

Use of second person point of view (you) draws reader into scene.

Specific details make description vivid.

Transitional sentence leads to next part of paper.

tiful in a different way and houses the more contemporary part of the collection.

As you enter the new wing, you will feel a
quickening, a transition from yesterday to today.
Gone are the lovely mantelpieces and views of the
charming walled garden. Here all is clean and uncluttered to display to best advantage the blazing
colors and stark lines of the modern masters. You
will find Picasso and Pollock and Dalí and Braque in
profusion.

Don't miss the Rothko room. Here, against a
black background, are hung Mark Rothko's huge color
paintings. As you sit here, you will find yourself
surrounded by pure, pulsating, sensuous color. Relax. Clear your thoughts and allow yourself to ab-
sorb the impact of the blazing reds and yellows, the
soothing tranquillity of the blues and greens. The
results are unforgettable.

> Sensory details
> help reader ex-
> perience gallery
> as writer did.

Assuming that you now can't wait to visit the
Phillips Collection and claim it for your own, I
must warn you that getting there is not half the
fun. The neighborhood, while interesting and charming, is a maze of narrow one-way streets totally de-
void of parking spaces. However, there is a Metro
stop within two or three blocks, and I promise you
the walk will be interesting.

In any event, go and see the Phillips Collection. On Sunday afternoons at five, there is the
bonus of a free concert by talented young musicians.
If you are an art lover, you can't miss. If you are
not an art lover, you just might become one.

> Conclusion en-
> courages reader
> to visit museum.

— Mary Kenny

Explaining an insight

THE ASSIGNMENT

When you explain an insight on a topic, you offer readers a fresh or
interesting way of looking at the topic. In other words, you give them
a way of understanding something that they may have understood
differently before.

You might challenge a conventional view that has not been validated by your own experience: the view, for example, that growing up in a small town is idyllic or that work as a flight attendant is glamorous. You might explain an insight about a group with which you are familiar: Harley-Davidson bikers, farmers, the physically challenged, people from another culture. You might give readers a new way of looking at some aspect of the media: maybe by poking fun at the language of sports announcers, revealing stereotypes in a television series, explaining why *Star Trek* has had such lasting appeal, or showing that the history of rap music is more complex than most people think. Or you might give readers an insight into one of your special interests, such as photography, mountain climbing, or one of the martial arts.

Your insight should appear in a thesis sentence early in the essay, most likely at the end of the introductory paragraph (see section 2a). For this assignment, your information should come from personal knowledge, interviews, or direct observation. Aim for an essay from 500 to 1,000 words long—from two to four typed pages, double-spaced.

STUDENT PAPER: EXPLAINING AN INSIGHT

E-mail--Return to Sender?

For many of us, turning on the computer and checking for e-mail messages has become as much a part of our daily routine as a trip to the mailbox. The growing popularity of e-mail makes us wonder how we ever survived without it. E-mail has many advantages over regular mail, including speed, low cost, and convenience. In our enthusiasm for e-mail, however, we would be unwise to abandon the post office altogether. For some purposes, e-mail is a poor substitute for "snail mail," both in our personal lives and in the business world.

Thesis appears at end of introduction.

There is no denying that e-mail has certain advantages over regular mail. The most obvious advantage is speed. We can send e-mail around the world in a matter of minutes with no more effort than it takes to press a few keys on the computer. It is this speed that has led to our calling regular mail "snail mail."

Second paragraph opens with clear topic sentence.

E-mail also has the advantage of being less expensive, for most people, than regular mail. Many

Topic sentence focuses on expense.

people have access to e-mail for free through their
work or school. And while some people may pay for
e-mail through an online service, there is no increase in cost relative to the number of messages
sent. It is the same price to send one message to
one person as it is to send messages back and forth
all day or to a hundred people. Finally, if we consider the costs saved in long-distance phone bills
in addition to the costs saved in postage, most
e-mail users surely come out ahead.

*Topic sentence
focuses on con-
venience.*

There is no question that e-mail is convenient.
It allows us to send the same message to many people
at the same time with little more effort than it
takes to send a message to one person. When sending
multiple copies of a message, we avoid the trouble
of photocopying the letter, printing out additional
copies, addressing envelopes, and posting the mail.
E-mail is also convenient because it lends itself to
an informal style that makes composing a message
relatively easy; in addition, readers of e-mail tol-
erate more mistakes than readers of conventional
mail, and their tolerance saves us time.

*Transitional
topic sentence
helps reader
move to second
part of paper.*

Despite the many benefits that e-mail provides,
it is not always appropriate. Before dashing off another piece of e-mail--in our private lives or in
the business world--we need to pause and consider
whether the post office or a carrier such as Federal
Express or UPS might be more fitting.

*Details show
appeal of tradi-
tional mail.*

It would be sad to think that letters from
friends might become obsolete. With e-mail, unfortunately, all messages look very much alike, and this
sameness removes some of the wonder of getting a
message in the first place. We have no handwriting
to scrutinize, no perfumed envelope to smell, no
colors or textures to enjoy. E-mail is also limited
by what we can send. Attached files might let us
send a copy of a photo, but we wouldn't want to put
it in a frame. We will never receive an e-mail care
package from home or an e-mail pop-up birthday card.

For these more personal things we must still rely on regular mail. Besides, opening old computer files is never as much fun as pulling a musty shoebox out of the closet to browse through old letters and photos.

In the business world, as in our personal lives, e-mail is not always an appropriate medium. First, there is the issue of privacy. Because of its electronic transmission in networked systems, e-mail may be accessible to co-workers and supervisors. It's probably not a good idea to complain about the boss on the company e-mail or to write anything that shouldn't be shared with strangers or potential enemies. A second problem with e-mail is its informality. For much company business, a certain level of courtesy and formality is desirable; e-mail can seem inappropriate because of its relatively slapdash quality. And finally, because of its speed, e-mail encourages "flaming," sending off rapid-fire emotional messages that can get a businessperson in serious trouble.

Details show dangers of e-mail in business world.

While e-mail gives us the ability to send messages with convenience, speed, and little expense, it lacks the personality and authority of regular mail. Luckily, however, we needn't always choose one over the other. Instead we should take advantage of both, using each to its best advantage: e-mail for quick notes, multiple mailings, and routine business correspondence; regular mail for personal messages and for formal or private business correspondence. Regular mail will always take a bit longer, but at times good things are worth waiting for.

Conclusion summarizes main points.

— Lauren Pent

Narrating an event

THE ASSIGNMENT

A narrative essay re-creates an experience for a central purpose: usually to reveal an insight about the action or people involved. You might write about an experience in which you encountered people from a culture different from your own. You might write about a turning point in your life—perhaps a time when you were forced suddenly to grow up, a time when you faced a difficult challenge, or a time when you reassessed your values. You might describe an experience in which you learned to do something new: coaching a Little League team, designing stage sets for a play, forming a musical group. Or you might recount an adventure that tested you in some way. If you have experienced work in an emergency room, on an ambulance or fire truck, or as a police officer, you might describe in vivid detail one day or evening at work to give readers an inside view of this stressful job.

A narrative should have a central focus, but it is not always necessary to express the focus in a thesis sentence early in the essay (see pp. 24–25); at times you will want to get right to the action. A narrative should of course be based on personal experience. Aim for an essay from 500 to 1,000 words long—two to four typed pages, double-spaced.

STUDENT PAPER: NARRATING AN EVENT

Michelle on Tape

Writer starts with action. No thesis is needed.

As I pulled into my parents' driveway, I realized how loud the radio was. I turned it down, peeled my legs off the blue vinyl seat, and lugged my pile of laundry up to the front door. The doorknob wouldn't turn and I still hadn't gotten around to making myself a duplicate key.

I rang the bell and waited. Nothing.

Specific details help reader visualize scene.

Leaving my basket of dirty clothes on the steps, I tramped through the bushes in front of the living room window. Pep was across the room sitting in his usual chair and reading the paper. He was a familiar sight in his plaid flannel shirt, striped clip-on bow tie, and tweed cabby hat.

I knocked on the window. He turned around, startled, and focused his eyes on me. I smiled and waved at him, but he just stared at me. I gestured toward the front door. His face had that hollow look, but something made him get up and let me in.

"Hi, Pep." I kissed him on the cheek. He made way for me and my laundry.

"Hello, how are you?"

I headed for the washing machine. Pep trailed closely behind.

Dialogue adds personality to characters.

"Kevin and Clare aren't home, but they should be here soon. Do you want to wait for them?"

"Yah, I'll be here." I began separating whites from darks.

"Do you want anything to eat? There's meat and bread in the ice box and some cookies in there."

"No thanks."

"I don't know where Kevin and Clare are. They took Katie out somewhere. Do you know Katie?"

I paused. Here we go. This was going to be one of those conversations. I should just say, "Why, yes, I know Katie." But perhaps if I venture a bit further, something might jog his memory and we wouldn't have to go through the whole routine. Dad says that Pep has a tape recorder in his brain, and bits and pieces keep getting erased.

Writer uses tape-recorder image for the first time.

I decided to give it a shot. "Pep, Katie is my sister."

It didn't work. Pep responded as though I hadn't said a word. "Yah. Well, they went down to . . ." He doubled his chin and scratched his chest with both hands.

"You know, down . . ."

"To the Donnellys'?"

"Yah, that's it. What did you say?"

I repeated, "Donnellys'," loud and clear. It was usually best to speak with as few words as possible. The name Donnelly had a vague significance in Pep's mind, but he had no idea that the Donnellys were my mother's sister and her family.

"Yes, that's right, they went to the Donnellys'. How did you know? What did you say your name was?"

Dialogue further illustrates Pep's memory loss.

"Michelle."

He smiled politely. "Oh, are you a friend of Clare's?"

"Pep! I'm her daughter."

"Yah, well, I just want to tell Kevin and Clare who was here in case you leave before they get back."

"I'm home for the weekend. I'm not going anywhere."

"Okay," he said, with an offended tone that left me feeling guilty. He turned around and headed for his chair. He truly did not know who I was. He had let a perfect stranger into our house to wash clothes.

Writer reminisces to add significance to event.

When I was a child, Pep would spend hours with me, patiently teaching me all fifty states and their capitals. When I had those down, we moved on to state flowers, birds, and slogans. He would read me his poetry and tell me never-ending bedtime stories about giants and fairies and magical castles. We would sit in front of the Christmas tree and try to guess which ornament the other was thinking of. On this day, though, I had more important things on my mind. Whites. Darks. Delicates.

Pep returned a few minutes later with a pen and his notebook.

Writer recounts internal thoughts as well as external events.

"Here, write down your name so I can tell Kevin and Clare you were here." The prospect scared me. I was hoping he would realize who I was after a while and forget that he had forgotten me. But this was putting everything on the line. What if he saw my name and still couldn't recognize me? As he eagerly offered me the pen and paper, I couldn't say no. I wrote M-i-c-h-e-l-l-e in his notebook and gave it back to him.

He looked at it for a few seconds and then wrinkled his eyebrows and bit his lip. He looked at me with a hint of disbelief.

"Michelle."

He said it with the expression of a disappointed but amused parent. The name seemed to hang in space. I imagined what would come next. He might say, "You're not Michelle" or "Who in the world is Michelle?"

But he said, "All this time you were Michelle?"

"Yes." That giant lump shot into my throat and tears crept into my eyes.

"Well, thank God for you."

I smiled. He patted me on the shoulder and walked away, shaking his head and chuckling. I was relieved. I did still exist in his mind, on his tape. But I was only a part-time visitor now, and I couldn't help wondering how long it would be before I was permanently erased.

Conclusion makes the significance of the title clear.

— Michelle Fitzpatrick

Summarizing two readings

THE ASSIGNMENT

Find two readings that take opposing positions on a debatable issue (or use two readings provided by your instructor). Choose readings that consider the issue in some detail. Also, make sure that your readings have named authors; in other words, avoid unsigned articles or anonymous Web sites.

Summarize each reading in 150 to 200 words using the following guidelines:

— In the first sentence or two, mention the title of the reading, the name of the author (or authors), and the author's thesis or central purpose.

— Use a neutral tone; be objective and fair. The goal of a summary is to report the author's views as accurately as possible.

— Write from the third-person point of view, and use the present tense: Tooley argues that . . . [not *I thought that* or *You will see that* or *Tooley argued that*].

— Put all or most of the summary in your own words; if you borrow a phrase or a sentence from the author, put it in quotation marks. (See pp. 303–10 and 394 for advice on integrating quotations.)

— Limit yourself to presenting the author's key points.

— Though you must work within a word limit, give enough details to suggest the author's evidence for his or her key points.

— Edit your draft for wordy sentences. A good summary is short but informative; every word should count.

If you selected your own readings, provide your instructor with photocopies. For this assignment, you do not need to submit a works cited page.

STUDENT ESSAY: SUMMARY OF A READING

First sentence states Bennett's central purpose.

In his speech "Drug Policy and the Intellectuals," William Bennett chides intellectuals who claim that our drug problem can be solved by legalization. Bennett finds all of their arguments unconvincing. According to some intellectuals, legalization would remove the profit motive from the drug

Summary focuses on Bennett's refutations of opposing views.

business. Bennett disagrees, claiming that most drug dealers profit very little because they are small-time "runners." Bennett also disagrees with the view that legalizing drugs would reduce the crime rate; most criminals, he says, were committing crimes before they became hooked on drugs. Some intellectuals argue that drug use would not rise upon legalization. Citing the crack epidemic as an example of what happens when a drug becomes widely available, Bennett argues that drug use would skyrocket. Some intellectuals declare that it costs too much to enforce drug laws; Bennett reasons that the cost of not enforcing them would be higher. He mentions costs to society such as drug-related accidents, lost productivity, hospitalizations, and the births of premature infants. He also cites the personal costs to addicts--the loss of dignity, of a sense of responsibility, of intellectual acuity. And drug users don't just hurt themselves, asserts Bennett:

Borrowed language appears in quotation marks and is followed by a page citation.

"They hurt parents, they destroy families, they ruin friendships" (519). To intellectuals who claim that the war on drugs is a lost cause, Bennett counters with examples of cities and communities in which the war is being won, sometimes block by

Last sentence echoes Bennett's central purpose.

block. Bennett calls upon intellectuals to use their mental talents to help communities combat the deadly problem of drugs.

— Greg Cohen

Analyzing a reading

THE ASSIGNMENT
Find a reading that takes a stand on a debatable issue (or use a reading provided by your instructor). Choose a reading that considers the

issue in some detail. Also, make sure that your reading has a named author; in other words, avoid unsigned articles or anonymous Web sites.

Analyze the reading in 500 to 1,000 words using the following guidelines:

—In the opening paragraph, mention the title of the reading and the name of the author (or authors) and describe the author's thesis and overall argumentative strategy. Then state your own thesis. Your thesis should sum up your evaluation of the author's argument.

—If the article is aimed at a particular audience (not just readers in general), show how the author attempts to persuade this audience.

—Show how the author structures the main arguments in support of the thesis.

—Evaluate the evidence the author gives in support of his or her main arguments. If the author makes unproven assumptions or uses logical fallacies, point these out (see pp. 358–60). If the author's reasoning strikes you as largely sound, explain why you find it persuasive.

—Write your analysis from the third-person point of view, and use the present tense: *Bennett argues that . . .* [not *I thought that* or *You will see that*].

—Put most of the analysis in your own words, but include some quotations from the article to illustrate your points. Document these quotations with MLA citations, and include a works cited page (see pp. 412–47).

If you selected your own reading, provide your instructor with a photocopy.

STUDENT ESSAY: ANALYSIS OF A READING

William Bennett and the Intellectuals

In his speech "Drug Policy and the Intellectuals," William Bennett challenges his audience at
Harvard daringly, by attacking intellectuals. It is
easy to imagine the tension in the room. Bennett
wins over his audience of intellectuals, however, in
two ways: (1) by calling upon their talents in his
opening and closing remarks and (2) by delivering an
impassioned, yet largely fair, attack on the arguments of intellectuals who favor legalizing drugs.

Introduction gives title of speech and name of author and describes Bennett's thesis and strategy.

Writer uses headings to help reader follow organization.

Bennett's opening and closing remarks

In his opening remarks, Bennett comes close to insulting his audience of intellectuals, stopping short of an insult by referring to those he is attacking as "they" (not "you"). Early in the speech, he diplomatically praises some intellectuals, especially in medicine and science, who are using their talents to combat the drug problem. In a further diplomatic move, Bennett makes clear that his speech will not be politically partisan. Bennett will be criticizing intellectuals, whether on the left or the right, who hold either or both of these views: that the drug problem can be solved by legalization and that the problem is so hopeless we should give up trying to fix it.

Writer comments on Bennett's attempt to persuade his audience.

Quotations documented with citations.

In his closing remarks, Bennett calls upon the talents of the intellectuals sitting in his audience. People living in drug-plagued neighborhoods are the "real drug experts," he says, and they haven't given up the fight: In city after city they are "reclaiming their neighborhoods, working with police, setting up community activities, getting addicts into treatment, saving their children" (362). Why, he wonders, would the intellectuals want to do less? He asks, "Isn't it time we had more drug control scholars?" (364).

In a final diplomatic move, Bennett ends his speech not with condemnation but with an invitation: "We are grappling with complicated, stubborn policy issues, and I encourage you to join us. [. . .] I invite America's deep thinkers to get with the program, or at the very least, to get in the game" (364).

Bennett's arguments

Writer analyzes effectiveness of Bennett's arguments.

The opening and closing sections of Bennett's speech, which focus on the intellectuals, act as a frame for the longer central section. In this central section Bennett attacks the arguments in favor of legalizing drugs, calling them "a recipe for a public policy disaster" (360). Although some of Bennett's counterarguments are stronger than others,

on the whole they are a fair assessment of the views
Bennett opposes.

Bennett's least convincing arguments attempt to
counter the claims that legalization would eliminate
the drug dealers' profit motive, that legalization
would reduce the crime rate, and that drug laws restrict our liberty. Bennett barely discusses the
liberty issue. As for the drug dealers' profit motive, he suggests--oddly, I think--that most drug
dealers aren't making much of a profit right now. He
means that over a long time, they don't profit; but
we all know that in the short run many of them make
very large profits.

Writer criticizes some of Bennett's arguments.

Bennett's argument concerning the crime rate is
only partly convincing. He refers vaguely to "research" showing that most drug criminals were doing
crime before they "got into drugs" and says that
most addicts would continue to commit crimes if
drugs were legal (362). While this could be true,
surely the extent and seriousness of the crimes
would be reduced. Bennett makes one argument about
crime, however, that is hard to refute: If drugs
were legal for adults, many dealers would shift
their market to teenagers, who would be restricted
from buying drugs.

One of Bennett's strongest arguments challenges
those who claim that legalization is a simple way to
eliminate the drug problem. He rightly criticizes
them for failing to describe the kind of world they
are proposing, for failing to answer questions like
these:

Writer shows strengths of some of Bennett's arguments.

> Would crack be legal? How about PCP? Or
> smokable heroin? Or ice? Would they all be
> stocked at the local convenience store,
> perhaps just a few blocks from an elemen-
> tary school? And how much would they
> cost? (360-61)

Long quotation displayed by indenting. Quotation marks not needed.

Bennett also argues convincingly that, contrary
to the claims of legalization advocates, drug use
would go up if drugs were legal. When cocaine was

available only in expensive powder form, he says, it
was not widely used; but when it became available in
inexpensive vials of crack, cocaine use skyrocketed.
If drugs were legal, they would be easy to get, and
they would be cheaper as well. Common sense tells us
that more people would use drugs.

Legalization advocates focus on the high cost of
enforcing drug laws. Bennett correctly chides them
for not asking an important question: What would be
the costs of legalization? Bennett tells us:

> We would have more drug-related accidents
> at work, on the highways, and in the air-
> ways. We would have even bigger losses
> in worker productivity. Our hospitals
> would be filled with drug emergencies. We
> would have more school kids on dope, and
> that means dropouts. More pregnant women
> would buy legal cocaine, and then deliver
> tiny, premature infants. (361)

And to these costs, says Bennett, we can add the costs
of "treatment, social welfare, and insurance" (361).

Legalization advocates assume that drug use
hurts only the user. Bennett questions this assumption. In addition to the high costs to society just
mentioned, Bennett points out that drugs "destroy
families" and "ruin friendships" and "are a threat
to the life of the mind" (362).

Finally, Bennett addresses the issue of drug
enforcement, which his opponents say doesn't--and
can't--work. His evidence here is anecdotal and
therefore only partly convincing. But at this point
in the speech, Bennett has given us reason for
thinking that we must make it work.

Conclusion

Bennett's speech began with some tension--a
conservative thinker facing a largely liberal audience of intellectuals. Bennett overcomes this tension first through diplomacy, then through a series
of largely solid arguments, and finally with the
positive appeal: a call for using the intellectuals'

*Quotation marks
used around
quotations that
are run into text.*

*Conclusion sums
up analysis.*

```
collective intelligence to solve a problem that is
not beyond hope.
```

[NEW PAGE]

```
                         Work Cited
Bennett, William J. "Drug Policy and the Intellectu-
    als." Current Issues and Enduring Questions: A
    Guide to Critical Thinking and Argument, with
    Readings. Ed. Sylvan Barnet and Hugo Bedau.
    Boston: Bedford, 1999. 515-22.
                              — Claire Tarvin
```

Writer includes works cited page.

Arguing a point

THE ASSIGNMENT

Choose a debatable issue about which you have some knowledge—either through personal experience, televised newscasts, the Internet, or reading. In a paper of 500 to 1,000 words, take a stand on the issue and defend your position to a general audience of intelligent but skeptical readers. If you need more information, track it down in the library or on the Internet; in a paper of this length, however, use secondary sources sparingly.

Here are some general guidelines for an argument paper:

—State your thesis clearly (usually at the end of your introduction). In your introduction, be careful to avoid alienating readers who may be in initial disagreement with your views.

—Strike a reasonable tone.

—Develop your arguments with as much specific and relevant evidence as possible.

—Attempt to refute opposing arguments—or at least to explain why they are less weighty than your own arguments.

—Where possible, build common ground with readers who may not be inclined to agree with you.

—Avoid common mistakes in reasoning (see pp. 355–61).

—If you quote from a source or use information from a source that is not common knowledge, cite it with an MLA in-text citation and include the source in a list of works cited at the end of the paper. (See 55a and 55b.)

See sections 46 and 47 for detailed advice on writing an argument paper.

STUDENT ESSAY: ARGUING A POINT

For a student argument paper, see pages 361–64.

Writing a research paper

THE ASSIGNMENT

Conduct research on a debatable political or scholarly issue. A debatable issue is one about which intelligent, well-meaning people might disagree; it does not need to be a highly controversial topic. (See 48a for guidelines on choosing a topic.) Keep an open mind as you read a variety of sources reflecting different points of view.

After weighing the evidence, form a tentative thesis that sums up your position on the issue (see 51a). Then write a six-to-ten-page paper that supports your thesis with valid and well-documented evidence (feel free to revise your tentative thesis as your paper begins to take shape). Envision an audience of intelligent but skeptical readers—readers who might not be inclined to agree with you but are willing to listen to evidence on all sides of the issues.

Unless your instructor suggests otherwise, adhere to the following guidelines:

—Base your paper on at least eight relevant sources. Most of these sources should be more than one or two pages long. Also, most of these sources should have named authors; do not rely heavily on unsigned articles or anonymous Web sites.

—Include at least five quotations from sources, but do not quote excessively. Also, keep the quoted material brief; only in exceptional circumstances should a quotation be more than four lines long.

—Integrate all quoted material with clear signal phrases (see pp. 402–08). Put quoted material in quotation marks (except for long quotations set off from the text), and document all quotations with MLA in-text citations. (See pp. 394 and 410–17.)

—Avoid plagiarism. Enclose borrowed language in quotation marks, put summaries and paraphrases in your own words, and document sources with MLA citations (see pp. 399 and 400). Note: Copying strings of words without putting them in quotation marks is plagiarism—even if you cite the source.

—Provide your instructor with a photocopy or printout of each page from a source that you have cited. Highlight the sentences or passages that you are citing. That way your instructor can see whether you have handled sources appropriately. For a quick checklist on appropriate use of sources, see page 409.

—In preparing the final manuscript, follow the MLA guidelines in section 55.

See sections 48 through 56 for detailed advice on writing a research paper.

STUDENT RESEARCH PAPER

For a sample student research paper, see pages 438–47.

Document
Design

The term *document* is broad enough to describe anything you might write in an English class, in other classes across the curriculum, in the business world, and in everyday life. How you design a document (format it on the page) can affect how it is received.

Instructors have certain expectations about how a college paper should look (see 6a). Employers too expect documents such as business letters and memos to be formatted in standard ways (see 6b). Even peers who read your e-mail and World Wide Web pages will appreciate an effective document design (see 7).

5

Become familiar with the principles of document design.

Good document design promotes readability, but what this means depends on your purpose and audience and perhaps on other elements of your writing situation, such as your subject and any length restrictions. (See the checklist on pp. 10–11.) All of your design choices — word processing options and use of headings, displayed lists, and other visuals — should be made in light of your specific writing situation.

5a Select appropriate format options.

Word processing programs present you with abundant format options. Before you begin typing, you should make sure that your margins, line spacing, and justification are set appropriately. If a number of fonts (typeface styles and sizes) are available, you should also determine which is most appropriate for your purposes.

Margins, line spacing, and justification

For documents written on 8½″ × 11″ paper, you should leave a margin of between one and one and a half inches on all sides of the page. These margins prevent the text from looking too crowded, and they allow room for annotations, such as an instructor's comments or an editor's suggestions.

Most manuscripts-in-progress are double-spaced to allow room for editing. Final copy is often double-spaced as well, since single-spacing is less inviting to read. But at times the advantages of double-spacing are offset by other considerations. In a business memo, for example, you may single-space to fit the memo on one easily scanned page. And in a technical report, you might single-space to save paper, for both ecological and financial reasons.

Word processing programs usually give you a choice between a justified and an unjustified (ragged) right margin. When the text is justified, all of the words line up against the right margin, as they do on a typeset page like the one you are now reading. Unfortunately, text that has been justified on a computer can be hard to read. The problem is that extra space is added between words in some lines, creating "rivers" of white that can be quite distracting. In addition, right-justified margins may create a need for excessive hyphenation at the ends of lines. Unless your computer can create the real look of a typeset page, you should turn off the right-justification feature.

Fonts

If you have a choice of fonts, you should select a normal size (10 to 12 points) and a style that is not too offbeat. Although unusual styles of type, such as those that look handwritten, may seem attractive, they slow readers down. We all read more efficiently when a text meets our usual expectations.

CAUTION: Never write or type a college essay or any other document in all capital letters. Research shows that readers experience much frustration when they are forced to read more than a few words in a row printed in all capital letters.

5b Consider using headings.

There is little need for headings in short essays, especially if the writer uses paragraphing and clear topic sentences to guide readers. In more complex documents, however, such as research papers, grant proposals, business reports, and Web-based documents, headings can be a useful visual cue for readers.

Headings help readers see at a glance the organization of a document. If more than one level of heading is used, the headings also indicate the hierarchy of ideas—as they do throughout this book.

Headings serve a number of functions, depending on the needs of different readers. When readers are simply looking up information, headings will help them find it quickly. When readers are scanning, hoping to pick up the gist of things, headings will guide them. Even when readers are committed enough to read every word, headings can help. Efficient readers preview a document before they begin reading; when previewing and while reading, they are guided by any visual cues the writer provides.

CAUTION: Avoid using more headings (or more levels of headings) than you really need. Excessive use of headings can make a text choppy.

Phrasing headings

Headings should be as brief and as informative as possible. Certain styles of headings—the most common being *-ing* phrases, noun phrases, questions, and imperative sentences—work better for some purposes, audiences, and subjects than others.

Whatever style you choose, use it consistently for headings on the same level. In other words, headings on the same level of organization should be written in parallel structure (see 9), as in the following examples. The first set of headings appeared in a report written for an environmental think tank, the second in a history textbook, the third in a mutual fund brochure, and the fourth in a garden designer's newsletter.

-*ING* HEADINGS
Safeguarding the earth's atmosphere

Charting the path to sustainable energy

Conserving global forests

Triggering the technological revolution

Strengthening international institutions

NOUN PHRASE HEADINGS
The economics of slavery

The sociology of slavery

Psychological effects of slavery

QUESTIONS AS HEADINGS
How do I buy shares?

How do I redeem shares?

What is the history of the fund's performance?

What are the tax consequences of investing in the fund?

IMPERATIVE SENTENCES AS HEADINGS
Fertilize roses in the fall.

Feed them again in the spring.

Prune roses when dormant and after flowering.

Spray roses during their growing season.

Placing and highlighting headings

Headings on the same level of organization should be positioned and highlighted in a consistent way. For example, you might center your first-level headings and print them in boldface; then you might place the second-level headings flush left (against the left margin) and underline them, like this:

First-level heading

<u>Second-level heading</u>

Headings are usually centered or placed flush left, but at times you might decide to indent them a half inch or five spaces from the left margin, like a paragraph indent. Or in a business document, you might place headings in a column to the left of the text.

To highlight headings, you might use boldface, italics or underlining, all capital letters, color, a larger or smaller typeface than the text, a different font, or some combination of these:

boldface	color
italics	larger typeface
<u>underlining</u>	smaller typeface
ALL CAPITAL LETTERS	**different font**

On the whole, it is best to use restraint. Excessive highlighting results in a page that looks too busy, and it defeats its own purpose, since readers have trouble sorting out which headings are more important than others.

Important headings can be highlighted by using white space around them. Less important headings can be downplayed by using less white space or by running them into the text (as with the small all-capitals heading on p. 5).

5c Consider using displayed lists.

Lists are easy to read or scan when they are displayed rather than run into your text. You might reasonably choose to display the following kinds of lists:

— steps in a process
— materials needed for a project
— parts of an object
— advice or recommendations
— items to be discussed
— criteria for evaluation (as in checklists)

Displayed lists should usually be introduced with an independent clause followed by a colon (see 35a and the preceding list). Periods are not used after items in a list unless the items are sentences.

Lists are most readable when they are presented in parallel grammatical form (see 9). In the sample list, for instance, the items are all noun phrases. As with headings, some kinds of lists might be more appropriately presented as *-ing* phrases, as imperative sentences, or as questions.

To draw the reader's eye to a list, you might use bullets (circles or squares) or dashes if there is no need to number the items. If there is some reason to number the items, use an arabic number followed by a period for each item.

Although displayed lists can be a useful visual cue, they should not be overdone. Too many of them will give a document a choppy, cluttered look. And lists that are very long (sometimes called "laundry lists") should be avoided as well. Readers can hold only so many ideas in their short-term memory, so if a list grows too long, you should find some way of making it more concise or clustering similar items.

5d Consider adding visuals.

Visuals such as charts, graphs, tables, diagrams, maps, and photographs convey information concisely and vividly. In a student
essay not intended for publication, you can use another person's visuals as long as you credit the borrowing (see 50). And
with access to computer graphics, you can create your own visuals to enhance an essay, a report, or an electronic document.

　　This section suggests when charts, graphs, tables, and diagrams might be appropriate for your purposes. It also discusses
where you might place such visuals.

Using charts, graphs, tables, and diagrams

In documents that help readers follow a process or make a decision, flow charts can be useful; for an example, see page 169
in this book. Pie charts are appropriate for indicating ratios or
apportionment, as in the following example.

PIE CHART

Sales Breakdown for 1999

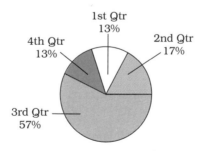

　　Line graphs and bar graphs illustrate disparities in numerical data. Line graphs are appropriate when you want to illu-
minate trends over a period of time, such as trends in sales, in
unemployment, or in population growth. Bar graphs can be
used for the same purpose. In addition, bar graphs are useful

LINE GRAPH

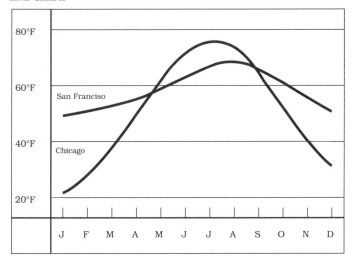

MONTHLY MEAN TEMPERATURE IN
SAN FRANCISCO AND CHICAGO

BAR GRAPH

SALES BREAKDOWN BY REGION, 1999

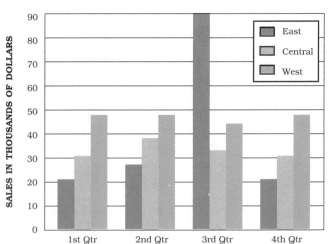

for highlighting comparisons, such as vote totals for rival political candidates or the number of refugees entering the United States during different time periods.

Tables are not as visually interesting as line graphs or charts, but they allow for inclusion of specific numerical data, such as exact percentages. The following table presents the responses of students and faculty to one question on a campus-wide questionnaire.

TABLE

Is American education based too much on European history and values?

| | PERCENT | | |
	NO	UNDECIDED	YES
Nonwhite students	21	25	54
White students	55	29	16
Nonwhite faculty	15	20	65
White faculty	57	27	16

Diagrams are useful—and sometimes indispensable—in scientific and technical writing. It is more concise, for example, to use the following diagram than to explain the chemical formula in words.

DIAGRAM

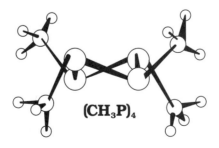

$(CH_3P)_4$

Placing visuals

A visual may be placed in the text of a document, near a discussion to which it relates, or it can be put in an appendix, labeled, and referred to in the text.

Placing visuals in the text of a document can be tricky. Usually you will want the visual to appear close to the sentences that relate to it, but page breaks won't always allow this placement. At times you may need to insert the visual at a later point and tell readers where it can be found or, with the help of software, you may be able to make the text flow around the visual.

In newsletters and in business and technical documents, page layout is both an art and a science. The best way to learn how to lay out pages is to work with colleagues who have had experience solving the many problems that can arise.

6

Use standard academic and business formats.

6a Use MLA format unless you have been asked to follow other guidelines.

If your instructor provides formal guidelines for formatting an essay—or a more specialized document such as a lab report, a case study, or a research paper—you should of course follow them. Otherwise, use the manuscript format that is standard for the discipline in which you are writing.

In most English and humanities classes, you will be asked to use the MLA (Modern Language Association) format. The following sample essay illustrates this format. For more detailed advice about MLA manuscript guidelines, along with a sample MLA research paper, see 55d. If you have been asked to use APA (American Psychological Association) manuscript guidelines, see 56c.

MLA ESSAY FORMAT

1″

Weitzel 1   ½″

Double-
spacing
throughout

Tom Weitzel

Dr. Fry

English 101

16 April 1999

Title,
centered

Who Goes to the Races?

½″
indent

A favorite pastime of mine is observing
people, and my favorite place to observe is at
the horse races. After many encounters with the
racing crowd, I have discovered that there are four
distinct groups at the track: the once-a-year
bunch, the professionals, the clubhouse set, and the
unemployed.

The largest group at the track consists of
those who show up once a year. They know little
about horses or betting and rely strictly on race-
track gimmick sheets and newspaper predictions
for selecting possible winners. If that strategy

1″

doesn't work, they use intuition, lucky numbers,

1″

favorite colors, or appealing names. They bet
larger amounts as the day goes along, gambling on
every race, including long-shot bets on exactas
and daily doubles. The vast majority go home broke
and frustrated.

More subtle and quiet are the professionals.
They follow the horses from track to track and
live in campers and motor homes. Many are married
couples, some are retired, and all are easily
spotted with their lunch sacks, water jugs, and
binoculars. Since most know one another, they section themselves off in a particular area of the
stadium. All rely on the racing form and on personal knowledge of each horse, jockey, and track
in making the proper bet. They bet only on the

1″

MLA ESSAY FORMAT *(continued)*

smart races, rarely on the favorites. Never do
they bet on exactas or daily doubles. More often
than not they either break even or go home
winners.

Isolated from the others is the clubhouse
set. Found either at the cocktail lounge or in the
restaurant, usually involved in business transac-
tions, these racing fans rarely see a race in person and do their betting via the waiter. It's
difficult to tell whether they go home sad, happy,
or in between. They keep their emotions to
themselves.

The most interesting members of the race-
track population are the unemployed. They will be
found not in the clubhouse, but right down at the
rail next to the finish line. Here one can discover the real emotion of the racetrack--the
screaming, the cursing, and the pushing. The unemployed are not in it for the sport. Betting is not
a game for them, but a battle for survival. If
they lose, they must borrow enough money to carry
them until the next check comes in, and then, of
course, they head right back to the track. This
particular group arrives at the track beaten and
leaves beaten.

I have probably lost more money than I have
won at the track, but observing these four interesting groups of people makes it all worthwhile.

1″ ←→   1″ ←→

6b Use standard business formats.

This section provides guidelines for preparing business letters, résumés, and memos. For a more detailed discussion of these and other business documents—proposals, reports, executive summaries, and so on—consult a business writing textbook or take a look at examples currently being written at the organization for which you are writing.

Business letters

In writing a business letter, be direct, clear, and courteous, but do not hesitate to be firm if necessary. State your purpose or request at the beginning of the letter and include only pertinent information in the body. By being as direct and concise as possible, you show that you value your reader's time.

A sample business letter appears on page 90. This letter is typed in what is known as "block" style. The return address at the top and the close and signature at the bottom are lined up just to the right of the center of the width of the page. The inside address, the salutation, and the body of the letter are flush left (against the left margin). The paragraphs are not indented.

If you choose to indent your paragraphs, you are using "semiblock" style, which is considered less formal. If you choose to move all elements of the letter flush left, you are using the most formal style, "full block." This style is usually preferred when the letter is typed on letterhead stationery that gives the return address of the writer or the writer's company.

When writing to a woman, use the abbreviation *Ms.* in the salutation unless you know that the woman prefers another form of address. If you are not writing to a particular person, you can use the salutation *Dear Sir or Madam* or you can address the company itself—*Dear Solar Technology.*

Below the signature, flush left, you may include the abbreviation *Enc.* to indicate that something is enclosed with the letter or the abbreviation *cc* followed by a colon and the name of someone who is receiving a copy of the letter.

BUSINESS LETTER IN BLOCK FORM

Return address ⎯⎯⎯ 121 Knox Road, #6
College Park, MD 20740
March 4, 1999

Linda Hennessee, Managing Editor ⎯
World Discovery
1650 K Street, NW   Inside address
Washington, DC 20036

Dear Ms. Hennessee: ⎯⎯ Salutation

Please accept my application for the summer editorial internship listed with
the Career Development Center at the University of Maryland. Currently I
am a junior at the University of Maryland, with a double major in English
and Latin American studies.

Over the past three years I have gained considerable experience in newspaper and magazine journalism, as you will see on my enclosed résumé. I am
familiar with the basic procedures of editing and photographic development, but my primary interests lie in feature writing and landscape photogra-   Body
phy. My professional goal is to work as a photojournalist with an international focus, preferably for a major magazine. I cannot imagine a better introduction to that career than a summer at *World Discovery*.

I am available for an interview almost any time and can be reached at
301-555-2651. My e-mail address is jrichard@umdcp.edu.

I look forward to hearing from you.

Close ⎯⎯ Sincerely,

Signature ⎯⎯ *Jeffrey Richardson*

Jeffrey Richardson

Enc.

Résumés

An effective résumé gives relevant information in a clear and concise form. The trick is to present yourself in the best possible light without going on at length and wasting your reader's time.

A sample résumé appears on page 92. Notice that the writer has used bullets to make his résumé easy to scan. Notice too that he presents his work experience in reverse chronological order—to highlight his most recent accomplishments.

When you send out your résumé, you should include a letter that tells what position you seek and where you learned about it (see p. 90). The letter should also summarize your education and past experience, relating them to the job you are applying for. End the letter with a suggestion for a meeting, and tell your prospective employer when you will be available.

Memos

Business memos (short for *memorandums*) are a form of communication used within a company or organization. Usually brief and to the point, a memo reports information, makes a request, or recommends an action. The format of a memo, which varies from company to company, is designed for easy distribution, quick reading, and efficient filing.

Most memos display the date, the name of the recipient, the name of the sender, and the subject on separate lines at the top of the page. Many companies have preprinted forms for memos, and some word processing programs allow you to call up a memo template that prints standard memo lines—"To," "cc" (for others receiving a copy of the memo), "From," and "Subject"—at the top of the page.

Because readers of the memos are busy people, you cannot assume that they will read your memo word for word. Therefore the subject line should describe the subject as clearly and concisely as possible, and the introductory paragraph should get right to the point. In addition, the body of the memo should be well organized and easy to scan. To promote scanning, use headings where possible and display any items that deserve special attention by setting them off from the text. A sample memo with headings and a displayed list appears on page 93.

RÉSUMÉ

Jeffrey Richardson

121 Knox Road, #6
College Park, MD 20740
301–555–2651

OBJECTIVE   To obtain an editorial internship with a magazine

EDUCATION
Fall 1995–   University of Maryland
present
- B.A. expected in June 1999
- Double major: English and Latin American studies
- GPA: 3.7 (on a 4-point scale)

EXPERIENCE
Fall 1996–   Photo editor, *The Diamondback*, college paper
present
- Shoot and print photographs
- Select and lay out photographs and other visuals

Summer   Intern, *The Globe,* Fairfax, Virginia
1997
- Wrote stories about local issues and personalities
- Interviewed political candidates
- Edited and proofread copy
- Contributed photographs
- Coedited "The Landscapes of Northern Virginia: A Photoessay"

Summer   Tutor, Fairfax County ESL Program
1996
- Tutored Latino students in English as a Second Language
- Trained new tutors

ACTIVITIES   Photographers' Workshop, Spanish Club

REFERENCES   Available upon request

BUSINESS MEMO

Commonwealth Press

MEMORANDUM

March 1, 1999

To: Production, promotion, and editorial assistants

cc: Stephen Chapman

From: Helen Brown

Subject: New computers for staff

We will receive the new computers next week for the assistants in production, promotion, and editorial. In preparation, I would like you to take part in a training program and to rearrange your work areas to accommodate the new equipment.

Training Program

A computer consultant will teach in-house workshops on how to use our spreadsheet program. If you have already tried the program, be prepared to discuss any problems you have encountered.

Workshops for our three departments will be held in the training room at the following times:

- Production: Monday, March 8, 10:00 a.m. to 2:00 p.m.
- Promotion: Wednesday, March 10, 10:00 a.m. to 2:00 p.m.
- Editorial: Friday, March 12, 10:00 a.m. to 2:00 p.m.

Lunch will be provided in the cafeteria. If you cannot attend, please let me know by March 5.

Allocation and Setup

To give everyone access to a computer, we will set up the new computers as follows: two in the assistants' workspace in production; two in the area outside the conference room for the promotion assistants; and two in the library for the editorial assistants.

Assistants in all three departments should see me before March 5 to discuss preparation of the spaces for the new equipment.

7

Create effective electronic documents.

7a Follow the conventions of e-mail.

Communicating by electronic mail (or e-mail) has many benefits. Unlike conventional "snail" mail messages, e-mail messages are sent and received immediately after they are written—to and from anywhere in the world at any time. And although e-mail can be as quick as a telephone call, it provides a bit more time than conversation allows for framing ideas and thoughtful responses. As with all writing, you should keep your audience and purpose clearly in mind as you draft e-mail. But you should also be aware of the special conventions of this fast-paced form of communication.

Keeping messages brief and direct

Because the purpose of e-mail is to relay and receive information quickly, it is a courtesy to keep each message as brief as possible and to state your point early. Your message may be just one of many that your reader has to wade through. Always fill in the subject line with a clear, concise description of what your message is about (*Dec. 4 meeting agenda* is clearer than *Committee notes*). If you are making a request or a recommendation, state it right away, if possible in the first few sentences (*Can you get your report to me by Monday?* or *I think we need two committees to study the impact of the proposed building*). For long, detailed messages that may fill more than two computer screens, consider providing a summary at the beginning, such as the following:

> The study on improving the work environment at DeVincent Company includes four key recommendations:
>
> 1. Acquire additional space for the customer service division
> 2. Improve lighting and reduce background noise in cubicle areas
> 3. Add another break room for the third and fourth floors
> 4. Purchase coffee machines and water coolers for all break rooms

Maintaining an appropriate tone

It is appropriate for e-mail to be more informal than other types of writing; you may even alienate your reader if your tone sounds too formal. In general, maintain a tone that is friendly and conversational, yet respectful. The first-person (*I*) and second-person (*you*) points of view are standard in e-mail, and contractions are nearly always acceptable.

Though you should always try to keep messages as brief as possible, you can avoid a blunt tone by including an appropriate greeting and closing. You may also want to open with a brief personal note or include a bit of humor when communicating with friends and colleagues.

> **TOO FORMAL AND BLUNT**
> Now that the regional conference has concluded, it is my responsibility to assemble the agenda for the 2000 planning meeting. In order to do so in a timely fashion, I need your ideas about issues to cover in the meeting by October 25.

Expressions like *it is my responsibility* and *in order to do so in a timely fashion* make this message sound formal and stilted, and the lack of a greeting and closing give it a cold, blunt tone.

> **REVISED**
> Dear Carolyn,
>
> I enjoyed seeing you and the other members of the steering committee at the regional conference. Now that I'm back in the office, I need to start putting together the agenda for our 2000 planning meeting. If you have any preliminary thoughts about issues to cover, could you please e-mail them to me by October 25? Thanks, Carolyn. I look forward to hearing from you.
>
> Best,
> Ada

As with all forms of writing, your tone in e-mail should suit your subject and audience. In business and academic contexts or in writing to someone you don't know well, you will probably want to use a more formal tone than you would when, say, making social plans with friends. Regardless of your subject and audience, you should always avoid harsh or flippant language in e-mail.

NOTE: Some e-mailers use emoticons (combinations of symbols that look like faces turned sideways) and acronyms (such as *TIA* for "thanks in advance"). Though you may be tempted to use these shortcuts, it is usually better to convey your tone and meaning through words, especially in business and academic contexts. Readers who are unfamiliar with emoticons and e-mail abbreviations may be confused by them, and even readers who understand these shortcuts may be annoyed by them.

Following e-mail etiquette

E-mail, like other forms of communication, has its own etiquette, which varies slightly depending on your purpose and audience. Essentially, when writing and responding to others, you should take care to be prompt, clear, and courteous. Here are some principles to keep in mind:

—Check your e-mail frequently and respond to messages promptly.
—Fill in subject lines to help readers sort through their messages and set priorities.
—Include a brief greeting (such as *Hi, Gloria* or *Dear Professor Hartley*) and a brief closing (such as *Bye for now* or *Sincerely*).
—Avoid writing in all capital letters or all lowercase letters.
—Resist "flaming" — spouting off angry or insulting messages.
—Forward messages from others only when you are certain the original sender would approve.
—Restrict your use of copyrighted materials to short passages, and always name the author, title, and publication source.

Revising e-mail

Although standards for revision are not as high for fast-paced e-mail as for other forms of written communication, resist the temptation to send off a message without reading it first. Check

E-MAIL MESSAGE

Return-Path: <dportes@umass-boston.edu>
Date: Fri, 19 Nov 1999 22:31:45-0500
To: rdayson@newhoriz.org
From: Danielle Portes <dportes@umass-boston.edu>
Subject: Telephone interview on Dec. 4
cc: Helen Tran <htran@umass-boston.edu>

Dear Ms. Dayson:

Thank you for taking the time to speak with me last week about my research project. As we agreed, I am sending some questions for you to consider before our phone interview on December 3 at 2 p.m.

QUESTIONS ABOUT GUESTS

--What symptoms of stress do guests--both women and their children-- show when they first arrive at the shelter?

--What problems, in addition to the abuse itself, must guests deal with (for example, lack of support from family or friends, financial concerns, problems in dealing with police and courts)?

–Can you think of any past or current guests who might agree to an interview?

QUESTIONS ABOUT STAFFERS

--What are the main stresses that staffers face? How do they cope with these stresses?

--What do staffers see as the rewards as well as the drawbacks of the job?

--On average, how many guests does each staffer work with every day? every week?

--Can you think of any past or current staffers who might agree to an interview?

I appreciate your considering these questions and look forward to our interview.

Sincerely,
Danielle Portes
Phone: 617-555-7777

to make sure that your tone is tactful, that your main point is clear and concise, and that your message is free of errors in grammar, punctuation, spelling, and mechanics.

7b Create effective Web sites.

At some point you may be asked to create a World Wide Web site as part of a school or work assignment, or you may decide to build one for your personal use. Although this book can't begin to explain all the technical aspects of creating a Web site, included here are design and organizational hints to help you make the most of this new medium. For more detailed information on creating a Web site, see *Style Guide for Online Hypertext* < http://www.w3.org/pub/WWW/Provider/Style >, written by Web founder Tim Berners-Lee.

Organizing information

If you have browsed the World Wide Web, you may have noticed that the most effective sites are the simplest ones—those that give you quick and easy access to what you're looking for. The overall organization of a Web site can be found on its home page, which welcomes visitors, introduces them to the site, and gives them an overview of its contents (see the sample on p. 99).

From the home page, visitors navigate via "links," words or visual images that, at the click of the mouse, send them to other pages within the site or to other locations on the Web. In a typical Web site, the home page contains the most general information, and internal pages are more specific.

Before creating a Web site, make an outline of the hierarchy of the information you will present: a home page linked to internal pages, which can in turn be linked to other pages in your site or on the Web. As is true in print documents, important items, such as a company name, should receive more prominence than items of lesser importance, such as a copyright date. To help you weigh the relative importance of material, think about what your readers will most likely be looking for. Why are they visiting your site in the first place? What are they expecting to find?

Breaking up text

Because the Internet is so vast, online surfers move quickly from page to page. Visitors to your page won't have the patience to scroll through long passages of text. To keep your readers' attention, present your material as concisely as possible, and break up text with headings and displayed lists (see 5b). And, where appropriate, highlight information with visuals such as clip art, photos, or even animation.

Linking to other sites

One of the most useful features of World Wide Web documents is the ability to create links to other Internet locations. You will probably decide to add some links to other sites from your Web page, but use care when doing so. Especially when creating academic or professional Web sites, keep in mind that any links you include should be relevant to your subject.

A link to another site is an implicit endorsement of that site, so you should evaluate potential sites before linking to

SAMPLE WEB PAGE

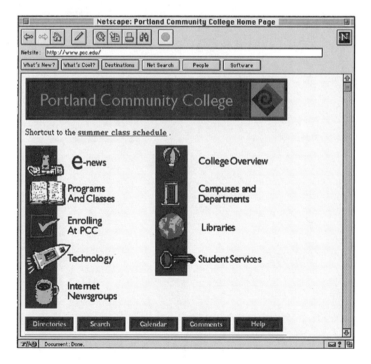

them. As a courtesy to readers, periodically visit the sites you have links to; remove any links to sites that are outdated or non-functioning, and reroute links to sites that have moved.

Testing your site

When you create a Web site, you are publishing a document that represents you or your organization. Therefore, before you upload your new site to the Web, you should be certain that all your links are working and that all your text has been properly coded.

As you would in a print document, you should use a clear and grammatical writing style, carefully proofread your text, and give proper credit to any material you may have borrowed from other sources.

Clarity

8

Coordinate equal ideas; subordinate minor ideas.

When combining two or more ideas in one sentence, use co-ordination to create equal emphasis and use subordination to create unequal emphasis.

 GRAMMAR CHECKERS do not catch the problems with coordination and subordination discussed in this section. Not surprisingly, computer programs have no way of sensing the relative importance of ideas.

Coordination

Coordination draws attention equally to two or more ideas. To coordinate single words or phrases, join them with a coordinating conjunction or with a pair of correlative conjunctions (see 57g). To coordinate independent clauses—word groups that could stand alone as a sentence—join them with a comma and a coordinating conjunction or with a semicolon:

| , and | , but | , or | , nor |
| , for | , so | , yet | ; |

The semicolon is often accompanied by a conjunctive adverb such as *moreover*, *furthermore*, *therefore*, or *however* or by a transitional phrase such as *for example*, *in other words*, or *as a matter of fact*. (See the chart on p. 104 for a more complete list.)

Assume, for example, that your intention is to draw equal attention to the following two ideas.

Grandmother lost her sight. Her hearing sharpened.

To coordinate these ideas, you can join them with a comma and the coordinating conjunction *but* or with a semicolon and the conjunctive adverb *however*.

Grandmother lost her sight, but her hearing sharpened.

Grandmother lost her sight; however, her hearing sharpened.

It is important to choose a coordinating conjunction or conjunctive adverb appropriate to your meaning. In the preceding example, the two ideas contrast with one another, calling for *but* or *however*.

Subordination

To give unequal emphasis to two or more ideas, express the major idea in an independent clause and place any minor ideas in subordinate clauses or phrases. (For specific subordination strategies, see the chart on p. 105.)

Deciding which idea to emphasize is not a matter of right and wrong but is determined by the meaning you intend. Consider the two ideas about Grandmother's sight and hearing.

> Grandmother lost her sight. Her hearing sharpened.

If your purpose is to stress your grandmother's acute hearing rather than her blindness, subordinate the idea about her blindness.

> *As she lost her sight,* Grandmother's hearing sharpened.

To focus on your grandmother's growing blindness, subordinate the idea about her hearing.

> *Though her hearing sharpened*, Grandmother gradually lost her sight.

8a Combine choppy sentences.

Short sentences demand attention, so you should use them primarily for emphasis. Too many short sentences, one after the other, make for a choppy style.

If an idea is not important enough to deserve its own sentence, try combining it with a sentence close by. Put any minor ideas in subordinate structures such as phrases or subordinate clauses.

▶ We keep our use of insecticides, herbicides, and fungicides to
a minimum/ ~~We~~ *because we* are concerned about the environment.

A minor idea is now expressed in a subordinate clause beginning with *because*.

Using coordination to combine sentences of equal importance

1. Consider using a comma and a coordinating conjunction. (See 32a.)

, and	, but	, or	, nor
, for	, so	, yet	

▶ **In Orthodox Jewish funeral ceremonies, the shroud is a simple**

and the

linen vestment. The coffin is plain wood with no adornment.

2. Consider using a semicolon and a conjunctive adverb or transitional phrase. (See 34b.)

also	in addition	of course
as a result	in fact	on the other hand
besides	in other words	otherwise
consequently	in the first place	still
finally	meanwhile	then
for example	moreover	therefore
for instance	nevertheless	thus
furthermore	next	
however	now	

therefore, she

▶ **My mother is lactose intolerant. She must avoid milk, cheese,**

yogurt, and ice cream.

3. Consider using a semicolon alone. (See 34a.)

▶ **Most hospitals in the United States offer Western methods of**

hospitals

treatment. Hospitals in China provide both Western and Chinese

medicine.

Using subordination to combine sentences of unequal importance

1. Consider putting the less important idea in a subordinate clause beginning with one of the following words. (See 59b.)

after	before	that	which
although	even though	unless	while
as	if	until	who
as if	since	when	whom
because	so that	where	whose

▶ *When my*   *she*
  ~~My~~ son asked his great-grandmother if she had been a slave~~.~~ ~~She~~

  became very angry.

▶ My sister owes much of her recovery to a bodybuilding program~~.~~
  that she
  ~~She~~ began the program three years ago.

2. Consider putting the less important idea in an appositive phrase. (See 59d.)

▶ Karate~~,~~ is a discipline based on the philosophy of nonviolence~~.~~ ~~It~~

  teaches the art of self-defense.

3. Consider putting the less important idea in a participial phrase. (See 59c.)

  Noticing
▶ ~~I noticed~~ that smoke had filled the backyard~~.~~ I ran out to see

  where it was coming from.

       E
▶ ~~Alvin~~ was encouraged by his professor to apply for the job~~.~~
  Alvin
  ~~He~~ filed an application on Monday morning.

▶ The Chesapeake and Ohio Canal, ~~is~~ a 184-mile waterway

                  ^

constructed in the 1800s/. ~~It~~ was a major source of

               ^

transportation for goods during the Civil War.

A minor idea is now expressed in an appositive phrase (*a 184-mile waterway constructed in the 1800s*).

              E

▶ ~~Sister Consilio was~~ ɇnveloped in a black robe with only her

                      Sister Consilio

face and hands visible/. ~~She~~ was an imposing figure.

               ^

A minor idea is now expressed in a participial phrase beginning with *Enveloped*.

Although subordination is ordinarily the most effective technique for combining short, choppy sentences, coordination is appropriate when the ideas are equal in importance.

▶ The hospital decides when patients will sleep and wake/. ~~It~~

                                   ^

                           and

dictates what and when they will eat/. ~~It~~ tells them when they

                           ^

may be with family and friends.

Equivalent ideas are expressed in a coordinate series.

ESL

When combining sentences, do not repeat the subject of the sentence; also do not repeat an object or an adverb in an adjective clause. See 31b and 31c.

▶ The apartment that we moved into ~~it~~ needed many

   repairs.

▶ Tanya climbed into the tree house that the boys were

   playing in. ~~it.~~

     ^

8b Avoid ineffective or excessive coordination.

Coordinate structures are appropriate only when you intend to draw the reader's attention equally to two or more ideas: *Professor Naake praises loudly, and she criticizes softly*. If one idea is more important than another—or if a coordinating conjunction does not clearly signal the relation between the ideas—you should subordinate the less important idea.

▶ *When*
Jason walked over to his new Miata, ~~and~~ he saw that its

windshield had been smashed.

The minor idea has become a subordinate clause beginning with *When*.

▶ My uncle, *noticing* ~~noticed~~ my frightened look, ~~and~~ told me that the

dentures in the glass were not real teeth.

The less important idea has become a participial phrase modifying the noun *uncle*.

▶ *After four hours,*
~~Four hours went by, and~~ a rescue truck finally arrived, but

by that time we had been evacuated in a helicopter.

Three independent clauses were excessive. The least important idea has become a prepositional phrase.

EXERCISE 8–1

Combine or restructure the following sentences by subordinating minor ideas or by coordinating ideas of equal importance. You must decide which ideas are minor because the sentences are given out of context. Revisions of lettered sentences appear in the back of the book. Example:

where they
The crew team finally returned to shore, ~~and~~ had a party on
to celebrate
the beach and ~~celebrated~~ the start of the season.

a. An instruction manual is enclosed with your computer, and it is user-friendly.

b. Part of my earnings went toward the purchase of a ten-speed bicycle. I hoped the bicycle would serve as my primary form of transportation.
c. There are five fishing piers on the island. Each pier has a bait and tackle shop.
d. Student volunteers from Baltimore City Community College help the younger children with reading and math. These are the children's weakest subjects.
e. The home study course seemed to have everything I was looking for, and I thought my troubles were over, but in reality they were just beginning.

1. Mary will graduate from high school in June. She has not yet decided on a college.
2. I noticed that the sky was glowing orange and red. I bent down to crawl into the bunker.
3. The Market Inn is located at 2nd and E Streets. It doesn't look very impressive from the outside. The food, however, is excellent.
4. Cocaine is an addictive drug, and it can seriously harm you both physically and mentally, if death doesn't get you first.
5. These particles are known as "stealth liposomes," and they can hide in the body for a long time without detection.
6. Our waitress was costumed in a kimono. She had painted her face white. She had arranged her hair in an upswept lacquered beehive.
7. He walked up to the pitcher's mound. He dug his toe into the ground. He swung his arm around backward and forward. Then he threw the ball and struck the batter out.
8. Agnes was another girl I worked with. She was a hyperactive child.
9. The lift chairs were going around very fast. They were bumping the skiers into their seats.
10. The first football card set was released by the Goudey Gum Company in 1933. The set featured only three football players. They were Red Grange, Bronko Nagurski, and Knute Rockne.

8c Do not subordinate major ideas.

If a sentence buries its major idea in a subordinate construction, readers may not give the idea enough attention. Express the major idea in an independent clause and subordinate any minor ideas.

▶ Lanie, who now walks with the help of braces, *had polio as a child,* ~~had polio as a child.~~

The writer wanted to focus on Lanie's ability to walk, but the original sentence buried this information in an adjective clause. The revision puts the major idea in an independent clause and tucks the less important idea into an adjective clause (*who had polio as a child*).

▶ *As*
I was driving home from my new job, heading down Ranchitos
^

Road, ~~when~~ my car suddenly overheated.

The writer wanted to emphasize that the car was overheating, not the fact of driving home. The revision expresses the major idea in an independent clause, the less important idea in an adverb clause (*As I was driving home from my new job*).

8d Do not subordinate excessively.

In attempting to avoid short, choppy sentences, writers sometimes go to the opposite extreme, putting more subordinate ideas into a sentence than its structure can bear. If a sentence collapses of its own weight, occasionally it can be restructured. More often, however, such sentences must be divided.

▶ Our job is to stay between the stacker and the tie machine

If they do,
watching to see if the newspapers jam /. ~~in which case~~ we
^

pull the bundles off and stack them on a skid, because

otherwise they would back up in the stacker.

EXERCISE 8–2

In each of the following sentences, the idea that the writer wished to emphasize is buried in a subordinate construction. Restructure each sentence so that the independent clause expresses the major idea and lesser ideas are subordinated. Revisions of lettered sentences appear in the back of the book. Example:

Although
Catherine has weathered many hardships, ~~although~~ she has
^

rarely become discouraged. [*Emphasize that Catherine has*

rarely become discouraged.]

a. We experienced a routine morning at the clinic until an infant in cardiac arrest arrived by ambulance. [*Emphasize the arrival of the infant.*]

b. My 1969 Camaro, which is no longer street legal, is an original SS396. [*Emphasize the fact that the car is no longer street legal.*]

c. This highly specialized medical training, which usually takes four years to complete, is called a "residency." [*Emphasize the length of time.*]

d. Although native Hawaiians try to preserve their ancestors' sacred customs, outsiders have forced changes on them. [*Emphasize the Hawaiians' attempt to preserve their customs.*]

e. Ash Lawn, the restored home of our fifth president, James Monroe, is located only two miles from Monticello. [*Emphasize that Ash Lawn is the restored home of our fifth president.*]

1. The ivy-covered dormitories, located about a mile from most of the classrooms, date from the early nineteenth century. [*Emphasize where the dormitories are located.*]

2. I was losing consciousness when my will to live kicked in. [*Emphasize the will to live.*]

3. Louis's team worked with the foreign mission by building new churches and restoring those damaged by hurricanes. [*Emphasize the building and restoring.*]

4. The rotor hit, gouging a hole about an eighth of an inch deep in my helmet. [*Emphasize that the rotor gouged a hole in the helmet.*]

5. Although Sarah felt that we lacked decent transportation, our family owned a Jeep, a pickup truck, and a sports car. [*Emphasize Sarah's feeling that the family lacked decent transportation.*]

9

Balance parallel ideas.

If two or more ideas are parallel, they are easier to grasp when expressed in parallel grammatical form. Single words should be balanced with single words, phrases with phrases, clauses with clauses.

A kiss can be a comma, a question mark, or an exclamation point.

—Mistinguett

This novel is not to be tossed lightly aside, but to be hurled

with great force.   —Dorothy Parker

In matters of principle, stand like a rock; in matters of taste,

swim with the current.   —Thomas Jefferson

Writers often use parallelism to create emphasis. (See 14c.)

 GRAMMAR CHECKERS do not flag faulty parallelism. Because computer programs have no way of assessing whether two or more ideas are parallel in meaning, they fail to catch the faulty parallelism in sentences such as this: *In my high school, boys were either jocks, preppies, or studied constantly.*

9a Balance parallel ideas in a series.

Readers expect items in a series to appear in parallel grammatical form. When one or more of the items violate readers' expectations, a sentence will be needlessly awkward.

▶ Abused children commonly exhibit one or more of the

following symptoms: withdrawal, rebelliousness,
                                          depression.
restlessness, and ~~they are depressed~~.
                        ^

The revision presents all of the items as nouns.

▶ Hooked on romance novels, I learned that there is nothing
                                                      having
more important than being rich, looking good, and ~~to~~
                                                      ^

~~have~~ a good time.

The revision uses *-ing* forms for all items in the series.

▶ After assuring us that he was sober, Sam drove down the
                                          went through
middle of the road, ran one red light, and two stop signs.
                                          ^

The revision adds a verb to make the three items parallel: *drove . . . , ran . . . , went through. . . .*

NOTE: In headings and lists, aim for as much parallelism as the content allows. (See 5b.)

9b Balance parallel ideas presented as pairs.

When pairing ideas, underscore their connection by expressing them in similar grammatical form. Paired ideas are usually connected in one of these ways:

- —with a coordinating conjunction such as *and, but,* or *or*
- —with a pair of correlative conjunctions such as *either . . . or* or *not only . . . but also*
- —with a word introducing a comparison, usually *than* or *as*

Parallel ideas linked with coordinating conjunctions

Coordinating conjunctions (*and, but, or, nor, for, so,* and *yet*) link ideas of equal importance. When those ideas are closely parallel in content, they should be expressed in parallel grammatical form.

▶ At Lincoln High School, vandalism can result in suspension
        expulsion
or even ~~being expelled~~ from school.
   ^

The revision balances the nouns *suspension* and *expulsion*.

▶ Many states are reducing property taxes for homeowners
    extending
and ~~extend~~ financial aid in the form of tax credits to renters.
  ^

The revision balances the verb *reducing* with the verb *extending*.

Parallel ideas linked with correlative conjunctions

Correlative conjunctions come in pairs: *either . . . or, neither . . . nor, not only . . . but also, both . . . and, whether . . . or.* Make sure that the grammatical structure following the second half of the pair is the same as that following the first half.

▶ Thomas Edison was not only a prolific inventor but also ~~was~~

a successful entrepreneur.

The words *a prolific inventor* follow *not only*, so *a successful entrepreneur* should follow *but also*. Repeating *was* creates an unbalanced effect.

▶ I was advised either to change my flight or ^*to* take the train.

To change my flight, which follows *either*, should be balanced with *to take the train*, which follows *or*.

Comparisons linked with *than* or *as*

In comparisons linked with *than* or *as*, the elements being compared should be expressed in parallel grammatical structure.

▶ It is easier to speak in abstractions than ^*to ground* ~~grounding~~ one's

thoughts in reality.

▶ Mother could not persuade me that giving is as much a joy
as ^*receiving.* ~~to receive.~~

To speak in abstractions is balanced with *to ground one's thoughts in reality*. *Giving* is balanced with *receiving*.

NOTE: Comparisons should also be logical and complete. (See 10c.)

9c Repeat function words to clarify parallels.

Function words such as prepositions (*by*, *to*) and subordinating conjunctions (*that*, *because*) signal the grammatical nature of the word groups to follow. Although they can sometimes be omitted, include them whenever they signal parallel structures that might otherwise be missed by readers.

▶ Many smokers try switching to a brand they find distasteful
  to
  or a low tar and nicotine cigarette.
  ^

In the original sentence the prepositional phrase was too complex for easy reading. The repetition of the preposition *to* prevents readers from losing their way.

▶ The ophthalmologist told me that Julie was extremely
                    that
  farsighted but corrective lenses would help considerably.
  ^

A second subordinating conjunction helps readers sort out the two parallel ideas: *that* Julie was extremely farsighted and *that* corrective lenses would help.

EXERCISE 9–1

Edit the following sentences to correct faulty parallelism. Revisions of lettered sentences appear in the back of the book. Example:

We began the search by calling the Department of Social
            requesting
Services and ~~requested~~ a list of licensed day care centers in
  ^

our area.

a. The system has capabilities such as communicating with other computers, processing records, and mathematical functions.
b. The personnel officer told me that I would answer the phone, welcome visitors, distribute mail, and some typing.
c. The African elephants are endangered primarily because poachers kill them and having less and less space to live in.
d. How ideal it seems to raise a family here in Winnebago instead of the air-polluted suburbs.
e. In combat the soldiers were brave but sometimes foolish—because of poor training, lack of confidence, and having little experience.

1. The summer of our engagement, we saw a few plays, attended family outings, and a few parties.
2. Roger explained to the immigration officer that his visa had expired and of his applying to have it renewed.
3. The examiners observed us to see if we could stomach the grotesque accidents and how to cope with them.
4. During basic training, I was not only told what to do but also what to think.

5. Activities on Wednesday afternoons include fishing trips, dance lessons, and computers.
6. Tony found that it was faster to ride his bike than driving into the city.
7. More plants fail from improper watering than any other cause.
8. Your adviser familiarizes you with the school and how to select classes appropriate for your curriculum.
9. The winner of the gluttony contest swallowed six large pancakes, slurped down a cream pie, gobbled six waffles, and four pastries in front of the dumbfounded judges.
10. Esperanza is responsible for stocking merchandise, writing orders for delivery, and sales of computers.

10

Add needed words.

Do not omit words necessary for grammatical or logical completeness. Readers need to see at a glance how the parts of a sentence are connected.

Languages sometimes differ in the need for certain words. In particular, be alert for missing verbs, articles, subjects, or expletives. See 29e, 30, and 31a.

ESL

GRAMMAR CHECKERS do not flag the vast majority of missing words. They can, however, catch some missing verbs (see 27e). Although they can flag some missing articles (*a*, *an*, and *the*), they often suggest that an article is missing when in fact it is not. (See also 30.)

10a Add words needed to complete compound structures.

In compound structures, words are often omitted for economy: *Tom is a man who means what he says and [who] says what he means.* Such omissions are perfectly acceptable as long as the omitted words are common to both parts of the compound structure.

If the shorter version is not grammatical or idiomatic because an omitted word is not common to both parts of the compound structure, the word must be put back in.

▶ Some of the regulars are acquaintances whom we see at

       who

work or live in our community.
      ^

The word *who* must be included because *whom . . . live in our community* is not grammatically correct.

            accepted

▶ Mayor Davis never has and never will accept a bribe.
                ^

Has . . . accept is not grammatically correct.

                   in

▶ Many South Pacific islanders still believe and live by ancient
                        ^

laws.

Believe . . . by is not idiomatic in English.

10b   Add the word *that* if there is any danger of misreading without it.

If there is no danger of misreading, the word *that* may be omitted when it introduces a subordinate clause. *The value of a principle is the number of things* [*that*] *it will explain.* Occasionally, however, a sentence might be misread without *that.*

                  that

▶ Looking out the family room window, Sarah saw her
                                ^

favorite tree, which she had climbed so often as a child,

was gone.

Sarah didn't see the tree; she saw that the tree was gone.

10c   Add words needed to make comparisons logical and complete.

Comparisons should be made between items that are alike. To compare unlike items is illogical and distracting.

▶ Henry preferred the hotels in Pittsburgh to Philadelphia.

    those in (inserted before Philadelphia)

Hotels must be compared with hotels.

▶ Some say that Ella Fitzgerald's renditions of Cole Porter's
songs are better than any other ~~singer~~.

    singer's. (replacing *singer*)

Ella Fitzgerald's renditions cannot be logically compared to a singer. The revision uses the possessive form *singer's*, with the word *renditions* being implied.

Sometimes the word *other* must be inserted to make a comparison logical.

▶ Chicago is larger than any city in Illinois.

    other (inserted before *city*)

Since Chicago is not larger than itself, the original comparison was not logical.

Sometimes the word *as* must be inserted to make a comparison grammatically complete.

▶ Ben is as talented, if not more talented than, the other

    as, (inserted after *talented*)

actors.

The construction *as talented* is not complete without a second *as*: *as talented as . . . the other actors*.

Comparisons should be complete enough to ensure clarity. The reader should understand what is being compared.

INCOMPLETE   Brand X is less salty.

COMPLETE   Brand X is less salty than Brand Y.

Also, there should be no ambiguity. In the following sentence, two interpretations are possible.

AMBIGUOUS   Ken helped me more than my roommate.

CLEAR   Ken helped me more than *he helped* my roommate.

CLEAR   Ken helped me more than my roommate *did*.

10d Add the articles *a, an,* and *the* where necessary for grammatical completeness.

Articles are sometimes omitted in recipes and other instructions that are meant to be followed while they are being read. Such omissions are inappropriate, however, in nearly all other forms of writing, whether formal or informal.

▶ Blood can be drawn only by doctor or by authorized person
  who has been trained in procedure.

(a inserted before doctor, an before authorized, the before procedure)

It is not always necessary to repeat articles with paired items: *We bought a computer and printer.* However, if one of the items requires *a* and the other requires *an*, both articles must be included.

▶ We bought a computer and ink-jet printer.

(an inserted before ink-jet)

ESL

Articles can cause special problems for speakers of English as a second language. See 30.

EXERCISE 10–1

Add any words needed for grammatical or logical completeness in the following sentences. Revisions of lettered sentences appear in the back of the book. Example:

> The officer at the desk feared *that* the prisoner in the interroga-
>
> tion room would escape.

a. Dip paintbrush into paint remover and spread thick coat on small section of door.
b. Christopher had an attention span longer than the other students.
c. SETI (the Search for Extraterrestrial Intelligence) has and will continue to excite interest among space buffs.
d. Samantha got along better with the chimpanzees than Albert.

e. We were glad to see Yellowstone National Park was recovering from the devastating forest fire.

1. Producers of violent video games are not capable or interested in regulating themselves.
2. Our nursing graduates are as skilled, if not more skilled than, those of any other state college.
3. Very few black doctors were allowed to serve in the Civil War, and their qualifications had to be higher than white doctors.
4. Hector understood the problem with the engine would not go away.
5. It was obvious that the students liked the new teacher more than the principal.

11

Untangle mixed constructions.

A mixed construction contains parts that do not sensibly fit together. The mismatch may be a matter of grammar or of logic.

> **GRAMMAR CHECKERS** can flag *is when, is where,* and *reason . . . is because* constructions (11c), but they fail to identify nearly all other mixed constructions, including sentences as tangled as this one: *Depending on the number and strength of drinks, the amount of time that has passed, and one's body weight determines the concentration of alcohol in the blood.*

11a Untangle the grammatical structure.

Once you head into a sentence, your choices are limited by the range of grammatical patterns in English. (See 58 and 59.) You cannot begin with one grammatical plan and switch without warning to another.

MIXED   For most drivers who have a blood alcohol concentration of .05 percent increase their risk of causing an accident.

> **REVISED** For most drivers who have a blood alcohol concentration of .05 percent, the risk of causing an accident is increased.

> **REVISED** Most drivers who have a blood alcohol concentration of .05 percent increase their risk of causing an accident.

The prepositional phrase beginning the sentence (*For most drivers who . . .*) can serve only as a modifier, not as the subject of the sentence. To begin with the prepositional phrase, the writer must finish with a subject and verb (*risk . . . is increased*). To stay with the original verb (*increase*), the writer must provide a subject (*most drivers*).

▶ *Being*
~~When an employee is~~ promoted without warning can be alarming.

The adverb clause *When an employee is promoted without warning* cannot serve as the subject of the sentence. The revision replaces the adverb clause with a gerund phrase, a word group that can function as the subject. (See 59b and 59c.)

▶ Although the United States is one of the wealthiest nations in the world, ~~but~~ almost 20 percent of American children live in poverty.

The *Although* clause is subordinate, so it cannot be linked to an independent clause with the coordinating conjunction *but*.

Occasionally a mixed construction is so tangled that it defies grammatical analysis. When this happens, back away from the sentence, rethink what you want to say, and then say it again as clearly as you can.

> **MIXED** In the whole-word method children learn to recognize entire words rather than by the phonics method in which they learn to sound out letters and groups of letters.

> **REVISED** The whole-word method teaches children to recognize entire words; the phonics method teaches them to sound out letters and groups of letters.

ESL English does not allow double subjects; nor does it allow an object or an adverb to be repeated in an adjective clause. See 31b and 31c.

▶ The squirrel that came down our chimney ~~it~~ did much damage.

▶ Hearing screams, Serena ran over to the pool that her daughter was swimming in. ~~it.~~
                                                ^

11b Straighten out the logical connections.

The subject and the predicate should make sense together; when they don't, the error is known as *faulty predication.*

▶ We decided that ~~Tiffany's welfare~~ would not be safe living
            Tiffany
            ^
with her mother.

Tiffany, not her welfare, may not be safe.

▶ Under the revised plan, the elderly, ~~who now receive a double~~
                            the double personal exemption for
                                        ^
~~personal exemption,~~ will be abolished.

The exemption, not the elderly, will be abolished.

An appositive and the noun to which it refers should be logically equivalent. When they are not, the error is known as *faulty apposition.*

▶ ~~The tax accountant,~~ a very lucrative field, requires
   Tax accounting,
   ^
intelligence, patience, and attention to mathematical

detail.

The tax accountant is a person, not a field.

11c Avoid *is when, is where,* and *reason . . . is because* constructions.

In formal English many readers object to *is when, is where,* and *reason . . . is because* constructions on either grammatical or logical grounds.

▶ Anorexia nervosa is ~~where people,~~ *a disorder suffered by people who,* believing they are too fat,
∧

diet to the point of starvation.

Anorexia nervosa is a disorder, not a place.

▶ ~~The reason~~ I missed the exam ~~is~~ because my motorcycle

broke down.

The writer might have changed *because* to *that* (*The reason I missed the exam is that my motorcycle broke down*), but the revision above is more concise.

EXERCISE 11–1

Edit the following sentences to untangle mixed constructions. Revisions of lettered sentences appear in the back of the book. Example:

~~By~~ *l*oosening the soil around your jade plant will help the air

and nutrients penetrate to the roots.

a. The name of the song is called "Words Unspoken."
b. A cloverleaf is when traffic on limited-access freeways can change direction.
c. Bowman established the format in which future football card companies would emulate for years to come.
d. Early diagnosis of prostate cancer is often curable.
e. Depending on the number and strength of drinks, the amount of time that has passed since the last drink, and one's body weight determines the concentration of alcohol in the blood.

1. Dyslexia is where people have a learning disorder that impairs reading ability.
2. The reason the Inuit were forced to eat their dogs was because the caribou, on which they depended for food, migrated out of reach.

3. Although I feel that Mr. Dawe is an excellent calculus instructor, but a few minor changes in his method would benefit both him and his class.
4. In this box contains the key to your future.
5. Using surgical gloves is a precaution now worn by dentists to prevent contact with the patients' blood and saliva.

12

Repair misplaced and dangling modifiers.

Modifiers, whether they are single words, phrases, or clauses, should point clearly to the words they modify. As a rule, related words should be kept together.

> GRAMMAR CHECKERS can flag split infinitives, such as *to carefully and thoroughly sift* (12d). However, they don't alert you to other misplaced modifiers or dangling modifiers, including danglers like this one: *When a young man, my mother enrolled me in tap dance classes, hoping I would become the next Gregory Hines.*

12a Put limiting modifiers such as *only* in front of the words they modify.

Limiting modifiers such as *only, even, almost, nearly,* and *just* should appear in front of a verb only if they modify the verb: *At first, I couldn't even touch my toes, much less grasp them.* If they limit the meaning of some other word in the sentence, they should be placed in front of that word.

▶ Lasers ~~only~~ destroy the target, leaving the surrounding
    only
    ^

healthy tissue intact.

Only limits the meaning of *the target*, not *destroy*.

▶ Although they played their best, the Beaumont Bluejays
  even
  didn't ~~even~~ score once.
            ^

Even modifies *once*, not *score*.

The limiting modifier *not* is frequently misplaced, suggesting a meaning the writer did not intend.

                          not
▶ In the United States in 1860, all black southerners were ~~not~~
                            ^
  slaves.

The original sentence means that no black southerners were
slaves. The revision makes the writer's real meaning clear: Some
(but not all) black southerners were slaves.

12b Place phrases and clauses so that readers can see at a glance what they modify.

Although phrases and clauses can appear at some distance from
the words they modify, make sure your meaning is clear. When
phrases or clauses are oddly placed, absurd misreadings can
result.

> **MISPLACED**   The king returned to the clinic where he had
>   undergone heart surgery in 1998 in a limousine
>   sent by the White House.
>
> **REVISED**   Traveling in a limousine sent by the White House,
>   the king returned to the clinic where he had
>   undergone heart surgery in 1998.

The revision corrects the false impression that the king under-
went heart surgery in a limousine.

     On the walls
▶ ~~There~~ are many pictures of comedians who have performed
   ^
  at Gavin's, ~~on the walls.~~
             ^

The comedians weren't performing on the walls; the pictures were
on the walls.

▶ The robber was described as a six-foot-tall man with a heavy 150-pound,

mustache. ~~weighing 150 pounds.~~

The robber, not the mustache, weighed 150 pounds.

Occasionally the placement of a modifier leads to an ambiguity, in which case two revisions will be possible, depending on the writer's intended meaning.

AMBIGUOUS	The exchange students we met for coffee occasionally questioned us about our latest slang.
CLEAR	The exchange students we occasionally met for coffee questioned us about our latest slang.
CLEAR	The exchange students we met for coffee questioned us occasionally about our latest slang.

In the original version, it was not clear whether the meeting or the questioning happened occasionally. The revisions eliminate the ambiguity.

12c Move awkwardly placed modifiers.

As a rule, a sentence should flow from subject to verb to object, without lengthy detours along the way. When a long adverbial element separates a subject from its verb, a verb from its object, or a helping verb from its main verb, the result is usually awkward.

▶ ~~Our son,~~ After doctors told him that he would never walk
our son
without a cane, began an intensive program of

rehabilitation.

There is no reason to separate the subject *Our son* from the verb *began* with a long adverb clause.

I
▶ ~~Oscar Lewis spent,~~ in researching *The Children of Sanchez,*
Oscar Lewis spent
hundreds of hours living with the Sanchez family in a slum
^
of Mexico City.

The *in* phrase needlessly separated the verb *spent* from its object, *hundreds of hours.*

ESL

English does not allow an adverb to appear between a verb and its object. See 31d.

easily.
▶ Yolanda lifted ~~easily~~ the fifty-pound weight./

12d Do not split infinitives needlessly.

An infinitive consists of *to* plus a verb: *to think, to breathe, to dance.* When a modifier appears between *to* and the verb, an infinitive is said to be "split": *to carefully balance.* If a split infinitive is obviously awkward, it should be revised.

If possible, the
▶ ~~The~~ patient should try to,/~~if possible,~~ avoid going up and
^
down stairs.

Usage varies when a split infinitive is less awkward than the preceding one. To be on the safe side, however, you should not split such infinitives, especially in formal writing.

formally.
▶ The candidate decided to ~~formally~~ launch her campaign./
^

When a split infinitive is more natural and less awkward than alternative phrasing, most readers find it acceptable: *We decided to actually enforce the law* is a perfectly natural construction in English. *We decided actually to enforce the law* is not.

EXERCISE 12–1

Edit the following sentences to correct misplaced or awkwardly placed modifiers. Revisions of lettered sentences appear in the back of the book. Example:

> *in a telephone survey*
> Answering questions can be annoying. ~~in a telephone~~
> ^   ^
>
> ~~survey.~~

a. At our warehouse sale, cash, MasterCard, or Visa will only be accepted.
b. All thin people are not anorexic or bulimic.
c. Celia received a flier about a workshop on making a kimono from a Japanese nun.
d. Jurors are encouraged to thoroughly sift through the evidence.
e. All passengers were, as the train reached the border, asked to have their passports ready.

1. Several recent studies have encouraged heart patients to more carefully watch their cholesterol levels.
2. He promised never to remarry at her deathbed.
3. The recordings were all done at the studio of the late Jimi Hendrix named Electric Ladyland.
4. The old Marlboro ads depicted a man on a horse smoking a cigarette.
5. The smog was so bad that we could only see a hundred yards ahead.

12e Repair dangling modifiers.

A dangling modifier fails to refer logically to any word in the sentence. Dangling modifiers are easy to repair, but they can be hard to recognize, especially in your own writing.

Recognizing dangling modifiers

Dangling modifiers are usually word groups (such as verbal phrases) that suggest but do not name an actor. When a sentence opens with such a modifier, readers expect the subject of the next clause to name the actor. If it doesn't, the modifier dangles.

> *When the driver opened*
> ~~Opening~~ the window to let out a huge bumblebee, the car
>   ^
>
> accidentally swerved into an oncoming car.

The car didn't open the window; the driver did.

>   *women have often been denied*
> After completing seminary training, ~~women's~~ access to the
>   ^
>
> pulpit. ~~has often been denied~~.
>   ^

The women (not their access to the pulpit) complete the training.

The following sentences illustrate four common kinds of dangling modifiers.

DANGLING	*Deciding to join the navy*, the recruiter enthusiastically pumped Joe's hand. [Participial phrase]
DANGLING	*Upon entering the doctor's office*, a skeleton caught my attention. [Preposition followed by a gerund phrase]
DANGLING	*To please the children*, some fireworks were set off a day early. [Infinitive phrase]
DANGLING	*Though only sixteen*, UCLA accepted Martha's application. [Elliptical clause with an understood subject and verb]

These dangling modifiers falsely suggest that the recruiter decided to join the navy, that the skeleton entered the doctor's office, that the fireworks intended to please the children, and that UCLA is only sixteen years old.

Repairing dangling modifiers

To repair a dangling modifier, you can revise the sentence in one of two ways:

1. Name the actor in the subject of the sentence, or
2. name the actor in the modifier.

Depending on your sentence, one of these revision strategies may be more appropriate than the other.

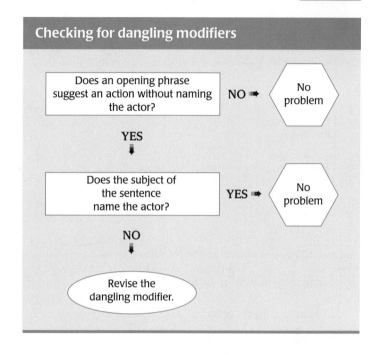

Checking for dangling modifiers

Does an opening phrase suggest an action without naming the actor? → **NO** → No problem

YES
↓

Does the subject of the sentence name the actor? → **YES** → No problem

NO
↓

Revise the dangling modifier.

ACTOR NAMED IN SUBJECT

I noticed
► Upon entering the doctor's office, a skeleton~~, caught my~~
                                          ^   ^

~~attention.~~

we set off
► To please the children, some fireworks ~~were set off~~ early.
                                          ^

ACTOR NAMED IN MODIFIER

When Joe decided
► ~~Deciding~~ to join the navy, the recruiter enthusiastically
  ^
        his
pumped ~~Joe's~~ hand.
       ^

Martha was   *her*
► Though only sixteen, UCLA accepted ~~Martha's~~ application.
  ^   ^

NOTE: You cannot repair a dangling modifier just by moving it. Consider, for example, the sentence about the skeleton. If you put the modifier at the end of the sentence (*A skeleton* *caught my attention upon entering the doctor's office*), you are still suggesting—absurdly, of course—that the skeleton entered the office. The only way to avoid the problem is to put the word *I* in the sentence, either as the subject or in the modifier.

▶ Upon entering the doctor's office, a skeleton. ~~caught my~~ *I noticed*
　　　　　　　　　　　　　　　　　　　　^　　　　　　^

~~attention.~~

▶ ~~Upon entering~~ the doctor's office, a skeleton caught my *As I entered*
　　　　　^

attention.

EXERCISE 12–2

Edit the following sentences to correct dangling modifiers. Most sentences can be revised in more than one way. Revisions of lettered sentences appear in the back of the book. Example:

　　　　　　　　　　　　　　　　　　　　　　　a student must complete
To acquire a degree in almost any field, two science courses.
　　　　　　　　　　　　　　　　　　　　^　　　　　　　　　　^

~~must be completed.~~

a. Reaching the heart, a bypass was performed on the severely blocked arteries.
b. To enter college early, more than good grades are required.
c. While dining at night, the lights along the Baja coastline created a romantic atmosphere perfect for our first anniversary.
d. While still a beginner at tennis, the coaches recruited my sister to train for the Olympics.
e. After returning to Jamaica, Marcus Garvey's Back to Africa movement slowly died.

1. By following this new procedure, our mailing costs will decrease significantly.
2. As president of the missionary circle, one of Grandmother's duties is to raise money for the church.
3. When investigating burglaries and thefts, it was easy for me to sympathize with the victims because I had been a victim myself.
4. As a child growing up in Nigeria, my mother taught me to treat all elders with respect.
5. While working as a ranger in Everglades National Park, a Florida panther crossed the road in front of my truck one night.

13

Eliminate distracting shifts.

GRAMMAR CHECKERS do not flag the shifts discussed in this section: shifts in point of view; shifts in verb tense, mood, or voice; and shifts between direct and indirect questions or quotations. Even the most obvious errors like this one will slip right past most grammar checkers: *My three-year-old fell into the pool and to my surprise she swims to the shallow end.*

13a Make the point of view consistent in person and number.

The point of view of a piece of writing is the perspective from which it is written: first person (*I* or *we*), second person (*you*), or third person (*he/she/it/one* or *they*). The *I* (or *we*) point of view, which emphasizes the writer, is a good choice for informal letters and writing based primarily on personal experience. The *you* point of view, which emphasizes the reader, works well for giving advice or explaining how to do something. The third-person point of view, which emphasizes the subject, is appropriate in formal academic and professional writing.

Writers who are having difficulty settling on an appropriate point of view sometimes shift confusingly from one to another. The solution is to choose a suitable perspective and then stay with it.

▶ One week our class met in a junkyard to practice rescuing a

victim trapped in a wrecked car. We learned to dismantle the

We   *our*
car with the essential tools. ~~You~~ were graded on ~~your~~ speed
                                          ^   ^
our
and ~~your~~ skill in extricating the victim.
        ^

The writer should have stayed with the *we* point of view. *You* is inappropriate because the writer is not addressing readers directly. *You* should not be used in a vague sense meaning "anyone." (See 23d.)

▶ *You*
~~Everyone~~ should purchase a lift ticket unless you plan to
   ∧

spend most of your time walking or crawling up a steep hill.

Here *you* is an appropriate choice because the writer is giving advice directly to readers.

▶ *Police officers are*
~~A police officer is~~ often criticized for always being there when
   ∧

they aren't needed and never being there when they are.

Although the writer might have changed *they* to *he* or *she* (to match the singular *officer*), the revision in the plural is more concise. (See also 22a and 17f.)

13b Maintain consistent verb tenses.

Consistent verb tenses clearly establish the time of the actions being described. When a passage begins in one tense and then shifts without warning and for no reason to another, readers are distracted and confused.

▶ There was no way I could fight the current and win. Just as I
                                jumped   *swam*
was losing hope, a stranger ~~jumps~~ off a passing boat and ~~swims~~
                              ∧   ∧

toward me.

Writers often encounter difficulty with verb tenses when writing about literature. Because fictional events occur outside the time frames of real life, the past and the present tenses may seem equally appropriate. The literary convention, however, is to describe fictional events consistently in the present tense.

▶ The scarlet letter is a punishment sternly placed upon
                                                    is
Hester's breast by the community, and yet it ~~was~~ an
                                               ∧

extremely fanciful and imaginative product of Hester's own

needlework.

13c Make verbs consistent in mood and voice.

Unnecessary shifts in the mood of a verb can be as distracting
as needless shifts in tense. There are three moods in English:
the *indicative,* used for facts, opinions, and questions; the *imperative,* used for orders or advice; and the *subjunctive,* used in
certain contexts to express wishes or conditions contrary to fact
(see 28b).

The following passage shifts confusingly from the indicative to the imperative mood.

▶ The officers advised us against allowing anyone into our

homes without proper identification. ~~Also,~~ alert neighbors to
                                                    ^
                                    They also suggested that we

vacation schedules.

Since the writer's purpose was to report the officers' advice, the
revision puts both sentences in the indicative.

A verb may be in either the active voice (with the subject
doing the action) or the passive voice (with the subject receiving the action). (See 28c.) If a writer shifts without warning from
one to the other, readers may be left wondering why.

▶ When the tickets are ready, the travel agent notifies the

client./ ~~Each ticket is then listed~~ on a daily register form, and
        ^   ^
    lists each ticket

a copy of the itinerary, ~~is filed.~~
^   ^
files

The passage began in the active voice (*agent notifies*) and then
switched to the passive (*ticket is listed, copy is filed*). Because the
active voice is clearer and more direct, the writer changed all the
verbs to the active voice.

13d Avoid sudden shifts from indirect to direct questions or quotations.

An indirect question reports a question without asking it: *We
asked whether we could take a swim.* A direct question asks directly: *Can we take a swim?* Sudden shifts from indirect to

direct questions are awkward. In addition, sentences containing such shifts are impossible to punctuate because indirect questions must end with a period and direct questions must end with a question mark. (See 38b.)

▶ I wonder whether the sister knew of the theft and, if so, ~~did~~
whether she reported
~~she report~~ it to the police.
^

The revision poses both questions indirectly. The writer could also ask both questions directly: *Did the sister know of the theft and, if so, did she report it to the police?*

An indirect quotation reports someone's words without quoting word for word: *Annabelle said that she is a Virgo.* A direct quotation presents the exact words of a speaker or writer, set off with quotation marks: *Annabelle said, "I am a Virgo."* Unannounced shifts from indirect to direct quotations are distracting and confusing, especially when the writer fails to insert the necessary quotation marks, as in the following example.

asked me not to
▶ Mother said that she would be late for dinner and ~~please do~~
^
came
~~not~~ leave for choir practice until Dad ~~comes~~ home.
^

The revision reports all of the mother's words. The writer could also quote directly: *Mother said, "I will be late for dinner. Please do not leave for choir practice until Dad comes home."*

EXERCISE 13–1

Edit the following sentences to eliminate distracting shifts. Revisions of lettered sentences appear in the back of the book. Example:

they
For most people, quitting smoking is not easy once ~~you~~ are
^
hooked.

a. My hopes rise and fall as Joseph's heart started and stopped. The doctors insert a large tube into his chest, and the blood flowed from the incision onto the floor.

b. A minister often has a hard time because they have to please so many different people.

c. We drove for eight hours until we reached the South Dakota Badlands. You could hardly believe the eeriness of the landscape at dusk.

d. The question is whether ferrets bred in captivity have the instinct to prey on prairie dogs or is this a learned skill.

e. Everyone should protect yourself from the sun, especially on the first day of extensive exposure.

1. A courtroom lawyer has more than a touch of theater in their blood.

2. The artist has often been seen as a threat to society, especially when they refuse to conform to conventional standards of taste.

3. Phil said that he would be happy to set up the new computer and when could he come over and get started.

4. Rescue workers put water on her face and lifted her head gently onto a pillow. Finally, she opens her eyes.

5. With a little self-discipline and a desire to improve oneself, you too can enjoy the benefits of running.

14

Emphasize your point.

Within each sentence, emphasize your point by expressing it in the subject and verb, the words that receive the most attention from readers. As a rule, choose an active verb and pair it with a subject that names the person or thing doing the action.

Within longer stretches of prose, you can draw attention to ideas deserving special emphasis by using a variety of techniques, often involving an unusual twist or some element of surprise.

14a Prefer active verbs.

Active verbs express meaning more emphatically and vigorously than their weaker counterparts—forms of the verb *be* or verbs in the passive voice. Forms of the verb *be* (*be, am, is, are, was, were, being, been*) lack vigor because they convey no action. Verbs in the passive voice lack strength because their subjects receive the action instead of doing it. (See also 28c and 58c.)

Although the forms of *be* and passive verbs have legitimate uses, if an active verb can carry your meaning, use it.

> **BE VERB** A surge of power *was* responsible for the destruction of the pumps.
>
> **PASSIVE** The pumps *were destroyed* by a surge of power.
>
> **ACTIVE** A surge of power *destroyed* the pumps.

Even among active verbs, some are more active—and therefore more vigorous and colorful—than others. Carefully selected verbs can energize a piece of writing.

▶ The goalie crouched low, ~~reached~~ *swept* out his stick, and ~~sent~~ *hooked* the

rebound away from the mouth of the net.

When to replace be *verbs*

Not every *be* verb needs replacing. The forms of *be* (*be, am, is, are, was, were, being, been*) work well when you want to link a subject to a noun that clearly renames it or to an adjective that describes it: *History is a bucket of ashes. Scoundrels are always sociable.* And when used as helping verbs before present participles (*is flying, are disappearing*) to express ongoing action, *be* verbs are fine: *Derrick was plowing the field when his wife went into labor.* (See 29a.)

If using a *be* verb makes a sentence needlessly wordy, however, consider replacing it. Often a phrase following the verb will contain a word (such as *violation*) that suggests a more vigorous, active alternative (*violate*).

▶ Burying nuclear waste in Antarctica would ~~be in violation of~~ *violate*

an international treaty.

Violate is less wordy and more vigorous than *be in violation of.*

▶ When Rosa Parks ~~was resistant to~~ giving up her seat on the
       resisted
^

  bus, she became a civil rights hero.

Resisted is more active than *was resistant to*.

When to replace passive verbs

In the active voice, the subject of the sentence does the action;
in the passive, the subject receives the action.

ACTIVE   Hernando *caught* the fly ball.

PASSIVE The fly ball *was caught* by Hernando.

In passive sentences, the actor (in this case *Hernando*) frequently
disappears from the sentence: *The fly ball was caught.*

In most cases, you will want to emphasize the actor, so you
should use the active voice. To replace a passive verb with an
active alternative, make the actor the subject of the sentence.

▶ ~~The transformer was struck by a bolt of lightning,~~ plunging
     A bolt of lightning struck the transformer,
^

  us into darkness.

The active verb (*struck*) makes the point more forcefully than the
passive verb (*was struck*).

▶ As the patient undressed, scars ~~were seen~~ on her back,
                       the doctor saw
^

  stomach, and thighs.

The active version is clearer because it names the actor: the
doctor.

The passive voice is appropriate if you wish to emphasize the
receiver of the action or to minimize the importance of the
actor.

APPROPRIATE Many native Hawaiians *are forced* to leave their
PASSIVE   beautiful beaches to make room for hotels and
                 condominiums.

APPROPRIATE	As the time for harvest approaches, the tobacco
PASSIVE	plants *are sprayed* with a chemical to retard the
	growth of suckers.

The writer of the first sentence wished to emphasize the receiver of the action, *Hawaiians.* The writer of the second sentence wished to focus on the tobacco plants, not on the people spraying them.

In much scientific writing, the passive voice properly emphasizes the experiment or process being described, not the researcher.

APPROPRIATE	The solution *was heated* to the boiling point, and
PASSIVE	then it *was reduced* in volume by 50 percent.

 Some speakers of English as a second language avoid the passive voice even when it is appropriate. For advice on trans-**ESL** forming an active-voice sentence to the passive, see page 137.

 GRAMMAR CHECKERS are fairly good at flagging passive verbs, such as *were given.* However, because passive verbs are sometimes appropriate, you—not the computer program—must decide whether to make a passive verb active.

14b As a rule, choose a subject that names the person or thing doing the action.

In weak, unemphatic prose, both the actor and the action may be buried in sentence elements other than the subject and the verb. In the following sentence, for example, the actor and the action both appear in prepositional phrases, word groups that do not receive much attention from readers.

WEAK	Exposure to Dr. Martinez's excellent teaching had the
	effect of inspiring me to major in education.
EMPHATIC	Dr. Martinez's excellent teaching inspired me to major in education.

Consider the subjects and verbs of the two versions—
exposure had versus *teaching inspired.* Clearly the latter expresses the writer's point more emphatically.

> *Cocaine used*   *cause*
> ~~The use of cocaine~~ by pregnant women can ~~be a major~~
>   ^   ^
>
> ~~contributor to~~ severe brain damage in infants.

In the original version, the subject and verb—*use can be*—express
the point blandly. *Cocaine can cause* alerts readers to the dangers
of cocaine more emphatically than *use can be.*

EXERCISE 14–1

Revise any weak, unemphatic sentences by replacing *be* verbs or passive verbs with active alternatives and, if necessary, by naming in the
subject the person or thing doing the action. Some sentences are emphatic; do not change them. Revisions of lettered sentences appear in
the back of the book. Example:

> *The ranger doused the campfire before giving us*
> ~~The campfire was doused by the ranger before we were given~~
> ^
>
> a ticket for unauthorized use of a campsite.

a. The Prussians were victorious over the Saxons in 1745.
b. The entire operation is managed by Ahmed, the producer.
c. Finally the chute caught air and popped open with a jolt at about
   2,000 feet.
d. There were fighting players on both sides of the rink.
e. At recess, Ms. Robinson joined us in our games. She jumped rope,
   played dodgeball, and even climbed on the jungle gym.

1. Just as the police closed in, two shots were fired by the terrorists
   from the roof of the hotel.
2. Julia was successful in her first attempt to pass the bar exam.
3. The bomb bay doors rumbled open and freezing air whipped
   through the plane.
4. Listening to the music of Charlie Parker and John Coltrane had the
   effect of inspiring me to take up the saxophone.
5. The only responsibility I was given by my parents was putting gas
   in the brand-new Mitsubishi they bought me my senior year.

14c Experiment with techniques for gaining special emphasis.

By experimenting with certain techniques, usually involving some element of surprise, you can draw attention to ideas that deserve special emphasis. Use such techniques sparingly, however, or they will lose their punch. The writer who tries to emphasize everything ends up emphasizing nothing.

Using sentence endings for emphasis

You can highlight an idea simply by withholding it until the end of a sentence. The technique works something like a punch line. In the following example, the sentence's meaning is not revealed until its very last word.

> The only completely consistent people are the dead.
> —Aldous Huxley

Using parallel structure for emphasis

Parallel grammatical structure draws special attention to paired ideas or to items in a series (See 9). When parallel ideas are paired, the emphasis falls on words that underscore comparisons or contrasts, especially when they occur at the end of a phrase or clause.

> We must *stop talking* about the *American dream* and *start listening* to the *dreams of Americans*.   —Reubin Askew

In a parallel series, the emphasis falls at the end, so it is generally best to end with the most dramatic or climactic item in the series.

> Sister Charity enjoyed passing out writing punishments: translate the Ten Commandments into Latin, type a thousand-word essay on good manners, copy the New Testament with a quill pen.   —Marie Visosky, student

Using punctuation for emphasis

Obviously the exclamation point can add emphasis, but you should not overuse it. As a rule, the exclamation point is more appropriate in dialogue than in ordinary prose.

> I oozed a glob of white paint onto my palette, whipped some medium into it, loaded my brush, and announced to the class, "Move over, Michelangelo. Here I come!"
> —Carolyn Goff, student

A dash or a colon may be used to draw attention to word groups worthy of special attention. (See 35a, 35b, and 39a.)

> The middle of the road is where the white line is—and that's the worst place to drive.　　　　　—Robert Frost

> I turned to see what the anemometer read: The needle had pegged out at 106 knots.　　　　　—Jonathan Shilk, student

Occasionally, a pair of dashes may be used to highlight a word or an idea.

> [My friend] was a gay and impudent and satirical and delightful young black man—a slave—who daily preached sermons from the top of his master's woodpile, with me for sole audience.
> —Mark Twain

Using an occasional short sentence for emphasis

Too many short sentences in a row will fast become monotonous (see 8a), but an occasional short sentence, when played off against longer sentences in the same passage, will draw attention to an idea.

> The great secret, known to internists and learned early in marriage by internists' wives [or husbands], but still hidden from the general public, is that most things get better by themselves. Most things, in fact, are better by morning.
> —Lewis Thomas

15

Provide some variety.

When a rough draft is filled with too many same-sounding sentences, try injecting some variety—as long as you can do so without sacrificing clarity or ease of reading.

GRAMMAR CHECKERS are of little help with sentence variety. It takes a human ear to know when and why sentence variety is needed.

Some programs tell you when you have used the same word to open several sentences, but sometimes it is a good idea to do so — if you are trying to highlight parallel ideas, for example (see p. 52).

15a Vary your sentence openings.

Most sentences in English begin with the subject, move to the verb, and continue along to the object, with modifiers tucked in along the way or put at the end. For the most part, such sentences are fine. Put too many of them in a row, however, and they become monotonous.

Adverbial modifiers, being easily movable, can often be inserted ahead of the subject. Such modifiers might be single words, phrases, or clauses.

▶ *Eventually a*
A few drops of sap ~~eventually~~ began to trickle into the

bucket.

Like most adverbs, *eventually* does not need to appear close to the verb it modifies (*began*).

▶ *Just as we were heading to work, the*
~~The~~ earthquake rumbled through the valley ~~. just as we were~~

~~heading to work.~~

The adverb clause, which modifies the verb *rumbled,* is as clear at the beginning of the sentence as it is at the end.

Adjectives and participial phrases can frequently be moved to the beginning of a sentence without loss of clarity.

▶ *Discouraged*
~~The~~ university, ~~discouraged~~ by the researchers' apparent lack

the university
of progress, nearly withdrew funding for these prize-winning

experiments.

▶ ~~John and I,~~ anticipating a peaceful evening, sat down at

the campfire to grill a couple of steaks and brew a pot of

coffee.

> *A*
>
> *John and I*

CAUTION: When beginning a sentence with a participial phrase, make sure that the subject of the sentence names the person or thing described in the introductory phrase. If it doesn't, the phrase will dangle. (See 12e.)

15b Use a variety of sentence structures.

A writer should not rely too heavily on simple sentences and compound sentences, for the effect tends to be both monotonous and choppy. (See 8a and 8b.) Too many complex or compound-complex sentences, however, can be equally monotonous. If your style tends to one or the other extreme, try to achieve a better mix of sentence types. (See 60a.)

15c Try inverting sentences occasionally.

A sentence is inverted if it does not follow the normal subject-verb-object pattern. (See 58c.) Many inversions sound artificial and should be avoided except in the most formal contexts. But if an inversion sounds natural, it can provide a welcome touch of variety.

▶ *Opposite the produce section is a*

~~A~~ refrigerated case of mouth-watering cheeses~~, is opposite~~

~~the produce section;~~ a friendly attendant will cut off just the

amount you want.

▶ *Set at the top two corners of the stage were huge*

~~Huge~~ lavender hearts outlined in bright white lights~~, were set~~

~~at the top two corners of the stage.~~

EXERCISE 15–1

Edit the following paragraph to increase variety in sentence structure.

> I have spent thirty years of my life on a tobacco farm, and I cannot understand why people smoke. The whole process of raising tobacco involves deadly chemicals. The ground is treated for mold and chemically fertilized before the tobacco seed is ever planted. The seed is planted and begins to grow, and then the bed is treated with weed killer. The plant is then transferred to the field. It is sprayed with poison to kill worms about two months later. Then the time for harvest approaches, and the plant is sprayed once more with a chemical to retard the growth of suckers. The tobacco is harvested and hung in a barn to dry. These barns are havens for birds. The birds defecate all over the leaves. After drying, these leaves are divided by color, and no feces are removed. They are then sold to the tobacco companies. I do not know what the tobacco companies do after they receive the tobacco. I do not need to know. They cannot remove what I know is in the leaf and on the leaf. I don't want any of it to pass through my mouth.

16

Tighten wordy sentences.

Long sentences are not necessarily wordy, nor are short sentences always concise. A sentence is wordy if it can be tightened without loss of meaning.

GRAMMAR CHECKERS can flag some, but not all, wordy constructions. Most programs alert you to common redundancies, such as *true fact,* and empty or inflated phrases, such as *in my opinion* or *in order that.* In addition, they alert you to possible wordiness caused by passive verbs, such as *was encouraged* (see also 14a). They are less helpful in identifying sentences with needlessly complex structures.

16a Eliminate redundancies.

Redundancies such as *cooperate together, close proximity, basic essentials*, and *true fact* are a common source of wordiness. There is no need to say the same thing twice.

▶ Black slaves were ~~thought of or~~ stereotyped as lazy

  even though they were the main labor force of the

  South.

        works
▶ Daniel ~~is now employed~~ at a private rehabilitation center

  ~~working~~ as a registered physical therapist.

    Though modifiers ordinarily add meaning to the words they modify, occasionally they are redundant.

▶ Sylvia ~~very hurriedly~~ scribbled her name, address, and phone

  number on the back of a greasy napkin.

▶ Joel was determined ~~in his mind~~ to lose weight.

    The words *scribbled* and *determined* already contain the notions suggested by the modifiers *very hurriedly* and *in his mind.*

16b Avoid unnecessary repetition of words.

Though words may be repeated deliberately, for effect, repetitions will seem awkward if they are clearly unnecessary. When a more concise version is possible, choose it.

▶ Our fifth patient, in room six, is a mentally ill. ~~patient.~~

                                   grow
▶ The best teachers help each student to ~~become a better~~

  ~~student~~ both academically and emotionally.

16C Cut empty or inflated phrases.

An empty phrase can be cut with little or no loss of meaning. Common examples are introductory word groups that apologize or hedge: *in my opinion, I think that, it seems that, one must admit that,* and so on.

▶ ~~In my opinion,~~ *O*ur current immigration policy is misguided

on several counts.

▶ ~~It seems that~~ *Lonesome Dove* is one of Larry McMurtry's

most ambitious novels.

Inflated phrases can be reduced to a word or two without loss of meaning.

INFLATED	CONCISE
along the lines of	like
as a matter of fact	in fact
at all times	always
at the present time	now, currently
at this point in time	now, currently
because of the fact that	because
by means of	by
by virtue of the fact that	because
due to the fact that	because
for the purpose of	for
for the reason that	because
have the ability to	be able to, can
in light of the fact that	because
in the nature of	like
in order to	to
in spite of the fact that	although, though
in the event that	if
in the final analysis	finally
in the neighborhood of	about
until such time as	until

▶ We will file the appropriate papers ~~in the event that~~ *if* we are

unable to meet the deadline.

16d Simplify the structure.

If the structure of a sentence is needlessly indirect, try simplifying it. Look for opportunities to strengthen the verb.

▶ The financial analyst claimed that because of volatile market

conditions she could not ~~make an~~ estimate ~~of~~ the company's

future profits.

The verb *estimate* is more vigorous and more concise than *make an estimate of.*

The colorless verbs *is, are, was,* and *were* frequently generate excess words.

monitors and balances
▶ The secretary ~~is responsible for monitoring and balancing~~
  ^

the budgets for travel, contract services, and personnel.

The revision is more direct and concise.

The expletive constructions *there is* and *there are* (or *there was* and *there were*) can also generate excess words. The same is true of expletive constructions beginning with *it.* (See 58c.)

      A
▶ ~~There is~~ another module ~~that~~ tells the story of Charles

Darwin and introduces the theory of evolution.

        H   *must*
▶ ~~It is important that~~ hikers remain inside the park
            ^

boundaries.

Expletive constructions are appropriate, however, when a writer has a good reason for delaying the subject. (See 58c.)

Finally, verbs in the passive voice may be needlessly indirect. When the active voice expresses your meaning as well, use it. (See 14a and 28c.)

>   *our coaches have recruited*
> All too often, athletes with marginal academic skills. ~~have~~
>   ^   ^
>
> ~~been recruited by our coaches.~~

16e Reduce clauses to phrases, phrases to single words.

Word groups functioning as modifiers can often be made more compact. Look for any opportunities to reduce clauses to phrases or phrases to single words.

> We took a side trip to Monticello, ~~which was~~ the home of
>
> Thomas Jefferson.

>   *silk*
> For her birthday we gave Jess a stylish vest. ~~made of silk.~~
>   ^   ^

EXERCISE 16–1

Edit the following sentences for wordiness. Revisions of lettered sentences appear in the back of the book. Example:

>   *even though*
> The Wilsons moved into the house ~~in spite of the fact that~~
>   ^
>
> the back door was only ten yards from the train tracks.

a. The drawing room in the west wing is the room that is said to be haunted.
b. Even the placement of ten terry cloth towels stuffed under the door did nothing to stop the flow.
c. In my opinion, Bloom's race for the governorship is a futile exercise.
d. In the heart of Beijing lies the Forbidden City, which is an imperial palace built in very ancient times during the Ming dynasty.
e. Seeing the barrels, the driver immediately slammed on his brakes.

1. The thing data sets are used for is communicating with other computers.
2. Martin Luther King, Jr., was a man who set a high standard for future leaders to meet.
3. A typical autocross course consists of at least two straightaways, and the rest of the course is made up of numerous slaloms and several sharp turns.

4. We are asking for your help and cooperation in reducing the cost of our mailings.
5. The price of driving while drunk or while intoxicated can be extremely high.

17

Choose appropriate language.

Language is appropriate when it suits your subject, engages your audience, and blends naturally with your own voice.

To some extent, your choice of language will be governed by the conventions of the genre in which you are writing. When in doubt about the conventions of a particular genre — lab reports, informal essays, business memos, and so on — take a look at models written by experts in the field.

17a Stay away from jargon.

Jargon is specialized language used among members of a trade, profession, or group. Use jargon only when readers will be familiar with it; even then, use it only when plain English will not do as well.

JARGON   For years the indigenous body politic of South Africa attempted to negotiate legal enfranchisement without result.

REVISED   For years the indigenous people of South Africa negotiated in vain for the right to vote.

Broadly defined, jargon includes puffed-up language designed more to impress readers than to inform them. The following are common examples from business, government, higher education, and the military, with plain English translations in parentheses.

ameliorate (improve)	indicator (sign)
commence (begin)	optimal (best, most favorable)
components (parts)	parameters (boundaries, limits)
endeavor (try)	peruse (read, look over)
exit (leave)	prior to (before)
facilitate (help)	utilize (use)
factor (consideration, cause)	viable (workable)
impact (v.) (affect)	

Sentences filled with jargon are hard to read, and they are often wordy as well.

▶ All ~~employees functioning in the capacity of~~ work-study
must prove that they are currently enrolled.
students ~~are required to give evidence of current enrollment.~~
^

begin
▶ Mayor Summers will ~~commence~~ his term of office by
^
improving   *poor neighborhoods.*
~~ameliorating~~ living conditions in ~~economically deprived zones.~~
^   ^

17b Avoid pretentious language, most euphemisms, and "doublespeak."

Hoping to sound profound or poetic, some writers embroider their thoughts with large words and flowery phrases, language that in fact sounds pretentious. Pretentious language is so ornate and often so wordy that it obscures the thought that lies beneath.

parents become old,
▶ When our ~~progenitors reach their silver-haired and golden~~
^
entomb   *old-age homes*
~~years,~~ we frequently ~~ensepulcher~~ them in ~~homes for~~
^   ^
dead.
~~senescent beings~~ as if they were already among the ~~deceased.~~
^

Related to pretentious language are euphemisms, nice-sounding words or phrases substituted for words thought to sound harsh or ugly. Like pretentious language, euphemisms are wordy and indirect. Unlike pretentious language, they are sometimes appropriate. It is our social custom, for example, to use euphemisms when speaking or writing about death (*Her sister passed on*), excretion (*I have to go to the bathroom*), sexual intercourse (*They did not sleep together until they were married*), and the like. We may also use euphemisms out of concern for someone's feelings. Telling parents, for example, that their daughter is "unmotivated" is more sensitive than saying she's lazy. Tact or politeness, then, can justify an occasional euphemism.

Most euphemisms, however, are needlessly evasive or even deceitful. Like pretentious language, they obscure the intended meaning.

EUPHEMISM	PLAIN ENGLISH
adult entertainment	pornography
preowned automobile	used car
economically deprived	poor
selected out	fired
negative savings	debts
strategic withdrawal	retreat or defeat
revenue enhancers	taxes
chemical dependency	drug addiction
downsize	lay off
correctional facility	prison

The term *doublespeak,* coined by George Orwell in his novel *1984,* applies to any deliberately evasive or deceptive language, including euphemisms. Doublespeak is especially common in politics, where missiles are named "Peacekeepers," airplane crashes are termed "uncontrolled contact with the ground," and a military retreat is described as "tactical redeployment." Business also gives us its share of doublespeak. When the manufacturer of a pacemaker writes that its product "may result in adverse health consequences in pacemaker-dependent patients as a result of sudden 'no output' failure," it takes an alert reader to grasp the message: The pacemaker might suddenly stop functioning and cause a heart attack or even death.

GRAMMAR CHECKERS can be helpful in identifying jargon and pretentious language. For example, they commonly advise against using words such as *utilize, finalize, facilitate,* and *effectuate.* You may find, however, that a program advises you to "simplify" language that is not jargon or pretentious language and may in fact be appropriate in academic writing. Sometimes you can direct the program to change the style level from standard to formal.

Clarity

EXERCISE 17-1

Edit the following sentences to eliminate jargon, pretentious or flowery language, euphemisms, and doublespeak. You may need to make substantial changes in some sentences. Revisions of lettered sentences appear in the back of the book. Example:

> *mastered*
> After two weeks in the legal department, Sue has ~~worked~~
> ^
> *office* *performance has*
> ~~into~~ the routine, ~~of the office,~~ and her ~~functional and self-~~
> ^ ^ ^
>
> ~~management skills have~~ exceeded all expectations.

a. Pay no heed to those who attempt to dissuade you from attaining what you desire.
b. In order that I may increase my expertise in the area of delivery of services to clients, I feel that participation in this conference will be beneficial.
c. Have you ever been accused of flagellating a deceased equine?
d. When Sal was selected out from his high-paying factory job, he learned what it was like to be economically depressed.
e. Passengers should endeavor to finalize the customs declaration form prior to exiting the aircraft.

1. We learned that the mayor had been engaging in a creative transfer of city employees' pension funds.
2. As I approached the edifice of confinement where my brother was incarcerated, several inmates loudly vocalized a number of lewd remarks.
3. The nurse announced that there had been a negative patient-care outcome due to a therapeutic misadventure on the part of the surgeon.
4. When we returned from our evening perambulation, we shrank back in horror as we surmised that our domestic dwelling was being swallowed up in hellish flames.
5. The bottom line is that the company is experiencing a negative cash flow.

17c Avoid obsolete, archaic, and invented words.

Obsolete words are words found in the writing of the past that have dropped out of use entirely. Archaic words are old words that are still used, but only in special contexts such as literature or advertising. Although dictionaries list obsolete words such as *recomfort* and *reechy* and archaic words such as *anon* and *betwixt,* these words are not appropriate for current use.

Invented words (also called *neologisms*) are words too recently created to be part of standard English. Many invented words fade out of use without becoming standard. *Netizen* and *digerati* are neologisms that may not last. *Printout, flextime,* and *e-mail* are no longer neologisms; they have become standard English. Avoid using invented words in your writing unless they are given in the dictionary as standard or unless no other word expresses your meaning.

17d In most contexts, avoid slang, regional expressions, and nonstandard English.

Slang is an informal and sometimes private vocabulary that expresses the solidarity of a group such as teenagers, rock musicians, or football fans; it is subject to more rapid change than standard English. For example, the slang teenagers use to express approval changes every few years; *cool, groovy, neat, wicked,* and *awesome* have replaced one another within the last three decades. Sometimes slang becomes so widespread that it is accepted as standard vocabulary. *Jazz,* for example, started out as slang but is now generally accepted to describe a style of music.

Although slang has a certain vitality, it is a code that not everyone understands, and it is very informal. Therefore, it is inappropriate in most written work.

▶ If we don't begin studying for the final, a whole semester's

    will be wasted.

    work ~~is going down the tubes.~~

      ^

                                disgust you.

▶ The government's "filth" guidelines for food will ~~gross you~~

                                           ^

    ~~out.~~

Regional expressions are common to a group in a geographical area. *Let's talk with the bark off* (for *Let's speak frankly*) is an expression in the southern United States, for example. Regional expressions have the same limitations as slang and are therefore inappropriate in most writing.

▶ John was four blocks from the house before he remembered

      turn on

to ~~cut~~ the headlights. ~~on.~~
  ^   ^

▶ I'm not ~~for~~ sure, but I think the dance has been postponed.

Standard English is the language used in all academic, business, and professional fields. Nonstandard English is spoken by people with a common regional or social heritage. Although nonstandard English may be appropriate when spoken within a close group, it is out of place in most formal and informal writing.

        has

▶ The counselor ~~have~~ so many problems in her own life that
                ^

    doesn't

she ~~don't~~ know how to advise anyone else.
  ^

If you speak a nonstandard dialect, try to identify the ways in which your dialect differs from standard English. Look especially for the following features of nonstandard English, which commonly cause problems in writing.

Misuse of verb forms such as *began* and *begun* (See 27a.)

Omission of *-s* endings on verbs (See 27c.)

Omission of *-ed* endings on verbs (See 27d.)

Omission of necessary verbs (See 27e.)

Double negatives (See 26d.)

17e Choose an appropriate level of formality.

In deciding on a level of formality, consider both your subject and your audience. Does the subject demand a dignified treatment, or is a relaxed tone more suitable? Will readers be put off if you assume too close a relationship with them, or might you alienate them by seeming too distant?

For most college and professional writing, some degree of formality is appropriate. In a letter applying for a job, for example, it is a mistake to sound too breezy and informal.

TOO INFORMAL	I'd like to get that receptionist's job you've got in the paper.
MORE FORMAL	I would like to apply for the receptionist's position listed in the *Peoria Journal Star*.

Informal writing is appropriate for private letters, e-mail, articles in popular magazines, and business correspondence between close associates. Like spoken conversation, it allows contractions (*don't, I'll*) and colloquial words (*kids, buddy*). Vocabulary and sentence structure are rarely complex.

In choosing a level of formality, above all be consistent. When a writer's voice shifts from one level of formality to another, readers receive mixed messages.

▶ Once a pitcher for the Cincinnati Reds, Bob shared with me

                           began

the secrets of his trade. His lesson ~~commenced~~ with his
                                    ^

                 thrown

famous curveball, ~~implemented~~ by tucking the little finger
                ^

behind the ball instead of holding it straight out. Next he
revealed
~~elucidated~~ the mysteries of the sucker pitch, a slow ball
^

coming behind a fast windup.

Words such as *commenced* and *elucidated* are inappropriate for the subject matter, and they clash with informal terms such as *sucker pitch* and *fast windup*.

GRAMMAR CHECKERS can flag slang and some informal language. Be aware, though, that they tend to be conservative on the matter of using contractions. If your ear tells you that a contraction such as *isn't* or *doesn't* strikes the right tone, stay with it.

EXERCISE 17–2

Edit the following paragraph to eliminate slang and maintain a consistent level of formality.

The graduation speaker really blew it. He should have discussed the options and challenges facing the graduating class. Instead, he shot his mouth off at us and trashed us for being lazy and pampered. He did make some good points, however. Our profs have certainly babied us by not holding fast to deadlines, by dismissing assignments that the class ragged them about, by ignoring our tardiness, and by handing out easy C's like hotcakes. Still, we resented this speech as the final word from the college establishment. It should have been the orientation speech when we started college.

17f Avoid sexist language.

Sexist language is language that stereotypes or demeans men or women, usually women. Using nonsexist language is a matter of courtesy—of respect for and sensitivity to the feelings of others.

Recognizing sexist language

Some sexist language is easy to recognize because it reflects genuine contempt for women: referring to a woman as a "broad," for example, or calling a lawyer a "lady lawyer," or saying in an advertisement, "If our new sports car were a lady, it would get its bottom pinched."

Other forms of sexist language are less blatant. The following practices, while they may not result from conscious sexism, reflect stereotypical thinking: referring to nurses as women and doctors as men, using different conventions when naming or identifying women and men, or assuming that all of one's readers are men.

STEREOTYPICAL LANGUAGE

After the nursing student graduates, *she* must face a difficult state board examination. [Not all nursing students are women.]

Running for city council are Jake Stein, an attorney, and *Mrs. Cynthia Jones*, a professor of English and *mother of three*. [The title *Mrs.* and the phrase *mother of three* are irrelevant.]

Wives of senior government officials are required to report any gifts they receive that are valued at more than $100. [Not all senior government officials are men.]

Still other forms of sexist language result from outmoded traditions. The pronouns *he, him,* and *his,* for instance, were traditionally used to refer generically to persons of either sex.

GENERIC *HE* OR *HIS*

When a senior physician is harassed by managed care professonals, *he* may be tempted to leave the profession.

A journalist is stimulated by *his* deadline.

Today, however, such usage is widely viewed as sexist because it excludes women and encourages sex-role stereotyping—the view that men are somehow more suited than women to be doctors, journalists, and so on.

Like the pronouns *he, him,* and *his,* the nouns *man* and *men* were once used indefinitely to refer to persons of either sex. Current usage demands gender-neutral terms for references to both men and women.

INAPPROPRIATE	APPROPRIATE
chairman	chairperson, moderator, chair, head
clergyman	member of the clergy, minister, pastor
congressman	member of Congress, representative, legislator
fireman	firefighter
foreman	supervisor
mailman	mail carrier, postal worker, letter carrier
mankind	people, humans
manpower	personnel
policeman	police officer
salesman	salesperson, sales associate, salesclerk, sales representative
to man	to operate, to staff
weatherman	weather forecaster, meteorologist
workman	worker, laborer

GRAMMAR CHECKERS are good at flagging sexist words, such as *mankind,* but they may also flag words, such as *girl* and *woman,* when they aren't being used in a sexist manner. It's sexist to call a woman a girl or a doctor a woman doctor, but you don't need to avoid the words *girl* and *woman* entirely and replace them with needlessly abstract terms like *female* and *individual.* All in all, just use your common sense. It's usually easy to tell when a word is offensive—and when it is not.

Although grammar checkers can flag sexist words, they cannot flag other kinds of sexist language, such as inconsistent treatment of men and women.

Clarity

Revising sexist language

When revising sexist language, be sparing in your use of the wordy constructions *he or she* and *his or her.* Although these constructions are fine in small doses, they become awkward when repeated throughout an essay. A better revision strategy, many writers have discovered, is to write in the plural; yet another strategy is to recast the sentence so that the problem does not arise.

> **ACCEPTABLE BUT WORDY**
> When a senior physician is harassed by managed care professionals, *he or she* may be tempted to leave the profession.
>
> A journalist is stimulated by *his or her* deadline.

> **BETTER: USING THE PLURAL**
> When senior *physicians* are harassed by managed care professionals, *they* may be tempted to leave the profession.
>
> *Journalists* are stimulated by *their* deadlines.

> **BETTER: RECASTING THE SENTENCE**
> When harassed by managed care professionals, *a senior physician* may be tempted to leave the profession.
>
> A journalist is stimulated by *a* deadline.

For more examples of these revision strategies, see section 22.

EXERCISE 17–3

Edit the following sentences to eliminate sexist language or sexist assumptions. Revisions of lettered sentences appear in the back of the book. Example:

> *Scholarship athletes* *their*
> ~~A scholarship athlete~~ must be as concerned about ~~his~~
>
> *they are* *their*
> academic performance as ~~he is~~ about ~~his~~ athletic
>
> performance.

a. Mrs. Geralyn Farmer, who is a mayor's wife, is the chief surgeon at University Hospital. Dr. Paul Green is her assistant.
b. If a young graduate is careful about investments, he can accumulate a significant sum in a relatively short period.
c. An elementary school teacher should understand the concept of nurturing if she intends to be a success.

d. The vice president for community affairs asked Elizabeth and Joseph to serve as cochairmen of the Red Cross blood drive.

e. If man does not stop polluting his environment, mankind will perish.

1. I have been trained to doubt an automobile mechanic, even if he has an excellent reputation.

2. If a high school graduate makes a career in the armed forces, he can retire with a comfortable pension before the age of fifty.

3. In the gubernatorial race, Lena Weiss, a defense lawyer and mother of two, easily defeated Harvey Tower, an architect.

4. My brother hired a lady lawyer who is a partner in the firm of Harris and Porter.

5. Peter Atlas and Dorea Smith own a large and successful bookstore. Peter handles the financial affairs, and Dorea, who is charming and attractive, directs all marketing efforts and manages the employees.

17g Revise language that may offend groups of people.

Obviously it is impolite to use offensive terms such as *Polack* or *redneck*. But biased language can take more subtle forms. Because language evolves over time, names once thought acceptable may become offensive. When describing groups of people, choose names that the groups currently use to describe themselves.

▶ North Dakota takes its name from the ~~Indian~~ *Sioux* word meaning

"friend" or "ally."

▶ Many ~~Oriental~~ *Asian* immigrants have recently settled in our small

town in Tennessee.

Negative stereotypes (such as "drives like a teenager" or "haggard as an old crone") are of course offensive. But you should avoid stereotyping a person or a group even if you believe your generalization to be positive.

▶ It was no surprise that Greer, ~~a Chinese American,~~ *an excellent math and science student,* was

selected for the honors chemistry program.

18

Find the exact words.

Two reference works will help you find words to express your meaning exactly: a good dictionary and a book of synonyms and antonyms such as *Roget's International Thesaurus*.

 GRAMMAR CHECKERS can flag some nonstandard idioms, such as *comply to*, and many clichés, such as *leave no stone unturned*. In addition, they can flag commonly confused words such as *principal* and *principle* or *affect* and *effect*, although you must decide which word is correct in your context. Grammar checkers are less helpful with the other problems discussed in section 18: choosing words with appropriate connotations, using concrete language, and using figures of speech appropriately.

18a Select words with appropriate connotations.

In addition to their strict dictionary meanings (or *denotations*), words have *connotations*, emotional colorings that affect how readers respond to them. The word *steel* denotes "made of or resembling commercial iron that contains carbon," but it also calls up a cluster of images associated with steel, such as the sensation of touching it. These associations give the word its connotations—cold, smooth, unbending.

If the connotation of a word does not seem appropriate for your purpose, your audience, or your subject matter, you should change the word. When a more appropriate synonym does not come quickly to mind, consult a dictionary or a thesaurus.

▶ The model was ~~skinny~~ and fashionable.
      slender
      ^

The connotation of the word *skinny* is too negative.

▶ As I covered the boats with marsh grass, the ~~perspiration~~ *sweat* I

had worked up evaporated in the wind, and the cold morning

air seemed even colder.

The term *perspiration* is too dainty for the context, which suggests vigorous exercise.

EXERCISE 18–1

Use a dictionary or thesaurus to find at least four synonyms for each of the following words. Be prepared to explain any slight differences in meaning.

1. decay (verb)   3. hurry (verb)   5. secret (adjective)
2. difficult (adjective)   4. pleasure (noun)   6. talent (noun)

18b Prefer specific, concrete nouns.

Unlike general nouns, which refer to broad classes of things, specific nouns point to definite and particular items. *Film*, for example, names a general class, *science fiction film* names a narrower class, and *Jurassic Park* is more specific still. Other examples: *team, football team, Denver Broncos; music, symphony, Beethoven's Ninth; work, carpentry, cabinetmaking.*

Unlike abstract nouns, which refer to qualities and ideas (*justice, beauty, realism, dignity*), concrete nouns point to immediate, often sensory experience and to physical objects (*steeple, asphalt, lilac, stone, garlic*).

Specific, concrete nouns express meaning more vividly than general or abstract ones. Although general and abstract language is sometimes necessary to convey your meaning, ordinarily prefer specific, concrete alternatives.

▶ The senator spoke about the challenges of the future:

problems ~~concerning the environment and world peace~~ *of famine, pollution, dwindling resources, and terrorism.*

Nouns such as *thing, area, aspect, factor,* and *individual* are especially dull and imprecise.

Clarity

> *rewards.*
> A career in transportation management offers many ~~things~~.
> ⌃

> *experienced technician.*
> Try pairing a trainee with an ~~individual with technical~~
> ⌃
>
> ~~experience.~~

18c Do not misuse words.

If a word is not in your active vocabulary, you may find yourself misusing it, sometimes with embarrassing consequences. When in doubt, check the dictionary.

> *climbing*
> The fans were ~~migrating~~ up the bleachers in search of seats.
> ⌃

> *avail.*
> Mrs. Johnson tried to fight but to no ~~prevail~~.
> ⌃

> *permeated*
> Drugs have so ~~diffused~~ our culture that they touch all
> ⌃
>
> segments of society.

Be especially alert for misused word forms—using a noun such as *absence, significance,* or *persistence,* for example, when your meaning requires the adjective *absent, significant,* or *persistent.*

> *persistent*
> Most dieters are not ~~persistence~~ enough to make a permanent
> ⌃
>
> change in their eating habits.

EXERCISE 18–2

Edit the following sentences to correct misused words. Revisions of lettered sentences appear in the back of the book. Example:

> *all-absorbing.*
> The training required for a ballet dancer is ~~all-absorbent~~.
> ⌃

a. We regret this delay; thank you for your patients.
b. Those who believe that books written for children are all sweetness and light are suffering from an allusion.

c. Liu Kwan began his career as a lawyer, but now he is a real estate mongrel.
d. When Robert Frost died at age eighty-eight, he left a legacy of poems that will make him immoral.
e. In general, the Internet has had a positive affect on our society.

1. Waste, misuse of government money, security and health violations, and even pilfering have become major dilemmas at the FBI.
2. Did you understand the significant of the list?
3. Grand Isle State Park is surrounded on three sides by water.
4. The Old World nuance of the restaurant intrigued us.
5. Tom Jones is an illegal child who grows up under the care of Squire Allworthy.

18d Use standard idioms.

Idioms are speech forms that follow no easily specified rules. The English say "Maria went *to hospital*," an idiom strange to American ears, which are accustomed to hearing *the* in front of *hospital*. Native speakers of a language seldom have problems with idioms, but prepositions sometimes cause trouble, especially when they follow certain verbs and adjectives. When in doubt, consult a good desk dictionary.

UNIDIOMATIC	IDIOMATIC
abide with (a decision)	abide by (a decision)
according with	according to
agree to (an idea)	agree with (an idea)
angry at (a person)	angry with (a person)
capable to	capable of
comply to	comply with
desirous to	desirous of
different than (a person or thing)	different from (a person or thing)
intend on doing	intend to do
off of	off
plan on doing	plan to do
preferable than	preferable to
prior than	prior to
superior than	superior to
sure and	sure to
try and	try to
type of a	type of

Clarity

 Because idioms follow no particular rules, you must learn them individually. You may find it helpful to keep a list of idioms **ESL** that you frequently encounter in conversation and in reading.

EXERCISE 18–3

Edit the following sentences to eliminate errors in the use of idiomatic expressions. If a sentence is correct, write "correct" after it. Answers to lettered sentences appear in the back of the book. Example:

> We agreed to abide ~~with~~ *by* the decision of the judge.

a. Queen Anne was so angry at Sarah Churchill that she dismissed her once faithful servant.

b. Prior to the Russians' launching of *Sputnik,* *-nik* was not an English suffix.

c. Dad told us to be sure and visit the ghost towns of Nevada.

d. For the frightened refugees, the dangerous trek across the mountains was preferable than life in a war zone.

e. The baby fell off of the couch and landed on the soft cushion of the dog's bed.

1. Be sure and report on the danger of releasing genetically engineered bacteria into the atmosphere.

2. Why do you assume that embezzling bank assets is so different than robbing the bank?

3. Most of the class agreed to Sylvia's view that domestic terrorism is a very dangerous problem.

4. It was hard to predict what type of a prank Luis would play next.

5. Andrea intends on joining the Peace Corps after graduation.

18e Avoid worn-out expressions (clichés).

The frontiersman who first announced that he had "slept like a log" no doubt amused his companions with a fresh and unlikely comparison. Today, however, that comparison is a cliché, a saying that has lost its dazzle from overuse. No longer can it surprise.

To see just how dully predictable clichés are, put your hand over the right column on the next page and then finish the phrases on the left.

cool as a	cucumber
beat around	the bush
blind as a	bat
busy as a	bee, beaver
crystal	clear
dead as a	doornail
out of the frying pan and	into the fire
light as a	feather
like a bull	in a china shop
playing with	fire
nutty as a	fruitcake
selling like	hotcakes
starting out at the bottom	of the ladder
water under the	bridge
white as a	sheet, ghost
avoid clichés like the	plague

The cure for clichés is frequently simple: Just delete them. When this won't work, try adding some element of surprise. One student, for example, who had written that she had butterflies in her stomach, revised her cliché like this:

> If all of the action in my stomach is caused by butterflies, there must be a horde of them, with horseshoes on.

The image of butterflies wearing horseshoes is fresh and unlikely, not dully predictable like the original cliché.

18f Use figures of speech with care.

A figure of speech is an expression that uses words imaginatively (rather than literally) to make abstract ideas concrete. Most often, figures of speech compare two seemingly unlike things to reveal surprising similarities.

In a *simile,* the writer makes the comparison explicitly, usually by introducing it with *like* or *as:* "By the time cotton had to be picked, grandfather's neck was as red as the clay he plowed." In a *metaphor,* the *like* or *as* is omitted, and the comparison is implied. For example, in the Old Testament Song of Solomon, a young woman compares the man she loves to a fruit tree: "With great delight I sat in his shadow, and his fruit was sweet to my taste."

Writers sometimes use figures of speech without thinking carefully about the images they evoke. This can result in a *mixed metaphor,* the combination of two or more images that don't make sense together.

▶ Crossing Utah's salt flats in his new Corvette, my father flew

at jet speed.
~~under a full head of steam.~~
⌃

Flew suggests an airplane, while *under a full head of steam* suggests a steamboat or a train. To clarify the image, the writer should stick with one comparison or the other.

▶ Our office had decided to put all controversial issues on a

back burner. ~~in a holding pattern.~~
⌃

Here the writer is mixing stoves and airplanes. Simply deleting one of the images corrects the problem.

EXERCISE 18–4

Edit the following sentences to replace worn-out expressions and clarify mixed figures of speech. Revisions of lettered sentences appear in the back of the book. Example:

the color drained from his face.
When he heard about the accident, ~~he turned white as a~~
⌃

~~sheet.~~

a. John stormed into the room like a bull in a china shop.
b. The president thought that the scientists were using science as a sledgehammer to grind their political axes.
c. The Cubs easily beat the Mets, who were in the soup early in the game today at Wrigley Field.
d. We ironed out the sticky spots in our relationship.
e. Sasha told us that he wasn't willing to put his neck out on a limb.

1. I could read him like a book; he had egg all over his face.
2. Tears were strolling down the child's face.
3. The dean of students acted like a big fish in a little pond.
4. There are too many cooks in the broth here at corporate headquarters.
5. We told Al that he was playing with fire when we learned that he intended to spy on the trustees' meeting.

Grammar

19

Repair sentence fragments.

A sentence fragment is a word group that pretends to be a sentence. Sentence fragments are easy to recognize when they appear out of context, like these:

> On the old wooden stool in the corner of my grandmother's kitchen.

> And immediately popped their flares and life vests.

When fragments appear next to related sentences, however, they are harder to spot.

> On that morning I sat in my usual spot. On the old wooden stool in the corner of my grandmother's kitchen.

> The pilots ejected from the burning plane, landing in the water not far from the ship. And immediately popped their flares and life vests.

Recognizing sentence fragments

To be a sentence, a word group must consist of at least one full independent clause. An independent clause has a subject and a verb, and it either stands alone or could stand alone.

To test a word group for sentence completeness, use the flow chart on page 169. For example, by using the flow chart, you can see exactly why *On the old wooden stool in the corner of my grandmother's kitchen* is a fragment: It lacks both a subject and a verb. *And immediately popped their flares and life vests* is a fragment because it lacks a subject. If you have difficulty identifying subjects and verbs, see 58a and 57c.

ESL Unlike some languages, English does not allow omission of subjects (except in imperative sentences in which the subject *you* is understood); nor does it allow omission of verbs. See 31a and 29e.

Test for sentence completeness

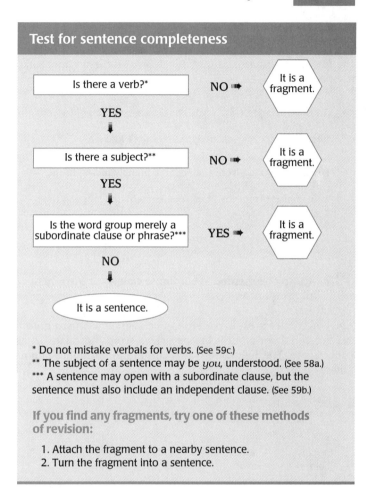

Is there a verb?* NO → It is a fragment.

YES ↓

Is there a subject?** NO → It is a fragment.

YES ↓

Is the word group merely a subordinate clause or phrase?*** YES → It is a fragment.

NO ↓

It is a sentence.

* Do not mistake verbals for verbs. (See 59c.)
** The subject of a sentence may be *you,* understood. (See 58a.)
*** A sentence may open with a subordinate clause, but the sentence must also include an independent clause. (See 59b.)

If you find any fragments, try one of these methods of revision:

1. Attach the fragment to a nearby sentence.
2. Turn the fragment into a sentence.

GRAMMAR CHECKERS can flag as many as half of the sentence fragments in a sample; but that means, of course, that they miss half or more of them. If fragments are a serious problem for you, you will still need to proofread for them.

Sometimes you will get "false positives," sentences that have been flagged but are not fragments. For example, one program flagged this complete sentence as a possible fragment: *I bent down to crawl into the bunker.* When a program spots a possible fragment, you should check to see if it is really a fragment. You can do this by using the flow chart on this page.

Repairing sentence fragments

You can repair most fragments in one of two ways: Either pull the fragment into a nearby sentence or turn the fragment into a sentence.

▶ On that morning I sat in my usual spot/, ~~On~~ the old wooden

stool in the corner of my grandmother's kitchen.

▶ The pilots ejected from the burning plane, landing in the

water not far from the ship. ~~And~~ immediately popped their

flares and life vests.

19a Attach fragmented subordinate clauses or turn them into sentences.

A subordinate clause is patterned like a sentence, with both a subject and a verb, but it begins with a word that marks it as subordinate. The following words commonly introduce subordinate clauses:

after	even though	so that	when	whom
although	how	than	where	whose
as	if	that	whether	why
as if	in order that	though	which	
because	rather than	unless	while	
before	since	until	who	

Subordinate clauses function within sentences as adjectives, as adverbs, or as nouns. They cannot stand alone. (See 59b.)

Most fragmented clauses beg to be pulled into a sentence nearby.

▶ Jane will address the problem of limited on-campus parking/
if
~~If~~ she is elected special student adviser.

If introduces a subordinate clause that modifies the verb *will address*. (For punctuation of subordinate clauses appearing at the end of a sentence, see 33f.)

▶ Although we seldom get to see wildlife in the city/, ~~At~~ the zoo   *at*

we can still find some of our favorites.

Although introduces a subordinate clause that modifies the verb *can find*. (For punctuation of subordinate clauses appearing at the beginning of a sentence, see 32b.)

If a fragmented clause cannot be attached to a nearby sentence or if you feel that attaching it would be awkward, try rewriting it. The simplest way to turn a subordinate clause into a sentence is to delete the opening word or words that mark it as subordinate.

▶ Population increases and uncontrolled development are taking

a deadly toll on the environment. ~~So that~~ ɪn many parts of   *I*

the world, fragile ecosystems are collapsing.

19b Attach fragmented phrases or turn them into sentences.

Like subordinate clauses, phrases function within sentences as adjectives, as adverbs, or as nouns. They cannot stand alone. Fragmented phrases are often prepositional or verbal phrases; sometimes they are appositives, words or word groups that rename nouns or pronouns. (See 59a, 59c, and 59d.)

Often a fragmented phrase may simply be pulled into a nearby sentence.

▶ The panther lay quite motionless behind the rock/, ~~Waiting~~   *waiting*

silently for its prey.

Waiting silently for its prey is a verbal phrase. (For punctuation of verbal phrases, see 32e.)

▶ Mary is suffering from agoraphobia/, Ⱥ fear of the outside   *a*

world.

Grammar

A fear of the outside world is an appositive renaming the noun *ago-raphobia.* (For punctuation of appositives, see 32e.)

If a fragmented phrase cannot be pulled into a nearby sentence effectively, turn the phrase into a sentence. You may need to add a subject, a verb, or both.

▶ In the computer training session, Eugene explained how to
    He also taught us
install our new software. ~~Also~~ how to organize our files,
                        ^

connect to the Internet, and back up our hard drives.

The word group beginning with *Also how to organize* is a fragmented verbal phrase. The revision turns the fragment into a sentence by adding a subject and a verb.

19c Attach other fragmented word groups or turn them into sentences.

Other word groups that are commonly fragmented include parts of compound predicates, lists, and examples introduced by *such as, for example,* or similar expressions.

Parts of compound predicates

A predicate consists of a verb and its objects, complements, and modifiers (see 58b). A compound predicate includes two or more predicates joined by a coordinating conjunction such as *and, but,* or *or.* Because the parts of a compound predicate share the same subject, they should appear in the same sentence.

▶ The woodpecker finch of the Galápagos Islands carefully
                                        and
selects a twig of a certain size and shape. ~~And~~ then uses
                                           ^

this tool to pry out grubs from trees.

Notice that no comma appears between the parts of a compound predicate. (See 33a.)

Lists

When a list is mistakenly fragmented, it can often be attached to a nearby sentence with a colon or a dash. (See 35a and 39a.)

▶ It has been said that there are only three indigenous
American art forms. ~~:~~ *musical* ~~Musical~~ comedy, jazz, and soap opera.

Examples introduced by such as, for example, *or similar expressions*

Expressions that introduce examples (or explanations) can lead to unintentional fragments. Although you may begin a sentence with some of the following words or phrases, make sure that what you have written is a sentence, not a fragment.

also	for instance	or
and	in addition	such as
but	like	that is
especially	mainly	
for example	namely	

Sometimes fragmented examples can be attached to the preceding sentence.

▶ The South has produced some of our greatest twentieth-
century writers. ~~,~~ *such* ~~Such~~ as Flannery O'Connor, William Faulkner,

Alice Walker, Tennessee Williams, and Thomas Wolfe.

At times, however, it may be necessary to turn the fragment into a sentence.

▶ If Eric doesn't get his way, he goes into a fit of rage. ~~For~~
he lies *opens*
~~example,~~ ~~lying~~ on the floor screaming or ~~opening~~ the cabinet
slams
doors and then ~~slamming~~ them shut.

The writer corrected this fragment by adding a subject—*he*—and substituting verbs for the verbals *lying, opening,* and *slamming.*

19d Exception: Occasionally a fragment may be used deliberately, for effect.

Skilled writers occasionally use sentence fragments for the following special purposes.

FOR EMPHASIS	Following the dramatic Americanization of their children, even my parents grew more publicly confident. *Especially my mother.*
	—Richard Rodriguez
TO ANSWER A QUESTION	Are these new drug tests 100 percent reliable? *Not in the opinion of most experts.*
AS A TRANSITION	*And now the opposing arguments.*
EXCLAMATIONS	*Not again!*
IN ADVERTISING	*Fewer calories. Improved taste.*

Although fragments are sometimes appropriate, writers and readers do not always agree on when they are appropriate. Therefore you will find it safer to write in complete sentences.

EXERCISE 19–1

Repair any fragment by attaching it to a nearby sentence or by rewriting it as a complete sentence. If a word group is correct, write "correct" after it. Revisions of lettered sentences appear in the back of the book. Example:

> One Greek island that should not be missed is Mykonos. ~~/~~ A
>
> vacation spot for Europeans and a playpen for the rich.

a. As I stood in front of the microwave, I recalled my grandmother bending over her old black stove. And remembered what she taught me: that any food can have soul if you love the people you are cooking for.

b. The resort was full of attractions. Three swimming pools, four restaurants, five bars, and every game imaginable, including a life-sized chess set.

c. I stepped on some frozen moss and started sliding down the face of a flat rock toward the falls. Suddenly I landed on another rock.

d. We need to stop believing myths about drinking. That strong black coffee will sober you up, for example, or that a cold shower will straighten you out.

e. On Sundays, James scrupulously read the newspaper's employment listings. Scrutinizing every position that held even the remotest possibility.

1. Sitting at a sidewalk café near the Sorbonne, I could pass as a French student. As long as I kept my mouth shut.

2. Mother loved to play all our favorite games. Canasta, Monopoly, hide-and-seek, and even kick-the-can.

3. The horses were dressed up with hats and flowers. Some even wore sunglasses.

4. The archaeologists worked very slowly. Examining and labeling every pottery shard they uncovered.

5. The geologists were interested in visiting the Seychelles. The only midocean islands in the world that are formed of granite.

6. If a woman from the desert tribe showed anger toward her husband, she was whipped in front of the whole village. And shunned by the rest of the women.

7. A tornado is a violent whirling wind. One that produces a funnel-shaped cloud and moves over land in a slim path of destruction.

8. Keiko arrived in the village of Futagami. Where she was to spend the summer with her grandparents.

9. In my three years of driving, I have never had an accident. Not one wreck, not one fender bender, not even a little dent.

10. Aspiring bodybuilders must first ascertain their strengths and weaknesses. And then decide what they want to achieve.

EXERCISE 19–2

Repair each fragment in the following paragraphs by attaching it to a sentence nearby or by rewriting it as a complete sentence.

Surfing the Internet now competes with watching television as our national pastime. People, it seems, have a natural ability to sit for hour upon hour. Passively watching images flit before their eyes. Whether these appear on a TV screen or a computer screen doesn't seem to make much difference. What counts are the images themselves. Not where they come from.

Web surfing is the cyber-age equivalent of channel surfing. Both of which appeal to us because of their constant promise of something better around the corner. When 1950s TV viewers got bored with Howdy Doody, they turned off the set. Or switched to a channel with no programming and stared at the test pattern. Today, with eighty or more channels to choose from, the demanding spectator is no longer forced to watch anything uninteresting. The Internet is the next logical step in this constant broadening of choice. Taking us from eighty channels to an almost infinite number of screens.

But there is at least one major risk of a culture based on images. That the written word may become an endangered species. As our brains eventually adapt to greater and greater levels of stimulation. Will we continue to be able to focus on a page of print? Already, members of the TV generation have a much harder time reading than their parents did. What, many people are wondering, will become of the Internet generation?

Before we send out too many alarms, however, we should remember that the Internet is still in its infancy. Already, Web browsers are helping us limit the dizzying number of choices that face us on the World Wide Web. By giving us powerful search tools that zero in on whatever aspect of a topic we are most interested in. And there is some evidence that those who spend time surfing the Net are doing more, not less, reading. Unlike TV viewers. Some Net surfers prefer to run their eyes over the words on the screen. An activity that is, after all, reading. Others download information and read the printouts. While it is true that television has reduced our nation's level of literacy, the Internet could well advance it. Only the future will tell.

20

Revise run-on sentences.

Run-on sentences are independent clauses that have not been joined correctly. An independent clause is a word group that can stand alone as a sentence (see section 60). When two independent clauses appear in one sentence, they must be joined in one of these ways:

—with a comma and a coordinating conjunction (*and, but, or, nor, for, so, yet*)
—with a semicolon (or occasionally a colon or a dash)

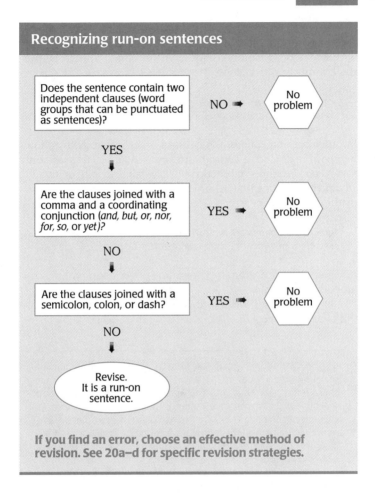

Recognizing run-on sentences

Does the sentence contain two independent clauses (word groups that can be punctuated as sentences)?   NO ➡ ⬡ No problem

YES ⬇

Are the clauses joined with a comma and a coordinating conjunction (*and, but, or, nor, for, so,* or *yet*)?   YES ➡ ⬡ No problem

NO ⬇

Are the clauses joined with a semicolon, colon, or dash?   YES ➡ ⬡ No problem

NO ⬇

Revise. It is a run-on sentence.

If you find an error, choose an effective method of revision. See 20a–d for specific revision strategies.

Recognizing run-on sentences

There are two types of run-on sentences. When a writer puts no mark of punctuation and no coordinating conjunction between independent clauses, the result is called a *fused sentence.*

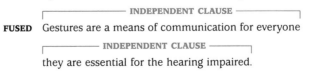

┌─────────── INDEPENDENT CLAUSE ───────────┐
FUSED   Gestures are a means of communication for everyone

┌─────────── INDEPENDENT CLAUSE ───────────┐
they are essential for the hearing impaired.

A far more common type of run-on sentence is the *comma splice*—two or more independent clauses joined by a comma without a coordinating conjunction. In some comma splices, the comma appears alone.

> **COMMA**   Gestures are a means of communication for everyone,
> **SPLICE**   they are essential for the hearing impaired.

In other comma splices, the comma is accompanied by a joining word that is *not* a coordinating conjunction. There are only seven coordinating conjunctions in English: *and, but, or, nor, for, so,* and *yet.* Notice that all of these words are short—only two or three letters long.

> **COMMA**   Gestures are a means of communication for everyone,
> **SPLICE**   however, they are essential for the hearing-impaired.

However is a transitional expression, not a coordinating conjunction (see 20b).

To review your writing for possible run-on sentences, use the chart on page 177.

GRAMMAR CHECKERS can flag only about 20 to 50 percent of the run-on sentences in a sample. The programs tend to be cautious, telling you that you "may have" a run-on sentence; you will almost certainly get a number of "false positives," sentences that have been flagged but are not run-ons. For example, a grammar checker flagged the following acceptable sentence as a possible run-on: *They believe that requiring gun owners to purchase a license is sufficient.*

If you have a problem with run-ons, you will need to proofread for them even after using a grammar checker. Also, if your program spots a "possible" run-on, you will need to check to see if it is in fact a run-on, perhaps by using the flow chart on page 177.

Revising run-on sentences

To revise a run-on sentence, you have four choices:

1. Use a comma and a coordinating conjunction (*and, but, or, nor, for, so, yet*).

▶ Gestures are a means of communication for everyone, they *but*
are essential for the hearing-impaired.

2. Use a semicolon (or, if appropriate, a colon or a dash). A semicolon may be used alone; it can also be accompanied by a transitional expression such as *however.*

▶ Gestures are a means of communication for everyone*;* they
are essential for the hearing-impaired.

▶ Gestures are a means of communication for everyone*; however,* they
are essential for the hearing-impaired.

3. Make the clauses into separate sentences.

▶ Gestures are a means of communication for everyone*. They* ~~they~~
are essential for the hearing-impaired.

4. Restructure the sentence, perhaps by subordinating one of the clauses.

▶ *Although gestures*
~~Gestures~~ are a means of communication for everyone, they
are essential for the hearing-impaired.

One of these revision techniques usually works better than the others for a particular sentence. The fourth technique, the one requiring the most extensive revision, is often the most effective.

20a Consider separating the clauses with a comma and a coordinating conjunction.

There are seven coordinating conjunctions in English: *and, but, or, nor, for, so,* and *yet.* When a coordinating conjunction joins independent clauses, it is usually preceded by a comma. (See 32a.)

▶ The paramedic asked where I was hurt, *and* as soon as I told

him, he cut up the leg of my favorite pair of jeans.

▶ Many government officials privately admit that the polygraph

is unreliable, ~~however,~~ *yet* they continue to use it as a security

measure.

> *However* is a transitional expression, not a coordinating conjunction, so it cannot be used with only a comma to join independent clauses. (See 20b.)

20b Consider separating the clauses with a semicolon (or, if appropriate, with a colon or a dash).

When the independent clauses are closely related and their relation is clear without a coordinating conjunction, a semicolon is an acceptable method of revision. (See 34a.)

▶ Tragedy depicts the individual confronted with the fact of

death/; comedy depicts the adaptability and ongoing survival

of human society.

A semicolon is required between independent clauses that have been linked with a transitional expression (such as *however, therefore, moreover, in fact,* or *for example*). For a longer list, see 34b.

▶ The timber wolf looks much like a large German shepherd/;

however, the wolf has longer legs, larger feet, a wider head,

and a long, bushy tail.

If the first independent clause introduces the second or if the second clause summarizes or explains the first, a colon or a dash may be an appropriate method of revision. (See sections

35b and 39a.) In formal writing, the colon is usually preferred to the dash.

                   : This
▶ Nuclear waste is hazardous ~~this~~ is an indisputable fact.

                                —
▶ The female black widow spider is often a widow of her own

making, she has been known to eat her partner after mating.

If the first independent clause introduces a quoted sentence, a colon is an appropriate method of revision.

                                             :
▶ Carolyn Heilbrun has this to say about the future, "Today's

shocks are tomorrow's conventions."

20c Consider making the clauses into separate sentences.

                      We
▶ Why should we spend money on expensive space

exploration, we have enough underfunded programs here

on earth.

Since one independent clause is a question and the other is a statement, they should be separate sentences.

                                       Then
▶ I gave the necessary papers to the police officer, ~~then~~ he said

I would have to accompany him to the police station, where

a counselor would talk with me and call my parents.

Because the second independent clause is quite long, a sensible revision is to use separate sentences.

NOTE: When two quoted independent clauses are divided by explanatory words, make each clause its own sentence.

▶ "It's always smart to learn from your mistakes," quipped my
                 It's
boss, "~~it's~~ even smarter to learn from the mistakes of others."

20d Consider restructuring the sentence, perhaps by subordinating one of the clauses.

If one of the independent clauses is less important than the other, turn it into a subordinate clause or phrase. (For more about subordination, see 8, especially the chart on p. 105.)

▶ Of the many geysers in Yellowstone National Park, the most
                       which
   famous is Old Faithful, ~~it~~ sometimes reaches 150 feet in
                       ^

   height.

   Although many
▶ ~~Many~~ scholars dismiss the abominable snowman of the
  ^

   Himalayas as a myth, others claim it may be a kind of ape.

▶ Mary McLeod Bethune, ~~was~~ the seventeenth child of former
                  ^

   slaves, ~~she~~ founded the National Council of Negro Women in

   1935.

   Minor ideas in these sentences are now expressed in subordinate clauses or phrases.

EXERCISE 20–1

Revise any run-on sentences using the method of revision suggested in brackets. Revisions of lettered sentences appear in the back of the book. Example:

   Because
   Orville was obsessed with his weight, he rarely ate anything
  ^

   sweet and delicious. [*Restructure the sentence.*]

a. The city had one public swimming pool, it stayed packed with children all summer long. [*Restructure the sentence.*]
b. The building is being renovated, therefore at times we have no heat, water, or electricity. [*Use a comma and a coordinating conjunction.*]
c. Why shouldn't a divorced wife receive half of her husband's pension and retirement benefits, she was her husband's partner for many years. [*Make two sentences.*]

d. Suddenly there was a loud silence, the shelling had stopped. [*Use a semicolon.*]

e. The experience taught Juanita a lesson, she could not always rely on her parents to bail her out of trouble. [*Use a colon.*]

1. For the first time in her adult life, Lucia had time to waste, she could spend a whole day curled up with a good book. [*Use a semicolon.*]

2. The city government had good reason to fear a major earthquake, most of the business district was built on a landfill. [*Restructure the sentence.*]

3. The next time an event is canceled because of bad weather, don't blame the meteorologist, blame nature. [*Make two sentences.*]

4. Mr. Romero is an excellent linguist he has been studying Chinese dialects for twenty years. [*Restructure the sentence.*]

5. The president of Algeria was standing next to the podium he was waiting to be introduced. [*Restructure the sentence.*]

6. On most days I had only enough money for bus fare, lunch was a luxury I could not afford. [*Use a semicolon.*]

7. There was one major reason for John's wealth, his grandfather had been a multimillionaire. [*Use a colon.*]

8. The neighborhood was ruled by gangs, what kind of environment was this for my ten-year-old son? [*Make two sentences.*]

9. Lindsey is a top competitor she has been riding since the age of seven. [*Restructure the sentence.*]

10. Wind power for the home is a supplementary source of energy, it can be combined with electricity, gas, or solar energy. [*Restructure the sentence.*]

EXERCISE 20–2

Revise any run-on sentences using a technique that you find effective. If a sentence is correct, write "correct" after it. Revisions of lettered sentences appear in the back of the book. Example:

but
I ran the three blocks as fast as I could, ~~however,~~ I missed
⌃

the bus.

a. Ted never drove the vintage cars that he had inherited, however, he could not bring himself to sell them.

b. The duck hunter set out his decoys in the shallow bay and then settled in to wait for the first real bird to alight.

c. In the Middle Ages, the streets of London were dangerous places, it was safer to travel by boat along the Thames.

d. Researchers were studying the fertility of Texas land tortoises they X-rayed all the female tortoises to see how many eggs they had.

e. We had planned to spend the last few days of our vacation at the beach, the hurricane, however, brought us home in a hurry.

1. Are you able to endure boredom, isolation, and potential violence, then the army may well be the adventure for you.
2. Jet funny cars are powered by jet engines, these engines are the same type that are used on fighter aircraft and helicopters.
3. If one of the dogs should happen to fall through the ice, it would be cut loose from the team and left to its fate, the sled drivers could not endanger the rest of the team for just one dog.
4. The volunteers worked hard to clean up and restore calm after the tornado, as a matter of fact, many of them did not sleep for the first three days of the emergency.
5. Nuclear power plants produce energy by fission, a process that generates radioactive waste.
6. The floor around the refreshment stand was sticky, I was lucky to make it away with both shoes on my feet.
7. The center of the French Quarter of New Orleans is Jackson Square, this square is one of the most beautiful urban spaces in the United States.
8. We didn't trust her, she had lied before.
9. I pushed open the first door with my back, turning to open the second door, I encountered a young woman in a wheelchair holding it open for me.
10. If you want to lose weight and keep it off, consider this advice, don't try to take it off faster than you put it on.

EXERCISE 20–3

In the following rough draft, revise any run-on sentences.

Some parents and educators argue that requiring uniforms in public schools would improve student behavior and performance. They think that uniforms give students a more professional attitude toward school, moreover they believe that uniforms help create a sense of community among students from diverse backgrounds. Parents and educators holding these views are well meaning, however they should take a second look at the arguments against requiring school uniforms in public schools.

Uniforms do create a sense of community, they do this, however, by stamping out individuality. People spend most of their working lives having to conform to one dress code or another. Youth is a time to express originality, it is a time to develop a sense of self. One important way young people express their identities is through the clothes they wear. Of course, it could be argued that the self-patrolled dress code of high school students is ultimately stricter than that of any company, never-

theless, trying to control dress habits from above will lead to re-
sentment or to mindless conformity.

If children are going to act like adults, they need to be
treated like adults, they need to be made responsible for their
own choices. Telling young people what to wear to school
merely prolongs their childhoods. Education is not just a matter
of learning facts and figures, it also involves growing up and understanding how to function in the real world.

Most public schools must take everyone who applies, this
includes students and parents who are opposed to school uniforms. Uniforms may be a good idea for private schools, they
may even be a good idea for a few public "alternative" schools
that parents and their children can choose. In most public
schools, however, school uniforms should not be required.

21

Make subjects and verbs agree.

Native speakers of standard English know by ear that *he talks,*
she has, and *it doesn't* (not *he talk, she have,* and *it don't*) are
standard subject-verb combinations. For such speakers, problems with subject-verb agreement arise only in certain tricky
situations, which are detailed in 21b–21k.

If you don't trust your ear—perhaps because you speak
English as a second language, perhaps because you speak or
hear nonstandard English in your community—you will need
to learn the standard forms explained in 21a. Even if you do
trust your ear, take a quick look at 21a to see what "subject-
verb agreement" means.

GRAMMAR CHECKERS attempt to flag faulty subject-verb agreement, but they have mixed success. They fail to flag many problems; in addition, they flag a number of correct sentences, usually because they have misidentified the subject, the verb, or
both. For example, one program flagged the following correct
sentence: *Nearly everyone on the panel favors the health care reform proposal.* The program identified the subject as *care* and
the verb as *reform;* in fact, the subject is *everyone* and the verb
is *favors.*

Grammar

Subject-verb agreement at a glance

PRESENT-TENSE FORMS OF *LOVE*
(A TYPICAL VERB)

	SINGULAR		PLURAL	
FIRST PERSON	I	love	we	love
SECOND PERSON	you	love	you	love
THIRD PERSON	he/she/it	loves	they	love

PRESENT-TENSE FORMS OF *HAVE*

	SINGULAR		PLURAL	
FIRST PERSON	I	have	we	have
SECOND PERSON	you	have	you	have
THIRD PERSON	he/she/it	has	they	have

PRESENT-TENSE FORMS OF *DO*

	SINGULAR		PLURAL	
FIRST PERSON	I	do/don't	we	do/don't
SECOND PERSON	you	do/don't	you	do/don't
THIRD PERSON	he/she/it	does/doesn't	they	do/don't

PRESENT-TENSE AND PAST-TENSE
FORMS OF *BE*

	SINGULAR		PLURAL	
FIRST PERSON	I	am/was	we	are/were
SECOND PERSON	you	are/were	you	are/were
THIRD PERSON	he/she/it	is/was	they	are/were

21a Consult this section for standard subject-verb combinations.

In the present tense, verbs agree with their subjects in number (singular or plural) and in person (first, second, or third). The present-tense ending *-s* (or *-es*) is used on a verb if its subject is third-person singular; otherwise the verb takes no ending. Consider, for example, the present-tense forms of the verb *love*, given at the beginning of the chart above.

The verb *be* varies from this pattern; unlike any other verb, it has special forms in *both* the present and the past tense. These forms appear at the end of the chart on this page.

When to use the *-s* (or *-es*) form of a present-tense verb

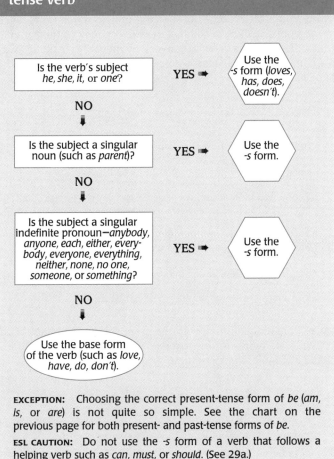

Is the verb's subject *he, she, it,* or *one*? YES ⟹ Use the *-s* form (*loves, has, does, doesn't*).

NO ↓

Is the subject a singular noun (such as *parent*)? YES ⟹ Use the *-s* form.

NO ↓

Is the subject a singular indefinite pronoun—*anybody, anyone, each, either, everybody, everyone, everything, neither, none, no one, someone,* or *something*? YES ⟹ Use the *-s* form.

NO ↓

Use the base form of the verb (such as *love, have, do, don't*).

EXCEPTION: Choosing the correct present-tense form of *be* (*am, is,* or *are*) is not quite so simple. See the chart on the previous page for both present- and past-tense forms of *be*.

ESL CAUTION: Do not use the *-s* form of a verb that follows a helping verb such as *can, must,* or *should*. (See 29a.)

If you aren't confident that you know the standard forms, use the charts on this and the previous page as you proofread for subject-verb agreement. You may also want to take a look at 27c, which discusses the matter of *-s* endings in some detail.

Grammar

21b Make the verb agree with its subject, not with a word that comes between.

Word groups often come between the subject and the verb. Such word groups, usually modifying the subject, may contain a noun that at first appears to be the subject. By mentally stripping away such modifiers, you can isolate the noun that is in fact the subject.

> The *samples* on the tray in the lab *need* testing.

▶ High levels of air pollution causes damage to the respiratory

tract.

The subject is *levels,* not *pollution.* Strip away the phrase *of air pollution* to hear the correct verb: *levels cause.*

▶ The slaughter of pandas for their pelts have caused the
has

panda population to decline drastically.

The subject is *slaughter,* not *pandas* or *pelts.*

NOTE: Phrases beginning with the prepositions *as well as, in addition to, accompanied by, together with,* and *along with* do not make a singular subject plural.

▶ The governor, as well as his press secretary, were shot.
was

To emphasize that two people were shot, the writer could use *and* instead: *The governor and his press secretary were shot.*

21c Treat most subjects joined with *and* as plural.

A subject with two or more parts is said to be compound. If the parts are connected by *and,* the subject is nearly always plural.

> *Leon and Jan* often *jog* together.

▶ Jill's natural ability and her desire to help others ~~has~~ led to
  have

a career in the ministry.

Ability and desire is a plural subject, so its verb should be *have*.

EXCEPTIONS: When the parts of the subject form a single unit or when they refer to the same person or thing, treat the subject as singular.

Strawberries and cream was a last-minute addition to the menu.

Sue's friend and adviser was surprised by her decision.

When a compound subject is preceded by *each* or *every,* treat it as singular.

Each tree, shrub, and vine needs to be sprayed.

Every car, truck, and van is required to pass inspection once a year.

21d With subjects joined with *or* or *nor* (or by *either . . . or* or *neither . . . nor*), make the verb agree with the part of the subject nearer to the verb.

A driver's *license* or credit *card is* required.

A driver's *license* or two credit *cards are* required.

▶ If a relative or neighbor ~~are~~ abusing a child, notify the police
  is

immediately.

▶ Neither the lab assistant nor the students ~~was~~ able to down-
  were

load the program.

The verb must be matched with the part of the subject closer to it: *neighbor is* in the first sentence, *students were* in the second.

NOTE: If one part of the subject is singular and the other is plural, put the plural one last to avoid awkwardness.

21e Treat most indefinite pronouns as singular.

Indefinite pronouns are pronouns that do not refer to specific persons or things. The following commonly used indefinite pronouns are singular:

anybody	each	everyone	nobody	somebody
anyone	either	everything	none	someone
anything	everybody	neither	no one	something

Many of these words appear to have plural meanings, and they are often treated as such in casual speech. In formal written English, however, they are nearly always treated as singular.

> *Everyone* on the team *supports* the coach.

> Each of the furrows ~~have~~ been seeded.
> ^{has}

> Everybody who signed up for the ski trip ~~were~~ taking
> ^{was}
>
> lessons.

The subjects of these sentences are *Each* and *Everybody*. These indefinite pronouns are third-person singular, so the verbs must be *has* and *was*.

The indefinite pronouns *none* and *neither* are considered singular when used alone.

Three rooms are available; *none has* a private bath.

Neither is able to attend.

When these pronouns are followed by prepositional phrases with a plural meaning, however, usage varies. Some experts insist on treating the pronouns as singular, but many writers disagree. It is safer to treat them as singular.

> *None* of these trades *requires* a college education.

> *Neither* of those pejoratives *fits* Professor Brady.

A few indefinite pronouns (*all, any, some*) are singular or plural depending on the noun or pronoun they refer to.

Some of the *lemonade has* disappeared.

Some of the *rocks were* slippery.

21f Treat collective nouns as singular unless the meaning is clearly plural.

Collective nouns such as *jury, committee, audience, crowd, class, troop, family,* and *couple* name a class or a group. In American English, collective nouns are nearly always treated as singular: They emphasize the group as a unit. Occasionally, when there is some reason to draw attention to the individual members of the group, a collective noun may be treated as plural. (Also see 22b.)

SINGULAR   The *class respects* the teacher.

PLURAL   The *class are* debating among themselves.

To underscore the notion of individuality in the second sentence, many writers would add a clearly plural noun such as *members:*

PLURAL   The class *members are* debating among themselves.

▶ The scout troop ~~meet~~ *meets* in our basement on Tuesdays.

The troop as a whole meets in the basement; there is no reason to draw attention to its individual members.

▶ A young couple ~~was~~ *were* arguing about politics while holding

hands.

The meaning is clearly plural. Only individuals can argue and hold hands.

NOTE: The phrase *the number* is treated as singular, *a number* as plural.

SINGULAR   *The number* of school-age children *is* declining.

PLURAL   *A number* of children *are* attending the wedding.

NOTE: When units of measurement are used collectively, treat them as singular; when they refer to individual persons or things, treat them as plural.

SINGULAR   *Three-fourths* of the pie *has* been eaten.

PLURAL   *One-fourth* of the drivers *were* drunk.

21g Make the verb agree with its subject even when the subject follows the verb.

Verbs ordinarily follow subjects. When this normal order is reversed, it is easy to become confused. Sentences beginning with *there is* or *there are* (or *there was* or *there were*) are inverted; the subject follows the verb.

There *are* surprisingly few *children* in our neighborhood.

▶ There ~~was~~ *were* a social worker and a crew of twenty volunteers at

the scene of the accident.

The subject *worker and crew* is plural, so the verb must be *were.*

Occasionally you may decide to invert a sentence for variety or effect. When you do so, check to make sure that your subject and verb agree.

▶ At the back of the room ~~is~~ *are* a small aquarium and an enormous

terrarium.

The subject *aquarium and terrarium* is plural, so the verb must be *are.* If the correct sentence seems awkward, begin with the subject: *A small aquarium and an enormous terrarium are at the back of the room.*

21h Make the verb agree with its subject, not with a subject complement.

One basic sentence pattern in English consists of a subject, a linking verb, and a subject complement: *Jack is a securities lawyer.* Because the subject complement (*lawyer*) names or describes the subject (*Jack*), it is sometimes mistaken for the subject. (See 58b on subject complements.)

These *problems are* a way to test your skill.

> A tent and a sleeping bag ~~is~~ *are* the required equipment for all campers.

Tent and bag is the subject, not *equipment.*

> A major force in today's economy ~~are~~ *is* women—as earners, consumers, and investors.

Force is the subject, not *women.* If the corrected version seems awkward, make *women* the subject: *Women are a major force in today's economy—as earners, consumers, and investors.*

21i *Who, which,* and *that* take verbs that agree with their antecedents.

Like most pronouns, the relative pronouns *who, which,* and *that* have antecedents, nouns or pronouns to which they refer. Relative pronouns used as subjects of subordinate clauses take verbs that agree with their antecedents.

Pick a *stock* that *pays* good dividends.

Problems can arise with the constructions *one of the* and *only one of the.* As a rule, treat *one of the* constructions as plural, *only one of the* constructions as singular.

▶ Our ability to use language is one of the things that set̶s̶ us

apart from animals.

The antecedent of *that* is *things*, not *one*. Several things set us apart from animals.

▶ Dr. Barker knew that Frank was the only one of his sons who
was
w̶e̶r̶e̶ responsible enough to handle the estate.
∧
The antecedent of *who* is *one*, not *sons*. Only one son was responsible enough.

21j Words such as *athletics, economics, mathematics, physics, statistics, measles, mumps,* and *news* are usually singular, despite their plural form.

is
▶ Statistics a̶r̶e̶ among the most difficult courses in our program.
∧

EXCEPTION: When they describe separate items rather than a collective body of knowledge, words such as *athletics, mathematics, physics,* and *statistics* are plural: *The statistics on school retention rates are impressive.*

21k Titles of works, company names, words mentioned as words, and gerund phrases are singular.

describes
▶ *Lost Cities* d̶e̶s̶c̶r̶i̶b̶e̶ the discoveries of many ancient
∧
civilizations.

specializes
▶ Delmonico Brothers s̶p̶e̶c̶i̶a̶l̶i̶z̶e̶ in organic produce and
∧
additive-free meats.

is
▶ *Controlled substances* a̶r̶e̶ a euphemism for illegal drugs.
∧

A gerund phrase consists of an *-ing* verb form followed by any objects, complements, or modifiers (see 59c). Treat gerund phrases as singular.

▶ Encountering busy signals ~~are~~ troublesome to our clients,
_{is}

so we have hired two new switchboard operators.

EXERCISE 21–1

Underline the subject (or compound subject) and then select the verb that agrees with it. (If you have difficulty identifying the subject, consult 58a.) Answers to lettered sentences appear in the back of the book. Example:

<u>Someone</u> in the audience (has/have) volunteered to partici-

pate in the experiment.

a. The city's rich history and its exciting cultural life (has/have) made Paris a popular tourist destination.
b. Shelters for teenage runaways (offers/offer) a wide variety of services.
c. Each of the twenty-five actors (was/were) given a five-minute tryout, and only three were called back for a more intensive audition.
d. The chances of your being promoted (is/are) excellent.
e. When Governor John White returned to Roanoke, he found that there (was/were) no signs of life or traces of the settlers he had left behind.

1. Neither the professor nor his assistants (was/were) able to solve the mystery of the eerie glow in the laboratory.
2. Four years of research (has/have) gone into making our software suitable for the Japanese market.
3. Located at the south end of the complex (was/were) an Olympic-size pool, two basketball courts, and four tennis courts.
4. The most significant lifesaving device in automobiles (is/are) air bags.
5. The old iron gate and the brick wall (makes/make) our courthouse appear older than its fifty years.
6. The dangers of smoking (is/are) well documented.
7. Every year, during the midsummer festival, the smoke of village bonfires (fills/fill) the sky.

8. When food supplies (was/were) scarce, the slaves had to make do with the less desirable parts of the animals.
9. There (is/are) several pots of herbs on the balcony.
10. Hidden under the floorboards (was/were) a bag of coins and a rusty sword.

EXERCISE 21-2

Edit the following sentences to eliminate problems with subject-verb agreement. If a sentence is correct, write "correct" after it. Answers to lettered sentences appear in the back of the book. Example:

> were
> Jack's first days in the infantry ~~was~~ grueling.
>   ^

a. High concentrations of carbon monoxide results in headaches, dizziness, unconsciousness, and even death.
b. Not until my interview with Dr. Hwang were other possibilities opened to me.
c. After hearing the evidence and the closing arguments, the jury was sequestered.
d. Crystal chandeliers, polished floors, and a new oil painting has transformed Sandra's apartment.
e. The board of directors, ignoring the wishes of the neighborhood, has voted to allow further development.

1. Fully 30 percent of the channel's programming consist of commercials.
2. Of particular concern are penicillin and tetracycline, antibiotics used to make animals more resistant to disease.
3. The presence of certain bacteria in our bodies is one of the factors that determine our overall health.
4. No one who has ever seen the northern lights has forgotten the experience.
5. Every year a number of kokanee salmon, not native to the region, is introduced into Flathead Lake.
6. Mathematics has always been one of my strongest subjects.
7. Neither the explorer nor his companions was ever seen again.
8. At MGM Studios at Disney World, the wonders of moviemaking comes alive.
9. SEACON is the only one of our war games that emphasize scientific and technical issues.
10. The key program of Alcoholics Anonymous are the twelve steps to recovery.

22

Make pronouns and antecedents agree.

A pronoun is a word that substitutes for a noun. (See 57b.) Many pronouns have antecedents, nouns or pronouns to which they refer. A pronoun and its antecedent agree when they are both singular or both plural.

> **SINGULAR**   *Dr. Sarah Simms* finished *her* rounds.
>
> **PLURAL**   The *doctors* finished *their* rounds.

ESL

The pronouns *he, his, she, her, it,* and *its* must agree in gender (masculine, feminine, or neuter) with their antecedents, not with the words they modify.

Jane visited *her* [not *his*] brother in Denver.

GRAMMAR CHECKERS usually miss problems with pronoun-antecedent agreement. It takes a human eye to see that a singular noun, such as *logger,* does not agree with a plural pronoun, such as *their,* in a sentence like this: *The logger in the Northwest relies on the old forest growth for their living.*

22a Do not use plural pronouns to refer to singular antecedents.

Writers are frequently tempted to use plural pronouns to refer to two kinds of singular antecedents: indefinite pronouns and generic nouns.

Indefinite pronouns

Indefinite pronouns refer to nonspecific persons or things. Even though some of the following indefinite pronouns may seem to have plural meanings, treat them as singular in formal English.

anybody	either	neither	somebody
anyone	everybody	nobody	someone
anything	everyone	none	something
each	everything	no one	

In class *everyone* performs at *his or her* [not *their*] own fitness level.

When a plural pronoun refers mistakenly to a singular indefinite pronoun, you can usually choose one of three options for revision.

1. Replace the plural pronoun with *he or she* (or *his or her*).
2. Make the antecedent plural.
3. Rewrite the sentence so that no problem of agreement exists.

▶ When someone has been drinking, ~~they are~~ likely to speed.
   he or she is

▶ When ~~someone has~~ been drinking, they are likely to speed.
   drivers have

▶ ~~When someone~~ has been drinking, ~~they are~~ likely to speed.
   A driver who   *is*

Because the *he or she* construction is wordy, often the second or third revision strategy is more effective. Be aware that the traditional use of *he* (or *his*) to refer to persons of either sex is now widely considered sexist. (See 17f.)

Generic nouns

A generic noun represents a typical member of a group, such as a typical student, or any member of a group, such as any lawyer. Although generic nouns may seem to have plural meanings, they are singular.

Every *runner* must train rigorously if *he or she wants* [not *they want*] to excel.

When a plural pronoun refers mistakenly to a generic noun, you will usually have the same three revision options as just mentioned for indefinite pronouns.

▶ A medical student must study hard if ~~they want~~ to succeed.
he or she wants

▶ ~~A medical student~~ must study hard if they want to succeed.
Medical students

▶ A medical student must study hard ~~if they want~~ to succeed.

22b Treat collective nouns as singular unless the meaning is clearly plural.

Collective nouns such as *jury, committee, audience, crowd, class, troop, family, team,* and *couple* name a class or a group. Ordinarily the group functions as a unit, so the noun should be treated as singular; if the members of the group function as individuals, however, the noun should be treated as plural. (See also 21f.)

AS A UNIT The *committee* granted *its* permission to build.

AS INDIVIDUALS The *committee* put *their* signatures on the document.

Above all, be consistent in your treatment of a collective noun. For example, in the following sentence the verb *has* signals that *jury* is singular, so for consistency the pronoun referring to *jury* must be *its.*

▶ The jury has reached ~~their~~ decision.
its

There is no reason to draw attention to the individual members of the jury, so *jury* should be treated as singular.

▶ The audience shouted "Bravo" and stamped ~~its~~ feet.
their

It is difficult to see how the audience as a unit can stamp *its* feet. The meaning here is clearly plural, requiring *their.*

22c Treat most compound antecedents connected by *and* as plural.

Joanne and John moved to the mountains, where *they* built a log cabin.

22d With compound antecedents connected by *or* or *nor* (or by *either . . . or* or *neither . . . nor*), make the pronoun agree with the nearer antecedent.

Either *Bruce* or *James* should receive first prize for *his* sculpture.

Neither the *mouse* nor the *rats* could find *their* way through the maze.

NOTE: If one of the antecedents is singular and the other plural, as in the second example, put the plural one last to avoid awkwardness.

EXCEPTION: If one antecedent is male and the other female, do not follow the traditional rule. The sentence *Either Bruce or Ann should receive the blue ribbon for her sculpture* makes no sense. The best solution is to recast the sentence: *The blue ribbon for best sculpture should go to Bruce or Ann.*

EXERCISE 22–1

Edit the following sentences to eliminate problems with pronoun-antecedent agreement. Most of the sentences can be revised in more than one way, so experiment before choosing a solution. If a sentence is correct, write "correct" after it. Revisions of lettered sentences appear in the back of the book. Example:

> *Recruiters*
> ~~The recruiter~~ may tell the truth, but there is much that they
> ^
> choose not to tell.

a. The sophomore class elects its president tomorrow.
b. The instructor has asked everyone to bring their own tools to carpentry class.

c. An eighteenth-century architect was also a classical scholar; they were often at the forefront of archaeological research.

d. If anyone is caught smoking on the premises, they will be severely reprimanded.

e. Why should we care about the timber wolf? One answer is that they have proven beneficial to humans by killing off weakened prey.

1. Seven qualified Hispanic agents applied, each hoping for a career move that would let them use their language and cultural training on more than just translations; the job went to a non-Hispanic who was taking a crash course in Spanish.

2. If anyone notices any suspicious activity, they should report it to the police.

3. The troop was expected to operate as a unit and carry out their orders without discussion.

4. David lent his motorcycle to someone who allowed their friend to use it.

5. The applicant should be bilingual if they want to qualify for this position.

23

Make pronoun references clear.

Pronouns substitute for nouns; they are a kind of shorthand. In a sentence like *After Andrew intercepted the ball, he kicked it as hard as he could,* the pronouns *he* and *it* substitute for the nouns *Andrew* and *ball.* The word a pronoun refers to is called its *antecedent.*

GRAMMAR CHECKERS do not flag problems with faulty pronoun reference. Although a computer program can identify pronouns, it has no way of knowing which words, if any, they refer to. For example, grammar checkers miss the fact that the pronoun *it* has an ambiguous reference in the following sentence: *The thief stole the woman's purse and her car and then destroyed it.* Did the thief destroy the purse or the car? It takes human judgment to realize that readers might be confused.

23a Avoid ambiguous or remote pronoun reference.

Ambiguous pronoun reference occurs when the pronoun could refer to two possible antecedents.

▶ *The pitcher broke when Gloria set it*
~~When Gloria set the pitcher~~ on the glass-topped table⸝ ~~it~~

~~broke.~~

▶ Tom told James, *"You have* ~~that he had~~ won the lottery*."*

What broke—the table or the pitcher? Who won the lottery—Tom or James? The revisions eliminate the ambiguity.

Remote pronoun reference occurs when a pronoun is too far away from its antecedent for easy reading.

▶ After the court ordered my ex-husband to pay child support,

he refused. Approximately eight months later, we were back

in court. This time the judge ordered him to make payments

directly to the Support and Collections Unit, which would in

turn pay me. For the first six months I received regular

payments, but then they stopped. Again ~~he~~ *my ex-husband* was summoned

to appear in court; he did not respond.

The pronoun *he* was too distant from its antecedent, *ex-husband*, which appeared several sentences earlier.

23b Generally, avoid broad reference of *this, that, which,* and *it.*

For clarity, the pronouns *this, that, which,* and *it* should ordinarily refer to specific antecedents rather than to whole ideas or sentences. When a pronoun's reference is needlessly broad, either replace the pronoun with a noun or supply an antecedent to which the pronoun clearly refers.

▶ More and more often, especially in large cities, we are finding

ourselves victims of serious crimes. We learn to accept ~~this~~ *our fate*

with minor gripes and groans.

For clarity the writer substituted a noun (*fate*) for the pronoun *this,* which referred broadly to the idea expressed in the preceding sentence.

▶ Romeo and Juliet were both too young to have acquired much

a fact
wisdom, which accounts for their rash actions.

The writer added an antecedent (*fact*) that the pronoun *which* clearly refers to.

EXCEPTION: Many writers view broad reference as acceptable when the pronoun refers clearly to the sense of an entire clause.

> If you pick up a starving dog and make him prosperous, he will not bite you. This is the principal difference between a dog and a man.   —Mark Twain

23c Do not use a pronoun to refer to an implied antecedent.

A pronoun should refer to a specific antecedent, not to a word that is implied but not present in the sentence.

the braids
▶ After braiding Ann's hair, Sue decorated ~~them~~ with ribbons.

The pronoun *them* referred to Ann's braids (implied by the term *braiding*), but the word *braids* did not appear in the sentence.

Modifiers, such as possessives, cannot serve as antecedents. A modifier may strongly imply the noun that the pronoun might logically refer to, but it is not itself that noun.

Euripides
▶ In ~~Euripides'~~ *Medea*, ~~he~~ describes the plight of a woman

rejected by her husband.

The pronoun *he* cannot refer logically to the possessive modifier *Euripides'*, which functions as an adjective. The revision substitutes the noun *Euripides* for the pronoun *he*, thereby eliminating the problem.

23d Avoid the indefinite use of *they*, *it*, and *you*.

Do not use the pronoun *they* to refer indefinitely to persons who have not been specifically mentioned. *They* should always refer to a specific antecedent.

▶ Sometimes a list of ways to save energy is included with the
    the gas company suggests
  gas bill. For example, ~~they suggest~~ setting a moderate
                          ^

  temperature for the hot water heater.

The word *it* should not be used indefinitely in constructions such as "It is said on television . . ." or "In the article it says that. . . ."

                  T
▶ In ~~t~~he report ~~it~~ points out that lifting the ban on Compound

  1080 would prove detrimental, possibly even fatal, to the

  bald eagle.

The pronoun *you* is appropriate when the writer is addressing the reader directly: *Once you have kneaded the dough, let it rise in a warm place for at least twenty-five minutes.* Except in informal contexts, however, the indefinite *you* (meaning "anyone in general") is inappropriate.

          one doesn't
▶ In Ethiopia ~~you don't~~ need much property to be considered
             ^

  well-off.

If the pronoun *one* seems too stilted, the writer might recast the sentence: *In Ethiopia a person doesn't need much property to be considered well-off.*

23e To refer to persons, use *who, whom,* or *whose,* not *that* or *which.*

In most contexts, use *who, whom,* or *whose* to refer to persons, *that* or *which* to refer to animals or things. Although *that* is occasionally used to refer to persons, it is more polite to use a form of *who.* *Which* is reserved only for animals or things, so it is impolite to use it to refer to persons.

▶ When he heard about my seven children, four of ~~which~~ *whom*

were still living at home, Vincent smiled and said,

"I love children."

▶ Fans wondered how an out-of-shape old man ~~that~~ *who* walked

with a limp could play football.

NOTE: Occasionally *whose* may be used to refer to animals and things to avoid the awkward *of which* construction.

▶ A major corporation, ~~the~~ *whose* name ~~of which~~ will be in tomorrow's

paper, has been illegally dumping toxic waste in the harbor

for years.

EXERCISE 23–1

Edit the following sentences to correct errors in pronoun reference. In some cases you will need to decide on an antecedent that the pronoun might logically refer to. Revisions of lettered sentences appear in the back of the book. Example:

> Following the breakup of AT&T, many other companies
>
> began to offer long-distance phone service. ~~This~~ *The competition* has led to
>
> lower long-distance rates.

a. The detective removed the bloodstained shawl from the body and then photographed it.
b. In Professor Jamal's class, you are lucky to earn a C.
c. The Comanche braves' lifestyle was particularly violent; they gained respect for their skill as warriors.
d. All students can secure parking permits from the campus police office; they are open from 8 A.M. until 8 P.M.
e. Our German conversation group is made up of six people, three of which I had never met before.

1. Many people believe that the polygraph test is highly reliable if you employ a licensed examiner.
2. Because of Paul Robeson's outspoken attitude toward fascism, he was labeled a Communist.
3. In the encyclopedia it states that male moths can smell female moths from several miles away.
4. When Aunt Harriet put the cake on the table, it collapsed.
5. Be sure to visit Istanbul's bazaar, where they sell everything from Persian rugs to electronic calculators.

24

Distinguish between pronouns such as *I* and *me.*

The personal pronouns in the following chart change what is known as case form according to their grammatical function in a sentence. Pronouns functioning as subjects (or subject complements) appear in the *subjective* case; those functioning as objects appear in the *objective* case; and those showing ownership appear in the *possessive* case.

	SUBJECTIVE CASE	OBJECTIVE CASE	POSSESSIVE CASE
SINGULAR	I	me	my
	you	you	your
	he/she/it	him/her/it	his/her/its
PLURAL	we	us	our
	you	you	your
	they	them	their

Pronouns in the subjective and objective cases are frequently confused. Most of the rules in this section specify when to use one or the other of these cases (*I* or *me, he* or *him,* and so on). Rule 24g details a special use of pronouns and nouns in the possessive case.

> GRAMMAR CHECKERS can flag some incorrect pronouns and ex-
> plain the rules for using *I* or *me, he* or *him, she* or *her, we* or *us,*
> and *they* or *them.* For example, grammar checkers correctly
> flagged *we* in the following sentence, suggesting that *us* should
> be used as the object of the preposition *for: I say it is time for*
> *we parents to revolt.*
>
>   You should not assume, however, that a computer program
> will catch all incorrect pronouns. For example, grammar check-
> ers did not flag *more than I* in this sentence, where the writer's
> meaning requires *me: I get a little jealous that our dog likes my*
> *neighbor more than I.*

24a Use the subjective case (*I, you, he, she, it, we, they*) for
subjects and subject complements.

When personal pronouns are used as subjects, ordinarily your
ear will tell you the correct pronoun. Problems sometimes arise,
however, with compound word groups containing a pronoun,
so it is not always safe to trust your ear.

> *he*
> ▶ Joel ran away from home because his stepfather and ~~him~~
>   ^
> had quarreled.

His stepfather and he is the subject of the verb *had quarreled.* If we
strip away the words *his stepfather and,* the correct pronoun becomes clear: *he had quarreled* (not *him had quarreled*).

When a pronoun is used as a subject complement (a word
following a linking verb), your ear may mislead you, since the
incorrect form is frequently heard in casual speech. (See subject complement, 58b.)

> *she.*
> ▶ Sandra confessed that the artist was ~~her.~~
>   ^

The pronoun *she* functions as a subject complement with the linking verb *was.* In formal, written English, subject complements must
be in the subjective case. If your ear rejects *artist was she* as too stilted,
try rewriting the sentence: *Sandra confessed that she was the artist.*

24b Use the objective case (*me, you, him, her, it, us, them*) for all objects.

When a personal pronoun is used as a direct object, an indirect object, or the object of a preposition, ordinarily your ear will lead you to the correct pronoun. When an object is compound, however, you may occasionally become confused.

▶ Janice was indignant when she realized that the salesclerk

was insulting her mother and ~~she~~.
                                  her.

Her mother and her is the direct object of the verb *was insulting.* Strip away the words *her mother and* to hear the correct pronoun: *was insulting her* (not *was insulting she*).

▶ Geoffrey went with my family and ~~I~~ to King's Dominion.
                                   me

Me is the object of the preposition *with.* We would not say *Geoffrey went with I.*

When in doubt about the correct pronoun, some writers try to avoid making the choice by using a reflexive pronoun such as *myself.* Such evasions are nonstandard, even though they are used by some educated persons.

▶ The Egyptian cab driver gave my husband and ~~myself~~ some
                                               me

good tips on traveling in North Africa.

My husband and me is the indirect object of the verb *gave.* For correct uses of *myself,* see the Glossary of Usage which begins on page 503.

24c Put an appositive and the word to which it refers in the same case.

Appositives are noun phrases that rename nouns or pronouns. A pronoun used as an appositive has the same function (usually subject or object) as the word(s) the appositive renames.

▶ At the drama festival, two actors, Christina and ~~me,~~ were *I,*

selected to do the last scene of *King Lear.*

The appositive *Christina and I* renames the subject, *actors.*

▶ The college interviewed only two applicants for the job,
Professor Stevens and ~~I.~~ *me.*

The appositive *Professor Stevens and me* renames the direct object *applicants.*

24d Following *than* or *as,* choose the pronoun that expresses your meaning.

When a comparison begins with *than* or *as,* your choice of a pronoun will depend on your intended meaning. Consider, for example, the difference in meaning between these sentences:

My husband likes football better than I.

My husband likes football better than me.

Finish each sentence mentally and its meaning becomes clear: *My husband likes football better than I* [do]. *My husband likes football better than* [he likes] *me.*

▶ Even though he is sometimes ridiculed by the other boys,
Norman is much better off than ~~them.~~ *they.*

They is the subject of the verb *are,* which is understood: *Norman is much better off than they* [are]. If the correct English seems too formal, you can always add the verb.

▶ We respected no other candidate as much as ~~she.~~ *her.*

This sentence means that we respected no other candidate as much as *we respected her. Her* is the direct object of the understood verb *respected.*

24e When deciding whether *we* or *us* should precede a noun, choose the pronoun that would be appropriate if the noun were omitted.

We
▶ ~~Us~~ tenants would rather fight than move.
      ^

                                        us
▶ Management is short-changing ~~we~~ tenants.
                                        ^

No one would say *Us would rather fight than move* or *Management is short-changing we*.

24f Use the objective case for subjects and objects of infinitives.

An infinitive is the word *to* followed by the base form of a verb. (See 59c.) Subjects of infinitives are an exception to the rule that subjects must be in the subjective case. Whenever an infinitive has a subject, it must be in the objective case. Objects of infinitives also are in the objective case.

                                me   *him*
▶ The crowd expected Chris and ~~I~~ to defeat Tracy and ~~he~~ in the
                                ^   ^

doubles championship.

Chris and me is the subject of the infinitive *to defeat; Tracy and him* is the direct object of the infinitive.

24g Use the possessive case to modify a gerund.

A pronoun that modifies a gerund or a gerund phrase should appear in the possessive case (*my, our, your, his/her/its, their*). A gerund is a verb form ending in *-ing* that functions as a noun. Gerunds frequently appear in phrases, in which case the whole gerund phrase functions as a noun. (See 59c.)

                        your
▶ The chances of ~~you~~ being hit by lightning are about two
                        ^

million to one.

Your modifies the gerund phrase *being hit by lightning*.

Nouns as well as pronouns may modify gerunds. To form the possessive case of a noun, use an apostrophe and an -s (*a victim's rights*) or just an apostrophe (*victims' rights*). (See 36a.)

▶ **The old order in France paid a high price for the** ~~aristocracy~~ *aristocracy's*

exploiting the lower classes.

The possessive noun *aristocracy's* modifies the gerund phrase *exploiting the lower classes.*

EXERCISE 24–1

Edit the following sentences to eliminate errors in case. If a sentence is correct, write "correct" after it. Answers to lettered sentences appear in the back of the book. Example:

Grandfather cuts down trees for neighbors much younger
he.
than ~~him.~~

a. My Ethiopian neighbor was puzzled by the dedication of we joggers.
b. The jury was astonished when the witness suddenly confessed that the murderer was none other than he.
c. Sue's husband is ten years older than her.
d. Everyone laughed whenever Sandra described how her brother and her had seen the Loch Ness monster and fed it sandwiches.
e. We appreciate you bringing this problem to our attention.

1. The chain stores are threatening the survival of us shopkeepers.
2. The mysterious old woman handed Natasha and him a gold coin each.
3. The patient began suffering from the delusion that him and his family were constantly being followed and observed.
4. A professional counselor advised the division chief that Marco, Fidelia, and myself should be allowed to apply for the opening.
5. My adjustment to a new career was compounded by me becoming a single parent.
6. For a moment, I thought the farmer's dogs were going to attack Danny and I.
7. The swirling cyclone caused he and his horse to race for shelter.
8. The winners of the art competition, Justine and I, will spend a month studying painting in Florence.

9. During the testimony the witness pointed directly at the defendant and announced that the thief was him.
10. Despite our different backgrounds, a close friendship developed between Esperanza and I.

25

Distinguish between *who* and *whom*.

The choice between *who* and *whom* (or *whoever* and *whomever*) occurs primarily in subordinate clauses and in questions. *Who* and *whoever,* subjective-case pronouns, are used for subjects and subject complements. *Whom* and *whomever,* objective-case pronouns, are used for objects. (For more about pronoun case, see 24.)

> GRAMMAR CHECKERS can flag some sentences with a misused *who* or *whom* and explain the nature of the error. For example, grammar checkers flagged the subject pronoun *who* in the following sentence, suggesting correctly that the context calls for the object pronoun *whom*: *One of the women who Martinez hired became the most successful lawyer in the agency.*
>
> However, at times the programs skip past a misused *who* or *whom,* as they did with this sentence: *Now that you have studied with both musicians, whom in your opinion is the better teacher?* The programs could not tell that the object pronoun *whom* functions incorrectly as the subject of the verb *is.*

25a In subordinate clauses, use *who* and *whoever* for subjects or subject complements, *whom* and *whomever* for all objects.

When *who* and *whom* (or *whoever* and *whomever*) introduce subordinate clauses, their case is determined by their function *within the clause they introduce.* To choose the correct pronoun, you must isolate the subordinate clause and then decide how the pronoun functions within it. (See subordinate clauses, 59b.)

In the following two examples, the pronouns *who* and *whoever* function as the subjects of the clauses they introduce.

> *who*
> **The prize goes to the runner ~~whom~~ collects the most points.**
>   ^

The subordinate clause is *who collects the most points.* The verb of the clause is *collects,* and its subject is *who.*

> *whoever*
> **He tells that story to ~~whomever~~ will listen.**
>   ^

The writer selected the pronoun *whomever,* thinking that it was the object of the preposition *to.* However, the object of the preposition is the entire subordinate clause *whoever will listen.* The verb of the clause is *will listen,* and its subject is *whoever.*

Who occasionally functions as a subject complement in a subordinate clause. Subject complements occur with linking verbs (usually *be, am, is, are, was, were, being,* and *been*). (See 58b.)

> *who*
> **The receptionist knows ~~whom~~ you are.**
>   ^

The subordinate clause is *who you are.* Its subject is *you,* and its subject complement is *who.*

When functioning as an object in a subordinate clause, *whom* (or *whomever*) appears out of order, before both the subject and the verb. To choose the correct pronoun, you must mentally restructure the clause.

> *whom*
> **You will work with our senior industrial engineers, ~~who~~ you**
>   ^
> **will meet later.**

The subordinate clause is *whom you will meet later.* The subject of the clause is *you,* the verb is *will meet,* and *whom* is the direct object of the verb. This becomes clear if you mentally restructure the clause: *you will meet whom.*

When functioning as the object of a preposition in a subordinate clause, *whom* is often separated from its preposition.

> *whom*
> **The tutor ~~who~~ I was assigned to was very supportive.**
>   ^

Whom is the object of the preposition *to.* In this sentence, the writer might choose to drop *whom: The tutor I was assigned to was very supportive.*

Grammar

NOTE: Inserted expressions such as *they know, I think,* and *she says* should be ignored in determining whether to use *who* or *whom.*

▶ All of the show-offs, bullies, and tough guys in school want

                   who
to take on a big guy ~~whom~~ they know will not hurt them.
                            ^

Who is the subject of *will hurt,* not the object of *know.*

25b In questions, use *who* and *whoever* for subjects, *whom* and *whomever* for all objects.

When *who* and *whom* (or *whoever* and *whomever*) are used to open questions, their case is determined by their function within the question. In the following example, *who* functions as the subject of the question.

    Who
▶ ~~Whom~~ was responsible for creating that computer virus?
   ^

When *whom* functions as the object of a verb or the object of a preposition in a question, it appears out of normal order. To choose the correct pronoun, you must mentally restructure the question.

    Whom
▶ ~~Who~~ did the committee select?
  ^

Whom is the direct object of the verb *did select.* To choose the correct pronoun, restructure the question: *The committee did select whom?*

    Whom
▶ ~~Who~~ did you enter into the contract with?
  ^

Whom is the object of the preposition *with,* as is clear if you recast the question: *You did enter into the contract with whom?*

USAGE NOTE: In spoken English, *who* is frequently used to open a question even when it functions as an object: *Who did Joe replace?* Although some readers will accept such constructions in informal written English, it is safer to use *whom: Whom did Joe replace?*

EXERCISE 25–1

Edit the following sentences to eliminate errors in the use of *who* and *whom* (or *whoever* and *whomever*). If a sentence is correct, write "correct" after it. Answers to lettered sentences appear in the back of the book. Example:

> *whom*
> What is the name of the person ~~who~~ you are sponsoring for
>   ^
>
> membership in the club?

a. In his first production of *Hamlet,* who did Laurence Olivier replace?
b. Who was Martin Luther King's mentor?
c. Datacall allows you to talk to whoever needs you no matter where you are in the building.
d. The bank doors were locked, and whomever was inside remained there until the police officers arrived.
e. One of the women who Martinez hired became the most successful lawyer in the agency.

1. When medicine is scarce and expensive, physicians must give it to whomever has the best chance to survive.
2. Who was accused of receiving Mafia funds?
3. According to the Greek myth, the Sphinx devoured those who could not answer her riddles.
4. The only interstate travelers who get pulled over for speeding are the ones whom cannot afford a radar detector.
5. I was introduced to Jake's brother, who I had never met before.

26

Choose adjectives and adverbs with care.

Adjectives ordinarily modify nouns or pronouns; occasionally they function as subject complements following linking verbs. Adverbs modify verbs, adjectives, or other adverbs. (See 57d and 57e.)

Many adverbs are formed by adding *-ly* to adjectives (*normal, normally; smooth, smoothly*). But don't assume that all words ending in *-ly* are adverbs or that all adverbs end in *-ly.* Some adjectives end in *-ly* (*lovely, friendly*) and some adverbs don't (*always, here, there*). When in doubt, consult a dictionary.

ESL

In English, adjectives are not pluralized to agree with the words they modify: *The red* [not *reds*] *roses were a wonderful surprise.*

GRAMMAR CHECKERS can flag a number of problems with adjectives and adverbs: some misuses of *bad* or *badly* and *good* or *well*; some double comparisons, such as *more meaner;* some absolute comparisons, such as *most unique;* and some double negatives, such as *can't hardly.* However, the programs slip past more problems than they find. Programs ignored errors like these: *could have been handled more professional* and *hadn't been bathed regular.*

26a Use adverbs, not adjectives, to modify verbs, adjectives, and adverbs.

When adverbs modify verbs (or verbals), they nearly always answer the question When? Where? How? Why? Under what conditions? How often? or To what degree? When adverbs modify adjectives or other adverbs, they usually qualify or intensify the meaning of the word they modify. (See 57e.)

The incorrect use of adjectives in place of adverbs to modify verbs occurs primarily in casual or nonstandard speech.

> *perfectly*
> ▶ The arrangement worked out ~~perfect~~ for everyone.

> *smoothly*
> ▶ The manager must see that the office runs ~~smooth~~ and
> *efficiently.*
> ~~efficient.~~

The adverb *perfectly* modifies the verb *worked out;* the adverbs *smoothly* and *efficiently* modify the verb *runs.*

The incorrect use of the adjective *good* in place of the adverb *well* is especially common in casual and nonstandard speech.

> *well*
> ▶ We were surprised to hear that Louise had done so ~~good~~ on
> the CPA exam.

The adverb *well* (not the adjective *good*) should be used to modify the verb *had done*.

NOTE: The word *well* is an adjective when it means "healthy," "satisfactory," or "fortunate": *I am very well, thank you. All is well. It is just as well.*

Adjectives are sometimes used incorrectly to modify adjectives or adverbs.

▶ In the early 1970s, chances for survival of the bald eagle

     really
looked ~~real~~ slim.
     ^

Only adverbs can be used to modify adjectives or other adverbs. *Really* intensifies the meaning of the adjective *slim*.

Placement of adjectives and adverbs can be a tricky matter for second-language speakers. See 31c.

ESL

26b Use adjectives, not adverbs, as subject complements.

A subject complement follows a linking verb and completes the meaning of the subject. (See 58b.) When an adjective functions as a subject complement, it describes the subject.

    Justice is *blind*.

Problems can arise with verbs such as *smell, taste, look,* and *feel,* which sometimes, but not always, function as linking verbs. If the word following one of these verbs describes the subject, use an adjective; if it modifies the verb, use an adverb.

    ADJECTIVE   The detective looked *cautious*.

    ADVERB   The detective looked *cautiously* for fingerprints.

The adjective *cautious* describes the detective; the adverb *cautiously* modifies the verb *looked*.

Linking verbs suggest states of being, not actions. Notice, for example, the different meanings of *looked* in the preceding examples. To look cautious suggests the state of being cautious; to look cautiously is to perform an action in a cautious way.

▶ The lilacs in our backyard smell especially ~~sweetly~~ *sweet* this year.

▶ Lori looked ~~well~~ *good* in her new raincoat.

▶ We all felt ~~badly~~ *bad* about the play's cancellation.

The verbs *smell*, *looked*, and *felt* suggest states of being, not actions. Therefore, they should be followed by adjectives, not adverbs.

26c Use comparatives and superlatives with care.

Most adjectives and adverbs have three forms: the positive, the comparative, and the superlative.

POSITIVE	COMPARATIVE	SUPERLATIVE
soft	softer	softest
fast	faster	fastest
careful	more careful	most careful
bad	worse	worst
good	better	best

Comparative versus superlative

Use the comparative to compare two things, the superlative to compare three or more.

▶ Which of these two brands of toothpaste is ~~best?~~ *better?*

▶ Though Shaw and Jackson are impressive, Hobbs is the ~~more~~ *most* qualified of the three candidates running for mayor.

Form of comparatives and superlatives

To form comparatives and superlatives of most one- and two-syllable adjectives, use the endings *-er* and *-est: smooth, smoother, smoothest; easy, easier, easiest.* With longer adjectives, use *more* and *most* (or *less* and *least* for downward comparisons): *exciting, more exciting, most exciting; helpful, less helpful, least helpful.*

Some one-syllable adverbs take the endings *-er* and *-est* (*fast, faster, fastest*), but longer adverbs and all of those ending in *-ly* form the comparative and superlative with *more* and *most* (or *less* and *least*).

The comparative and superlative forms of the following adjectives and adverbs are irregular: *good, better, best; well, better, best; bad, worse, worst; badly, worse, worst.*

▶ The Kirov is the ~~talentedest~~ *most talented* ballet company we have seen.

▶ Lloyd's luck couldn't have been ~~worser~~ *worse* than David's.

Double comparatives or superlatives

Do not use a double comparative (an *-er* ending and the word *more*) or a double superlative (an *-est* ending and the word *most*).

▶ All the polls indicated that Dewey was more ~~likelier~~ *likely* to win

than Truman.

▶ Of all her family, Julia is the ~~most~~ happiest about the move.

Absolute concepts

Avoid expressions such as *more straight, less perfect, very round,* and *most unique.* Either something is unique or it isn't. It is illogical to suggest that absolute concepts come in degrees.

▶ That is the most ~~unique~~ *unusual* wedding gown I have ever seen.

▶ The painting would have been even more ~~priceless~~ *valuable* had it

been signed.

26d Avoid double negatives.

Standard English allows two negatives only if a positive meaning is intended: *The orchestra was not unhappy with its performance.* Double negatives used to emphasize negation are nonstandard.

Negative modifiers such as *never, no,* and *not* should not be paired with other negative modifiers or with negative words such as *neither, none, no one, nobody,* and *nothing.*

▶ Management is not doing ~~nothing~~ *anything* to see that the trash is

picked up.

▶ George won't ~~never~~ *ever* forget that day.

▶ I enjoy living alone because I don't have to answer to ~~nobody.~~ *anybody.*

The double negatives *not . . . nothing, won't never,* and *don't . . . nobody* are nonstandard.

The modifiers *hardly, barely,* and *scarcely* are considered negatives in standard English, so they should not be used with negatives such as *not, no one,* or *never.*

▶ Maxine is so weak she ~~can't~~ *can* hardly climb stairs.

EXERCISE 26–1

Edit the following sentences to eliminate errors in the use of adjectives and adverbs. If a sentence is correct, write "correct" after it. Answers to lettered sentences appear in the back of the book. Example:

> When I watched Carl run the 440 on Saturday, I was amazed
> at how ~~good~~ *well* he paced himself.

a. When Tina began breathing normal, we could relax.
b. All of us on the team felt badly about our performance.
c. This incident could have been handled more professional if lines of communication had been kept open.
d. The vaulting box, more commonly known as the horse, is the easiest of the four pieces of equipment to master.
e. Fiona has developed the most unique Web site I've ever seen.

1. When answering the phone, you should speak clearly and courteous.
2. The green bagels looked and tasted real peculiar.
3. After checking to see how bad I had been hurt, my sister dialed 911.
4. With the budget deadline approaching, our office hasn't hardly had time to handle routine correspondence.
5. Marcia performed very well at her Drama Club audition.

27

Choose standard English verb forms.

In nonstandard English, spoken by those who share a regional or cultural heritage, verb forms sometimes differ from those of standard English. In writing, use standard English verb forms unless you are quoting nonstandard speech or using nonstandard forms for literary effect. (See 17d.)

Except for the verb *be,* all verbs in English have five forms. The following chart lists the five forms and provides a sample sentence in which each might appear.

BASE FORM	Usually I (*walk, ride*).
PAST TENSE	Yesterday I (*walked, rode*).
PAST PARTICIPLE	I have (*walked, ridden*) many times before.
PRESENT PARTICIPLE	I am (*walking, riding*) right now.
-S FORM	He/she/it (*walks, rides*) regularly.

Both the past-tense and past-participle forms of regular verbs end in *-ed* (*walked, walked*). Irregular verbs form the past tense and past participle in other ways (*rode, ridden*).

The verb *be* has eight forms instead of the usual five: *be, am, is, are, was, were, being, been.*

27a Use the correct forms of irregular verbs.

For all regular verbs, the past-tense and past-participle forms are the same (ending in *-ed* or *-d*), so there is no danger of confusion. This is not true, however, for irregular verbs, such as the following.

BASE FORM	PAST TENSE	PAST PARTICIPLE
go	went	gone
fight	fought	fought
fly	flew	flown

The past-tense form, which never has a helping verb, expresses action that occurred entirely in the past. The past participle is used with a helping verb—either with *has, have,* or *had* to form one of the perfect tenses or with *be, am, is, are, was, were, being,* or *been* to form the passive voice.

PAST TENSE	Last July, we *went* to Paris.
PAST PARTICIPLE	We have *gone* to Paris twice.

When you aren't sure which verb form to choose (*went* or *gone, began* or *begun,* and so on), consult the list of common irregular verbs that starts on the next page. Choose the past-tense form if the verb in your sentence doesn't have a helping verb; choose the past-participle form if it does.

In nonstandard English speech, the past-tense and past-participle forms may differ from those of standard English, as in the following sentences.

▶ Yesterday we ~~seen~~ *saw* an unidentified flying object.

▶ The reality of the situation finally ~~sunk~~ *sank* in.

The past-tense forms *saw* and *sank* are required because there are no helping verbs.

▶ The truck was apparently ~~stole~~ *stolen* while the driver ate lunch.

▶ By the end of the day the stock market had ~~fell~~ *fallen* two hundred

points.

Because of the helping verbs, the past-participle forms are required: *was stolen, had fallen.*

When in doubt about the standard English forms of irregular verbs, consult the following list or look up the base form of the verb in the dictionary, which also lists any irregular forms. (If no additional forms are listed in the dictionary, the verb is regular, not irregular.)

Common irregular verbs

BASE FORM	PAST TENSE	PAST PARTICIPLE
arise	arose	arisen
awake	awoke, awaked	awaked, awoke
be	was, were	been
beat	beat	beaten, beat
become	became	become
begin	began	begun
bend	bent	bent
bite	bit	bitten, bit
blow	blew	blown
break	broke	broken
bring	brought	brought
build	built	built
burst	burst	burst
buy	bought	bought
catch	caught	caught
choose	chose	chosen
cling	clung	clung
come	came	come
cost	cost	cost
deal	dealt	dealt
dig	dug	dug
dive	dived, dove	dived
do	did	done
drag	dragged	dragged
draw	drew	drawn
dream	dreamed, dreamt	dreamed, dreamt

Grammar

BASE FORM	PAST TENSE	PAST PARTICIPLE
drink	drank	drunk
drive	drove	driven
eat	ate	eaten
fall	fell	fallen
fight	fought	fought
find	found	found
fly	flew	flown
forget	forgot	forgotten, forgot
freeze	froze	frozen
get	got	gotten, got
give	gave	given
go	went	gone
grow	grew	grown
hang (suspend)	hung	hung
hang (execute)	hanged	hanged
have	had	had
hear	heard	heard
hide	hid	hidden
hurt	hurt	hurt
keep	kept	kept
know	knew	known
lay (put)	laid	laid
lead	led	led
lend	lent	lent
let (allow)	let	let
lie (recline)	lay	lain
lose	lost	lost
make	made	made
prove	proved	proved, proven
read	read	read
ride	rode	ridden
ring	rang	rung
rise (get up)	rose	risen
run	ran	run
say	said	said
see	saw	seen
send	sent	sent
set (place)	set	set
shake	shook	shaken
shoot	shot	shot
shrink	shrank	shrunk
sing	sang	sung
sink	sank	sunk
sit (be seated)	sat	sat
slay	slew	slain

BASE FORM	PAST TENSE	PAST PARTICIPLE
sleep	slept	slept
speak	spoke	spoken
spin	spun	spun
spring	sprang	sprung
stand	stood	stood
steal	stole	stolen
sting	stung	stung
strike	struck	struck, stricken
swear	swore	sworn
swim	swam	swum
swing	swung	swung
take	took	taken
teach	taught	taught
throw	threw	thrown
wake	woke, waked	waked, woken
wear	wore	worn
wring	wrung	wrung
write	wrote	written

27b Distinguish among the forms of *lie* and *lay*.

Writers and speakers frequently confuse the various forms of *lie* (meaning "to recline or rest on a surface") and *lay* (meaning "to put or place something"). *Lie* is an intransitive verb; it does not take a direct object: *The tax forms lie on the table.* The verb *lay* is transitive; it takes a direct object: *Please lay the tax forms on the coffee table.* (See 58b.)

In addition to confusing the meaning of *lie* and *lay*, writers and speakers are often unfamiliar with the standard English forms of these verbs.

BASE FORM	PAST TENSE	PAST PARTICIPLE	PRESENT PARTICIPLE
lie	lay	lain	lying
lay	laid	laid	laying

▶ Sue was so exhausted that she ~~laid~~ down for a nap.
lay

The past-tense form of *lie* ("to recline") is *lay*.

▶ The patient had ~~laid~~ *lain* in an uncomfortable position all night.

The past-participle form of *lie* ("to recline") is *lain*. If the correct English seems too stilted, recast the sentence: *The patient had been lying in an uncomfortable position all night.*

▶ The prosecutor ~~lay~~ *laid* the pistol on a table close to the jurors.

The past-tense form of *lay* ("to place") is *laid*.

▶ Letters dating from the Civil War were ~~laying~~ *lying* in the corner of the chest.

The present participle of *lie* ("to rest on a surface") is *lying*.

EXERCISE 27–1

Edit the following sentences to eliminate problems with irregular verbs. If a sentence is correct, write "correct" after it. Answers to lettered sentences appear in the back of the book. Example:

> Was it you I ~~seen~~ *saw* last night at the concert?

a. Noticing that my roommate was shivering and looking pale, I rung for the nurse.

b. When I get the urge to exercise, I lay down until it passes.

c. Grandmother had drove our new jeep to the sunrise church service on Savage Mountain, so we were left with the station wagon.

d. Last June my cousin Lucia swum the length of the lake in forty minutes.

e. In her attic, Sandra discovered Halloween costumes that had lain untouched for years.

1. How did the detective know that the suspect had went to the officer on the night of the murder?

2. Laying on the operating table, I could hear only the beating of my heart.

3. The burglar must have gone immediately upstairs, grabbed what looked good, and took off.

4. In just a week the ground had froze, and the first winter storm had left over a foot of snow.

5. Jet lag must have caught up with me; I lay down for a nap yesterday afternoon—and woke up this morning.

6. Lincoln took good care of his legal clients; the contracts he drew for the Illinois Central Railroad could never be broke.
7. Have you ever dreamed that you were falling from a cliff or flying through the air?
8. I locked my brakes, leaned the motorcycle to the left, and laid it down to keep from slamming into the fence.
9. In her junior year, Cindy run the 440-yard dash in 51.1 seconds.
10. Larry claimed that he had drank a bad soda, but Esther suspected the truth.

27c Use -*s* (or -*es*) endings on present-tense verbs that have third-person singular subjects.

All singular nouns (*child, tree*) and the pronouns *he, she,* and *it* are third-person singular; indefinite pronouns such as *everyone* and *neither* are also third-person singular. When the subject of a sentence is third-person singular, its verb takes an -*s* or -*es* ending in the present tense. (See also section 21.)

	SINGULAR		**PLURAL**	
FIRST PERSON	I	know	we	know
SECOND PERSON	you	know	you	know
THIRD PERSON	he/she/it	knows	they	know
	child	knows	parents	know
	everyone	knows		

In nonstandard speech, the -*s* ending required by standard English is sometimes omitted.

>   *turns*   *dissolves*   *eats*
> **Sulfur dioxide ~~turn~~ leaves yellow, ~~dissolve~~ marble, and ~~eat~~**
> **away iron and steel.**

The subject *sulfur dioxide* is third-person singular, so the verbs must end in -*s.*

CAUTION: Do not add the -*s* ending to the verb if the subject is not third-person singular.

The writers of the following sentences, knowing they sometimes dropped -*s* endings from verbs, overcorrected by adding the endings where they don't belong.

▶ I prepare̸ program specifications and logic diagrams.

The writer mistakenly concluded that the *-s* ending belongs on present-tense verbs used with *all* singular subjects, not just *third-person* singular subjects. The pronoun *I* is first-person singular, so its verb does not require the *-s*.

▶ The dirt floors require̸ continual sweeping.

The writer mistakenly thought that the *-s* ending on the verb indicated plurality. The *-s* goes on present-tense verbs used with third-person *singular* subjects. The subject *floors* is third-person plural, so its verb does not require the *-s*.

Has *versus* have

In the present tense, use *has* with third-person singular subjects; all other subjects require *have*.

	SINGULAR		**PLURAL**	
FIRST PERSON	I	have	we	have
SECOND PERSON	you	have	you	have
THIRD PERSON	he/she/it	has	they	have

In some dialects, *have* is used with all subjects. But standard English requires *has* for third-person singular subjects.

has

▶ This respected musician almost always ~~have~~ a message to
  ^

convey in his work.

has

▶ As for the retirement income program, it ~~have~~ finally been
  ^

established.

The subjects *musician* and *it* are third-person singular, so the verb should be *has* in each case.

CAUTION: Do not use *has* if the subject is not third-person singular. The writers of the following sentences were aware that they often wrote *have* when standard English requires *has*. Here they are using what appears to them to be the "more correct" form, but in an inappropriate context.

> *have*
> My business law classes ~~has~~ helped me to understand more
>   ^
>
> about contracts.

> *have*
> I ~~has~~ much to be thankful for.
>   ^

The subjects of these sentences—*classes* and *I*—are third-person plural and first-person singular, so standard English requires *have*. *Has* is used with third-person singular subjects only.

Does *versus* do *and* doesn't *versus* don't

In the present tense, use *does* and *doesn't* with third-person singular subjects; all other subjects require *do* and *don't*.

	SINGULAR		PLURAL	
FIRST PERSON	I	do/don't	we	do/don't
SECOND PERSON	you	do/don't	you	do/don't
THIRD PERSON	he/she/it	does/doesn't	they	do/don't

The use of *don't* instead of the standard English *doesn't* is a feature of many dialects in the United States. Use of *do* for *does* is rarer.

> *doesn't*
> Grandfather really ~~don't~~ have a place to call home.
>   ^

> *Does*
> ~~Do~~ he know the correct procedure for setting up the experiment?
> ^

Grandfather and *he* are third-person singular, so the verbs should be *doesn't* and *does*.

Am, is, *and* are; was *and* were

The verb *be* has three forms in the present tense (*am, is, are*) and two in the past tense (*was, were*). Use *am* and *was* with first-person singular subjects; use *is* and *was* with third-person singular subjects. With all other subjects, use *are* and *were*.

	SINGULAR		PLURAL	
FIRST PERSON	I	am/was	we	are/were
SECOND PERSON	you	are/were	you	are/were
THIRD PERSON	he/she/it	is/was	they	are/were

> Judy wanted to borrow Tim's notes, but she ~~were~~ *was* too shy to
ask for them.

The subject *she* is third-person singular, so the verb should be *was*.

> Did you think you ~~was~~ *were* going to drown?

The subject *you* is second-person singular, so the verb should be *were*.

GRAMMAR CHECKERS can catch some missing *-s* endings on verbs and some misused *-s* forms of the verb. Unfortunately, they flag quite a few correct sentences, so you need to know how to interpret what the programs tell you. See the grammar checker box on page 185 for more detailed information.

27d Do not omit *-ed* endings on verbs.

Speakers who do not fully pronounce *-ed* endings sometimes omit them unintentionally in writing. Failure to pronounce *-ed* endings is common in many dialects and in informal speech even in standard English. In the following frequently used words and phrases, for example, the *-ed* ending is not always fully pronounced.

advised	developed	prejudiced	supposed to
asked	fixed	pronounced	used to
concerned	frightened	stereotyped	

When a verb is regular, both the past tense and the past participle are formed by adding *-ed* to the base form of the verb.

Past tense

Use an *-ed* or *-d* ending to express the past tense of regular verbs. The past tense is used when the action occurred entirely in the past.

▶ Over the weekend, Ed ~~fix~~ his brother's skateboard and tuned
                fixed
                  ^

up his mother's 1955 Thunderbird.

▶ Last summer my counselor ~~advise~~ me to ask my chemistry
                       advised
                           ^

instructor for help.

Past participles

Past participles are used in three ways: (1) following *have, has,* or *had* to form one of the perfect tenses; (2) following *be, am, is, are, was, were, being,* or *been* to form the passive voice; and (3) as adjectives modifying nouns or pronouns. The perfect tenses are listed on page 235, and the passive voice is discussed in 28c. For a discussion of participles functioning as adjectives, see 59c.

▶ Robin has ~~ask~~ me to go to California with her.
        asked
        ^

    Has asked is present perfect tense (*have* or *has* followed by a past participle).

▶ Though it is not a new phenomenon, domestic violence is
    publicized
    ~~publicize~~ more frequently than before.
    ^

    Is publicized is a verb in the passive voice (a form of *be* followed by a past participle).

▶ All aerobics classes end in a cool-down period to stretch
    tightened
    ~~tighten~~ muscles.
    ^

    The past participle *tightened* functions as an adjective modifying the noun *muscles*.

 GRAMMAR CHECKERS can catch some missing *-ed* endings, but they tend to slip past as many as they catch. For example, although programs flagged *was accustom,* they ignored *has change* and *was pass.*

27e Do not omit needed verbs.

Although standard English allows some linking verbs and help-ing verbs to be contracted, at least in informal contexts, it does not allow them to be omitted.

Linking verbs, used to link subjects to subject complements, are frequently a form of *be: be, am, is, are, was, were, being, been.* (See 58b.) Some of these forms may be contracted (*I'm, she's, we're, you're, they're*), but they should not be omitted altogether.

▶ When we out there in the evening, we often hear the
  ^ *are*

  helicopters circling above.

▶ Alvin a man who can defend himself.
  ^ *is*

Helping verbs, used with main verbs, include forms of *be, do,* and *have* or the words *can, will, shall, could, would, should, may, might,* and *must.* (See 57c.) Some helping verbs may be contracted (*he's leaving, we'll celebrate, they've been told*), but they should not be omitted altogether.

▶ We been in Chicago since last Thursday.
  ^ *have*

▶ Do you know someone who be good for the job?
                       ^ *would*

Speakers of English as a second language sometimes have prob-lems with omitted verbs and correct use of helping verbs. See
ESL 29e and 29a.

GRAMMAR CHECKERS are fairly good at flagging omitted verbs, but they do not catch all of them. For example, programs caught the missing verb in this sentence: *He always talking.* But in the following, more complicated sentence, they did not catch the missing verb: *We often don't know whether he angry or just talking.*

EXERCISE 27-2

Edit the following sentences to eliminate problems with *-s* and *-ed* verb forms and with omitted verbs. If a sentence is correct, write "correct" after it. Answers to lettered sentences appear in the back of the book. Example:

> The psychologist ~~have~~ ^{has} so many problems in her own life that
> she ~~don't~~ ^{doesn't} know how to advise anyone else.

a. The cops was after my hot rod Lincoln. We was passing cars like they was standing still.

b. The museum visitors were not suppose to touch the exhibits.

c. Our church has all the latest technology, even a close-circuit television.

d. We often don't know whether he angry or just joking.

e. Have there ever been a time in your life when you were too depressed to get out of bed?

1. We were ask to sign a contract committing ourselves to not smoking for forty-eight hours.

2. Today a modern school building covers most of the old grounds.

3. The training for security checkpoint screeners, which takes place in an empty airplane hangar, consist of watching out-of-date videos.

4. Bettelheim claims that fairy tales stimulates the child's unconscious thoughts.

5. The ball was pass from one player to the other so fast that even the TV crew miss some of the exchanges.

28

Use verbs in the appropriate tense, mood, and voice.

28a Choose the appropriate verb tense.

Tenses indicate the time of an action in relation to the time of the speaking or writing about that action.

The most common problem with tenses—shifting confusingly from one tense to another—is discussed in section 13. Other problems with tenses are detailed in this section, after the following survey of tenses.

GRAMMAR CHECKERS do not flag the problems with tense discussed in this section. Although some programs may tell you that *had had* is incorrect, in fact it is often correct.

Survey of tenses

English has three simple tenses (past, present, and future) and three perfect tenses (present perfect, past perfect, and future perfect). In addition, there is a progressive form of each of these six tenses.

SIMPLE TENSES The simple present tense is used primarily to describe habitual actions (*Jane walks to work*) or to refer to actions occurring at the time of speaking (*I see a cardinal in our maple tree*). It is also used to state facts or general truths and to describe fictional events in a literary work (see p. 236). The present tense may even be used to express future actions that are to occur at some specified time (*The semester begins tomorrow*).

The simple past tense is used for actions completed entirely in the past (*Yesterday Jane walked to work*).

The simple future tense is used for actions that will occur in the future (*Tomorrow Jane will walk to work*) or for actions that are predictable, given certain causes (*Meat will spoil if not properly refrigerated*).

In the following chart, the simple tenses are given for the regular verb *walk,* the irregular verb *ride,* and the highly irregular verb *be.*

SIMPLE PRESENT

SINGULAR		PLURAL	
I	walk, ride, am	we	walk, ride, are
you	walk, ride, are	you	walk, ride, are
he/she/it	walks, rides, is	they	walk, ride, are

SIMPLE PAST

SINGULAR		PLURAL	
I	walked, rode, was	we	walked, rode, were
you	walked, rode, were	you	walked, rode, were
he/she/it	walked, rode, was	they	walked, rode, were

SIMPLE FUTURE

I, you, he/she/it, we, they   will walk, ride, be

PERFECT TENSES   More complex time relations are indicated by the perfect tenses. A verb in one of the perfect tenses (a form of *have* plus the past participle) expresses an action that was or will be completed by the time of another action.

PRESENT PERFECT
I, you, we, they   have walked, ridden, been
he/she/it   has walked, ridden, been

PAST PERFECT
I, you, he/she/it, we, they   had walked, ridden, been

FUTURE PERFECT
I, you, he/she/it, we, they   will have walked, ridden, been

PROGRESSIVE FORMS   The simple and perfect tenses already discussed have progressive forms that describe actions in progress. A progressive verb consists of a form of *be* followed by a present participle.

PRESENT PROGRESSIVE
I   am walking, riding, being
he/she/it   is walking, riding, being
you, we, they   are walking, riding, being

PAST PROGRESSIVE
I, he/she/it   was walking, riding, being
you, we, they   were walking, riding, being

FUTURE PROGRESSIVE
I, you, he/she/it, we, they   will be walking, riding, being

PRESENT PERFECT PROGRESSIVE
I, you, we, they   had been walking, riding, being
he/she/it   has been walking, riding, being

PAST PERFECT PROGRESSIVE
I, you, he/she/it, we, they   has been walking, riding, being

FUTURE PERFECT PROGRESSIVE
I, you, he/she/it, we, they   will have been walking, riding, being

ESL

The progressive forms are not normally used with mental activity verbs such as *believe*. See 29a.

Special uses of the present tense

Use the present tense when writing about events in a literary work, when expressing general truths, and when quoting, summarizing, or paraphrasing an author's views.

When writing about a work of literature, you may be tempted to use the past tense. The convention, however, is to describe fictional events in the present tense. (See also 13b.)

▶ In Masuji Ibuse's *Black Rain,* a child ~~reached~~ *reaches* for a pome-

granate in his mother's garden, and a moment later he

~~was~~ *is* dead, killed by the blast of the atomic bomb.

Scientific principles or general truths should appear in the present tense, unless such principles have been disproved.

▶ Galileo taught that the earth ~~revolved~~ *revolves* around the sun.

Since Galileo's teaching has not been discredited, the verb should be in the present tense. The following sentence, however, is acceptable: *Ptolemy taught that the sun revolved around the earth.*

When you are quoting, summarizing, or paraphrasing the author of a nonliterary work, use present-tense verbs such as *writes, reports, asserts,* and so on. This convention is usually followed even when the author is dead (unless a date or the context specifies the time of writing).

▶ Baron Bowan of Colwood ~~wrote~~ *writes* that a metaphysician is "one

who goes into a dark cellar at midnight without a light,

looking for a black cat that is not there."

EXCEPTION: When you are documenting a paper with the APA (American Psychological Association) style of in-text citations, which include a date after the author's name, use past-tense verbs such as *reported* or *demonstrated* or present perfect verbs such as *has reported* or *has demonstrated.*

> E. Wilson (1996) reported that positive reinforcement alone was a less effective teaching technique than a mixture of positive reinforcement and constructive criticism.

The past perfect tense

The past perfect tense consists of a past participle preceded by *had* (*had worked, had gone, had had*). (See page 235.) This tense is used for an action already completed by the time of another past action or for an action already completed at some specific past time.

> Everyone *had spoken* by the time I arrived.

> Everyone *had spoken* by 10:00 A.M.

Writers sometimes use the simple past tense when they should use the past perfect.

▶ We built our cabin high on a pine knoll, forty feet above an
  had been
  abandoned quarry that ~~was~~ flooded in 1920 to create a lake.
                            ^

  The building of the cabin and the flooding of the quarry both occurred
  in the past, but the flooding was completed before the time of building.

                                                          had
▶ By the time we arrived at the party, the guest of honor left.
                                                          ^

  The past perfect tense is needed because the action of leaving was
  completed at a specific past time (*by the time we arrived*).

Some writers tend to overuse the past perfect tense. Do not use the past perfect if two past actions occurred at the same time.

▶ When we arrived in Paris, Pauline ~~had~~ met us at the train

  station.

Sequence of tenses with infinitives and participles

An infinitive is the base form of a verb preceded by *to*. (See 59c.) Use the present infinitive to show action at the same time as or later than the action of the verb in the sentence.

                raise
▶ The club had hoped to ~~have raised~~ a thousand dollars by
                        ^

  April 1.

  The action expressed in the infinitive (*to raise*) occurred later than
  the action of the sentence's verb (*had hoped*).

Use the perfect form of an infinitive (*to have* followed by the past participle) for an action occurring earlier than that of the verb in the sentence.

▶ Dan would like to ~~join~~ *have joined* the navy, but he did not pass the

physical.

The liking occurs in the present; the joining would have occurred in the past.

Like the tense of an infinitive, the tense of a participle is also governed by the tense of the sentence's verb. Use the present participle (ending in *-ing*) for an action occurring at the same time as that of the sentence's verb.

Hiking the Appalachian Trail in early spring, we spotted many wildflowers.

Use the past participle (such as *given* or *helped*) or the present perfect participle (*having* plus the past participle) for an action occurring before that of the verb.

Discovered off the coast of Florida, the *Atocha* yielded many treasures.

Having worked her way through college, Melanie graduated debt-free.

28b Use the subjunctive mood in the few contexts that require it.

There are three moods in English: the *indicative,* used for facts, opinions, and questions; the *imperative,* used for orders or advice; and the *subjunctive,* used in certain contexts to express wishes, requests, or conditions contrary to fact. Of these moods, only the subjunctive causes problems for writers.

Forms of the subjunctive

In the subjunctive mood, present-tense verbs do not change form to indicate the number and person of the subject (see section 21). Instead, the subjunctive uses the base form of the verb (*be, drive, employ*) with all subjects.

It is important that you *be* [not *are*] prepared for the interview.

We asked that she *drive* [not *drives*] more slowly.

Also, in the subjunctive mood, there is only one past-tense form of *be: were* (never *was*).

If I *were* [not *was*] you, I'd proceed more cautiously.

Uses of the subjunctive

The subjunctive mood appears only in a few contexts: in contrary-to-fact clauses beginning with *if* or expressing a wish; in *that* clauses following verbs such as *ask, insist, recommend, request,* and *suggest;* and in certain set expressions.

IN CONTRARY-TO-FACT CLAUSES BEGINNING WITH *IF* When a subordinate clause beginning with *if* expresses a condition contrary to fact, use the subjunctive mood.

▶ If I ~~was~~ *were* a member of Congress, I would vote for that bill.

▶ We could be less cautious if Jake ~~was~~ *were* more trustworthy.

The verbs in these sentences express conditions that do not exist: The writer is not a member of Congress, and Jake is not trustworthy.

Do not use the subjunctive mood in *if* clauses expressing conditions that exist or may exist.

If Dana *wins* the contest, she will leave for Barcelona in June.

IN CONTRARY-TO-FACT CLAUSES EXPRESSING A WISH In formal English, the subjunctive is used in clauses expressing a wish or desire; in informal speech, however, the indicative is more common.

FORMAL I wish that Dr. Kurtinitis *were* my professor.

INFORMAL I wish that Dr. Kurtinitis *was* my professor.

IN *THAT* CLAUSES FOLLOWING VERBS SUCH AS *ASK, INSIST, RECOMMEND, REQUEST,* AND *SUGGEST* Because requests have not yet become reality, they are expressed in the subjunctive mood.

▶ Professor Moore insists that her students ~~are~~ *be* on time.

▶ We recommend that Lambert ~~files~~ *file* form 1050 soon.

IN CERTAIN SET EXPRESSIONS   The subjunctive mood, once more widely used in English, remains in certain set expressions: *be that as it may, as it were, come rain or shine, far be it from me,* and so on.

GRAMMAR CHECKERS rarely flag problems with the subjunctive mood. They may at times question your correct use of the subjunctive, since your correct use will seem to violate the rules of subject-verb agreement (see section 21). For example, one program suggested using *was* instead of *were* in the following correct sentence: *This isn't my dog; if it were, I would feed it.* Because the sentence describes a condition contrary to fact, the subjunctive form *were* is correct.

EXERCISE 28-1

Edit the following sentences to eliminate errors in verb tense or mood. If a sentence is correct, write "correct" after it. Answers to lettered sentences appear in the back of the book. Example:

After the path ~~was~~ *had been* plowed, we were able to walk through the park.

a. Watson and Crick discovered the mechanism that controlled inheritance in all life: the workings of the DNA molecule.
b. This isn't the Waldorf; if it were, we wouldn't be here.
c. In the feminist rewriting of "Sleeping Beauty," the girl was not awakened by a prince.
d. By the time we arrived, the cake had been eaten.
e. They had planned to have adopted a girl, but they got twin boys.

1. As soon as my aunt applied for the position of pastor, the post was filled by an inexperienced seminary graduate who had been so hastily snatched that his mortarboard was still in midair.
2. Don Quixote, in Cervantes's novel, was an idealist ill suited for life in the real world.

3. The hurricane tore up the palm trees, lifted them over the hotel roof, and had dropped them into the swimming pool.
4. When the doctor said "It's a girl," I was stunned. For nine months I dreamed about playing baseball with my son.
5. If men and women were angels, no government would be necessary.

28c Use the active voice unless you have a good reason for choosing the passive.

Transitive verbs (verbs that take a direct object) appear in either the active or the passive voice. (See 58c.) In the active voice, the subject of the sentence does the action; in the passive, the subject receives the action.

ACTIVE The committee *reached* a decision.

PASSIVE A decision *was reached* by the committee.

To transform a sentence from the passive to the active voice, make the actor the subject of the sentence.

▶ For the opening flag ceremony, ~~a dance was choreographed~~
  choreographed a dance
  ~~by~~ Mr. Martins to the song "Two Hundred Years and Still
  ∧

  a Baby."

The revision emphasizes Mr. Martins by making him the subject.

Active and passive verbs are both grammatically correct, but active verbs are usually more effective because they are simpler and more direct. For a full discussion of when to use active or passive verbs, see 14a.

  We did not take down the
▶ The Christmas decorations ~~were not taken down~~ until
  ∧

  Valentine's Day.

Very often the actor does not even appear in a passive-voice sentence. To turn such a sentence into the active voice, the writer must decide on an appropriate subject, in this case *We*.

Some speakers of English as a second language tend to avoid the passive voice even when it is appropriate. For advice on **ESL** transforming an active-voice sentence to the passive, see 58c.

GRAMMAR CHECKERS can flag many, but not all, passive verbs, and in some cases they flag verbs that aren't passive. Be aware, however, that passive verbs are sometimes appropriate, so you must decide whether to use an active verb instead.

EXERCISE 28-2

Change the following sentences from the passive to the active voice. You may need to invent an actor to be the subject in the active voice. Revisions of lettered sentences appear in the back of the book. Example:

> *We*
> ~~It was~~ learned from the test that our son was reading on the
> ^
> second-grade level.

a. Each cell in the monastery was painted by Fra Angelico.
b. Carbon dating is used by scientists to determine the approximate age of an object.
c. As the patient undressed, scars were seen on his back, stomach, and thighs. We suspected child abuse.
d. It was noted right away that the taxi driver had been exposed to Americans because he knew all the latest slang.
e. Diseases have been discovered by researchers more often than cures.

1. For as long as I can remember, grace has been said before every meal at our house.
2. No loyalty at all was shown by the dog to his owner, who had mistreated him.
3. It can be concluded that a college education provides a significant economic advantage.
4. The land was ruthlessly stripped of timber before the settlers realized the consequences of their actions.
5. Home equity loans were explained to me by the assistant manager.

ESL GRAMMAR

Sections 29, 30, and 31 of *Rules for Writers* have a special audience: speakers of English as a second language (ESL) who have
learned English but continue to have problems in a few trouble
spots.

29

Be alert to special problems with verbs.

Both native and nonnative speakers of English encounter the
following problems with verbs, which are treated elsewhere in
this handbook:

> problems with subject-verb agreement (section 21)
> misuse of verb forms (section 27)
> problems with tense, mood, and voice (section 28)

This section focuses on features of the English verb system that
cause special problems for second-language speakers.

29a Match helping verbs and main verbs appropriately.

Only certain combinations of helping verbs and main verbs are
allowed in English. The correct combinations are discussed in this
section, after the following review of helping verbs and main verbs.

Review of helping verbs and main verbs

Helping verbs always appear before main verbs. (See 57c.)

> HV MV   HV   MV
> We *will leave* for the picnic at noon. *Do* you *want* a ride?

Some helping verbs—*have, do,* and *be*—change form to indicate tense; others, known as modals, do not.

FORMS OF *HAVE, DO,* AND *BE*
have, has, had
do, does, did
be, am, is, are, was, were, being, been

MODALS
can, could, may, might, must, shall, should, will, would (*also* ought to)

Every main verb has five forms (except *be,* which has eight forms). The following list shows these forms for the regular verb *help* and the irregular verb *give.* (See 27a for a list of common irregular verbs.)

BASE FORM	help, give
PAST TENSE	helped, gave
PAST PARTICIPLE	helped, given
PRESENT PARTICIPLE	helping, giving
-*S* FORM	helps, gives

Modal + base form

After the modals *can, could, may, might, must, shall, should, will,* and *would,* use the base form of the verb.

▶   My cousin will send~~s~~ us photographs from her wedding.

        speak
▶   We could ~~spoke~~ Spanish when we were young.

CAUTION: Do not use *to* in front of a main verb that follows a modal. (*Ought to* is an exception.)

▶   Gina can ~~to~~ drive us home if we miss the bus.

Do, does, *or* did + base form

After helping verbs that are a form of *do,* use the base form of the verb.

The helping verbs *do, does,* and *did* are used in three ways: (1) to express a negative meaning with the adverb *not* or *never,* (2) to ask a question, and (3) to emphasize a main verb used in a positive sense.

▶ Mariko does not wants̸ any more dessert.

▶ Did Janice ~~bought~~ buy the gift for Katherine?

▶ We do ~~hoping~~ hope that you will come to the party.

Have, has, *or* had + *past participle (perfect tenses)*

After the helping verb *have, has,* or *had,* use the past participle to form one of the perfect tenses. (See 28a.) Past participles usually end in *-ed, -d, -en, -n,* or *-t.* (See 27a.)

▶ On cold nights many churches in the city have ~~offer~~ offered shelter

to the homeless.

▶ An-Mei has not ~~speaking~~ spoken Chinese since she was a child.

The helping verb *have* is sometimes preceded by a modal helping verb such as *will: By nightfall, we will have driven five hundred miles.* (See also perfect tenses, 28a.)

Form of be + *present participle (progressive forms)*

After the helping verb *be, am, is, are, was, were,* or *been,* use the present participle to express a continuing action. (See progressive forms, 28a.)

▶ Carlos is ~~build~~ building his house on a cliff overlooking the Pacific

Ocean.

▶ Uncle Roy was ~~driven~~ driving a brand-new red Corvette.

The helping verb *be* must be preceded by a modal (*can, could, may, might, must, shall, should, will,* or *would*): *Edith will be going to Germany soon.* The helping verb *been* must be preceded by *have, has,* or *had*: *Andy has been studying English for five years.* (See also progressive forms, 28a.)

CAUTION: Certain verbs are not normally used in the progressive sense in English. In general, these verbs express a state of being or mental activity, not a dynamic action. Common examples are *appear, believe, belong, contain, have, hear, know, like, need, see, seem, taste, think, understand,* and *want.*

>   *want*
> ▶ I ~~am wanting~~ to see August Wilson's *Fences* at Arena Stage.
>   ^

Some of these verbs, however, have special uses in which progressive forms are normal. (*We are thinking about going to the Bahamas.*) You will need to make a note of exceptions as you encounter them.

Form of be *+ past participle (passive voice)*

When a sentence is written in the passive voice, the subject receives the action instead of doing it: *Melissa was given a special award.* (See 28c.)

    To form the passive voice, use *be, am, is, are, was, were, being,* or *been* followed by a past participle (usually ending in *-ed, -d, -en, -n,* or *-t*).

>   *written*
> ▶ *Bleak House* was ~~write~~ by Charles Dickens.
>   ^

>   *honored*
> ▶ The scientists were ~~honor~~ for their work with dolphins.
>   ^

When the helping verb is *be, being,* or *been,* it must be preceded by another helping verb. *Be* must be preceded by a modal such as *will: Senator Dixon will be defeated. Being* must be preceded by *am, is, are, was,* or *were: The child was being teased. Been* must be preceded by *have, has,* or *had: I have been invited to a party.*

CAUTION: Although they may seem to have passive meanings, verbs such as *occur, happen, sleep, die,* and *fall* may not be used to form the passive voice because they are intransitive. Only transitive verbs, those that take direct objects, may be used to form the passive voice. (See transitive and intransitive verbs, 58b.)

▶ The earthquake ~~was~~ occurred last Wednesday.

> GRAMMAR CHECKERS can catch some mismatches of helping and main verbs. They can tell you, for example, that the base form of the verb should be used after certain helping verbs, such as *did* and *could*, in incorrect sentences like these: *Did you understood my question? Could Alan comes with us?*
>
> Programs can also catch some, but not all, problems with main verbs following forms of *have* or *be*. For example, grammar checkers flagged *have spend*, explaining that the past participle *spent* is required, and they flagged *are expose*, suggesting that either *exposed* or *exposing* is required. However, programs failed to flag problems in many sentences, such as these: *Sasha has change her major three times. The provisions of the contract were broke by both parties.*

EXERCISE 29–1

Revise any sentences in which helping and main verbs do not match. You may need to look at the list of irregular verbs in 27a to determine the correct form of some irregular verbs. Answers to lettered sentences appear in the back of the book. Example:

Maureen should find~~s~~ an apartment closer to campus.

a. We will making this a better country.
b. There is nothing in the world that TV has not touch on.
c. Did the landlord told you that he's going to raise the rent?
d. A hard wind was blown while we were climbing the mountain.
e. The child's innocent world has been taking away from him.

1. We haven't spoke to our cousins in several weeks, but we expect to hear from them during the holidays.
2. A serious accident was happened at the corner of Main Street and First Avenue last night.
3. Have you find your wallet yet?
4. I have ate Thai food only once before.
5. How often does Sandy takes her daughter to the doctor?

Grammar

29b In conditional sentences, choose verbs with care.

Conditional sentences state that one set of circumstances depends on whether another set of circumstances exists. Choosing verbs in such sentences can be tricky, partly because two clauses are involved: usually an *if* or a *when* or an *unless* clause and an independent clause.

Three kinds of conditional sentences are discussed in this section: factual, predictive, and speculative.

Factual

Factual conditional sentences express factual relationships. These relationships might be scientific truths, in which case the present tense is used in both clauses.

> If water *cools* to 32°, it *freezes*.

Or they might be present or past relationships that are habitually true, in which case the same tense is used in both clauses.

> When Sue *bicycles* along the canal, her dog *runs* ahead of her.

> Whenever the coach *asked* for help, I *volunteered*.

Predictive

Predictive conditional sentences are used to predict the future or to express future plans or possibilities. In such a sentence, an *if* or *unless* clause contains a present-tense verb; the verb in the independent clause usually consists of the modal *will, can, may, should,* or *might* followed by the base form of the verb.

> If you *practice* regularly, your tennis game *will improve.*

> We *will lose* our remaining wetlands unless we *act* now.

Speculative

Speculative conditional sentences are used for three purposes: (1) to speculate about unlikely possibilities in the present or future, (2) to speculate about events that did not happen in the past, and (3) to speculate about conditions that are contrary to fact. Each of these purposes requires its own combination of verbs.

UNLIKELY POSSIBILITIES Somewhat confusingly, English uses the past tense in an *if* clause to speculate about a possible but unlikely condition in the present or future. The verb in the independent clause consists of *would, could,* or *might* plus the base form of the verb.

> If I *had* the time, I *would travel* to Senegal.

> If Stan *studied* harder, he *could master* calculus.

In the *if* clause, the past-tense form *were* is used with subjects that would normally take *was: Even if I were* [not *was*] *invited, I wouldn't go to the picnic.* (See also 28b.)

EVENTS THAT DID NOT HAPPEN English uses the past perfect tense in an *if* clause to speculate about an event that did not happen in the past or to speculate about a state of being that was unreal in the past. (See past perfect tense, 28a.) The verb in the independent clause consists of *would have, could have,* or *might have* plus the past participle.

> If I *had saved* enough money, I *would have traveled* to Senegal last year.

> If Aunt Grace *had been* alive for your graduation, she *would have been* very proud.

CONDITIONS CONTRARY TO FACT To speculate about conditions that are currently unreal or contrary to fact, English usually uses the past-tense verb *were* (never *was*) in an *if* clause. (See 28b.) The verb in the independent clause consists of *would, could,* or *might* plus the base form of the verb.

> If Grandmother *were* alive today, she *would be* very proud of you.

> I *would make* children's issues a priority if I *were* president.

> **GRAMMAR CHECKERS** do not flag problems with conditional sentences. The programs miss even obvious errors, such as this one: *Whenever I washed my car, it rains.*

EXERCISE 29–2

Edit the following conditional sentences for problems with verbs. In some cases, more than one revision is possible. Suggested revisions of lettered sentences appear in the back of the book. Example:

had
If I ~~have~~ the money, I would meet my friends in Barcelona
^

next summer.

a. He would have won the election if he went to the port cities to campaign.
b. If Martin Luther King, Jr., was alive today, he would be appalled by the violence in our inner cities.
c. Whenever there is a fire in our neighborhood, everybody came out to watch.
d. We will lose our largest client unless we would update our computer system.
e. If I live in southern California, I wouldn't need to buy a winter coat.

1. If it would not be raining, we could go fishing.
2. If everyone has voted in the last election, the results would have been very different.
3. You would have met my cousin if you came to the party last night.
4. When dark gray clouds appeared on a hot summer afternoon, a thunderstorm often follows.
5. Our daughter would have drowned if Officer Blake didn't risk his life to save her.

29c Become familiar with verbs that may be followed by gerunds or infinitives.

A gerund is a verb form that ends in *-ing* and is used as a noun: *sleeping, dreaming.* (See 59c.) An infinitive is the base form of the verb preceded by the word *to: to sleep, to dream.* The word *to* is not a preposition in this use but an infinitive marker. (See 59c.)

A few verbs may be followed by either a gerund or an infinitive; others may be followed by a gerund but not by an infinitive; still others may be followed by an infinitive (either directly or with a noun or pronoun intervening) but not by a gerund.

Verb + gerund or infinitive

These commonly used verbs may be followed by a gerund or an infinitive, with little or no difference in meaning:

begin	continue	like	start
can't stand	hate	love	

I love *skiing.*
I love to *ski.*

With a few verbs, however, the choice of a gerund or infinitive changes the meaning dramatically:

forget	remember	stop	try

She stopped *speaking* to Lucia. [She no longer spoke to Lucia.]

She stopped *to speak* to Lucia. [She paused so that she could speak to Lucia.]

Verb + gerund

These verbs may be followed by a gerund but not by an infinitive:

admit	enjoy	postpone	resist
appreciate	escape	practice	risk
avoid	finish	put off	suggest
deny	imagine	quit	tolerate
discuss	miss	recall	

Have you finished *decorating* [not *to decorate*] the tree?

Bill enjoys *playing* [not *to play*] the piano.

Verb + infinitive

These verbs may be followed by an infinitive but not by a gerund:

agree	decide	manage	pretend	want
ask	expect	mean	promise	wish
beg	have	offer	refuse	
claim	hope	plan	wait	

We plan *to visit* [not *visiting*] the Yucatán next week.

Jill has offered *to water* [not *watering*] the plants while we are away.

Verb + noun or pronoun + infinitive

With certain verbs in the active voice, a noun or pronoun must come between the verb and the infinitive that follows it. The noun or pronoun usually names a person who is affected by the action.

advise	command	have	persuade	tell
allow	convince	instruct	remind	urge
cause	encourage	order	require	warn

The dean encourages *you to apply* for the scholarship.

The class asked *Luis to tell* the story of his escape.

A few verbs may be followed either by an infinitive directly or by an infinitive preceded by a noun or pronoun.

ask	expect	need	want	would like

We asked *to speak* to the congregation.

We asked *Rabbi Abrams to speak* to our congregation.

Verb + noun or pronoun + unmarked infinitive

An unmarked infinitive is an infinitive without *to*. A few verbs (known as "causative verbs") may be followed by a noun or pronoun and an unmarked (but not a marked) infinitive.

have ("cause")	let ("allow")	make ("force")

Absence makes *the heart grow* [not *to grow*] fonder.

Please let *me pay* [not *to pay*] for the tickets.

GRAMMAR CHECKERS can flag some, but not all, problems with gerunds and infinitives following verbs. For example, programs flagged many sentences with misused infinitives, such as these: *Have you finished to weed the garden? Chris enjoys to play tennis.* Programs were less successful at flagging sentences with misused present participles, skipping incorrect sentences like this one: *We want traveling to Hawaii next spring.*

EXERCISE 29-3

Form sentences by adding gerund or infinitive constructions to the following sentence openings. In some cases, more than one kind of construction may be possible. Possible sentences for lettered items appear in the back of the book. Example:

> **Please remind** *your sister to call me.*
>   ^

a. I enjoy
b. Will you encourage Samantha
c. The team hopes
d. Ricardo and his brothers miss
e. The babysitter let

1. Pollen makes
2. The club president asked
3. Next summer we plan
4. Waverly intends
5. Please stop

29d Use two-word verbs correctly.

Many verbs in English consist of a verb followed by a preposition or adverb known as a *particle*. (See 57c.) A two-word verb (also known as a *phrasal verb*) often expresses an idiomatic meaning that cannot be understood literally. Consider the verbs in the following sentences, for example.

> We *ran across* Professor Magnotto on the way to the bookstore.

> Calvin *dropped in* on his adviser this morning.

> Regina told me to *look* her *up* when I got to Seattle.

As you probably know, *ran across* means "encountered," *dropped in* means "paid an unexpected visit," and *look up* means "get in touch with." When you were first learning English, however, these two-word verbs must have suggested strange meanings.

Some two-word verbs are intransitive; they do not take direct objects. (See 58b.)

> This morning I *got up* at dawn.

Transitive two-word verbs (those that take direct objects) have particles that are either separable or inseparable. Separable particles may be separated from the verb by the direct object.

> Lucy *called* the wedding *off.*

Grammar

When the direct object is a noun, a separable particle may also follow the verb immediately.

> At the last minute, Lucy *called off* the wedding.

When the direct object is a pronoun, however, the particle must be separated from the verb.

> Why was there no wedding? Lucy *called* it *off* [not *called off* it].

Inseparable particles must follow the verb immediately. A direct object cannot come between the verb and the particle.

> The police will *look into* the matter [not *look* the matter *into*].

29e Do not omit needed verbs.

Some languages allow the omission of the verb when the meaning is clear without it; English does not.

▶ Jim *is* exceptionally intelligent.

▶ Many streets in San Francisco *are* very steep.

30

Use the articles *a, an,* and *the* appropriately.

Except for occasional difficulty in choosing between *a* and *an*, native speakers of English encounter few problems with articles. To speakers whose native language is not English, however, articles can prove troublesome, for the rules governing their use are surprisingly complex. This section summarizes those rules.

The articles a, an, and the

The indefinite articles *a* and *an* and the definite article *the* signal that a noun is about to appear. The noun may follow the article immediately, or modifiers may intervene (see 57a and 57d).

ART N	ART N
a sunset	an incredible sunset

ART N	ART N
the table	the round pine table

NOTE: *A* is used before a consonant sound: *a banana, a tree, a picture, a hand, a happy child. An* is used before a vowel sound: *an eggplant, an occasion, an uncle, an hour, an honorable person.* Notice that words beginning with *h* can have either a consonant sound (*hand, happy*) or a vowel sound (*hour, honorable*). (See also the Glossary of Usage: *a, an.*)

Other noun markers

Articles are not the only words used to mark nouns. Noun markers (sometimes called *determiners*) also include words such as the following, which identify or quantify nouns.

— possessive nouns, such as *Elena's*

— *my, your, his, her, its, our*

— *this, that, these, those*

— *all, any, each, either, every, few, many, more, most, much, neither, several, some*

— numbers: *one, two,* and so on

Usually an article is not used with another noun marker. Common exceptions include expressions such as *a few, the most,* and *all the.*

GRAMMAR CHECKERS can flag some missing or misused articles, pointing out, for example, that an article usually precedes a word such as *paintbrush* or *vehicle* or that the articles *a* and *an* are not usually used before a noncount noun such as *sugar* or *advice.*

However, the programs fail to flag many missing or misused articles. For example, in two paragraphs with eleven missing or misused articles, grammar checkers caught only two of the problems. In addition, the programs frequently suggest that an article is missing when it is not. For example, one program suggested that an article might be needed before *teacher* in this correct sentence: *My social studies teacher entered me in a public-speaking contest.*

30a Use *a* (or *an*) with singular count nouns whose specific identity is not known to the reader.

Count nouns refer to persons, places, or things that can be counted: *one girl, two girls; one city, three cities; one apple, four apples.* Noncount nouns refer to entities or abstractions that cannot be counted: *water, steel, air, furniture, patience, knowledge.* It is important to remember that noncount nouns vary from language to language. To see what nouns English categorizes as noncount nouns, refer to the list on the next page.

If a singular count noun names something not known to the reader—perhaps because it is being mentioned for the first time, perhaps because its specific identity is unknown even to the writer—the noun should be preceded by *a* or *an* unless it has been preceded by another noun marker. *A* (or *an*) usually means "one among many" but can also mean "any one."

▶ Mary Beth arrived in ^*a*^ limousine.

▶ We are looking for ^*an*^ apartment close to the lake.

30b Do not use *a* (or *an*) with noncount nouns.

A (or *an*) is not used to mark noncount nouns, such as *sugar, gold, honesty,* or *jewelry.* A list of commonly used noncount nouns is given in the chart on the next page.

▶ Claudia asked her mother for ~~an~~ advice.

If you want to express an approximate amount, you can often use one of the following quantifiers with a noncount noun.

QUANTIFIER	NONCOUNT NOUN
a great deal of	candy, courage
a little	salt, rain
any	sugar, homework
enough	bread, wood, money
less	meat, violence
little (*or* a little)	knowledge, time
more	coffee, information
much (*or* a lot of)	snow, pollution
plenty of	paper, lumber
some	tea, news, work

Commonly used noncount nouns

FOOD AND DRINK

bacon, beef, bread, broccoli, butter, cabbage, candy, cauliflower, celery, cereal, cheese, chicken, chocolate, coffee, corn, cream, fish, flour, fruit, ice cream, lettuce, meat, milk, oil, pasta, rice, salt, spinach, sugar, tea, water, wine, yogurt

NONFOOD SUBSTANCES

air, cement, coal, dirt, gasoline, gold, paper, petroleum, plastic, rain, silver, snow, soap, steel, wood, wool

ABSTRACT NOUNS

advice, anger, beauty, confidence, courage, employment, fun, happiness, health, honesty, information, intelligence, knowledge, love, poverty, satisfaction, truth, wealth

OTHER

biology (and other areas of study), clothing, equipment, furniture, homework, jewelry, luggage, lumber, machinery, mail, money, news, poetry, pollution, research, scenery, traffic, transportation, violence, weather, work

NOTE: A few noncount nouns may also be used as count nouns, especially in informal English: *Bill loves chocolate; Bill offered me a chocolate. I'll have coffee; I'll have a coffee.*

To express a more specific amount, you can often precede a noncount noun with a unit word that is typically associated with it. Here are some common combinations.

A OR AN + UNIT + *OF*	NONCOUNT NOUNS
a bottle of	water, vinegar
a carton of	ice cream, milk, yogurt
an ear of	corn
a head of	cabbage, lettuce
a loaf of	bread
a piece of	meat, furniture, advice
a pound of	butter, sugar
a quart of	milk, ice cream
a slice of	bread, bacon

CAUTION: Noncount nouns do not have plural forms, and they should not be used with numbers or words suggesting plurality (such as *several, many, a few, a couple of, a number of*).

▶ We need some information*s* about rain forests.

       much
▶ Do you have ~~many~~ money with you?
       ^

30c Use *the* with most nouns whose specific identity is known to the reader.

The definite article *the* is used with most nouns whose identity is known to the reader. (For exceptions, see 30d.) Usually the identity will be clear to the reader for one of the following reasons:

—The noun has been previously mentioned.
—A phrase or a clause following the noun restricts its identity.
—A superlative such as *best* or *most intelligent* makes the noun's identity specific.
—The noun describes a unique person, place, or thing.
—The context or situation makes the noun's identity clear.

▶ A truck loaded with dynamite cut in front of our van.
       the
When truck skidded a few seconds later, we almost plowed
     ^

into it.

The noun *truck* is preceded by *A* when it is first mentioned. When the noun is mentioned again, it is preceded by *the* since readers now know the specific truck being discussed.

          the
▶ Bob warned me that gun on the top shelf of the cupboard
         ^

was loaded.

The phrase *on the top shelf of the cupboard* identifies the specific gun.

▶ Stephanie's petite daughter dated ~~the~~ tallest boy in the

senior class.

The superlative *tallest* restricts the identity of the noun *boy*.

▶ During an eclipse, one should avoid the temptation to look

directly at *the* sun.

There is only one sun in our solar system, so its identity is clear.

▶ Please don't slam *the* door when you leave.

Both the speaker and the listener know which door is meant.

30d Do not use *the* with plural or noncount nouns meaning "all" or "in general"; do not use *the* with most singular proper nouns.

When a plural or a noncount noun means "all" or "in general," it is not marked with *the*.

▶ ~~The~~ *F*ountains are an attractive but expensive element of

landscape design.

▶ In some parts of the world, ~~the~~ rice is preferred to all other

grains.

As you probably know, proper nouns—which name specific people, places, or things—are capitalized. Although there are many exceptions, *the* is not used with most singular proper nouns, such as *Judge Ito, Spring Street,* or *Lake Huron.* However, *the* is used with plural proper nouns, such as *the United Nations, the Bahamas,* and *the Finger Lakes.*

Geographical names create problems because there are so many exceptions to the rules. When in doubt, consult the chart on the following page or ask a native speaker.

Geographical names

WHEN TO OMIT *THE*

streets, squares, parks	Ivy Street, Union Square, Denali National Park
cities, states, counties	Miami, Idaho, Bee County
most countries	Italy, Nigeria, China
continents	South America, Africa
bays, single lakes	Tampa Bay, Lake Geneva
single mountains, islands	Mount Everest, Crete

WHEN TO USE *THE*

united countries	the United States, the Republic of China
large regions, deserts	the East Coast, the Sahara
peninsulas	the Iberian Peninsula
oceans, seas, gulfs	the Pacific, the Dead Sea, the Persian Gulf
canals and rivers	the Panama Canal, the Amazon
mountain ranges	the Rocky Mountains, the Alps
groups of islands	the Solomon Islands

EXERCISE 30–1

Articles have been omitted from the following story, adapted from *Zen Flesh, Zen Bones*, compiled by Paul Reps. Insert the articles *a, an,* and *the* where English requires them and be prepared to explain the reasons for your choices.

Moon Cannot Be Stolen

Ryokan, who was Zen master, lived simple life in little hut at foot of mountain. One evening thief visited hut only to discover there was nothing in it to steal.

Ryokan returned and caught him. "You may have come long way to visit me," he told prowler, "and you should not return empty-handed. Please take my clothes as gift." Thief was bewildered. He took Ryokan's clothes and slunk away. Ryokan sat naked, watching moon. "Poor fellow," he mused, "I wish I could give him this beautiful moon."

31

Be aware of other potential trouble spots.

31a Do not omit subjects or the expletive *there* or *it*.

English requires a subject for all sentences except imperatives, in which the subject *you* is understood (*Give to the poor*). (See 58a.) If your native language allows the omission of an explicit subject in other sentences or clauses, be especially alert to this requirement in English.

▶ *I have*
Have a large collection of baseball cards.
^

▶ *she*
Your aunt is very energetic; seems young for her age.
^

When the subject has been moved from its normal position before the verb, English sometimes requires an expletive (*there* or *it*) at the beginning of the sentence or clause. (See 58c.) *There* is used at the beginning of a sentence or clause to draw the reader's (or listener's) attention to the location or existence of something.

▶ *There is*
Is an apple in the refrigerator.
^

▶ *there*
As you know, are many religious sects in India.
^

Notice that the verb agrees with the subject that follows it: *apple is, sects are.* (See 21g.)

In one of its uses, the word *it* functions as an expletive, to call attention to a subject following the verb.

▶ *It is*
Is healthy to eat fruit and grains.
^

▶ *It is*
Is clear that we must change our approach.
^

The subjects of these sentences are *to eat fruit and grains* (an infinitive phrase) and *that we must change our approach* (a noun clause). (See 59c and 59b.)

As you probably know, the word *it* is also used as the subject of sentences describing the weather or temperature, stating the time, indicating distance, or suggesting an environmental fact.

It is raining in the valley, and it is snowing in the mountains.

In July, it is very hot in Arizona.

It is 9:15 A.M.

It is three hundred miles to Chicago.

It gets noisy in our dorm on weekends.

> GRAMMAR CHECKERS can flag some sentences with a missing expletive (*there* or *it*), but they often misdiagnose the problem, suggesting that if a sentence opens with a word such as *Is* or *Are,* it may need a question mark at the end. Consider this sentence, which grammar checkers flagged: *Are two grocery stores on Elm Street.* Clearly, the sentence doesn't need a question mark. What it needs is an expletive: *There are two grocery stores on Elm Street.*

31b Do not repeat the subject of a sentence.

English does not allow a subject to be repeated in its own clause.

▶ The doctor ~~she~~ advised me to cut down on salt.

The pronoun *she* repeats the subject *doctor*.

The subject of a sentence should not be repeated even if a word group intervenes between the subject and the verb.

▶ The car that had been stolen ~~it~~ was found.

The pronoun *it* repeats the subject *car*.

31c Do not repeat an object or an adverb in an adjective clause.

In some languages an object or an adverb is repeated later in the adjective clause in which it appears; in English such repetitions are not allowed. Adjective clauses begin with relative pronouns (*who, whom, whose, which, that*) or relative adverbs (*when, where*), and these words always serve a grammatical function within the clauses they introduce. (See 59b.) Another word in the clause cannot also serve that same grammatical function.

When a relative pronoun functions as the object of a verb or the object of a preposition, do not add another word with the same function later in the clause.

▶ The puppy ran after the car that we were riding in, ~~it.~~
                                                    ^

The relative pronoun *that* is the object of the preposition *in,* so the object *it* is not allowed.

Even when the relative pronoun has been omitted, do not add another word with its same function.

▶ The puppy ran after the car we were riding in, ~~it.~~
                                                 ^

The relative pronoun *that* is understood even though it is not present in the sentence.

Like a relative pronoun, a relative adverb should not be echoed later in its clause.

▶ The place where I work ~~there~~ is one hour from my apartment

in the city.

The adverb *there* should not echo the relative adverb *where.*

GRAMMAR CHECKERS can flag certain sentences with repeated subjects or objects, but they misdiagnose the problem as two independent clauses incorrectly joined. For example, programs flagged this sentence: *The roses that they brought home they cost three dollars each.* The sentence does not have two independent clauses incorrectly joined. The problem with the sentence is that *they* repeats the subject *roses.*

EXERCISE 31–1

In the following sentences, add needed subjects or expletives and delete any repeated subjects, objects, or adverbs. Answers to lettered sentences appear in the back of the book. Example:

Nancy is the woman whom I talked to ~~her~~ last week.

a. Are some cartons of ice cream in the freezer.
b. Are several emergency telephone numbers listed next to the phones at the hotel.
c. The prime minister she is the most popular leader in my country.
d. Juana wants to travel to many countries that she has read about them.
e. The king, who had served since the age of sixteen, he was an old man when he died.

1. My cousin she is coming to visit this summer.
2. In this city is difficult to find a high-paying job.
3. The water is beautiful at the beach where we swim there.
4. Is a banyan tree in our backyard.
5. The neighbor we trusted he was a thief.

31d Place adjectives and adverbs with care.

Adjectives modify nouns or pronouns; adverbs modify verbs, adjectives, or other adverbs (see 57d and 57e). Both native and nonnative speakers encounter problems in the use of adjectives and adverbs (see section 26). For nonnative speakers, the placement of adjectives and adverbs can also be troublesome.

Placement of adjectives

No doubt you have already learned that in English, adjectives usually precede the nouns they modify and that they may also appear following linking verbs. (See 26b and 58b.)

Janine wore a *new* necklace. Janine's necklace was *new*.

When adjectives pile up in front of a noun, however, you may sometimes have difficulty arranging them. English is quite particular about the order of cumulative adjectives, those not separated by commas. (See 32d.)

Janine was wearing a *beautiful antique silver* necklace [not *silver antique beautiful* necklace].

The chart on the following page shows the order in which cumulative adjectives ordinarily appear in front of the noun they modify. This list is just a general guide; don't be surprised when you encounter exceptions.

NOTE: Long strings of cumulative adjectives tend to be awkward. As a rule, use no more than two or three of them between the article (or other noun marker) and the noun modified. Here are several examples:

a beautiful old pine table
two enormous French urns
an exotic purple jungle flower

Susan's large round painting
some small blue medicine
bottles

Usual order of cumulative adjectives

ARTICLE OR OTHER NOUN MARKER
a, an, the, her, Joe's, two, many, some

EVALUATIVE WORD
attractive, dedicated, delicious, ugly, disgusting

SIZE
large, enormous, small, little

LENGTH OR SHAPE
long, short, round, square

AGE
new, old, young, antique

COLOR
yellow, blue, crimson

NATIONALITY
French, Scandinavian, Vietnamese

RELIGION
Catholic, Protestant, Jewish, Muslim

MATERIAL
silver, walnut, wool, marble

NOUN/ADJECTIVE
tree (as in *tree house*), kitchen (as in *kitchen table*)

THE NOUN MODIFIED
house, sweater, bicycle, bread, woman, priest

Grammar

Placement of adverbs

Adverbs modifying verbs appear in various positions: at the beginning or end of the sentence, before or after the verb, or between a helping verb and its main verb.

> *Slowly*, we drove along the rain-slick road.

> Mia handled the teapot *very carefully.*

> Martin *always* wins our tennis matches.

> Christina is *rarely* late for our lunch dates.

> My daughter has *often* spoken of you.

An adverb may not, however, be placed between a verb and its direct object.

▶ Mother wrapped ~~carefully~~ the gift. *carefully.*

> The adverb *carefully* may be placed at the beginning or at the end of this sentence or before the verb. It cannot appear after the verb because the verb is followed by the direct object *the gift*.

 GRAMMAR CHECKERS do not flag problems with the placement of adjectives and adverbs. They can, however, flag a few other problems with adjectives and adverbs. See the grammar checker advice on page 216.

EXERCISE 31-2

Using the chart on page 265, arrange the following modifiers and nouns in their proper order. Answers to lettered items appear in the back of the book. Example:

two new French racing bicycles
new, French, two, bicycles, racing

a. woman, young, an, Vietnamese, attractive
b. dedicated, a, priest, Catholic
c. old, her, sweater, blue, wool
d. delicious, Joe's, Scandinavian, bread
e. many, feeders, bird, wooden, ornate

1. round, two, marble, tables, large
2. several, yellow, tulips, tiny
3. a, sports, classic, car
4. courtyard, a, square, small, brick
5. charming, restaurants, Italian, several

31e Distinguish between present participles and past participles used as adjectives.

Both present and past participles may be used as adjectives. The present participle always ends in *-ing*. Past participles usually end in *-ed*, *-d*, *-en*, *-n*, or *-t*. (See 27a.)

PRESENT PARTICIPLES confusing, speaking

PAST PARTICIPLES confused, spoken

Participles used as adjectives can precede the nouns they modify; they can also follow linking verbs, in which case they describe the subject of the sentence. (See 58b.)

It was a *depressing* movie. Jim was a *depressed* young man.

The essay was *confusing*. The student was *confused*.

A present participle should describe a person or thing causing or stimulating an experience; a past participle should describe a person or thing undergoing an experience.

The lecturer was *boring* [not *bored*].

The audience was *bored* [not *boring*].

In the first example, the lecturer is causing boredom, not experiencing it. In the second example, the audience is experiencing boredom, not causing it.

The participles that cause the most trouble for nonnative speakers are those describing mental states:

annoying / annoyed	exhausting / exhausted
boring / bored	fascinating / fascinated
confusing / confused	frightening / frightened
depressing / depressed	satisfying / satisfied
exciting / excited	surprising / surprised

GRAMMAR CHECKERS do not flag problems with present and past participles used as adjectives. Not surprisingly, the programs have no way of knowing the meaning a writer intends. For example, both of the following sentences could be correct, depending on the writer's meaning: *My roommate was annoying. My roommate was annoyed.*

EXERCISE 31–3

Edit the following sentences for proper use of present and past participles. If a sentence is correct, write "correct" after it. Answers to lettered sentences appear in the back of the book. Example:

> *excited*
> **Danielle and Monica were very ~~exciting~~ to be going to a**
>   ^
> **Broadway show for the first time.**

a. Listening to everyone's complaints all day was irritated.
b. During the long lecture, many students appeared tiring.
c. He was not pleased with his grades last semester.
d. The violence in recent movies is often disgusted.
e. He has been amazed by the skill of his opponent in chess.

1. After doing a great deal of research, the scientist made a fascinated discovery.
2. That blackout was the most frightened experience I've ever had.
3. I couldn't concentrate on my homework because I was distracted.
4. The directions for the new board game seem extremely complicating.
5. Do you think acting is a fulfilled career?

31f Become familiar with common prepositions that show time and place.

The most frequently used prepositions in English are *at, by, for, from, in, of, on, to,* and *with.* Each of these prepositions has a variety of uses that must be learned gradually, in context.

Prepositions that indicate time and place can be difficult to master because the differences among them are subtle and idiomatic. The chart on the opposite page is limited to four troublesome prepositions that show time and place: *at, on, in,* and *by.*

At, on, in, and *by* to show time and place

Showing time

AT   *at* a specific time: *at* 7:20, *at* dawn, *at* dinner

ON   *on* a specific day or date: *on* Tuesday, *on* June 4

IN   *in* a part of a 24-hour period: *in* the afternoon, *in* the daytime [but *at* night]

   in a year or month: *in* 1999, *in* July

   in a period of time: finished *in* three hours

BY   *by* a specific time or date: *by* 4:15, *by* Christmas

Showing place

AT   *at* a meeting place or location: *at* home, *at* the club

   at the edge of something: sitting *at* the desk

   at the corner of something: turning *at* the intersection

   at a target: throwing the snowball *at* Lucy

ON   *on* a surface: placed *on* the table, hanging *on* the wall

   on a street: the house *on* Spring Street

   on an electronic medium: *on* television, *on* the Internet

IN   *in* an enclosed space: *in* the garage, *in* the envelope

   in a geographic location: *in* San Diego, *in* Texas

   in a print medium: *in* a book, *in* a magazine

BY   *by* a landmark: *by* the fence, *by* the flagpole

Not every possible use is listed in the chart, so don't be surprised when you encounter exceptions and idiomatic uses that you must learn one at a time. For example, in English we ride *in* a car but *on* a bus, train, or subway. And when we fly *on* (not *in*) a plane, we are not sitting on top of the plane.

GRAMMAR CHECKERS are of little or no help with prepositions showing time and place. The conventions of preposition use do not have the kind of mathematical precision that a computer program requires.

EXERCISE 31–4

In the following sentences, replace any prepositions that are not used correctly. If a sentence is correct, write "correct" after it. Answers to lettered sentences appear in the back of the book. Example:

> *at*
> The play begins ~~on~~ 7:20 P.M.
> ^

a. Whenever we eat at the Centerville Diner, we sit at a small table on the corner of the room.
b. In the 1980s, the gap between the rich and the poor in the United States became wider.
c. Usually she met with her patients on the afternoon, but in that day she stayed at home to take care of her son.
d. The clock is hanging on the wall on the dining room.
e. Our rabbi moved to the Northwest on 1994 and has been with our temple at Seattle since 1996.

1. Exhausted, Jay fell asleep on the couch in his room at the hotel.
2. I don't feel safe walking on my neighborhood at night.
3. If the train is on time it will arrive on six o'clock at the morning.
4. She licked the stamp, stuck it in the envelope, put the envelope on her pocket, and walked to the nearest mailbox.
5. The mailbox was in the intersection of Laidlaw Avenue and Williams Street.

Punctuation

32

The comma

The comma was invented to help readers. Without it, sentence parts can collide into one another unexpectedly, causing misreadings.

> **CONFUSING**   If you cook Elmer will do the dishes.
>
> **CONFUSING**   While we were eating a rattlesnake approached our campsite.

Add commas in the logical places (after *cook* and *eating*), and suddenly all is clear. No longer is Elmer being cooked, the rattlesnake being eaten.

Various rules have evolved to prevent such misreadings and to speed readers along through complex grammatical structures. Those rules are detailed in this section.

 GRAMMAR CHECKERS do not offer much advice about commas. They can tell you that a comma is usually used before *which* but not before *that* (see 32e), but they fail to flag most other missing or misused commas. For example, in an essay with ten missing commas and five misused commas, a grammar checker spotted only one missing comma (after the word *therefore*).

32a Use a comma before a coordinating conjunction joining independent clauses.

When a coordinating conjunction connects two or more independent clauses—word groups that could stand alone as separate sentences—a comma must precede it. There are seven coordinating conjunctions in English: *and, but, or, nor, for, so,* and *yet.*

A comma tells readers that one independent clause has come to a close and that another is about to begin.

▶ Nearly everyone has heard of love at first sight, but I fell in

love at first dance.

EXCEPTION: If the two independent clauses are short and there is no danger of misreading, the comma may be omitted.

The plane took off and we were on our way.

CAUTION: As a rule, do *not* use a comma to separate coordinate word groups that are not independent clauses. (See 33a.)

▶ A good money manager controls expenses/ and invests

surplus dollars to meet future needs.

The word group following *and* is not an independent clause; it is the second half of a compound predicate.

32b Use a comma after an introductory clause or phrase.

The most common introductory word groups are clauses and phrases functioning as adverbs. Such word groups usually tell when, where, how, why, or under what conditions the main action of the sentence occurred. (See 59a–59c.)

A comma tells readers that the introductory clause or phrase has come to a close and that the main part of the sentence is about to begin.

▶ When Irwin was ready to eat, his cat jumped onto the table.

Without the comma, readers may have Irwin eating his cat. The comma signals that *his cat* is the subject of a new clause, not part of the introductory one.

▶ Near a small stream at the bottom of the canyon, we discov-

ered an abandoned shelter.

The comma tells readers that the introductory prepositional phrase has come to a close.

EXCEPTION: The comma may be omitted after a short adverb clause or phrase if there is no danger of misreading.

In no time we were at 2,800 feet.

Sentences also frequently begin with participial phrases describing the noun or pronoun immediately following them. The comma tells readers that they are about to learn the identity of the person or thing described; therefore, the comma is usually required even when the phrase is short. (See 59c.)

▶ **Thinking his motorcade drive through Dallas was routine,**

President Kennedy smiled and waved at the crowds.

▶ **Buried under layers of younger rocks, the earth's oldest**

rocks contain no fossils.

NOTE: Other introductory word groups include transitional expressions and absolute phrases. (See 32f.)

EXERCISE 32–1

Add or delete commas where necessary in the following sentences. If a sentence is correct, write "correct" after it. Answers to lettered sentences appear in the back of the book. Example:

Because it rained all Labor Day, our picnic was rather soggy.

a. When we arrived at Salou's beach, we saw immediately that we were overdressed for the occasion.
b. The man at the next table complained loudly and the waiter stomped off in disgust.
c. If you complete the enclosed card, and return it within two weeks, you will receive a free breakfast during your stay.
d. Nursing is physically, and mentally demanding, yet the pay is low.
e. Uncle Swen's dulcimers disappeared as soon as he put them up for sale but he always kept one for himself.

1. When the runaway race car crashed the gas tank exploded.
2. He pushed the car beyond the toll gate and poured a bucket of water on the smoking hood.
3. Lighting the area like a second moon the helicopter circled the scene.

4. As the concert began we heard a tremendous explosion.
5. Many musicians of Bach's time played several instruments, but few mastered them as early or played with as much expression as Bach.

32c Use a comma between all items in a series.

When three or more items are presented in a series, those items should be separated from one another with commas. Items in a series may be single words, phrases, or clauses.

▶ Bubbles of air, leaves, ferns, bits of wood, and insects are

often found trapped in amber.

Although some writers view the comma between the last two items as optional, most experts advise using the comma because its omission can result in ambiguity or misreading.

▶ Uncle David willed me all of his property, houses, and

warehouses.

Did Uncle David will his property *and* houses *and* warehouses— or simply his property, consisting of houses and warehouses? If the former meaning is intended, a comma is necessary to prevent ambiguity.

32d Use a comma between coordinate adjectives not joined with *and*. Do not use a comma between cumulative adjectives.

When two or more adjectives each modify a noun separately, they are coordinate.

Mother has become a *strong, confident, independent* woman.

Adjectives are coordinate if they can be joined with *and* (strong *and* confident *and* independent) or if they can be scrambled (an *independent, strong, confident* woman).

Adjectives that do not modify the noun separately are cumulative.

Three large gray shapes moved slowly toward us.

We cannot insert the word *and* between cumulative adjectives (three *and* large *and* gray shapes). Nor can we scramble them (*gray three large* shapes).

COORDINATE ADJECTIVES

▶ Roberto is a warm, gentle, affectionate father.

CUMULATIVE ADJECTIVES

▶ Ira ordered a rich/chocolate/layer cake.

EXERCISE 32–2

Add or delete commas where necessary in the following sentences. If a sentence is correct, write "correct" after it. Answers to lettered sentences appear in the back of the book. Example:

We gathered our essentials, took off for the great outdoors,

and ignored the fact that it was Friday the 13th.

a. She wore a black silk cape, a rhinestone collar, satin gloves and high-tops.
b. An ambulance threaded its way through police cars, fire trucks and irate citizens.
c. City Café is noted for its spicy vegetarian dishes and its friendly efficient service.
d. When air-conditioning arrived in the workplace, it had a large measurable impact on productivity.
e. My cat's pupils had constricted to small black shining dots.

1. My brother and I found a dead garter snake, picked it up and placed it on Miss Eunice's doorstep.
2. For breakfast the children ordered cornflakes, English muffins with peanut butter and cherry Cokes.
3. It was a small, unimportant part, but I was happy to have it.
4. Cyril was clad in a luminous orange rain suit and a brilliant white helmet.
5. Anne Frank and thousands like her were forced to hide in attics, cellars and secret rooms in an effort to save their lives.

32e Use commas to set off nonrestrictive elements. Do not use commas to set off restrictive elements.

Word groups describing nouns or pronouns (adjective clauses, adjective phrases, and appositives) are restrictive or nonrestrictive. A *restrictive* element defines or limits the meaning of the word it modifies and is therefore essential to the meaning of the sentence. Because it contains essential information, a restrictive element is not set off with commas.

> **RESTRICTIVE**   For camp the children needed clothes *that were washable.*

If you remove a restrictive element from a sentence, the meaning changes significantly, becoming more general than you intended. The writer of the example sentence does not mean that the children needed clothes in general. The intended meaning is more limited: the children needed *washable* clothes.

A *nonrestrictive* element describes a noun or pronoun whose meaning has already been clearly defined or limited. Because it contains nonessential or parenthetical information, a nonrestrictive element is set off with commas.

> **NONRESTRICTIVE**   For camp the children needed sturdy shoes, *which were expensive.*

If you remove a nonrestrictive element from a sentence, the meaning does not change dramatically. Some meaning is lost, to be sure, but the defining characteristics of the person or thing described remain the same as before. The children needed *sturdy shoes,* and these happened to be expensive.

Adjective clauses

Adjective clauses are patterned like sentences, containing subjects and verbs, but they function within sentences as modifiers of nouns or pronouns. They always follow the word they modify, usually immediately. Adjective clauses begin with a relative pronoun (*who, whom, whose, which, that*) or with a relative adverb (*where, when*).

Nonrestrictive adjective clauses are set off with commas; restrictive adjective clauses are not.

NONRESTRICTIVE CLAUSE

▶ Ed's house, which is located on thirteen acres, was completely
       ^   ^

furnished with bats in the rafters and mice in the kitchen.

The clause *which is located on thirteen acres* does not restrict the meaning of *Ed's house,* so the information is nonessential.

RESTRICTIVE CLAUSE

▶ An office manager for a corporation/that had government

contracts/asked her supervisor whether she could reprimand

her co-workers for smoking.

Because the clause *that had government contracts* identifies the corporation, the information is essential.

NOTE: Use *that* only with restrictive clauses. Many writers prefer to use *which* only with nonrestrictive clauses, but usage varies.

Phrases functioning as adjectives

Prepositional or verbal phrases functioning as adjectives may be restrictive or nonrestrictive. Nonrestrictive phrases are set off with commas; restrictive phrases are not.

NONRESTRICTIVE PHRASE

▶ The helicopter, with its 100,000-candlepower spotlight
              ^

illuminating the area, circled above.
                   ^

The *with* phrase is nonessential because its purpose is not to specify which of two or more helicopters is being discussed.

RESTRICTIVE PHRASE

▶ One corner of the attic was filled with newspapers/dating

from the turn of the century.

Dating from the turn of the century restricts the meaning of *newspapers,* so the comma should be omitted.

Appositives

An appositive is a noun or noun phrase that renames a nearby noun. Nonrestrictive appositives are set off with commas; restrictive appositives are not.

NONRESTRICTIVE APPOSITIVE

▶ Norman Mailer's first novel, *The Naked and the Dead,* was a

best-seller.

The term *first* restricts the meaning to one novel, so the appositive *The Naked and the Dead* is nonrestrictive.

RESTRICTIVE APPOSITIVE

▶ The song "Fire It Up" was blasted out of amplifiers ten

feet tall.

Once they've read *song,* readers still don't know precisely which song the writer means. The appositive following *song* restricts its meaning.

EXERCISE 32–3

Add or delete commas where necessary in the following sentences. If a sentence is correct, write "correct" after it. Answers to lettered sentences appear in the back of the book. Example:

My youngest sister, who plays left wing on the team, now

lives at The Sands, a beach house near Los Angeles.

a. B. B. King and Lucille, his customized black Gibson have electrified audiences all over the world.
b. The United States Coast Survey which was established in 1807 was the first scientific agency in this country.
c. The woman running for the council seat in the fifth district has a long history of community service.
d. Shakespeare's tragedy, *King Lear,* was given a splendid performance by the actor, Laurence Olivier.
e. Douglass's first autobiography, *Narrative of the Life of Frederick Douglass, an American Slave,* was published in 1845.

1. I had the pleasure of talking to a woman who had just returned from India where she had lived for ten years.
2. Sally's best friend Sid Phillips has been playing the guitar since the age of seven.
3. The gentleman waiting for a prescription is Mr. Rhee.
4. *Where the Wild Things Are,* the 1964 Caldecott Medal winner, is my nephew's favorite book.
5. The flame crawled up a few blades of grass to reach a low-hanging palmetto branch which quickly ignited.

32f Use commas to set off transitional and parenthetical expressions, absolute phrases, and elements expressing contrast.

Transitional expressions

Transitional expressions serve as bridges between sentences or parts of sentences. They include conjunctive adverbs such as *however, therefore,* and *moreover* and transitional phrases such as *for example, as a matter of fact,* and *in other words.* (For more complete lists, see 34b.)

When a transitional expression appears between independent clauses in a compound sentence, it is preceded by a semicolon and is usually followed by a comma. (See 34b.)

▶ Natural foods are not always salt free; for example, celery

contains more sodium than most people would imagine.

When a transitional expression appears at the beginning of a sentence or in the middle of an independent clause, it is usually set off with commas.

▶ As a matter of fact, nationalism is a relatively modern

concept.

▶ Rock and roll may be here to stay; the sad truth for some

rock musicians, however, is that their hearing may not be.

EXCEPTION: If a transitional expression blends smoothly with the rest of the sentence, calling for little or no pause in reading, it does not need to be set off with a comma. Expressions such as *also, at least, certainly, consequently, indeed, of course, moreover, no doubt, perhaps, then,* and *therefore* do not always call for a pause.

> Alice's bicycle is broken; *therefore* you will need to borrow Sue's.

NOTE: The conjunctive adverb *however* always calls for a pause, but it should not be confused with *however* meaning "no matter how," which does not: *However hard Bill tried, he could not match his previous record.*

Parenthetical expressions

Expressions that are distinctly parenthetical should be set off with commas. Providing supplemental information, they interrupt the flow of a sentence or appear at the end as afterthoughts.

▶ Evolution, as far as we know, doesn't work this way.

▶ The bass weighed about twelve pounds, give or take a few

ounces.

Absolute phrases

An absolute phrase, which modifies the whole sentence, usually consists of a noun followed by a participle or participial phrase. (See 59e.) Absolute phrases may appear at the beginning or at the end of a sentence. Wherever they appear, they should be set off with commas.

▶ Our grant having been approved, we were at last able to

begin the archaeological dig.

▶ Elvis Presley made music industry history in the 1950s,

his records having sold more than ten million copies.

In the first example, the absolute phrase appears at the beginning of the sentence; in the second example, it appears at the end.

CAUTION: Do not insert a comma between the noun and participle of an absolute construction.

▶ The next day,/being a school day, we turned down the

invitation.

Contrasted elements

Sharp contrasts beginning with words such as *not, never,* and *unlike* are set off with commas.

▶ The Epicurean philosophers sought mental, not bodily,

pleasures.

▶ Unlike Robert, Celia loved dance contests.

32g Use commas to set off nouns of direct address, the words *yes* and *no*, interrogative tags, and mild interjections.

▶ Forgive us, Dr. Spock, for reprimanding Jason.

▶ Yes, the loan will probably be approved.

▶ The film was faithful to the book, wasn't it?

▶ Well, cases like these are difficult to decide.

32h Use commas with expressions such as *he said* to set off direct quotations. (See also 37f.)

▶ Naturalist Arthur Cleveland Bent remarked, "In part the

peregrine declined unnoticed because it is not adorable."

▶ "Convictions are more dangerous foes of truth than lies,"

wrote philosopher Friedrich Nietzsche.

32i Use commas with dates, addresses, titles, and numbers.

Dates

In dates, the year is set off from the rest of the sentence with a pair of commas.

▶ On December 12, 1890, orders were sent out for the arrest

of Sitting Bull.

EXCEPTIONS: Commas are not needed if the date is inverted or if only the month and year are given.

> The recycling plan went into effect on 15 April 1999.

> January 1971 was an extremely cold month, according to the *World Almanac*.

Addresses

The elements of an address or place name are separated by commas. A zip code, however, is not preceded by a comma.

▶ John Lennon was born in Liverpool, England, in 1940.

▶ Please send the package to Greg Tarvin at 708 Spring Street,

Washington, Illinois 61571.

Titles

If a title follows a name, separate it from the rest of the sentence with a pair of commas.

▶ Sandra Belinsky, M.D., has been appointed to the board.

Punctuation

Numbers

In numbers more than four digits long, use commas to separate the numbers into groups of three, starting from the right. In numbers four digits long, a comma is optional.

> 3,500 [or 3500]
> 100,000
> 5,000,000

EXCEPTIONS: Do not use commas in street numbers, zip codes, telephone numbers, or years.

32j Use a comma to prevent confusion.

In certain contexts, a comma is necessary to prevent confusion. If the writer has omitted a word or phrase, for example, a comma may be needed to signal the omission.

▶ To err is human; to forgive, divine.
   ∧

If two words in a row echo each other, a comma may be needed for ease of reading.

▶ All of the catastrophes that we had feared might happen,
   ∧

   happened.

Sometimes a comma is needed to prevent readers from grouping words in ways that do not match the writer's intention.

▶ Patients who can, walk up and down the halls several times
   ∧

   a day.

EXERCISE 32–4: ALL USES OF THE COMMA

Add or delete commas where necessary in the following sentences. If a sentence is correct, write "correct" after it. Answers to lettered sentences appear in the back of the book. Example:

> "Yes, Virginia, there is a Santa Claus," wrote the editor.
>   ∧

a. April 16, 1999 is the final deadline for all applications.
b. The coach having bawled us out thoroughly, we left the locker room with his last harsh words ringing in our ears.
c. Good technique does not guarantee however, that the power you develop will be sufficient for Kyok Pa competition.
d. We all piled into Sadiq's car which we affectionately referred to as the "Blue Goose."
e. As a matter of fact our sales have far exceeded initial projections.

1. Mr. Mundy was born on July 22, 1939 in Arkansas, where his family had lived for four generations.
2. Swords flashing, our heroes dashed into action.
3. President Lincoln's original intention was to save the Union, not to destroy slavery.
4. We pulled into the first apartment complex we saw, and slowly patrolled the parking lots.
5. Eating raw limpets, I found out, is like trying to eat art gum erasers.
6. Fortunately science is creating many alternatives to research performed on animals.
7. While the machine was printing the oversized paper jammed.
8. "The last flight" she said with a sigh "went out five minutes before I arrived at the airport."
9. The Rio Grande, the border between Texas and Mexico lay before us. It was a sluggish mud-filled meandering stream that gave off an odor akin to sewage.
10. Pittsburgh, Pennsylvania is the home of several fine colleges and universities.

33

Unnecessary commas

Many common misuses of the comma result from an incomplete understanding of the major comma rules presented in section 32. In particular, writers frequently form misconceptions about rules 32a–32e, either extending the rules inappropriately or misinterpreting them. Such misconceptions can lead to the errors described in 33a–33e; rules 33f–33h list other common misuses of the comma.

33a Do not use a comma between compound elements that are not independent clauses.

Though a comma should be used before a coordinating conjunction joining independent clauses (see 32a), this rule should not be extended to other compound word groups.

▶ Marie Curie discovered radium,/and later applied her work

on radioactivity to medicine.

And links two verbs in a compound predicate: *discovered* and *applied*.

▶ Jake still doesn't realize that his illness is serious,/and

that he will have to alter his diet to improve his chances of

survival.

And links two subordinate clauses, each beginning with *that*.

33b Do not use a comma after a phrase that begins an inverted sentence.

Though a comma belongs after most introductory phrases (see 32b), it does not belong after phrases that begin an inverted sentence. In an inverted sentence, the subject follows the verb, and a phrase that ordinarily would follow the verb is moved to the beginning (see 58c).

▶ At the bottom of the sound,/lies a ship laden with gold

doubloons.

33c Do not use a comma before the first or after the last item in a series.

Though commas are required between items in a series (32c), do not place them either before or after the whole series.

▶ Other causes of asthmatic attacks are,/stress, change in

temperature, humidity, and cold air.

▶ Ironically, this job that appears so glamorous, carefree, and

easy,/carries a high degree of responsibility.

33d Do not use a comma between cumulative adjectives, between an adjective and a noun, or between an adverb and an adjective.

Commas are required between coordinate adjectives (those that can be joined with *and*), but they do not belong between cumulative adjectives (those that cannot be joined with *and*). (For a full discussion, see 32d.)

▶ In the corner of the closet we found an old,/maroon hatbox

from Sears.

A comma should never be used between an adjective and the noun that follows it.

▶ It was a senseless, dangerous,/mission.

Nor should a comma be used between an adverb and an adjective that follows it.

▶ The Hurst Home is unsuitable as a mental facility for

severely,/disturbed youths.

33e Do not use commas to set off restrictive or mildly parenthetical elements.

Restrictive elements are modifiers or appositives that restrict the meaning of the nouns they follow. Because they are essential to the meaning of the sentence, they are not set off with commas. (For a full discussion of both restrictive and nonrestrictive elements, see 32e.)

▶ Drivers,/who think they own the road,/make cycling a

dangerous sport.

The modifier *who think they own the road* restricts the meaning of *Drivers* and is therefore essential to the meaning of the sentence. Putting commas around the *who* clause falsely suggests that all drivers think they own the road.

▶ Margaret Mead's book,/*Coming of Age in Samoa,*/stirred up

considerable controversy when it was published.

Since Mead wrote more than one book, the appositive contains information essential to the meaning of the sentence.

Although commas should be used with distinctly parenthetical expressions (see 32f), do not use them to set off elements that are only mildly parenthetical.

▶ Charisse believes that the Internet is,/essentially,/a bastion of

advertising.

33f Do not use a comma to set off a concluding adverb clause that is essential to the meaning of the sentence.

When adverb clauses introduce a sentence, they are nearly always followed by a comma (see 32b). When they conclude a sentence, however, they are not set off by commas if their content is essential to the meaning of the earlier part of the sentence. Adverb clauses beginning with *after, as soon as, because, before, if, since, unless, until,* and *when* are usually essential.

▶ Don't visit Paris at the height of the tourist season,/unless

you have booked hotel reservations.

Without the *unless* clause, the meaning of the sentence would be broader than the writer intended.

When a concluding adverb clause is nonessential, it should be preceded by a comma. Clauses beginning with *although, even though, though,* and *whereas* are usually nonessential.

▶ The lecture seemed to last only a short time⌄ although the

clock said it had gone on for more than an hour.

33g Do not use a comma to separate a verb from its subject or object.

A sentence should flow from subject to verb to object without unnecessary pauses. Commas may appear between these major sentence elements only when a specific rule calls for them.

▶ Zoos large enough to give the animals freedom to roam⁄are

becoming more popular.

▶ Francesca explained to him⁄that she was busy and would

see him later.

In the first sentence, the comma should not separate the subject, *Zoos*, from the verb, *are becoming.* In the second sentence, the comma should not separate the verb, *explained*, from its object, the subordinate clause *that she was busy and would see him later.*

33h Avoid other common misuses of the comma.

Do not use a comma in the following situations.

AFTER A COORDINATING CONJUNCTION (*AND, BUT, OR, NOR, FOR, SO, YET*)

▶ Occasionally soap operas are performed live, but⁄more often

they are taped.

AFTER *SUCH AS* OR *LIKE*

▶ Many shade-loving plants, such as⁄begonias, impatiens, and

coleus, can add color to a shady garden.

BEFORE *THAN*

▶ Touring Crete was more thrilling for us,/than visiting the

Greek islands frequented by rich Europeans.

AFTER *ALTHOUGH*

▶ Although,/the air was balmy, the water was too cold for

swimming.

BEFORE A PARENTHESIS

▶ At MCI Sylvia began at the bottom,/(with only three and a

half walls and a swivel chair), but within five years she had

been promoted to supervisor.

TO SET OFF AN INDIRECT (REPORTED) QUOTATION

▶ Samuel Goldwyn once said,/that a verbal contract isn't worth

the paper it's written on.

WITH A QUESTION MARK OR AN EXCLAMATION POINT

▶ "Why don't you try it?,/" she coaxed. "You can't do any worse

than the rest of us."

EXERCISE 33–1

Delete commas where necessary in the following sentences. If a sentence is correct, write "correct" after it. Answers to lettered sentences
appear in the back of the book. Example:

Loretta Lynn has paved the way for artists such as,/Reba

McEntire and Wynonna Judd.

a. We'd rather spend our money on blue-chip stocks, than speculate
on pork bellies.

b. Being prepared for the worst, is one way to cope.
c. Please telephone me if you cannot send the information promptly, or if you have any questions.
d. The Marx Brothers made delightful, hilarious, movies.
e. I quickly accepted the fact that I was, literally, in third-class quarters.

1. As a child growing up in Jamaica, I often daydreamed about life in the United States.
2. He wore a thick, black, wool coat over army fatigues.
3. Often public figures, (Michael Jackson is a good example) go to great lengths to guard their private lives.
4. She loved early spring flowers such as, crocuses, daffodils, forsythia, and irises.
5. On Pam's wrist, was a tattoo of a dragon chasing a tiger.
6. Mesquite, the hardest of the softwoods, grows primarily in the Southwest.
7. Male supremacy was assumed by my father, and accepted by my mother.
8. The kitchen was covered with black soot, that had been deposited by the wood-burning stove, which stood in the middle of the room.
9. The lieutenant reported to his captain, that all of his men were present and accounted for.
10. The streets that three hours later would be bumper to bumper with commuters, were quiet and empty except for a few prowling cats.

34

The semicolon

The semicolon is used to connect major sentence elements of equal grammatical rank.

GRAMMAR CHECKERS flag some, but not all, misused semicolons (34d). In addition, they can alert you to some run-on sentences (34a). However, they miss more run-on sentences than they identify, and they sometimes flag correct sentences as possible run-ons. (See also the grammar checker advice on p. 178.)

34a Use a semicolon between closely related independent clauses not joined with a coordinating conjunction.

When related independent clauses appear in one sentence, they are ordinarily linked with a comma and a coordinating conjunction (*and, but, or, nor, for, so, yet*). The coordinating conjunction signals the relation between the clauses. If the clauses are closely related and the relation is clear without a conjunction, they may be linked with a semicolon instead.

> Injustice is relatively easy to bear; what stings is justice.
> —H. L. Mencken

> When I was a boy, I was told that anybody could become president; I'm beginning to believe it.   —Clarence Darrow

A semicolon must be used whenever a coordinating conjunction has been omitted between independent clauses. To use merely a comma creates a kind of run-on sentence known as a comma splice. (See section 20.)

▶ In 1800, a traveler needed six weeks to get from New York

City to Chicago; in 1860, the trip by railroad took only
              ^

two days.

CAUTION: Do not overuse the semicolon as a means of revising run-on sentences. For other revision strategies, see 20a, 20c, and 20d.

34b Use a semicolon between independent clauses linked with a transitional expression.

Transitional expressions include conjunctive adverbs and transitional phrases.

CONJUNCTIVE ADVERBS
accordingly, also, anyway, besides, certainly, consequently, conversely, finally, furthermore, hence, however, incidentally, indeed, instead, likewise, meanwhile, moreover, nevertheless, next, nonetheless, otherwise, similarly, specifically, still, subsequently, then, therefore, thus

TRANSITIONAL PHRASES

after all, as a matter of fact, as a result, at any rate, at the same time, even so, for example, for instance, in addition, in conclusion, in fact, in other words, in the first place, on the contrary, on the other hand

When a transitional expression appears between independent clauses, it is preceded by a semicolon and usually followed by a comma.

▶ Many corals grow very gradually; in fact, the creation of a

coral reef can take centuries.

When a transitional expression appears in the middle or at the end of the second independent clause, the semicolon goes *between the clauses.*

▶ Most singers gain fame through hard work and dedication;

Evita, however, found other means.

Transitional expressions should not be confused with the coordinating conjunctions *and, but, or, nor, for, so,* and *yet,* which are preceded by a comma when they link independent clauses. (See 32a.)

34c Use a semicolon between items in a series containing internal punctuation.

▶ Classic science fiction sagas are *Star Trek,* with Mr. Spock

and his large pointed ears; *Battlestar Galactica,* with its

Cylon Raiders; and *Star Wars,* with Han Solo, Luke

Skywalker, and Darth Vader.

Without the semicolons, the reader would have to sort out the major groupings, distinguishing between important and less important pauses according to the logic of the sentence. By inserting semicolons at the major breaks, the writer does this work for the reader.

34d Avoid common misuses of the semicolon.

Do not use a semicolon in the following situations.

BETWEEN A SUBORDINATE CLAUSE AND THE REST OF THE SENTENCE

▶ Unless you brush your teeth within ten or fifteen minutes after eating⨉, brushing does almost no good.

BETWEEN AN APPOSITIVE AND THE WORD IT REFERS TO

▶ Another delicious dish is the chef's special⨉, a roasted duck rubbed with spices and stuffed with wild rice.

TO INTRODUCE A LIST

▶ Some of my favorite film stars have home pages on the Web⨉: John Travolta, Susan Sarandon, Brad Pitt, and Emma Thompson.

BETWEEN INDEPENDENT CLAUSES JOINED BY *AND, BUT, OR, NOR, FOR, SO,* OR *YET*

▶ Five of the applicants had worked with spreadsheets⨉, but only one was familiar with database management.

EXCEPTIONS: If at least one of the independent clauses contains internal punctuation, you may use a semicolon even though the clauses are joined with a coordinating conjunction.

> As a vehicle [the model T] was hard-working, commonplace, and heroic; and it often seemed to transmit those qualities to the person who rode in it.   —E. B. White

Although a comma would also be correct in this sentence, the semicolon is more effective, for it indicates the relative weights of the pauses.

Occasionally, a semicolon may be used to emphasize a sharp contrast or a firm distinction between clauses joined with a coordinating conjunction.

> We hate some persons because we do not know them; and we will not know them because we hate them.
>
> — Charles Caleb Colton

EXERCISE 34–1

Add commas or semicolons where needed in the following well-known quotations. If a sentence is correct, write "correct" after it. Answers to lettered sentences appear in the back of the book. Example:

> **If an animal does something, we call it instinct; if we do the**
> ^   ^
>
> **same thing, we call it intelligence.**   —Will Cuppy
>   ^

a. When a woman behaves like a man why doesn't she behave like a nice man?   —Edith Evans

b. Do not ask me to be kind just ask me to act as though I were.   —Jules Renard

c. Don't talk about yourself it will be done when you leave.   —Wilson Mizner

d. The only sensible ends of literature are first the pleasurable toil of writing second the gratification of one's family and friends and lastly the solid cash.   —Nathaniel Hawthorne

e. I do not rule Russia ten thousand clerks do.   —Nicholas I

1. Everyone is a genius at least once a year a real genius has his [or her] original ideas closer together.   —G. C. Lichtenberg

2. When choosing between two evils I always like to try the one I've never tried before.   —Mae West

3. Once the children were in the house the air became more vivid and more heated every object in the house grew more alive.   —Mary Gordon

4. We don't know what we want but we are ready to bite someone to get it.   —Will Rogers

5. I've been rich and I've been poor rich is better.   —Sophie Tucker

EXERCISE 34–2

Edit the following sentences to correct errors in the use of the comma and the semicolon. If a sentence is correct, write "correct" after it. Answers to lettered sentences appear in the back of the book. Example:

> **Love is blind; envy has its eyes wide open.**
>   ^

a. At the outbreak of the American Civil War, many believed that the conflict would be over in a month, others had a dreadful premonition of the future.

b. America has been called a country of pragmatists; although the American devotion to ideals is legendary.

c. The first requirement is honesty, everything else follows.

d. I am not fond of opera, I must admit; however, that I was greatly moved by *Les Misérables*.

e. The Theban plays by Sophocles consist of *Antigone,* which deals with the conscience and the state, *King Oedipus,* which explores the question of fate and circumstance, and *Oedipus at Colonus,* which presents themes of suffering and redemption.

1. The scientists were fascinated by the species *Argyroneta aquatica;* a spider that lives underwater.

2. Martin Luther King, Jr., had not intended to be a preacher, initially, he had planned to become a lawyer.

3. Severe, unremitting pain is a ravaging force; especially when the patient tries to hide it from others.

4. The Victorians avoided the subject of sex but were obsessed with death, our contemporaries are obsessed with sex but avoid thinking about death.

5. Some educators believe that African American history should be taught in separate courses, others prefer to see it integrated into survey courses.

35

The colon

The colon is used primarily to call attention to the words that follow it.

 GRAMMAR CHECKERS can catch some misused colons. They are less helpful at telling you when you may need a colon. For example, the programs failed to note that a colon (not a comma) belongs after the word *items* in this sentence: *Every camper should consider carrying the following items, a first-aid kit, a Swiss army knife, and a flashlight.*

35a Use a colon after an independent clause to direct attention to a list, an appositive, or a quotation.

A LIST
The daily routine should include at least the following: twenty knee bends, fifty sit-ups, fifteen leg lifts, and five minutes of running in place.

AN APPOSITIVE
My roommate is guilty of two of the seven deadly sins: gluttony and sloth.

A QUOTATION
Consider the words of John F. Kennedy: "Ask not what your country can do for you; ask what you can do for your country."

For other ways of introducing quotations, see 37f.

35b Use a colon between independent clauses if the second summarizes or explains the first.

Faith is like love: It cannot be forced.

NOTE: When an independent clause follows a colon, it may begin with a lowercase or a capital letter.

35c Use a colon after the salutation in a formal letter, to indicate hours and minutes, to show proportions, between a title and subtitle, and between city and publisher in bibliographic entries.

Dear Sir or Madam:

5:30 P.M. (or p.m.)

The ratio of women to men was 2:1.

The Glory of Hera: Greek Mythology and the Greek Family

Boston: Bedford, 1997

NOTE: In biblical references, a colon is ordinarily used between chapter and verse (Luke 2:14). The Modern Language Association recommends a period instead (Luke 2.14).

35d Avoid common misuses of the colon.

A colon must be preceded by a full independent clause. Therefore, avoid using it in the following situations.

BETWEEN A VERB AND ITS OBJECT OR COMPLEMENT

▶ Some important vitamins found in vegetables are⫶ vitamin A, thiamine, niacin, and vitamin C.

BETWEEN A PREPOSITION AND ITS OBJECT

▶ The heart's two pumps each consist of⫶ an upper chamber, or atrium, and a lower chamber, or ventricle.

AFTER *SUCH AS, INCLUDING,* OR *FOR EXAMPLE*

▶ The trees on our campus include many fine Japanese specimens such as⫶ black pines, ginkgos, and weeping cherries.

EXERCISE 35–1

Edit the following sentences to correct errors in the use of the comma, the semicolon, or the colon. If a sentence is correct, write "correct" after it. Answers to lettered sentences appear in the back of the book. Example:

> Smiling confidently, the young man stated his major goal in
>
> life⫶ to be secretary of agriculture before he was thirty.
>   ∧

a. The Greeks were right, character is fate.
b. Some examples of reptiles are: lizards, snakes, crocodiles, and turtles.
c. There are only three seasons here: winter, July, and August.
d. For example: Teddy Roosevelt once referred to the wolf as "the beast of waste and desolation."
e. Remember the words of Thomas Gray: "The paths of glory lead but to the grave."

1. The patient survived for one reason, the medics got to her in time.
2. While traveling through France, Fiona visited: the Loire Valley, Chartres, the Louvre, and the McDonald's stand at the foot of the Eiffel Tower.
3. Minds are like parachutes, they function only when open.
4. Carl Sandburg once asked three important questions, "Who paid for my freedom? What was the price? And am I somehow beholden?"
5. Robin sorts the crabs into three groups: males, females, and crabs about to molt.

36

The apostrophe

GRAMMAR CHECKERS can flag some, but not all, missing or misused apostrophes. They can catch missing apostrophes in common contractions, such as *don't*. They can also flag some problems with possessives, although they miss others. The programs usually phrase their advice cautiously, telling you that you have a "possible possessive error" in a phrase such as *a days work* or *sled dogs feet*. Therefore, you—not the grammar checker— must decide whether to add an apostrophe and, if so, whether to put it before or after the *-s*.

36a Use an apostrophe to indicate that a noun is possessive.

Possessive nouns usually indicate ownership, as in *Tim's hat* or *the lawyer's desk*. Frequently, however, ownership is only loosely implied: *the tree's roots, a day's work*. If you are not sure whether a noun is possessive, try turning it into an *of* phrase: *the roots of the tree, the work of a day*.

When to add -'s

1. If the noun does not end in *-s*, add *-'s*.

   Roy managed to climb out on the driver's side.

   Thank you for refunding the children's money.

2. If the noun is singular and ends in -*s,* add -*'s.*

> Lois's sister spent last year in India.

EXCEPTION: If pronunciation would be awkward with the added -*'s,* some writers use only the apostrophe. Either use is acceptable.

> Sophocles' plays are among my favorites.

When to add only an apostrophe

If the noun is plural and ends in -*s,* add only an apostrophe.

> Both diplomats' briefcases were stolen.

Joint possession

To show joint possession, use -*'s* or (-*s'*) with the last noun only; to show individual possession, make all nouns possessive.

> Have you seen Joyce and Greg's new camper?

> John's and Marie's expectations of marriage couldn't have been more different.

In the first sentence, Joyce and Greg jointly own one camper. In the second sentence, John and Marie individually have different expectations.

Compound nouns

If a noun is compound, use -*'s* (or -*s'*) with the last element.

> My father-in-law's sculpture won first place.

36b Use an apostrophe and -*s* to indicate that an indefinite pronoun is possessive.

Indefinite pronouns refer to no specific person or thing: *everyone, someone, no one, something.* (See 57b.)

> This diet will improve almost anyone's health.

36c Use an apostrophe to mark omissions in contractions and numbers.

In contractions the apostrophe takes the place of missing letters.

It's a shame that Frank can't go on the tour.

It's stands for *it is*, *can't* for *cannot*.

The apostrophe is also used to mark the omission of the first two digits of a year (*the class of '99*) or years (*the '60s generation*).

We'll never forget the blizzard of '96.

36d Use an apostrophe and -s to pluralize numbers mentioned as numbers, letters mentioned as letters, words mentioned as words, and abbreviations.

Margarita skated nearly perfect figure 8's.

The bleachers in our section were marked with large red *J*'s.

We've heard enough *maybe*'s.

You must ask to see their I.D.'s.

Notice that the *-s* is not italicized when used with an italicized number, letter, or word.

EXCEPTION: An *-s* alone is often added to the years in a decade: *the 1980s.*

MLA NOTE: The Modern Language Association recommends no apostrophe in plurals of numbers and abbreviations: *figure 8s, VCRs.*

36e Avoid common misuses of the apostrophe.

Do not use an apostrophe in the following situations.

WITH NOUNS THAT ARE NOT POSSESSIVE

► Some ~~outpatient's~~ *outpatients* are given special parking permits.

IN THE POSSESSIVE PRONOUNS *ITS, WHOSE, HIS, HERS, OURS, YOURS,* AND *THEIRS*

▶ Each area has ~~it's~~ *its* own conference room.

It's means "it is." The possessive pronoun *its* contains no apostrophe despite the fact that it is possessive.

▶ This course was taught by a professional florist ~~who's~~ *whose*

technique was oriental.

Who's means "who is." The possessive pronoun *whose* contains no apostrophe despite the fact that it is possessive.

EXERCISE 36–1

Edit the following sentences to correct errors in the use of the apostrophe. If a sentence is correct, write "correct" after it. Answers to lettered sentences appear in the back of the book. Example:

Marietta lived above the only bar in town, Smiling ~~Jacks.~~ *Jack's.*

a. In a democracy, anyones vote counts as much as mine.
b. He received two A's, three B's, and a C.
c. The puppy's favorite activity was chasing it's tail.
d. After we bought J. J. the latest style pants and shirts, he decided that last years faded, ragged jeans were perfect for all occasions.
e. The snow does'nt rise any higher than the horse's fetlocks. [*More than one horse*]

1. For a bus driver, complaints, fare disputes, and robberies are all part of a days work.
2. We cleaned four years accumulation of trash out of the attic; its amazing how much junk can pile up.
3. Three teenage son's can devour about as much food as four full-grown field hands. The only difference is that they dont do half as much work.
4. Luck is an important element in a rock musicians career.
5. My sister-in-law's quilts are being shown at the Fendrick Gallery.

37

Quotation marks

 GRAMMAR CHECKERS are good at telling you to put commas and periods inside quotation marks; they are also fairly good at flagging "unbalanced quotes," an opening quotation mark that is not balanced with a closing quotation mark. The programs can't tell you, however, when you should or shouldn't use quotation marks.

37a Use quotation marks to enclose direct quotations.

Direct quotations of a person's words, whether spoken or written, must be in quotation marks.

> "A foolish consistency is the hobgoblin of little minds," wrote Ralph Waldo Emerson.

CAUTION: Do not use quotation marks around indirect quotations. An indirect quotation reports someone's ideas without using that person's exact words.

> Ralph Waldo Emerson believed that consistency for its own sake is the mark of a small mind.

NOTE: In dialogue, begin a new paragraph to mark a change in speaker.

> "Mom, his name is Willie, not William. A thousand times I've told you, it's *Willie*."
> "Willie is a derivative of William, Lester. Surely his birth certificate doesn't have Willie on it, and I like calling people by their proper names."
> "Yes, it does, ma'am. My mother named me Willie K. Mason." —Gloria Naylor

If a single speaker utters more than one paragraph, introduce each paragraph with quotation marks, but do not use closing quotation marks until the end of the speech.

37b Set off long quotations of prose or poetry by indenting.

When a quotation of prose runs to more than four typed lines in your paper, set it off by indenting one inch (or ten spaces) from the left margin. Quotation marks are not required because the indented format tells readers that the quotation is taken word for word from a source. Long quotations are ordinarily introduced by a sentence ending with a colon.

> After making an exhaustive study of the historical record, James Horan evaluates Billy the Kid like this:
>
> > The portrait that emerges of [the Kid] from the thousands of pages of affi-davits, reports, trial transcripts, his letters, and his testimony is neither the mythical Robin Hood nor the stereotyped adenoidal moron and pathological killer. Rather Billy appears as a disturbed, lonely young man, honest, loyal to his friends, dedicated to his beliefs, and betrayed by our institutions and the cor-rupt, ambitious, and compromising politi-cians of his time. (158)

The number in parentheses is a citation handled according to the Modern Language Association style. (See 53a.)

NOTE: When you quote two or more paragraphs from the source, indent the first line of each paragraph an additional one-half inch (or five spaces).

When you quote more than three lines of a poem, set the quoted lines off from the text by indenting one inch (or ten spaces) from the left margin. Use no quotation marks unless they appear in the poem itself. (To quote two or three lines of poetry, see 39e.)

> Although many anthologizers "modernize" her punctu-ation, Emily Dickinson relied heavily on dashes,

using them, perhaps, as a musical device. Here, for example, is the original version of the opening stanza from "The Snake":

> A narrow Fellow in the Grass
> Occasionally rides--
> You may have met Him--did you not
> His notice sudden is--

NOTE: The American Psychological Association has slightly different guidelines for setting off long quotations. (See 56c.)

37c Use single quotation marks to enclose a quotation within a quotation.

According to Paul Eliott, Eskimo hunters "chant an ancient magic song to the seal they are after: 'Beast of the sea! Come and place yourself before me in the early morning!' "

37d Use quotation marks around the titles of short works: newspaper and magazine articles, poems, short stories, songs, episodes of television and radio programs, and chapters or subdivisions of books.

Katherine Mansfield's "The Garden Party" provoked a lively discussion in our short-story class last night.

NOTE: Titles of books, plays, Web sites, television and radio programs, and films and names of magazines and newspapers are put in italics or underlined. (See 42a.)

37e Quotation marks may be used to set off words used as words.

Although words used as words are ordinarily underlined or italicized (see 42d), quotation marks are also acceptable. Just be sure to follow consistent practice throughout a paper.

The words "accept" and "except" are frequently confused.

The words *accept* and *except* are frequently confused.

37f Use punctuation with quotation marks according to convention.

This section describes the conventions used by American publishers in placing various marks of punctuation inside or outside quotation marks. It also explains how to punctuate when introducing quoted material.

Periods and commas

Always place periods and commas inside quotation marks.

> "This is a stick-up," said the well-dressed young couple. "We want all your money."

This rule applies to single quotation marks as well as double quotation marks. (See 37c.) It also applies to all uses of quotation marks: for quoted material, for titles of works, and for words used as words.

EXCEPTION: In the Modern Language Association's style of parenthetical in-text citations (see 53a), the period follows the citation in parentheses.

> James M. McPherson comments approvingly that the Whigs "were not averse to extending the blessings of American liberty, even to Mexicans and Indians" (48).

Colons and semicolons

Put colons and semicolons outside quotation marks.

> Harold wrote, "I regret that I am unable to attend the fundraiser for AIDS research"; his letter, however, came with a substantial contribution.

Question marks and exclamation points

Put question marks and exclamation points inside quotation marks unless they apply to the whole sentence.

> Contrary to tradition, bedtime at my house is marked by "Mommy, can I tell you a story now?"

> Have you heard the old proverb "Do not climb the hill until you reach it"?

In the first sentence, the question mark applies only to the quoted question. In the second sentence, the question mark applies to the whole sentence.

NOTE: Modern Language Association parenthetical citations create a special problem. According to MLA, the question mark or exclamation point should appear before the quotation mark, and a period should follow the parenthetical citation: *Rosie Thomas asks, "Is nothing in life ever straight and clear, the way children see it?" (77).* But because the question mark and period look rather odd so close together, perhaps it is best to restructure such a sentence: *"Is nothing in life ever straight and clear, the way children see it?" asks Rosie Thomas (77).*

Introducing quoted material

After a word group introducing a quotation, choose a colon, a comma, or no punctuation at all, whichever is appropriate in context.

FORMAL INTRODUCTION   If a quotation has been formally introduced, a colon is appropriate. A formal introduction is a full independent clause, not just an expression such as *he said* or *she remarked.*

> Morrow views personal ads in the classifieds as an art form: "The personal ad is like a haiku of self-celebration, a brief solo played on one's own horn."

EXPRESSION SUCH AS *HE SAID*   If a quotation is introduced with an expression such as *he said* or *she remarked*—or if it is followed by such an expression—a comma is needed.

> Stephan Leacock once said, "I am a great believer in luck, and I find the harder I work the more I have of it."

> "You can be a little ungrammatical if you come from the right part of the country," writes Robert Frost.

BLENDED QUOTATION   When a quotation is blended into the writer's own sentence, either a comma or no punctuation is appropriate, depending on the way in which the quotation fits into the sentence structure.

The future champion could, as he put it, "float like a butterfly and sting like a bee."

Charles Hudson notes that the prisoners escaped "by squeezing through a tiny window eighteen feet above the floor of their cell."

BEGINNING OF SENTENCE   If a quotation appears at the beginning of a sentence, set it off with a comma unless the question ends with a question mark or an exclamation point.

"We shot them like dogs," boasted Davy Crockett, who was among Jackson's troops.

"What is it?" I asked, bracing myself.

INTERRUPTED QUOTATIONS   If a quoted sentence is interrupted by explanatory words, use commas to set off the explanatory words.

"A great many people think they are thinking," observed William James, "when they are merely rearranging their prejudices."

If two successive quoted sentences from the same source are interrupted by explanatory words, use a comma before the explanatory words and a period after them.

"I was a flop as a daily reporter," admitted E. B. White. "Every piece had to be a masterpiece—and before you knew it, Tuesday was Wednesday."

37g   Avoid common misuses of quotation marks.

Do not use quotation marks to draw attention to familiar slang, to disown trite expressions, or to justify an attempt at humor.

▶   Between Thanksgiving and Super Bowl Sunday, many

American wives become ⁄"football widows."⁊

Do not use quotation marks around indirect quotations. (See also 37a.)

▶ After leaving the scene of the domestic quarrel, the officer

said that/"he was due for a coffee break.\'

Do not use quotation marks around the title of your own essay.

EXERCISE 37–1

Add or delete quotation marks as needed and make any other necessary changes in punctuation in the following sentences. If a sentence is correct, write "correct" after it. Answers to lettered sentences appear in the back of the book. Example:

Bill Cosby once said, "I don't know the key to success, but
                    ∧
the key to failure is trying to please everyone."
                                              ∧

a. My commanding officer said, "If we wanted you to have children, we would have issued them to you."
b. As Emerson wrote in 1849, "I hate quotations. Tell me what you know.
c. Andrew Marvell's most famous poem, To His Coy Mistress, is a tightly structured argument.
d. "Ladies and gentlemen," said the emcee, "I am happy to present our guest speaker.
e. Historians Segal and Stineback note that the English settlers considered these epidemics "the hand of God making room for His followers in the "New World"."

1. "Order in the court! Order in the court!" shouts the judge, banging her wooden spoon on the kitchen table.
2. "Kick the tires and light the fires" exclaimed the pilot, giving me my cue to start the engines.
3. Kara looked hopelessly around the small locked room. "If only I were a flea," she thought, "I could get out of here."
4. After winning the lottery, Juanita said that "she would give half the money to charity."
5. At recess we stayed inside to play a card game we called "Truth or Dare".
6. Gloria Steinem once twisted an old proverb like this, "A woman without a man is like a fish without a bicycle."
7. These newly rich young men often buy expensive cars, designer shoes, and "classy" European suits.

8. As David Anable has written: "The time is approaching when we will be able to select the news we want to read from a pocket computer."
9. "Even when freshly washed and relieved of all obvious confections," says Fran Lebowitz, "children tend to be sticky."
10. Have you heard the Cowboy Junkies' rendition of Hank Williams's "I'm So Lonesome I Could Cry?"

38

End punctuation

 GRAMMAR CHECKERS occasionally flag sentences beginning with words like *Why* or *Are* and suggest that a question mark may be needed. On the whole, however, grammar checkers are of little help with end punctuation. Most notably, they neglect to tell you when your sentence is missing end punctuation.

38a The period

Use a period to end all sentences except direct questions or genuine exclamations. Also use periods in abbreviations according to convention.

To end sentences

Everyone knows that a period should be used to end most sentences. The only problems that arise concern the choice between a period and a question mark or between a period and an exclamation point.

If a sentence reports a question instead of asking it directly, it should end with a period, not a question mark.

▶ Celia asked whether the picnic would be canceled?.
                                               ^

If a sentence is not a genuine exclamation, it should end with a period, not an exclamation point.

▶ After years of working her way through school, Pat finally

graduated with high honors‌!͜.

In abbreviations

A period is conventionally used in abbreviations such as these:

Mr.	B.A.	B.C.	i.e.	A.M. (or a.m.)
Mrs.	M.A.	B.C.E.	e.g.	P.M. (or p.m.)
Ms.	Ph.D.	A.D.	etc.	
Dr.	R.N.	C.E.		

A period is not used with U.S. Postal Service abbreviations for states: MD, TX, CA.

Ordinarily a period is not used in abbreviations of organization names:

NATO	UNESCO	UCLA	PUSH	IBM
TVA	IRS	AFL-CIO	NBA	FTC
USA (*or* U.S.A.)	NAACP	SEC	FCC	NIH

Usage varies, however. When in doubt, consult a dictionary, a style manual, or a publication by the agency in question. Even the yellow pages can help.

NOTE: If a sentence ends with a period marking an abbreviation, do not add a second period.

MLA NOTE: MLA prefers omitting periods in abbreviations made up of capital letters (BC, CE, PM, LLD).

38b The question mark

Obviously a direct question should be followed by a question mark.

What is the horsepower of a 747 engine?

If a polite request is written in the form of a question, it too is usually followed by a question mark, although usage varies.

Would you please send me your catalog of lilies?

CAUTION: Do not use a question mark after an indirect question, one that is reported rather than asked directly. Use a period instead.

▶ He asked me who was teaching the mythology course~~?~~.

NOTE: Questions in a series may be followed by question marks even when they are not complete sentences.

> We wondered where Calamity had hidden this time. Under the sink? Behind the furnace? On top of the bookcase?

38c The exclamation point

Use an exclamation point after a word group or sentence that expresses exceptional feeling or deserves special emphasis.

> When Gloria entered the room, I switched on the lights and we all yelled, "Surprise!"

CAUTION: Do not overuse the exclamation point.

▶ In the fisherman's memory the fish lives on, increasing in length and weight with each passing year, until at last it is big enough to shade a fishing boat~~!~~.

This sentence doesn't need to be pumped up with an exclamation point. It is emphatic enough without it.

▶ Whenever I see Steffi lunging forward to put away an overhead smash, it might as well be me~~!~~. She does it just the way that I would!

The first exclamation point should be deleted so that the second one will have more force.

EXERCISE 38–1

Add appropriate end punctuation in the following paragraph.

Although I am generally rational, I am superstitious I never walk under ladders or put shoes on the table If I spill the salt, I go into frenzied calisthenics picking up the grains and tossing them over my left shoulder As a result of these curious activities, I've always wondered whether knowing the roots of superstitions would quell my irrational responses Superstition has it, for example, that one should never place a hat on the bed This superstition arises from a time when head lice were quite common and placing a guest's hat on the bed stood a good chance of spreading lice through the host's bed Doesn't this make good sense And doesn't it stand to reason that if I know that my guests don't have lice I shouldn't care where their hats go Of course it does It is fair to ask, then, whether I have changed my ways and place hats on beds Are you kidding I wouldn't put a hat on a bed if my life depended on it

39

Other punctuation marks: the dash, parentheses, brackets, the ellipsis mark, the slash

GRAMMAR CHECKERS rarely flag problems with the punctuation marks in this section: the dash, parentheses, brackets, the ellipsis mark, and the slash. (For a general discussion of what grammar checkers can and cannot do, see p. 32.)

39a The dash

When typing, use two hyphens to form a dash (--). Do not put spaces before or after the dash. (If your word processing program has what is known as an "em-dash," you may use it instead, with no space before or after it.) Dashes are used for the following purposes.

To set off parenthetical material that deserves emphasis

Everything that went wrong—from the peeping Tom at her window last night to my head-on collision today—was blamed on our move.

To set off appositives that contain commas

An appositive is a noun or noun phrase that renames a nearby noun. Ordinarily most appositives are set off with commas (32e), but when the appositive contains commas, a pair of dashes helps the readers see the relative importance of all the pauses.

> In my hometown the basic needs of people—food, clothing, and shelter—are less costly than in Los Angeles.

To prepare for a list, a restatement, an amplification, or a dramatic shift in tone or thought

> Along the wall are the bulk liquids—sesame seed oil, honey, safflower oil, and that half-liquid "peanuts only" peanut butter.

> Consider the amount of sugar in the average person's diet—104 pounds per year, 90 percent more than that consumed by our ancestors.

> Everywhere we looked there were little kids—a box of Cracker Jacks in one hand and mommy or daddy's sleeve in the other.

> Kiere took a few steps back, came running full speed, kicked a mighty kick—and missed the ball.

In the first two examples, the writer could also use a colon. (See 35a.) The colon is more formal than the dash and not quite as dramatic.

CAUTION: Unless there is a specific reason for using the dash, avoid it. Unnecessary dashes create a choppy effect.

▶ Insisting that students use computers as instructional

tools⧸for information retrieval⧸makes good sense. Herding

them⧸sheeplike⧸into computer technology does not.

39b Parentheses

Use parentheses to enclose supplemental material, minor digressions, and afterthoughts.

> After taking her temperature, pulse, and blood pressure (routine vital signs), the nurse made Becky as comfortable as possible.

The weights James was first able to move (not lift, mind you) were measured in ounces.

Use parentheses to enclose letters or numbers labeling items in a series.

Regulations stipulated that only the following equipment could be used on the survival mission: (1) a knife, (2) thirty feet of parachute line, (3) a book of matches, (4) two ponchos, (5) an *E* tool, and (6) a signal flare.

CAUTION: Do not overuse parentheses. Rough drafts are likely to contain more afterthoughts than necessary. As writers head into a sentence, they often think of additional details, occasionally working them in as best they can with parentheses. Usually such sentences should be revised so that the additional details no longer seem to be afterthoughts.

> ▶ Researchers have said that ~~ten million (estimates run as~~ *from ten to fifty million*

> ~~high as fifty million)~~ Americans have hypoglycemia.

39c Brackets

Use brackets to enclose any words or phrases that you have inserted into an otherwise word-for-word quotation.

Audubon reports that "if there are not enough young to balance deaths, the end of the species [California condor] is inevitable."

The sentence quoted from the *Audubon* article did not contain the words *California condor* (since the context made clear what species was meant), so the writer needed to add the name in brackets.

The Latin word "sic" in brackets indicates that an error in a quoted sentence appears in the original source.

According to the review, k. d. lang's performance was brilliant, "exceding [sic] the expectations of even her most loyal fans."

Do not overuse "sic," however, since calling attention to others' mistakes can appear snobbish. The preceding quotation, for example, might have been paraphrased instead: *According to the review, even k. d. lang's most faithful fans were surprised by the brilliance of her performance.*

39d The ellipsis mark

The ellipsis mark consists of three spaced periods. Use an ellipsis mark to indicate that you have deleted words from an otherwise word-for-word quotation.

> Reuben reports that "when the amount of cholesterol circulating in the blood rises over . . . 300 milligrams per 100, the chances of a heart attack increase dramatically."

MLA NOTE: MLA now recommends putting brackets around ellipsis dots, like this: [. . .]. These brackets make clear that the ellipsis dots do not appear in the original work you are quoting (see pp. 404–05). You may wish to check with your instructor before following this new MLA guideline. If you are using a style other than MLA (such as APA), do not follow this guideline.

If you delete a full sentence or more in the middle of a quoted passage, use a period before the three ellipsis dots.

> "Most of our efforts," writes Dave Erikson, "are directed toward saving the bald eagle's wintering habitat along the Mississippi River. . . . It's important that the wintering birds have a place to roost, where they can get out of the cold wind and be undisturbed by man."

CAUTION: Do not use the ellipsis mark at the beginning of a quotation; do not use it at the end of a quotation unless you have cut some words from the final sentence quoted. (See also p. 405.)

In quoted poetry, use a full line of ellipsis dots to indicate that you have dropped a line or more from the poem.

> Had we but world enough, and time,
> This coyness, lady, were no crime.
> ....
> But at my back I always hear
> Time's wingèd chariot hurrying near;   —Andrew Marvell

The ellipsis mark may also be used to mark a hesitation or interruption in speech or to suggest unfinished thoughts.

> Before falling into a coma, the victim whispered, "It was a man with a tattoo on his . . ."

39e The slash

Use the slash to separate two or three lines of poetry that have been run in to your text. Add a space both before and after the slash.

> In the opening lines of "Jordan," George Herbert pokes gentle fun at popular poems of his time: "Who says that fictions only and false hair / Become a verse? Is there in truth no beauty?"

More than three lines of poetry should be handled as an indented quotation. (See 37b.)

The slash may occasionally be used to separate paired terms such as *pass/fail* and *producer/director.* Do not use a space before or after the slash.

> Roger, the producer/director, announced a casting change.

Be sparing, however, in this use of the slash. In particular, avoid the use of *and/or, he/she,* and *his/her.*

EXERCISE 39–1

Edit the following sentences to correct errors in punctuation, focusing especially on appropriate use of the dash, parentheses, brackets, ellipsis mark, and slash. If a sentence is correct, write "correct" after it. Answers to lettered sentences appear in the back of the book. Example:

> Social insects/—bees, for example/—are able to
>
> communicate quite complicated messages to one another.

a. I was born in Iowa (Davenport, to be specific).
b. Pat helped Jeff put the tail on his kite—which was made of scraps from old dresses—and off they went to the park.
c. *Infoworld* reports that "customers without any particular aptitude for computers can easily learn to use it [the Bay Area Teleguide] through simple, three-step instructions."
d. Every person there—from the youngest toddler to the oldest great-grandparent, was expected to sit through the three-hour sermon in respectful silence.
e. The class stood, faced the flag, placed hands over hearts, and raced through "I pledge allegiance—liberty and justice for all" in less than sixty seconds.

1. Of the three basic schools of detective fiction, the tea-and-crumpet, the hard-boiled detective, and the police procedural, I find the quaint, civilized quality of the tea-and-crumpet school the most appealing.
2. The professional pool player needs to contend not only with abstract theories of math and physics but also with concrete details like the nap of the felt (usually running lengthwise) and the resiliency of the rails.
3. There are three points of etiquette in poker: 1. always allow someone to cut the cards, 2. don't forget to ante up, and 3. never stack your chips.
4. The child sang her way through the alphabet—*A, B, C . . . Z*—and then waited for our applause.
5. The old Valentine verse we used to chant says it all: "Sugar is sweet, / And so are you."

Mechanics

40

Abbreviations

 GRAMMAR CHECKERS can flag a few inappropriate abbreviations, such as *Xmas* and *e.g.*, but do not assume that a program will catch all problems with abbreviations.

40a Use standard abbreviations for titles immediately before and after proper names.

TITLES BEFORE PROPER NAMES	TITLES AFTER PROPER NAMES
Mr. Rafael Zabala	William Albert, Sr.
Ms. Nancy Linehan	Thomas Hines, Jr.
Mrs. Edward Horn	Anita Lor, Ph.D.
Dr. Margaret Simmons	Robert Simkowski, M.D.
the Rev. John Stone	Margaret Chin, LL.D.
Prof. James Russo	Polly Stein, D.D.S.

Do not abbreviate a title if it is not used with a proper name.

▶ My history ~~prof.~~ professor was an expert on America's use of the

atomic bomb in World War II.

Avoid redundant titles such as *Dr. Amy Day, M.D.* Choose one title or the other: *Dr. Amy Day* or *Amy Day, M.D.*

MLA NOTE: MLA prefers omitting periods in abbreviations for academic degrees (PhD, MD, LLD).

40b Use abbreviations only when you are sure your readers will understand them.

Familiar abbreviations, often written without periods, are acceptable:

CIA	FBI	AFL-CIO	NAACP
NBA	UPI	NEA	CD-ROM
YMCA	CBS	USA (*or* U.S.A.)	ESL

The YMCA has opened a new gym close to my office.

While in New York City, the school group toured the NBC studios.

NOTE: When using an unfamiliar abbreviation (such as CBE for Council of Biology Editors) throughout a paper, write the full name followed by the abbreviation in parentheses at the first mention of the name. Then use the abbreviation throughout the rest of the paper.

40c Use B.C., A.D., A.M., P.M., No., and $ only with specific dates, times, numbers, and amounts.

The abbreviation B.C. ("before Christ") follows a date, and A.D. ("*anno Domini*") precedes a date. Acceptable alternatives are B.C.E. ("before the common era") and C.E. ("common era"), both of which follow the date.

40 B.C. (or B.C.E.)	4:00 A.M. (or a.m.)	No. 12 (or no. 12)
A.D. 44 (or 44 C.E.)	6:00 P.M. (or p.m.)	$150

Avoid using A.M., P.M., No., or $ when not accompanied by a specific figure.

▶ We set off for the lake early in the ~~A.M.~~ *morning.*

MLA NOTE: MLA prefers omitting periods in abbreviations made up of capital letters (BCE, AD, AM, PM).

40d Be sparing in your use of Latin abbreviations.

Latin abbreviations are acceptable in footnotes and bibliographies and in informal writing for comments in parentheses.

cf. (Latin *confer*, "compare")
e.g. (Latin *exempli gratia*, "for example")

et al. (Latin *et alii,* "and others")
etc. (Latin *et cetera,* "and so forth")
i.e. (Latin *id est,* "that is")
N.B. (Latin *nota bene,* "note well")

Harold Simms et al., *The Race for Space*

Alfred Hitchcock directed many classic thrillers (e.g., *Psycho, Rear Window,* and *Vertigo*).

In formal writing use the appropriate English phrases.

▶ Many obsolete laws remain on the books, e.g., a law in
                                                    for example,
                                                     ^

Vermont forbidding an unmarried man and woman to sit

closer than six inches apart on a park bench.

40e Avoid inappropriate abbreviations.

In formal writing, abbreviations for the following are not commonly accepted: personal names, units of measurement, days of the week, holidays, months, courses of study, divisions of written works, states, and countries (except in addresses and except Washington, D.C.). Do not abbreviate *Company* and *Incorporated* unless their abbreviated forms are part of an official name.

PERSONAL NAME   Charles (not Chas.)

UNITS OF MEASUREMENT   pound (not lb.)

DAYS OF THE WEEK   Monday (not Mon.)

HOLIDAYS   Christmas (not Xmas)

MONTHS   January, February, March (not Jan., Feb., Mar.)

COURSES OF STUDY   political science (not poli. sci.)

DIVISIONS OF WRITTEN WORKS   chapter, page (not ch., p.)

STATES AND COUNTRIES   Massachusetts (not MA or Mass.)

PARTS OF A BUSINESS NAME   Adams Lighting Company (not Adams Lighting Co.); Kim and Brothers, Inc. (not Kim and Bros., Inc.)

▶ Eliza promised to buy me one ~~lb.~~ of Godiva chocolate for my
pound

birthday, which was last ~~Fri.~~
Friday.^

EXERCISE 40–1

Edit the following sentences to correct errors in abbreviations. If a sentence is correct, write "correct" after it. Answers to lettered sentences appear in the back of the book. Example:

This year ~~Xmas~~ will fall on a ~~Tues.~~
Christmas^   *Tuesday.*^

a. Audrey Hepburn was a powerful spokesperson for UNICEF for many years.
b. A no. of govt. officials have been reviewing the records of some small brokerage firms in the area.
c. Mahatma Gandhi has inspired many modern leaders, including Martin Luther King, Jr.
d. The first discovery of America was definitely not in 1492 A.D.
e. Denzil spent all night studying for his psych. exam.

1. My favorite prof., Dr. Barker, is on sabbatical this semester.
2. When she arrived in Poughkeepsie to work at IBM, Pauline was overwhelmed by the sophistication and variety of product prototypes.
3. Some historians think that the New Testament was completed by A.D. 100.
4. Mark was born on Fri., May 13.
5. Many girls fall prey to a cult worship of great entertainers—e.g., in my mother's generation, girls worshiped the Beatles.

41

Numbers

 GRAMMAR CHECKERS can tell you to spell out certain numbers, such as *thirty-three* and numbers that begin a sentence, but they won't help you understand when it is acceptable to use figures.

41a Spell out numbers of one or two words or those that begin a sentence. Use figures for numbers that require more than two words to spell out.

▶ Now, some ~~8~~ *eight* years later, Muffin is still with us.

▶ I counted ~~one hundred seventy-six~~ *176* CD's on the shelf.

If a sentence begins with a number, spell out the number or rewrite the sentence.

▶ ~~150~~ *One hundred fifty* children in our program need expensive dental treatment.

Rewriting the sentence will also correct the error and may be less awkward if the number is long: *In our program 150 children need expensive dental treatment.*

EXCEPTIONS: In technical and some business writing, figures are preferred even when spellings would be brief, but usage varies.

When several numbers appear in the same passage, many writers choose consistency rather than strict adherence to the rule.

When one number immediately follows another, spell out one and use figures for the other: three 100-meter events, 125 four-poster beds.

41b Generally, figures are acceptable for dates, addresses, percentages, fractions, decimals, scores, statistics and other numerical results, exact amounts of money, divisions of books and plays, pages, identification numbers, and the time.

DATES   July 4, 1776, 56 B.C., A.D. 30

ADDRESSES   77 Latches Lane, 519 West 42nd Street

PERCENTAGES   55 percent (or 55%)

FRACTIONS, DECIMALS   ½, 0.047

SCORES   7 to 3, 21–18

STATISTICS   average age 37, average weight 180

SURVEYS   4 out of 5

EXACT AMOUNTS OF MONEY $105.37, $106,000

DIVISIONS OF BOOKS   volume 3, chapter 4, page 189

DIVISIONS OF PLAYS   act 3, scene 3 (or act III, scene iii)

IDENTIFICATION NUMBERS   serial number 10988675

TIME OF DAY   4:00 P.M., 1:30 A.M.

▶ Several doctors put up ~~two hundred fifty-five thousand dollars~~ *$255,000*
⌃

for the construction of a golf course.

NOTE: When not using A.M. or P.M., write out the time in words *(two o'clock in the afternoon, twelve noon, seven in the morning).*

EXERCISE 41–1

Edit the following sentences to correct errors in the use of numbers. If a sentence is correct, write "correct" after it. Answers to lettered sentences appear in the back of the book. Example:

By the end of the evening Ashanti had only ~~three dollars and~~ *$3.06*
⌃

~~six cents~~ left.

a. We have ordered 4 azaleas, 3 rhododendrons, and 2 mountain laurels for the back area of the garden.
b. Venezuelan independence from Spain was declared on July 5, 1811.
c. The score was tied at 5–5 when the momentum shifted and carried the Standards to a decisive 12–5 win.
d. We ordered three four-door sedans for company executives.
e. The Vietnam Veterans Memorial in Washington, D.C., had fifty-eight thousand one hundred thirty-two names inscribed on it when it was dedicated in 1982.

1. One of my favorite scenes in Shakespeare is the property division scene in act 1 of *King Lear.*
2. The botany lecture will begin at precisely 3:30 P.M.
3. 12 percent of all American marriages occur in June.
4. In nineteen hundred and forty-one, the United States entered World War II.
5. On a normal day, I spend at least 4 to 5 hours surfing the Internet.

42

Italics (underlining)

Italics, a slanting typeface used in printed material, can be produced by some word processing programs. In handwritten or typed papers, this typeface is indicated by <u>underlining</u>. Some instructors prefer underlining even if their students can produce italics.

NOTE: Some e-mail systems do not allow for italics or underlining. Many people indicate words that should be italicized by preceding and ending them with underscores. Punctuation should follow the coding.

    I am planning to write my senior thesis on _Anna
    Karenina_.

In less formal e-mail messages, normally italicized words aren't marked at all.

    I finally finished reading Anna Karenina--what a
    masterpiece!

GRAMMAR CHECKERS do not flag problems with italics or underlining. (For a general discussion of what grammar checkers can and cannot do, see p. 32.)

42a Underline or italicize the titles of works according to convention.

Titles of the following works should be underlined or italicized.

TITLES OF BOOKS   *The Great Gatsby, A Distant Mirror*

MAGAZINES   *Time, Scientific American*

NEWSPAPERS   the *St. Louis Post-Dispatch*

PAMPHLETS   *Common Sense, Facts about Marijuana*

LONG POEMS   *The Waste Land, Paradise Lost*

PLAYS   *King Lear, A Raisin in the Sun*

FILMS   *Casablanca, Saving Private Ryan*

TELEVISION PROGRAMS   *60 Minutes, Frasier*

RADIO PROGRAMS   *All Things Considered*

MUSICAL COMPOSITIONS   Gershwin's *Porgy and Bess*

CHOREOGRAPHIC WORKS   Twyla Tharp's *Brief Fling*

WORKS OF VISUAL ART   Rodin's *The Thinker*

COMIC STRIPS   *Dilbert*

SOFTWARE   *WordPerfect*

WEB SITES   *Barron's Online, ESPNET SportsZone*

The titles of other works, such as short stories, essays, episodes of radio and television programs, songs, and short poems, are enclosed in quotation marks. (See 37d.)

NOTE: Do not use underlining or italics when referring to the Bible, titles of books in the Bible (Genesis, not *Genesis*), or titles of legal documents (the Constitution, not the *Constitution*). Do not underline the title of your own paper.

42b Underline or italicize the names of spacecraft, aircraft, ships, and trains.

Challenger, Spirit of St. Louis, Queen Elizabeth II, Silver Streak

▶ The success of the Soviets' <u>Sputnik</u> galvanized the U.S.

space program.

42c Underline or italicize foreign words used in an English sentence.

▶ Although Joe's method seemed to be successful, I decided to

establish my own <u>modus operandi</u>.

EXCEPTION: Do not underline or italicize foreign words that have become a standard part of the English language — "laissez-faire," "fait accompli," "habeas corpus," and "per diem," for example.

42d Underline or italicize words mentioned as words, letters mentioned as letters, and numbers mentioned as numbers.

▶ Tim assured us that the howling probably came from

his bloodhound, Hill Billy, but his _probably_ stuck in

our minds.

▶ Sarah called her father by his given name, Johnny, but she

was unable to pronounce _J_.

▶ A big _3_ was painted on the door.

NOTE: Quotation marks may be used instead of underlining or italics to set off words mentioned as words. (See 37e.)

42e Avoid excessive underlining or italics for emphasis.

Underlining or italicizing to emphasize words or ideas is distracting and should be used sparingly.

▶ In-line skating is a sport that has become an _addiction_.

EXERCISE 42–1

Edit the following sentences to correct errors in the use of italics. If a sentence is correct, write "correct" after it. Answers to lettered sentences appear in the back of the book. Example:

> _Leaves of Grass_ by Walt Whitman was quite controversial
>
> when it was published a century ago.

a. Howard Hughes commissioned the Spruce Goose, a beautifully built but thoroughly impractical wooden aircraft.
b. The old man _screamed_ his anger, _shouting_ to all of us, "I will not leave my money to you worthless layabouts!"

c. Even though it is almost always hot in Mexico in the summer, you can usually find a cool spot on one of the park benches in the town's *zócalo*.

d. Cinema audiences once gasped at hearing the word *damn* in *Gone with the Wind*.

e. "The City and the Pillar" was an early novel by Gore Vidal.

1. Bernard watched as Eileen stood transfixed in front of Vermeer's *Head of a Young Girl*.

2. The monastery walls were painted with scenes described in the book of Genesis.

3. My per diem allowance was $200.

4. In her first calligraphy lesson, Suzanne learned how to make a Romanesque B.

5. Redford and Newman in the movie "The Sting" were amateurs compared with the seventeen-year-old con artist who lives at our house.

43

Spelling

You learned to spell from repeated experience with words in both reading and writing, but especially writing. Words have a look, a sound, and even a feel to them as the hand moves across the page. As you proofread, you can probably tell if a word doesn't look quite right. In such cases, the solution is obvious: Look up the word in the dictionary.

SPELL CHECKERS AND GRAMMAR CHECKERS are useful alternatives to a dictionary, but only to a point. A spell checker will not tell you how to spell words not listed in its dictionary; nor will it help you catch words commonly confused, such as *accept* and *except,* or some typographical errors, such as *own* for *won.* You will still need to proofread, and for some words you may need to turn to the dictionary.

Grammar checkers can flag commonly confused words such as *accept* and *except* or *principal* and *principle,* but they often do this when you have used the correct word. You will still need to think about the meaning you intend.

43a Become familiar with your dictionary.

A good desk dictionary—such as *The American Heritage Dictionary of the English Language, The Random House College Dictionary,* or *Merriam-Webster's Collegiate Dictionary* or *New World*

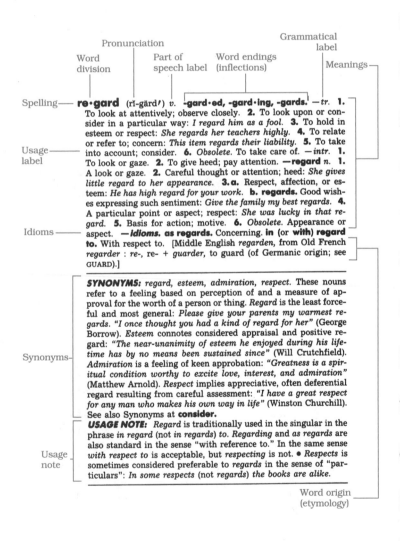

Pronunciation

Word division

Part of speech label

Word endings (inflections)

Grammatical label

Meanings

Spelling

Usage label

Idioms

re·gard (rĭ-gärd′) *v.* **-gard·ed, -gard·ing, -gards.** *—tr.* **1.** To look at attentively; observe closely. **2.** To look upon or consider in a particular way: *I regard him as a fool.* **3.** To hold in esteem or respect: *She regards her teachers highly.* **4.** To relate or refer to; concern: *This item regards their liability.* **5.** To take into account; consider. **6.** *Obsolete.* To take care of. *—intr.* **1.** To look or gaze. **2.** To give heed; pay attention. **—regard** *n.* **1.** A look or gaze. **2.** Careful thought or attention; heed: *She gives little regard to her appearance.* **3.a.** Respect, affection, or esteem: *He has high regard for your work.* **b. regards.** Good wishes expressing such sentiment: *Give the family my best regards.* **4.** A particular point or aspect; respect: *She was lucky in that regard.* **5.** Basis for action; motive. **6.** *Obsolete.* Appearance or aspect. **—*idioms.* as regards.** Concerning. **in** (or **with**) **regard to.** With respect to. [Middle English *regarden,* from Old French *regarder* : *re-,* re- + *guarder,* to guard (of Germanic origin; see GUARD).]

SYNONYMS: *regard, esteem, admiration, respect.* These nouns refer to a feeling based on perception of and a measure of approval for the worth of a person or thing. *Regard* is the least forceful and most general: *Please give your parents my warmest regards.* "*I once thought you had a kind of regard for her*" (George Borrow). *Esteem* connotes considered appraisal and positive regard: "*The near-unanimity of esteem he enjoyed during his lifetime has by no means been sustained since*" (Will Crutchfield). *Admiration* is a feeling of keen approbation: "*Greatness is a spiritual condition worthy to excite love, interest, and admiration*" (Matthew Arnold). *Respect* implies appreciative, often deferential regard resulting from careful assessment: "*I have a great respect for any man who makes his own way in life*" (Winston Churchill). See also Synonyms at **consider.**

Synonyms

Usage note

USAGE NOTE: *Regard* is traditionally used in the singular in the phrase *in regard* (not *in regards*) *to. Regarding* and *as regards* are also standard in the sense "with reference to." In the same sense *with respect to* is acceptable, but *respecting* is not. • *Respects* is sometimes considered preferable to *regards* in the sense of "particulars": *In some respects* (not *regards*) *the books are alike.*

Word origin (etymology)

Dictionary of the American Language—is an indispensable writer's aid.

A sample dictionary entry, taken from *The American Heritage Dictionary,* appears on page 330. Labels show where various kinds of information about a word can be found in that dictionary.

Spelling, word division, pronunciation

The main entry (*re•gard* in the sample entry) shows the correct spelling of the word. When there are two correct spellings of a word (as in *collectible, collectable,* for example), both are given, with the preferred spelling usually appearing first.

The main entry also shows how the word is divided into syllables. The dot between *re* and *gard* separates the word's two syllables and indicates where the word should be divided if it can't fit at the end of a line of type (see 44f). When a word is compound, the main entry shows how to write it: as one word (*crossroad*), as a hyphenated word (*cross-stitch*), or as two words (*cross section*).

The word's pronunciation is given just after the main entry. The accents indicate which syllables are stressed; the other marks are explained in the dictionary's pronunciation key. In some dictionaries this key appears at the bottom of every page or every other page.

Word endings and grammatical labels

When a word takes endings to indicate grammatical functions (called *inflections*), the endings are listed in boldface, as with *-garded, -garding,* and *-gards* in the sample entry.

Labels for the parts of speech and for other grammatical terms are abbreviated. The most commonly used abbreviations are these:

n.	noun	adj.	adjective
pl.	plural	adv.	adverb
sing.	singular	pron.	pronoun
v.	verb	prep.	preposition
tr.	transitive verb	conj.	conjunction
intr.	intransitive verb	interj.	interjection

Meanings, word origin, synonyms, and antonyms

Each meaning for the word is given a number. Occasionally a word's use is illustrated in a quoted sentence.

Sometimes a word can be used as more than one part of speech (*regard*, for instance, can be used as either a verb or a noun). In such a case, all the meanings for one part of speech are given before all the meanings for another, as in the sample entry. The entry also gives idiomatic uses of the word.

The origin of the word, called its *etymology*, appears in brackets after all the meanings (in some dictionaries it appears before the meanings).

Synonyms, words similar in meaning to the main entry, are frequently listed. In the sample entry, the dictionary draws distinctions in meaning among the various synonyms. Antonyms, which do not appear in the sample entry, are words having a meaning opposite from that of the main entry.

Usage

Usage labels indicate when, where, or under what conditions a particular meaning for a word is appropriately used. Common labels are *informal* (or *colloquial*), *slang, nonstandard, dialect, obsolete, archaic, poetic,* and *British.* In the sample entry, two meanings of *regard* are labeled *obsolete* because they are no longer in use.

Dictionaries sometimes include usage notes as well. In the sample entry, the dictionary offers advice on several uses of *regard* not specifically covered by the meanings. Such advice is based on the opinions of many experts and on actual usage in current magazines, newspapers, and books.

43b Discriminate between words that sound alike but have different meanings.

Words that sound alike or nearly alike but have different meanings and spellings are called homophones. The following sets of words are so commonly confused that a good proofreader will double-check their every use.

affect (verb: "to exert an influence")
effect (verb: "to accomplish"; noun: "result")

its (possessive pronoun: "of or belonging to it")
it's (contraction for "it is")

loose (adjective: "free, not securely attached")
lose (verb: "to fail to keep, to be deprived of")

principal (adjective: "most important"; noun: "head of a school")
principle (noun: "a general or fundamental truth")

their (possessive pronoun: "belonging to them")
they're (contraction for "they are")
there (adverb: "that place or position")

who's (contraction for "who is")
whose (possessive form of "who")

your (possessive form of "you")
you're (contraction of "you are")

To check for correct use of these and other commonly confused words, consult the Glossary of Usage, which begins on page 503.

43c Become familiar with the major spelling rules.

i *before* e *except after* c

Use *i* before *e* except after *c* or when sounded like *ay,* as in *neighbor* and *weigh.*

I **BEFORE** *E*	relieve, believe, sieve, niece, fierce, frieze
E **BEFORE** *I*	receive, deceive, sleigh, freight, eight
EXCEPTIONS	seize, either, weird, height, foreign, leisure

Suffixes

FINAL SILENT -*E* Generally, drop a final silent -*e* when adding a suffix that begins with a vowel. Keep the final -*e* if the suffix begins with a consonant.

combine, combination	achieve, achievement
desire, desiring	care, careful
prude, prudish	entire, entirety
remove, removable	gentle, gentleness

Words such as *changeable, judgment, argument,* and *truly* are exceptions.

FINAL *-y*　When adding *-s* or *-d* to words ending in *-y*, ordinarily change *-y* to *-ie* when the *-y* is preceded by a consonant but not when it is preceded by a vowel.

comedy, comedies	monkey, monkeys
dry, dried	play, played

With proper names ending in *-y*, however, do not change the *-y* to *-ie* even if it is preceded by a consonant: *the Dougherty family, the Doughertys*.

FINAL CONSONANTS　If a final consonant is preceded by a single vowel *and* the consonant ends a one-syllable word or a stressed syllable, double the consonant when adding a suffix beginning with a vowel.

bet, betting	occur, occurrence
commit, committed	

Plurals

-s OR *-es*　Add *-s* to form the plural of most nouns; add *-es* to singular nouns ending in *-s*, *-sh*, *-ch*, and *-x*.

table, tables	church, churches
paper, papers	dish, dishes

Ordinarily add *-s* to nouns ending in *-o* when the *-o* is preceded by a vowel. Add *-es* when it is preceded by a consonant.

radio, radios	hero, heroes
video, videos	tomato, tomatoes

OTHER PLURALS　To form the plural of a hyphenated compound word, add the *-s* to the chief word even if it does not appear at the end.

mother-in-law, mothers-in-law

English words derived from other languages such as Latin or French sometimes form the plural as they would in their original language.

medium, media	chateau, chateaux
criterion, criteria	

ESL

Spelling may vary slightly among English-speaking countries. This can prove particularly confusing for ESL students, who may have learned British or Canadian English. Following is a list of some common words spelled differently in American and British English. Consult a dictionary for others.

AMERICAN	BRITISH
canceled, traveled	cancelled, travelled
color, humor	colour, humour
judgment	judgement
check	cheque
realize, apologize	realise, apologise
defense	defence
anemia, anesthetic	anaemia, anaesthetic
theater, center	theatre, centre
fetus	foetus
mold, smolder	mould, smoulder
civilization	civilisation
connection, inflection	connexion, inflexion
licorice	liquorice

43d Be alert to commonly misspelled words.

absence	athlete	conqueror	exhaust
academic	athletics	conscience	existence
accidentally	attendance	conscientious	extraordinary
accommodate	basically	conscious	extremely
achievement	beginning	criticism	familiar
acknowledge	believe	criticize	fascinate
acquaintance	benefited	decision	February
acquire	bureau	definitely	foreign
address	business	descendant	forty
all right	calendar	dictionary	fourth
amateur	candidate	disastrous	friend
analyze	cemetery	eighth	government
answer	changeable	eligible	grammar
apparently	column	embarrass	guard
appearance	commitment	emphasize	harass
arctic	committed	entirely	height
argument	committee	environment	humorous
arithmetic	competitive	especially	incidentally
arrangement	conceivable	exaggerated	incredible
ascend	conferred	exercise	indispensable

inevitable	pamphlet	professor	sophomore
intelligence	parallel	pronunciation	strictly
irrelevant	particularly	quiet	subtly
irresistible	pastime	quite	succeed
knowledge	permissible	quizzes	surprise
license	perseverance	receive	thorough
lightning	phenomenon	referred	tragedy
loneliness	physically	restaurant	transferred
maintenance	picnicking	rhythm	tries
maneuver	playwright	roommate	truly
marriage	practically	sandwich	unnecessarily
mathematics	precede	schedule	usually
mischievous	preference	seize	vacuum
necessary	preferred	separate	vengeance
noticeable	prejudice	sergeant	villain
occasion	prevalent	siege	weird
occurred	privilege	similar	whether
occurrence	proceed	sincerely	writing

EXERCISE 43–1

The following memo has been run through a spell checker. Proofread it carefully, editing the spelling and typographical errors that remain.

November 2, 1998

To: Patricia Wise

cc: Richard Chang

Form: Constance Mayhew

Subject: Express Tours annual report

Thank you for agreeing to draft the annual report for Express Tours. Before you begin you're work, let me outline the initial steps.

First, its essential for you to include brief profiles of top management. Early next week, I'll provide profiles for all manages accept Samuel Heath, who's biographical information is being revised. You should edit these profiles carefully, than format them according to the enclosed instructions. We may ask you to include other employee's profiles at some point.

Second, you should arrange to get complete financial information for fiscal year 1998 from our comptroller, Richard Chang. (Helen Boyes, to, can provide the necessary figures.) When you get this information, precede according tot he plans we discuss

in yesterday's meeting. By the way, you will notice from the figures that the sale of our Charterhouse division did not significantly effect net profits.

Third, you should submit first draft of the report by December 15. I assume that you won a laser printer, but if you don't,
you can submit a disk and we'll print out a draft here. Of coarse,
you should proofread you writing.

I am quiet pleased that you can take on this project. If I or anyone else at Express Tours can answers questions, don't hesitate
to call.

44

The hyphen

GRAMMAR CHECKERS can flag some, but not all, missing or misused hyphens. For example, the programs can tell you that a
hyphen is needed in fractions and compound numbers, such
as *two-thirds* and *sixty-four.* They can also tell you how to spell
certain compound words, such as *breakup* (not *break-up*).

44a Consult the dictionary to determine how to treat a compound word.

Your dictionary will tell you whether to treat a compound
word as a hyphenated compound (*water-repellent*), one word
(*waterproof*), or two words (*water table*). If the compound word
is not in the dictionary, treat it as two words.

▶ The prosecutor chose not to cross–examine any witnesses.

▶ Grandma kept a small note book in her apron pocket.

▶ Alice walked through the looking/glass into a backward

world.

44b Use a hyphen to connect two or more words functioning together as an adjective before a noun.

▶ Mrs. Douglas gave Toshiko a seashell and some newspaper-

wrapped fish to take home to her mother.

▶ Priscilla Hood is not yet a well-known candidate.

Newspaper-wrapped and *well-known* are adjectives used before the nouns *fish* and *candidate*.

Generally, do not use a hyphen when such compounds follow the noun.

▶ After our television campaign, Priscilla Hood will be well/

known.

Do not use a hyphen to connect *-ly* adverbs to the words they modify.

▶ A slowly/moving truck tied up traffic.

NOTE: In a series, hyphens are suspended.

Do you prefer first-, second-, or third-class tickets?

44c Hyphenate the written form of fractions and of compound numbers from twenty-one to ninety-nine.

▶ One-fourth of my income goes to pay off the national debt.

44d Use a hyphen with the prefixes *all-*, *ex-* (meaning "former"), and *self-* and with the suffix *-elect*.

▶ The charity is funneling more money into self-help projects.

▶ Anne King is our club's president-elect.

44e A hyphen is used in some words to avoid ambiguity or to separate awkward double or triple letters.

Without the hyphen there would be no way to distinguish between words such as *re-creation* and *recreation.*

> Mountain biking in the country is my favorite summer recreation.

> The film was praised for its astonishing re-creation of nineteenth-century London.

Hyphens are sometimes used to separate awkward double or triple letters in compound words (*anti-intellectual, cross-stitch*). Always check a dictionary for the standard form of the word.

44f If a word must be divided at the end of a line, divide it correctly.

Divide words between syllables; never divide a one-syllable word.

▶ When I returned from my travels overseas, I didn't ~~reco-~~ *recog-*
~~gnize~~ *nize* one face on the magazine covers.

▶ Grandfather didn't have the courage or the ~~stren-~~ *strength*
~~gth~~ to open the door.

Never divide a word so that a single letter stands alone at the end of a line or fewer than three letters begin a line.

▶ She'll bring her brother with her when she comes ~~a-~~ *again.*
~~gain.~~

▶ As audience to *The Mousetrap*, Hamlet is a ~~watch-~~ *watcher*
~~er~~ watching watchers.

When dividing a compound word at the end of a line, either make the break between the words that form the compound or put the whole word on the next line.

▶ My niece is determined to become a long-~~dis-~~
distance
~~tance~~ runner when she grows up.
^

To divide long e-mail and Internet addresses, do not use a hyphen (because a hyphen could appear to be part of the address). If the address is mentioned in the text of your paper, break it at some convenient point, such as after a slash or before a period. For advice on breaking Internet addresses in an MLA works cited entry, see page 425.

EXERCISE 44–1

Edit the following sentences to correct errors in hyphenation. If a sentence is correct, write "correct" after it. Answers to lettered sentences appear in the back of the book. Example:

Zola's first readers were scandalized by his slice ⁻of ⁻life
^ ^

novels.

a. Gold is the seventy-ninth element in the periodic table.
b. The swiftly-moving tugboat pulled alongside the barge and directed it away from the oil spill in the harbor.
c. The Moche were a pre-Columbian people who established a sophisticated culture in ancient Peru.
d. Your dog is well-known in our neighborhood.
e. Road-blocks were set up along all the major highways leading out of the city.

1. We knew we were driving too fast when our tires skidded on the rain slick surface.
2. The Black Death reduced the population of some medieval villages by two thirds.
3. The flight attendant instructed us to fasten our seat belts before lift-off.
4. A well known actress who wishes to remain anonymous has contributed $10,000 toward our scholarship fund.
5. Joan had been brought up to be independent and self-reliant.

45

Capital letters

In addition to the rules in this section, you can use a good dictionary to tell you when to use capital letters.

> GRAMMAR CHECKERS remind you that sentences should begin with capital letters and that some words, such as *Cherokee,* are proper nouns. Many words, however, should be capitalized only in certain contexts, and you must determine when to do so.

45a Capitalize proper nouns and words derived from them; do not capitalize common nouns.

Proper nouns are the names of specific persons, places, and things. All other nouns are common nouns. The following types of words are usually capitalized: names for the deity, religions, religious followers, sacred books; words of family relationship used as names; particular places; nationalities and their languages, races, tribes; educational institutions, departments, degrees, particular courses; government departments, organizations, political parties; historical movements, periods, events, documents; specific electronic sources; and trade names.

PROPER NOUNS	COMMON NOUNS
God (used as a name)	a god
Book of Jeremiah	a sacred book
Uncle Pedro	my uncle
Father (used as a name)	my father
Lake Superior	a picturesque lake
the Capital Center	a center for advanced studies
the South	a southern state
Japan, a Japanese garden	an ornamental garden
University of Wisconsin	a good university
Geology 101	geology
Environmental Protection Agency	a federal agency

Mechanics

PROPER NOUNS	COMMON NOUNS
Phi Kappa Psi	a fraternity
a Democrat	an independent
the Enlightenment	the eighteenth century
the Declaration of Independence	a treaty
the World Wide Web, the Web	a home page
the Internet, the Net	a computer network
Kleenex	a tissue

Months, holidays, and days of the week are treated as proper nouns; the seasons and numbers of the days of the month are not.

> Our academic year begins on a Tuesday in early September, right after Labor Day.

> My mother's birthday is in early summer, on the second of June.

EXCEPTION: Capitalize Fourth of July (or July Fourth) when referring to the holiday.

Names of school subjects are capitalized only if they are names of languages. Names of particular courses are capitalized.

> This semester Austin is taking math, geography, geology, French, and English.

> Professor Anderson offers Modern American Fiction 501 to graduate students.

CAUTION: Do not capitalize common nouns to make them seem important: *Our company is currently hiring computer programmers* (not *Company, Computer Programmers*).

45b Capitalize titles of persons when used as part of a proper name but usually not when used alone.

> Professor Margaret Barnes; Dr. Harold Stevens; John Scott Williams, Jr.; Anne Tilton, LL.D.

> District Attorney Marshall was reprimanded for badgering the witness.

> The district attorney was elected for a two-year term.

Usage varies when the title of an important public figure is used alone: *The president* [or *President*] *vetoed the bill.*

45c Capitalize the first, last, and all major words in titles and subtitles of works such as books, articles, songs, and online documents.

In both titles and subtitles, major words such as nouns, pronouns, verbs, adjectives, and adverbs should be capitalized. Minor words such as articles, prepositions, and coordinating conjunctions are not capitalized unless they are the first or last word of a title or subtitle. Capitalize the second part of a hyphenated term in a title if it is a major word but not if it is a minor word.

To see why some of the following titles are italicized and some are put in quotation marks, see 42a and 37d.

> *The Impossible Theater: A Manifesto*
>
> *The F-Plan Diet*
>
> "Fire and Ice"
>
> "I Want to Hold Your Hand"
>
> *The Canadian Green Page*

Capitalize chapter titles and the titles of other major divisions of a work following the same guidelines used for titles of complete works.

> "Work and Play" in Santayana's *The Nature of Beauty*

45d Capitalize the first word of a sentence.

Obviously the first word of a sentence should be capitalized.

> When lightning struck the house, the chimney collapsed.

When a sentence appears within parentheses, capitalize its first word unless the parentheses appear within another sentence.

> Early detection of breast cancer significantly increases survival rates. (See table 2.)

> Early detection of breast cancer significantly increases survival rates (see table 2).

45e Capitalize the first word of a quoted sentence but not a quoted phrase.

In *Time* magazine Robert Hughes writes, "There are only about sixty Watteau paintings on whose authenticity all experts agree."

Russell Baker has written that in our country sports are "the opiate of the masses."

If a quoted sentence is interrupted by explanatory words, do not capitalize the first word after the interruption. (See 37f.)

"If you wanted to go out," he said sharply, "you should have told me."

When quoting poetry, copy the poet's capitalization exactly. Many poets capitalize the first word of every line of poetry; a few contemporary poets dismiss capitalization altogether.

When I consider everything that grows
Holds in perfection but a little moment —Shakespeare

it was the week   that
i felt the city's narrow breezes rush about
me —Don L. Lee

45f Do not capitalize the first word after a colon unless it begins an independent clause, in which case capitalization is optional.

Most of the bar's patrons can be divided into two groups: the occasional after-work socializers and the nothing-to-go-home-to regulars.

This we are forced to conclude: The [*or* the] federal government is needed to protect the rights of minorities.

45g Capitalize abbreviations for departments and agencies of government, other organizations, and corporations; capitalize the call letters of radio and television stations.

EPA, FBI, OPEC, IBM, WCRB, KNBC-TV

EXERCISE 45–1

Edit the following sentences to correct errors in capitalization. If a sentence is correct, write "correct" after it. Answers to lettered sentences appear in the back of the book. Example:

> On our trip to the West we visited the ~~g~~rand ~~c~~anyon and the
> *G*   *C*
> ~~g~~reat ~~s~~alt ~~d~~esert.
> *G*   *S*   *D*

a. District attorney Bax was disgusted when the jurors turned in a verdict of not guilty after only one hour of deliberation.
b. My mother has begun to research the history of her cherokee ancestors in Georgia.
c. W. C. Fields's epitaph reads, "On the whole, I'd rather be in Philadelphia."
d. Refugees from central America are finding it more and more difficult to cross the rio Grande into the United States.
e. I obtained profiles of both candidates from a useful web site called *Vote Smart Web.*

1. Whenever my brother took us to the movies, he gave us three choices: A brainless beach party flick, a foreign fluff film, or a blood-and-lust adventure movie.
2. The grunion is an unremarkable fish except for one curious habit: It comes ashore to spawn.
3. In our family, aunt Sandra was notorious for her biting tongue.
4. Historians have described Robert E. Lee as the aristocratic south personified.
5. Because Eileen enjoys working with handicapped children, she is pursuing a degree in Special Education.

Argument

In argumentative writing, you take a stand on a debatable issue. The issue being debated might be a matter of public policy: Should religious groups be allowed to meet on school property? What is the least dangerous way to dispose of nuclear waste? Should a state enact laws rationing medical care? On such questions, reasonable persons can disagree.

Reasonable men and women also disagree about many scholarly issues. Psychologists debate the validity of behaviorism; historians interpret the causes of the Civil War quite differently; biologists conduct genetic experiments to challenge the conclusions of other researchers.

46

Build a convincing case.

Your goal, in argumentative writing, is to change the way your readers think about a subject or to convince them to take an action that they might not otherwise be inclined to take. Do not assume that your audience already agrees with you; instead, envision skeptical readers who will make up their minds after listening to all sides of the debate.

46a Plan a strategy.

Planning a strategy for an argumentative essay is much like planning a debate for a speech class. A good way to begin is to list your arguments and the opposing arguments and then consider the likely impact of these arguments on your audience. If the opposing arguments look very powerful, you may want to rethink your position. By modifying your initial position — perhaps by claiming less or by proposing a less radical solution to a problem — you may have a greater chance of persuading readers to change their views.

Listing your arguments

Let's say that your tentative purpose (which may change as you think about your audience and the opposition) is to argue in favor of lowering the legal drinking age from twenty-one to eighteen. Here is a list of possible arguments in favor of this point of view.

— Society treats eighteen-year-olds as mature for most purposes.
  — They can vote.
  — They can go away to college.
  — At eighteen, men must register with Selective Service and be available for a possible draft.
— Age is not necessarily an indication of maturity.
— The current drinking age is unfair, since many older Americans were allowed to drink at eighteen.
— An unrealistic drinking age is almost impossible to enforce, and it breeds disrespect for the law.
— In European countries that allow eighteen-year-olds to drink, there is less irresponsible teenage drinking than in our country.

Listing the arguments of the opposition

The next step is to list the key arguments of the opposition. Here are some possible arguments *against* lowering the drinking age to eighteen.

— Teenage drinking frequently leads to drunk driving, which in turn leads to many deaths.
— Teenage drinking sometimes leads to date rape and gang violence.
— Alcoholism is a serious problem in our society, and a delayed drinking age can help prevent it.
— If the legal age were eighteen, many fifteen- and sixteen-year-olds would find a way to purchase alcohol illegally.

If possible, you should talk to someone who disagrees with your view or read some articles that are critical of your position. By familiarizing yourself with opposing viewpoints, you can be reasonably sure you have not overlooked an important argument that might be used against you.

Considering your audience

Once you have listed the major arguments on both (or all) sides, think realistically about the impact they are likely to have on your intended audience. If your audience is the voting age population in the United States, for example, consider how you might assess some of the arguments of each side of the drinking age question.

Looking at your list, you would see that your audience, which includes many older Americans, might not be impressed by the suggestion that age is no sign of maturity or by the argument that because eighteen-year-olds are old enough to attend college they should be allowed to drink. You would decide to emphasize your other arguments instead. Americans who remember a time when young men were drafted, for example, might be persuaded that it is unfair to ask a man to die for his country but not allow him to drink. And anyone who has heard of Prohibition might be moved by the argument that an unrealistic drinking regulation can breed disrespect for the law.

As for the opposing arguments, clearly the first one on the list is the most powerful. Statistics show that drunk driving by teenagers causes much carnage on our highways and that teenagers themselves are frequently the victims. To have any hope of convincing your audience, you would need to take this argument very seriously; it would be almost impossible to argue successfully that reducing highway deaths is not important.

Rethinking your position

After exploring all sides of an argument, you may decide to modify your initial position. Maybe your first thoughts about the issue were oversimplified, too extreme, or mistaken in some other respect. Or maybe, after thinking more about your readers, you see little hope of persuading them of the truth or wisdom of your position.

If you were writing about the drinking age, for example, you might decide to modify your position in light of your audience. To have a better chance of convincing the audience, you could argue that eighteen-year-olds *in the military* should be allowed to drink. Or you could argue that eighteen-year-olds should be allowed to drink beer and wine, not hard alcohol. Or you could link your proposal to new tough laws against drunk driving.

46b Frame a thesis and sketch an outline.

A thesis is a sentence that expresses the main point of an essay. (See 2a.) In argumentative writing, your thesis should clearly state your position on the issue you have chosen to write about. Let's say your issue is the high insurance rates that most companies set for young male drivers. After thinking carefully about your own views, the arguments of the opposition, and your audience (the general public), you might state your position like this:

> Although young male drivers have a high accident rate, insurance companies should not be allowed to discriminate against anyone who has driven for the past two years without a traffic violation.

Notice that this is a debatable point, one about which reasonable persons can disagree. It is not merely a fact (for example, that companies do set higher rates for young males). Nor is it a statement of belief (for example, that differing rates are always unfair). Neither facts nor beliefs can be substantiated by reasons, so they cannot serve as a thesis for an argument.

Once you have framed a thesis, try to state your major arguments, preferably in sentence form. Together, your thesis and your arguments will give you a rough outline of your essay, as in the following example:

> Thesis: Although young male drivers have a high accident rate, insurance companies should not be allowed to discriminate against anyone who has driven for the past two years without a traffic violation.
>
> —The current policy of insurance companies is unfair.
> —It is unfair to evaluate an individual driver on the basis of group statistics.
> —Group statistics are used to justify higher rates for young males but usually not for other groups.
> —Insurance companies could institute a more equitable policy at little expense.
> —Companies could charge higher rates for all newly licensed drivers (no matter their age or sex), in effect putting them on probation for a period such as two years.
> —Companies could keep individual records on all drivers and set rates yearly according to those records; the rates would apply to all drivers following the two-year probationary period.
> —With computer databases, records could be maintained at a reasonable cost.

Some of the sentences in your rough outline might become topic sentences of paragraphs in your final essay. (See 4a.)

46c Draft an introduction that states your position without alienating readers.

In argumentative writing, your introduction should state your position on an issue in a clear thesis sentence (see 2a), and it should do this without needlessly alienating the audience whom you hope to convince. Where possible, try to establish common ground with readers who may not be in initial agreement with your views.

One way to establish common ground with readers who disagree with your position is to show that you share common values. If your subject is school prayer, for instance, you might show that even though you oppose allowing prayer in schools, you believe in the value of prayer. The writer of the following introduction successfully used this strategy.

> Although the Supreme Court has ruled against prayer in public schools on First Amendment grounds, many people still feel that prayers should be allowed. These people, most of whom hold strong religious beliefs, are well intentioned. What they fail to realize is that the Supreme Court decision, although it was made on legal grounds, makes good sense on religious grounds as well. Prayer is too important to be trusted to our public schools. —Kevin Smith, student

Because Smith takes into consideration the values of those who disagree with him, readers are likely to approach his essay with an open mind.

46d Support each argument with specific evidence.

When presenting the arguments for your position, you will of course need to back them up with evidence: facts, statistics, examples and illustrations, expert opinion, and so on. Depending on the issue you have chosen to write about, you may or may not need to do some reading to gather evidence. Some argumentative topics, such as whether class attendance should be required at your college or university, can be developed through personal experience and maybe questionnaires or interviews. Most debatable topics, however, require some research.

If any of your evidence is based on reading, you will need to document your sources. Documentation gives credit to your sources and shows readers how to track down a source in case they want to assess its credibility or explore the issue further. (See 52a and 55.)

Using facts and statistics

A fact is something that is known with certainty because it has been objectively verified: The capital of Wyoming is Cheyenne. Carbon has an atomic weight of 12. John F. Kennedy was assassinated on November 22, 1963. Statistics are collections of numerical facts: More than three-quarters of U.S. households currently own a VCR. North America holds only 4 percent of the world's proven oil reserves; together, Iraq, Kuwait, and Saudi Arabia own 44 percent.

Most arguments are supported at least to some extent by facts and statistics. For example, if you were arguing against mandatory class attendance, you might include facts about the attendance policies of professors in several disciplines; you could also report statistics on the views of students.

Andrew Knutson, the student who wrote the argument paper on pages 361–64, gathered a few facts and statistics from two printed sources and one Internet source. When he used a statistic from one of these sources, he documented it with an MLA (Modern Language Association) citation in parentheses, like this:

> Currently the responsibility of educating about 75% of undocumented children is borne by just a few states—California, New York, Texas, and Florida (Edmondson 1).

Knutson got this statistic from an article by Brad Edmondson. The parenthetical citation at the end of the sentence names the author of the source and gives the page number. Complete information about the source appears in a works cited list at the end of the paper (see p. 364). (See sections 52 and 55 for more detailed information about citing sources.)

Using examples and anecdotes

Examples and anecdotes (illustrative stories) alone rarely prove a point, but when used in combination with other forms of evidence, they flesh out an argument and bring it to life. In an essay arguing against mandatory class attendance, you might give

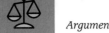

examples of class sessions that were obviously a waste of time, maybe because the professor simply read from the textbook or because you were asked to play games that had nothing to do with the subject.

In a research essay written for a psychology class, Karen Shaw used several examples from a variety of sources to show that apes are capable of using language creatively (see p. 461).

Citing expert opinion

Although they are no substitute for careful reasoning of your own, the views of an expert can contribute to the force of your argument. You might interview an educational psychologist on learning styles, for example, to help support your argument that class attendance is not the only way to learn. Or, if you were arguing in favor of mandatory class attendance, you might interview a dean to learn about academic goals (such as increased tolerance for persons from other cultures) that can be accomplished only through class attendance.

When you rely on expert opinion, you should be certain that your source is, in fact, an expert in the field you are covering. In some cases you may need to provide an explanation of what makes your source an expert. Use particular caution when gathering research from online sources (see section 49).

If you include expert testimony in your paper, you must document your sources. You can summarize or paraphrase the expert's opinion or you can quote the expert's exact words. For important advice on appropriate use of written sources, see the chart on page 409.

46e Anticipate objections; refute opposing arguments.

Readers who already agree with you need no convincing, although a well-argued case for their own point of view is always welcome. But indifferent and skeptical readers may resist your arguments because they have minds of their own. To give up a position that seems reasonable, a reader has to see that there is an even more reasonable one. In addition to presenting your own case, therefore, you should review the chief arguments of the opposition and explain what you think is wrong with them.

There is no best place in an essay to deal with the opposition. Often it is useful to summarize the opposing position early in your essay. After stating your thesis but before developing your own arguments, you might have a paragraph beginning *Critics of this view argue that. . . .* But sometimes a better plan is to anticipate objections as you develop your case paragraph by paragraph. Wherever you decide to deal with opposing arguments, do your best to refute them. Show that those who oppose you are not as persuasive as they claim because their arguments are flawed or because your arguments to the contrary have greater weight.

46f Establish common ground.

As you refute opposing arguments, try to establish common ground with readers who are not in initial agreement with your views. If you can show that you share your readers' values, they may be able to switch to your position without giving up what they feel is important. For example, to persuade people opposed to shooting deer that hunting is necessary, a state wildlife commission would have to show that it too cares about preserving deer and does not want them to die needlessly. Having established these values in common, the commission might be able to persuade critics that a carefully controlled hunting season is good for the deer population because it prevents starvation caused by overpopulation.

People believe that intelligence and decency support their side of an argument. To change sides, they must continue to feel intelligent and decent. Otherwise they will persist in their opposition.

47

Avoid common mistakes in reasoning.

Certain errors in reasoning occur frequently enough to deserve special attention. In both your reading and your writing, you will want to be alert to common mistakes in inductive and deductive reasoning and to certain mistakes known as logical fallacies.

47a Use inductive reasoning with care.

When you reason inductively, you draw a conclusion from an array of facts. For example, you might conclude that a professor is friendly because he or she smiles frequently and talks to students after class or that fifty-five miles per hour is a safer speed limit than sixty-five miles per hour because there are fewer deaths per accident at that speed.

Inductive reasoning deals in probability, not certainty. For a conclusion based on inductive reasoning to be highly probable, the evidence must be sufficient, representative, and relevant. Consider, for example, how you would evaluate the following conclusion, drawn from evidence gathered in a survey.

> **CONCLUSION** The majority of households in our city would subscribe to cable television if it were available.
>
> **EVIDENCE** In a recent survey, 356 of the 500 households questioned say they would subscribe to cable television.

Is the evidence sufficient? That depends. In a city of 10,000, the 500 households are a 5 percent sample, sufficient for the purposes of marketing research. But in a city of 2 million, the households would amount to one-fortieth of 1 percent of the population, an inadequate sample on which to base an important decision.

Is the evidence representative? Again, that depends. The cable company would trust the survey if it knew that the sample had been carefully constructed to reflect the age, sex, geographic distribution, and income of the city's population as a whole. If, however, the 500 households were concentrated in one wealthy neighborhood, the company would be wise to question the survey's conclusion.

Is the evidence relevant? The answer is a cautious yes. The survey question is directly linked to the conclusion. A question about the number of hours spent watching television, by contrast, would not be relevant, because it would not be about *subscribing* to *cable* television. In addition, a cautious interpreter of the evidence would want to know whether people who *say* they would subscribe tend to subscribe *in fact*. By looking at marketing research done in other cities, the cable television company could determine—through a new round of inductive reasoning—how many of the 356 households who say they would subscribe are likely in fact to subscribe.

47b Use deductive reasoning with care.

When you reason deductively, you draw a conclusion from two or more assertions (called *premises*).

> The police do not give speeding tickets to people driving less than five miles per hour over the limit. Sam is driving fifty-nine miles per hour in a fifty-five-mile-per-hour zone. Therefore, the police will not give Sam a speeding ticket.

The conclusion is true only if the premises are true. If the police sometimes give tickets for less than five-mile-per-hour violations or if the speedometer is inaccurate, Sam cannot safely conclude that he will avoid a ticket.

Deductive reasoning can often be structured in a three-step argument called a *syllogism*. The three steps are the major premise, the minor premise, and the conclusion:

1. Anything that increases radiation in the environment is dangerous to public health. (Major premise)
2. Nuclear reactors increase radiation in the environment. (Minor premise)
3. Therefore, nuclear reactors are dangerous to public health. (Conclusion)

The major premise is a generalization. The minor premise is a specific case. The conclusion follows from applying the generalization to the specific case.

Many deductive arguments do not state one of the premises but rather leave the reader to infer it, as in the following example:

> Violent crime is increasing.
>
> Therefore, we should reinstate the death penalty.

The minor premise, that violent crime is increasing, may be true, but the major premise, that the death penalty deters violent criminals, is a debatable issue. A careful reader will uncover this hidden major premise and question the whole argument.

 *Argument*

Deductive arguments break down if one of the premises is not true or if the conclusion does not logically follow from the premises. For example, consider this argument:

> The deer population in our state should be preserved. During hunting season hundreds of deer are killed. Therefore, the hunting season should be discontinued.

To challenge this argument, the state's wildlife commission might agree with both the major and minor premises but question whether the conclusion follows logically from them. True, the deer population should be preserved; true, deer are killed during hunting season. However, in an area where deer have no natural enemies, herds become too large for the forest vegetation to support them. The overpopulated herds strip the leaves and bark from the young trees, killing the trees before dying of starvation themselves. The commission might conclude, therefore, that a limited hunting season helps preserve a healthier and more stable population of deer.

47c Avoid logical fallacies.

Some errors in reasoning are so common that writers and readers call them by name: hasty generalization, non sequitur, false analogy, and so on. Such errors are known as *logical fallacies*. Some common fallacies are included in the following chart.

Common logical fallacies

HASTY GENERALIZATION

A generalization based on insufficient or unrepresentative evidence.

> Deaths from drug overdoses in Metropolis have doubled in the past three years. Therefore, more Americans than ever are dying from drug abuse.

NON SEQUITUR ("DOES NOT FOLLOW")

A conclusion that does not follow logically from preceding statements or that is based on irrelevant data.

> Mary loves children, so she will make an excellent elementary school teacher.

FALSE ANALOGY

The assumption that because two things are alike in some respects, they are alike in others.

> If we put humans on the moon, we should be able to find a cure for the common cold.

EITHER . . . OR FALLACY

The suggestion that only two alternatives exist when in fact there are more.

> Either learn how to program a computer or you won't be able to get a decent job after college.

FALSE CAUSE (*POST HOC*)

The assumption that because one event follows another, the first is the cause of the second.

> Since Governor Smith took office, unemployment for minorities in the state has decreased by 7 percent. Governor Smith should be applauded for reducing unemployment among minorities.

CIRCULAR REASONING

An argument in which the writer, instead of supplying evidence, simply restates the point in other language.

> Students should not be allowed to park in lots now reserved for faculty because those lots should be for faculty only.

BANDWAGON APPEAL

A claim that an idea should be accepted because a large number of people favor it or believe it is true.

> Everyone knows that smoking marijuana is physically addictive and psychologically harmful.

ARGUMENT TO THE PERSON (*AD HOMINEM*)

An attack on the person proposing an argument rather than on the argument itself.

> Senator Jones was a conscientious objector during the Vietnam War, so his proposal to limit military spending has no merit.

RED HERRING

An argument that focuses on an irrelevant issue to distract attention from the real issue.

> Reporters are out to get the president, so it's no wonder we are hearing rumors about all of these scandals.

BIASED LANGUAGE

Words with strong positive or negative connotations.

> Those narrow-minded, do-gooder environmentalists care more about trees than they do about people.

EXERCISE 47–1

Explain what is illogical in the following brief arguments. It may be helpful to identify the logical fallacy or fallacies by name. Answers to lettered sentences appear in the back of the book.

a. All of my blind dates have been embarrassing disasters, so I know this one will be too.
b. If you're old enough to vote, you're old enough to drink. Therefore, the drinking age should be lowered to eighteen.
c. This country has been run too long by old, out-of-date, out-of-touch, entrenched politicians protecting the special interests that got them elected.
d. It was possible to feed a family of four on $100 a week before Governor Leroy took office and drove up food prices.
e. If you're not part of the solution, you're part of the problem.

1. Whenever I wash my car, it rains. I have discovered a way to end all droughts—get all the people to wash their cars.
2. Our current war on drugs has not worked. Either we should legalize drugs or we should turn the drug war over to our armed forces and let them fight it.
3. College professors tend to be sarcastic. Three of my five professors this semester make sarcastic remarks.
4. Although Ms. Bell's book on Joe DiMaggio was well researched, I doubt that an Australian historian can contribute much to our knowledge of an American baseball player.
5. Self-righteous nonsmoking fanatics have eroded our basic individual freedoms by railroading the passage of oppressive anti-smoking laws that interfere with our natural right to make our own decisions.

6. If professional sports teams didn't pay athletes such high salaries, we wouldn't have so many kids breaking their legs at hockey and basketball camps.
7. Ninety percent of the students oppose a tuition increase; therefore, the board of trustees should not pass the proposed increase.
8. If the president had learned the lesson of Vietnam, he would realize that sending U.S. troops into a foreign country can only end in disaster.
9. A mandatory ten-cent deposit on bottles and cans will eliminate litter because everyone I know will return the containers for the money rather than throw them away.
10. Soliciting money to save whales and baby seals is irresponsible when thousands of human beings can't afford food and shelter.

SAMPLE ARGUMENT PAPER

In the following paper, student Andrew Knutson argues that Americans should continue to educate the children of illegal immigrants. Notice that Knutson is careful to establish common ground with readers who may hold a different view. Notice too that he attempts to refute the arguments of the opposition before laying out his own arguments.

In writing the paper, Knutson consulted two written sources and one Internet source. When he quotes from or uses statistics from a source, he cites the source with an MLA (Modern Language Association) in-text citation. Citations in the paper refer readers to the list of works cited at the end of the paper. (See sections 52 and 55 for detailed advice on citing sources.)

SAMPLE ARGUMENT PAPER

Why Educate the Children of Illegal Immigrants?

Immigration laws have been a subject of debate throughout American history, especially in states such as California and Texas, where immigrant populations are high. Recently, some citizens have been questioning whether we should continue to educate the children of illegal immigrants. While this issue is steeped in emotional controversy, we must not allow divisive "us against them" rhetoric to cloud our thinking. Yes, educating undocumented immigrants costs us, but not educating them would cost us much more.

Thesis, at end of introductory paragraph, doesn't alienate readers.

Writer addresses concerns of those who hold opposing views.

Those who propose barring the children of illegal immigrants from our schools have understandable worries. They worry that their state taxes will rise as undocumented children crowd their school systems. They worry about the crowding itself, given the loss of quality education that comes with large class sizes. They worry that school resources will be deflected from their children because of the linguistic and social problems that many of the newcomers face. And finally, they worry that even more illegal immigrants will cross our borders because of the lure of free education.

Writer refutes opposing arguments.

This last worry is probably unfounded. It is unlikely that many parents are crossing the borders solely to educate their children. More likely, they are in desperate need of work, economic opportunity, and possibly political asylum. As Charles Wheeler of

Quotation is cited using MLA style.

the National Immigration Law Center asserts, "There is no evidence that access to federal programs acts as a magnet to foreigners or that further restrictions would discourage illegal immigrants" (qtd. in "Exploiting").

Reasonable tone keeps argument from sounding biased.

Statistic is cited using MLA style.

The other concerns are more legitimate, but they can be addressed by less drastic measures than barring children from schools. Currently the responsibility of educating about 75% of undocumented children is borne by just a few states--California, New York, Texas, and Florida (Edmondson 1). One way to help these and other states is to have the federal government pick up the cost of educating undocumented children, with enough funds to alleviate the overcrowded classrooms that cause parents such concern. Such cost shifting could have a significant benefit, for if the federal government had to pay, it might work harder to stem the tide of illegal immigrants.

Writer uses evidence to support thesis.

So far, attempts to bar undocumented children from public schools have failed. In the 1982 case of Plyler v. Doe, the Supreme Court ruled on the issue.

In a 5-4 decision, it overturned a Texas law that allowed schools to deny education to illegal immigrants. Martha McCarthy reports that Texas had justified its law as a means of "preserving financial resources, protecting the state from an influx of illegal immigrants, and maintaining high quality education for resident children" (128). The Court considered these issues but concluded that in the long run the costs of educating immigrant children would pale in comparison to the costs--both to the children and to society--of not educating them.

Quotation is cited using MLA style.

It isn't hard to figure out what the costs of not educating these children would be. The costs to innocent children are obvious: loss of the opportunity to learn English, to understand American culture and history, to socialize with other children in a structured environment, and to grow up to be successful, responsible adults.

Transitional topic sentence leads readers to next part of paper.

The costs to society as a whole are fairly obvious as well. That is why we work so hard to promote literacy and prevent students from dropping out of school. An uneducated populace is dangerous to the fabric of society, contributing to social problems such as vandalism and crime, an underground economy, gang warfare, teenage pregnancy, substance abuse, and infectious and transmissible diseases. The health issue alone makes it worth our while to educate the children of undocumented immigrants, for when children are in school, we can make sure they are inoculated properly, and we can teach them the facts about health and disease.

Writer attempts to build common ground with readers.

Do we really want thousands of uneducated children growing up on the streets, where we have little control over them? Surely not. The lure of the streets is powerful enough already. Only by inviting all children into safe and nurturing and intellectually engaging schools can we combat that power. Our efforts will be well worth the cost.

Conclusion restates benefits of educating children of illegal immigrants.

[NEW PAGE]

Works cited page according to MLA style.

Works Cited

Edmondson, Brad. "Life without Illegal Immigrants."
American Demographics May 1996: 1.

"Exploiting Fears." Admissions Decisions: Should
Immigration Be Restricted? 7 Oct. 1996. Public Agenda. 10 Feb. 1999. <http://www.vote-
smart.org/issues/Immigration/chap2/
imm2itx.html>.

McCarthy, Martha M. "Immigrants in Public Schools:
Legal Issues." Educational Horizons 71
(1993): 128-30.

Research Guide

Most college assignments ask you to pose a question worth exploring, to read widely in search of possible answers, to interpret what you read, to draw reasoned conclusions, and to support those conclusions with valid and well-documented evidence.

Setting realistic deadlines

Admittedly, the process takes time: time for researching and time for drafting, revising, and documenting the paper in the style recommended by your instructor (see 55 and 56). Before beginning a research project, you should set a realistic schedule of deadlines. For example, one student constructed the following schedule for a paper assigned on October 1 and due October 29.

SCHEDULE	FINISHED BY
1. Take the college's library tour and get familiar with computer search tools.	October 2
2. Pose a research question and plan a search strategy.	3
3. Find sources.	5
4. Read and take notes.	10
5. Decide on a tentative thesis and outline.	15
6. Draft the paper.	16
7. Visit the writing center to get help with ideas for revision.	18
8. Do further research if necessary.	19
9. Revise the paper.	21
10. Prepare a list of works cited.	26
11. Type and proofread the final draft.	28

Notice that this student has budgeted more than a week for drafting and revising the paper. It's easy to spend too much of your available time gathering sources; make sure you allow a significant portion of your schedule for drafting and editing your work.

48

Conducting research

48a Pose possible questions worth exploring.

Working within the guidelines of your assignment, pose a few questions that seem worth researching. Here, for example, are some preliminary questions jotted down by students who were asked to write about a significant political or scholarly issue.

— Can a government-regulated rating system for television shows curb children's exposure to violent programming?

— Which geological formations are the safest repositories for nuclear waste?

— Will a ban on human cloning threaten important medical research?

— What was Marcus Garvey's contribution to the fight for racial equality?

— How can governments and zoos help preserve China's endangered panda?

— Why was amateur archaeologist Heinrich Schliemann such a controversial figure in his own time?

As you formulate possible questions, make sure that they are appropriate lines of inquiry for a research paper. Choose questions that are narrow (not too broad), challenging (not too bland), and grounded (not too speculative).

Choosing a narrow question

If your initial question is too broad, given the length of the paper you plan to write, look for ways to restrict your focus. Here, for example, is how some students narrowed their initial questions.

TOO BROAD

— What are the hazards of fad diets?

— Is the military seriously addressing the problem of sexual harassment?

NARROWER

—What are the hazards of liquid diets?

—To what extent has the army addressed the problem of sexual harassment since the Aberdeen scandal?

Choosing a challenging question

Your research paper will be more interesting to both you and your audience if you base it on an intellectually challenging line of inquiry. Avoid bland questions that fail to provoke thought or engage readers in a debate.

TOO BLAND

—What is obsessive-compulsive disorder?

—Where is wind energy being used?

CHALLENGING

—What treatments for obsessive-compulsive disorder show the most promise?

—Does investing in wind energy make economic sense?

You may well need to address a bland question in the course of answering a more challenging one. For example, if you were writing about promising treatments for obsessive-compulsive disorder, you would no doubt answer the question "What is obsessive-compulsive disorder?" at some point in your paper. It would be a mistake, however, to use the bland question as the focus for the whole paper.

Choosing a grounded question

Finally, you will want to make sure that your research question is grounded, not too speculative. Although speculative questions — such as those that address philosophical, ethical, or religious issues — are worth asking and may receive some attention in a research paper, they are inappropriate central questions. The central argument of a research paper should be grounded in evidence; it should not be based entirely on beliefs.

TOO SPECULATIVE

—Is capital punishment moral?

—What is the difference between a just and an unjust law?

GROUNDED

—Does capital punishment deter crime?

—Should we adjust our laws so that penalties for possession of powdered cocaine and crack cocaine are comparable?

48b Map out a search strategy.

A search strategy is a systematic system for tracking down sources. To create a search strategy appropriate for your research question, ask yourself two questions:

—What kinds of resources should I draw on?

—In what order should I conduct my search?

Appropriate resources

Before you start your search, consider what information you will need and where you are likely to find it (see the chart of possible resources on p. 371). If your research question addresses a historical issue, for example, you might look at reference works, books, scholarly articles (in print or online), and primary sources such as speeches. If your question addresses a current political issue, you might turn to magazine and newspaper articles, Web sites, government documents, discussion groups on the Internet, and possibly opinion surveys that you conduct yourself. With very current issues, books are not useful because by the time a book is published, it is already dated.

In addition to considering the currency of your proposed topic, take a careful look at your assignment. Most college assignments require you to seek out scholarly sources that challenge your intellect: books by authors who are experts in their field, specialized reference works (not just general encyclopedias), and articles in scholarly or technical journals (not just popular magazines). When in doubt about the kinds of sources you are expected to consult, check with your instructor.

Order of search

Often a good search strategy moves from sources that give you an overview of your subject to those that supply you with more specialized information. Some general reading will familiarize you with the ways in which scholars or debaters are framing issues related to your topic. Once you understand the intellectual or social context of your topic, you will be prepared to focus your search more narrowly.

48c Track down relevant library sources.

If you have not already done so, explore your library to find out what it offers. Most libraries provide maps and handouts that describe their services; many conduct orientation programs or offer tours or workshops. In addition, librarians can save you time by helping you define what you're looking for and then telling you where to find it.

Most of the searching you do at the library will take place at computer terminals with specific functions. Some terminals are for accessing the computerized book catalog, others contain CD-ROM databases of periodicals, and still others serve as gateways to the Internet.

NOTE: Many libraries make their catalogs available on the Internet, so you can search a library's holdings remotely. This does not necessarily mean that you will be able to access materials from your remote computer, but you will be able to see what is available before you visit the library.

Reference works

For some topics, you may want to begin your search by consulting general or specialized reference works. Check with a reference librarian to see which works are available in electronic format.

GENERAL REFERENCE WORKS General reference works include encyclopedias, biographical references, atlases, almanacs, and unabridged dictionaries. Here are just a few frequently used general references that you might want to consider.

> *Encyclopedia Americana*
> *The National Geographic Atlas of the World*
> *The New Encyclopædia Britannica*
> *The Oxford English Dictionary*

Resources to consider when creating a search strategy

LIBRARY RESOURCES

- General and specialized reference works
- Books
- Articles in scholarly journals
- Articles in magazines and newspapers
- Government documents
- Primary sources such as diaries and letters
- Audiovisual materials

INTERNET RESOURCES

- Web sites
- Reference works
- Electronic texts (books, poems, and so on)
- Government documents
- News articles
- Newsgroups and listservs
- MUD's and MOO's
- E-mail

FIELD RESOURCES

- Interviews
- Opinion surveys
- Discussion groups
- Literature from organizations
- Observations and experiments

Webster's New Biographical Dictionary
World Almanac and Book of Facts

For other titles, consult the computer catalog or check with a reference librarian.

NOTE: Although general encyclopedias are often a good place to learn background information about your topic, do not draw upon them in your final paper. Most instructors expect you to rely on more specialized sources.

SPECIALIZED REFERENCE WORKS Many specialized works are available: *Encyclopedia of the Environment, Contemporary Artists, The Historical and Cultural Atlas of African Americans, Almanac of American Politics, Anchor Bible Dictionary,* and so on. Some libraries provide handouts that list their specialized reference works, organized by academic discipline. If your library doesn't, ask a reference librarian for suggestions.

NOTE: A Bedford/St. Martin's Web site, *Research and Documentation in the Electronic Age,* lists many specialized reference works. If a work is available on the Web, the Bedford/St. Martin's site links you directly to the source. The address is < http://www.bedfordstmartins.com/hacker/resdoc >.

Books

Most libraries now use computer catalogs that allow you to search for books and often other materials—such as government documents and audiovisuals—at a computer terminal. While computer catalogs vary widely from library to library, most are easy to use, and a reference librarian will be available to help you if you get stuck. Most catalogs allow you to search for materials by subject, by author, or by title. The screens on this page and the next illustrate a subject search.

COMPUTER CATALOG SCREEN 1: LIST OF MATERIALS

```
PUMAS                        5    ITEMS
  1 Lawrence R D 192                        NU  SNELL  STACKS  1990
      The white puma : a novel              QL 795.P85L38 1990

  2 Shaw harley g                           NU  SNELL  STACKS  1989
      Soul among lions : the cougar as peaceful adv  QL 737.C23S52 1989

  3 Tinsley Jim Bob                         NU  SNELL  STACKS  1987
      The Puma : legendary lion of the Americas  QL 737.C2T5x  1987

  4                                         NU  SNELL  STACKS  1973
      Mountain lion social organization in the Idaho  QL 1.W54  no35

  5 Young Stanley Paul                      NU  SNELL  STACKS  1964
      The puma, mysterious American cat. Part I: Hist QL 737.C2Y56  1964

ALL ITEMS HAVE BEEN DISPLAYED..
Enter <Line number(s)> To Display Full Records (Number + B for Brief)
<Q>uit for New Search ▌
```

COMPUTER CATALOG SCREEN 2: DETAILS FOR A BOOK

```
-------------------------------------NU Libraries-------------
AUTHOR(s):      Tinsley, Jim Bob.
TITLE(s):       The Puma : legendary lion of the Americas /  Jim Bob
                   Tinsley.
                1st ed.

                El Paso, Tex. : Texas Western Press, University of Texas
                   at El Paso,  c1987.
                142 p, : ill. ; 29 cm.
                Includes index.
                Bibliography: p. [127]-136.

OTHER ENTRIES:  Pumas.

Format:         statedoc

LOCN:   SNELL STACKS    STATUS: Not checked out --
CALL #: QL 737.C2T5x 1987

----3 of 5--------------------------NU Libraries-------------
<R>epeat this display, <Q>uit,
<X> for Express,   <H> for Search History,   ? for Help   > █
```

The most common type of searching is by subject. Searching the catalog by subject involves the use of keywords or subject headings, which prompt the computer to retrieve information about relevant books and other source materials. If your search results in too few or too many finds (or "hits"), try refining your search by using one of the techniques listed in the chart on page 378.

Once you have narrowed your search to a list of relevant sources, you can usually command the computer to print out bibliographic information for a source, along with its call number. The call number is the book's address on the library shelf.

Periodicals

Periodicals are publications issued at regular intervals, such as magazines, newspapers, and scholarly or technical journals. To track down useful articles, consult a periodical index. Periodical indexes vary widely in their format and coverage, so you may wish to check with a reference librarian to find the resources that best suit your needs.

TYPES OF PERIODICAL INDEXES   Periodical indexes are usually available in both print and electronic formats. Most libraries now have a wide selection of electronic databases, either on CD-ROM's or through online subscription services. Be aware, however, that most electronic databases don't date back as far as the print versions do, so you may need to search print indexes for historical topics.

Some periodical indexes, such as *InfoTrac* and *Readers' Guide to Periodical Literature,* focus on popular periodicals and cover a wide range of subjects and publications. More specialized indexes, such as *Religion Index* and *Communication Abstracts,* focus on technical and scholarly journals in particular subject areas.

Periodical indexes also vary in the amount of information they provide. Some indexes contain only article titles and publication information, many include abstracts that summarize the articles, and a few contain the full text of the articles they list.

SEARCHING PERIODICAL INDEXES   You search for periodical articles in an electronic database just as you look for books in the library's computer catalog—by author, title, or subject keywords. Bibliographic records appear on the screen, and if further information is available (such as an abstract or the complete text), you can retrieve it by selecting the article you want. An example of a periodical index screen is on the next page.

If you are looking for periodical articles that appeared before the mid-1980s, you may need to turn to a print index. Like computer indexes, print indexes usually allow you to search by author, by title, or by subject.

Once you have found article titles that seem relevant to your topic, you will need to track down the periodicals that contain the actual articles. Most libraries provide either a print or an electronic listing of the periodicals they own. The listing tells you how each periodical has been preserved: on microfilm or microfiche, in bound volumes, or in unbound files. It also tells you which publication years the library owns.

CAUTION: Be careful not to confuse abstracts, which summarize articles, with actual articles.

PERIODICAL INDEX SCREEN: DETAILS FOR AN ARTICLE

```
1 RGA
   AUTHOR: Robinson, Jerome B.
   TITLE: Cat in the ballot box (California voters to decide on resumption
       of cougar hunting)
   SOURCE: Field & Stream (ISSN:8755-8580) v 100 p 30+ March'96
   CONTAINS: illustration(s)

SUBJECTS COVERED:
Puma attacks
Puma hunting
Game laws/California
ABSTRACT: For more than two decades, the California Department of Fish
and Game has been prohibited by law from taking measures to limit a
mountain lion population that has clearly overgrown its natural range and
is expanding into urban areas. Mountain lions usually eat deer, but in
locations where deer populations have become sparse, they have been
forced to find new food sources. Consequently, lions are killing
livestock, cats, dogs, and even people. Now, California voters are being
asked to decide if the "hands off" mountain lion policy should continue.
If voters pass a proposed referendum, the Fish and Game Department could
reintroduce limited sport hunting as a means of controlling mountain lion
populations.
```

Other library sources

Your library may have rare and unpublished manuscripts in a special collection. Holdings might also include government documents; records, tapes, and CD's; films and videos; and drawings, paintings, engravings, and slides.

If your research topic is especially complex or unusual, you may need greater resources than your library offers. In such a case, talk to a librarian about interlibrary loan, a process in which one library borrows materials from another. This procedure can take a week or more, so be sure to allow yourself plenty of time.

48d Track down relevant Internet sources.

Some of your research will probably take place on the Internet, a vast network of computers that can communicate with one another. When you are logged on to the Internet—often by using a browser such as Netscape Navigator or Microsoft Internet Explorer — you have access to countless online sources. The most common way to locate relevant online sources is to use the Internet search tools desribed in this section.

CAUTION: Because the Internet lacks quality control, be sure to evaluate online sources with special care (see 49).

Search engines

Millions of Internet sites are cataloged by search engines each day, so online searching can be a daunting process. To maximize your search efforts, consider your own needs and the specialties of the various search engines that are available.

SEARCHING BY CATEGORY Multilevel subject or topic directories arrange sites into manageable categories and allow you to find relevant sites without searching the entire Internet. (For an example, see the sample screens on page 377.) Subject directories can be stand-alone programs such as *Argus Clearinghouse* < http://www.clearinghouse.net >, or they can be part of a search engine such as *Yahoo!* < http://www.yahoo.com >.

The benefit of searching by category is that you are restricting your hits to those listed in the subject areas you think are most relevant, so you are less likely to be overwhelmed with possible sources. The downside of searching by category is that you may miss out on useful sites categorized under other subject headings or not included in the directory.

SEARCHING BY KEYWORD The amount of information returned by a simple keyword search, much of it irrelevant to your topic, can be overwhelming. To make the best use of your research time, spend a few minutes looking over the help screens or advanced search instructions on individual search engines. In addition, keep the following points in mind:

— Make your keywords as specific as possible.
— Check your spelling.
— Refine or broaden your search as needed (see the chart on page 378 for common techniques).

See the screens on pages 378–79 for a sample keyword search.

SCREEN 1: CHOOSING A CATEGORY

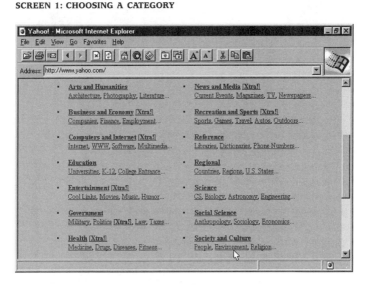

SCREEN 2: SEARCHING A CATEGORY

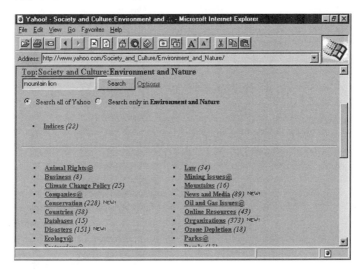

Refining keyword searches

Although command terms and characters vary among electronic databases and Internet search engines, some of the most commonly used functions are listed here.

- Use quotation marks around words that are part of a phrase: "Broadway muscials".

- Use AND to connect words that must appear in a document: Ireland AND peace. Some search engines require a plus sign instead: Ireland + peace

- Use NOT in front of words that must not appear in a document: Titanic NOT movie. Some search engines require a minus sign instead: Titanic − movie.

- Use OR if only one of the terms must appear in a document: "mountain lion" OR cougar.

- Use an asterisk as a substitute for letters that might vary: "marine biolog*".

- Use parentheses to group a search expression and combine it with another: (cigarettes OR tobacco OR smok*) AND lawsuits.

SCREEN 1: ENTERING A KEYWORD

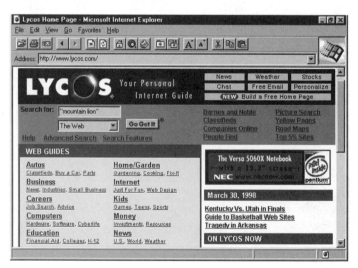

SCREEN 1: LIST OF HITS

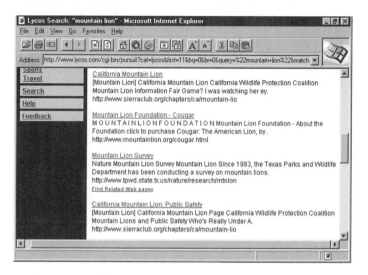

USING META SEARCH ENGINES Meta search engines such as *Dogpile* < http://www.dogpile.com > and *Metacrawler* < http://www.metacrawler.com > search multiple search engines at once. Meta search engines are useful tools for conducting a preliminary search to determine what types of online sources are available.

One drawback of using meta search engines is that a search will probably result in a number of redundant hits. Another drawback is that you won't be able to take advantage of the specialized commands offered by the individual search engines.

Other online research tools

Because they search the entire Web, search engines are likely to return a number of irrelevant hits and possibly bury relevant ones. To conduct a more focused search, turn to other online resources such as virtual libraries, text databases and archives, government sites, and news sites.

VIRTUAL LIBRARIES Virtual libraries are excellent resources for finding online references and useful research sites; some

Research Guide

Leading search engines and their specialties

ALTAVISTA <http://www.altavista.com> *AltaVista* is one of the most comprehensive search engines, so it is useful for finding obscure terms. This program allows you to restrict searches by date and to search only in particular fields—such as title, URL, or domain name (.com, .edu, and so on).

EXCITE <http://www.excite.com> *Excite* is good at ranking the probable relevance of a site, and it suggests sites that are similar to ones you found helpful.

HOTBOT <http://www.hotbot.com> The opening page of *HotBot* lets you customize your search. For example, it allows you to specify date restrictions, type of media desired, and domain names without having to go into an advanced search screen.

INFOSEEK <http://www.infoseek.com> *Infoseek* allows you to conduct a search on the results of a previous search. It also lets you search for terms only in a particular field, such as titles or URL's.

LYCOS <http://www.lycos.com> *Lycos* maintains a directory and searchable database of its top 5 percent rated sites. *Lycos* allows you to find sites similar to the ones you like best, and it offers advanced search features that allow you to set the relative importance of search parameters and choose the type of media desired.

YAHOO! <http://www.yahoo.com> *Yahoo!* has the most detailed subject directory of the leading search engines, so it is easy to click on a topic and see what's available. This program allows you to restrict a search by date.

even offer advice on writing and documenting research papers. Virtual libraries are usually organized like subject directories, with hierarchical categories. Here are some especially useful virtual libraries:

— *The Internet Public Library* < http://www.ipl.org >

— *THOR: Purdue University Libraries* < http:// thorplus.lib.purdue.edu >

— *The WWW Virtual Library* < http://vlib.org >

— *The Library of Congress* < http://lcweb.loc.gov >

— *The Webliography: Internet Subject Guides* < http:// www.lib.lsu.edu/weblio.html >

SAMPLE VIRTUAL LIBRARY SCREEN

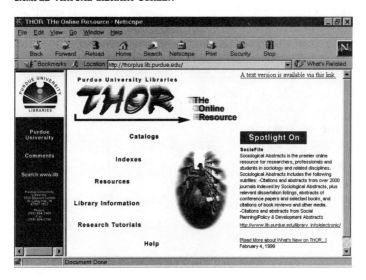

TEXT DATABASES AND ARCHIVES A number of useful online databases and archives house the complex texts of selected works such as poems, books, and speeches. The materials in these sites are usually limited to older works because of copyright laws. The following online archives are impressive collections:

— *Electronic Text Center* — University of Virginia Library < http://etext.lib.virginia.edu >

— *Project Bartleby Archive* < http://www.columbia.edu/acis/bartleby >

— *Project Gutenberg* < http://promo.net/pg >

GOVERNMENT SITES Many government agencies at every level provide online information services. Government-maintained sites include useful resources such as texts of laws, facts and statistics, government documents, and reference works. If your topic is a political issue, consider going to one of these sites:

— *U.S. Census Bureau: The Official Statistics* < http://www.census.gov >

— *Thomas: Legislative Information on the Internet* < http://thomas.loc.gov >

Useful online research sites

GENERAL REFERENCE SITES

- *Atlapedia Online* < http://www.atlapedia.com >
- *Britannica Online* < http://www.eb.com >
- *Encyclopedia Smithsonian* < http://www.si.edu/resource/faq >

DISCIPLINE-SPECIFIC SITES

- *Research and Documentation in the Electronic Age* (links to sites in a variety of academic disciplines) < http://www.bedfordstmartins.com/hacker/resdoc >
- *Bedford Links to Resources in Literature* < http://www.bedfordstmartins.com/litlinks >
- *Voice of the Shuttle: Web Page for Humanities Research* < http://humanitas.ucsb.edu >
- *H-net: Humanities and Social Sciences Online* < http://h-net2.msu.edu >
- *Social Science Information Gateway* < http://sosig.esrc.bris.ac.uk >
- *Stanford Encyclopedia of Philosophy* < http://plato.stanford.edu >
- "Famous Paintings Exhibition," *WebMuseum* < http://sunsite.unc.edu/wm/paint >
- *Perseus Project* < http://www.perseus.tufts.edu >
- *Bedford/St. Martin's Links to History Resources* < http://www.bedfordstmartins.com/history/historylinks.html >
- *Newsweek International Business Resource Center* < http://www.newsweek.int.com >
- *Science Online* < http://www.sciencemag.org >
- *Windows to the Universe* < http://www.windows.umich.edu >

SITES FOR EVALUATING SOURCES

- "Checklist for Evaluating Web Sites," *Canisius College Library & Internet* < http://www.canisius.edu/canhp/canlib/webcrit.htm >
- "Evaluating Web Sites: Criteria and Tools," *Olin Kroch Uris Libraries* < http://www.library.cornell.edu/okuref/research/webeval.html >
- "Evaluating Internet Information," *Internet Navigator* < http://sol.slcc.edu/lr/navigator/discovery/eval.html >

—*U.S. State & Local Gateway* < http://www.statelocal.gov >

—*U.S. Government Printing Office* < http://www.access.gpo.gov >

—*United Nations* < http://www.un.org >

NEWS SITES Many popular newspapers, magazines, and television networks have online sites that offer some of the most up-to-date information available on the Web. These online services, such as the following, often allow nonsubscribers or "guests" to search partial archives:

—*The New York Times on the Web* < http://www.nytimes.com >

—*The Washington Post* < http://www.washingtonpost.com >

—*U.S. News Online* < http://www.usnews.com/usnews/ home.htm >

—*nationalgeographic.com* < http://www.nationalgeographic.com/ main.html >

—*CNN Interactive* < http://www.cnn.com >

Online communications

The Internet offers several communications options for conducting your own field research. You might join a listserv, for example, to send and receive e-mail messages relevant to your topic. Or you may wish to search a particular newsgroup's postings. To find listservs and newsgroups related to your topic, go to one of these sites:

—*Tile.Net* < http://www.tile.net >

—*Liszt* < http://www.liszt.com >

—*Deja News* < http://www.dejanews.com >

In addition to listservs and newsgroups, you might log on to real-time discussion forums such as MUD's (multi-user dimensions) and MOO's (multi-user dimensions, object-oriented) to discuss your topic.

CAUTION: If you plan to use online communications to conduct field research, be aware that most of the people you contact will not be experts on your topic. Although you are more likely to find serious and worthwhile commentary in moderated listservs and scholarly discussion forums than in more freewheeling newsgroups, it is difficult to guarantee the credibility of anyone you "meet" online.

49

Evaluating sources

49a Select sources worth your attention.

By spending just an hour or two searching for information in the library or on the Internet, you can often locate dozens of potential sources for your topic—far more than you will have time to read. Your challenge will be to select a reasonable number of sources that are worth your time and attention.

As you conduct a library or Internet search, be alert for clues that indicate whether a book or article or Web site is worth tracking down. Titles often suggest the relevance of a source, and dates will help you rule out sources too old for consideration. In addition, many electronic indexes contain abstracts—brief summaries of articles—that can help you choose which ones to look at. Even the language used in a title or abstract can be a clue; the language might tell you, for example, that a source is too technical, too sensationalized, or not scholarly enough for your purposes.

Once you have tracked down a source, preview it quickly to see how much of your attention, if any, it is worth. Techniques for previewing a book, an article, and a Web site are a bit different. Suggested techniques appear in the chart on page 385.

49b Read with an open mind and a critical eye.

As you research your topic, keep an open mind. Do not let your personal beliefs prevent you from listening to new ideas and opposing viewpoints. Your research question — not a snap-judgment answer to the question—should guide your reading.

CAUTION: When researching on the Internet, it is easy to ignore views different from your own. Web pages that appeal to you will often link to other pages that support the same viewpoint. If your sources all seem to agree with you—and with one another—seek out opposing views and try to evaluate them with an open mind.

Previewing techniques

PREVIEWING A BOOK

— Scan the front and back covers for any information about the book's scope and its author's credentials.

— Glance through the table of contents, keeping your research question in mind.

— Skim the preface in search of a statement of the author's purposes.

— Using the index, look up a few words related to your research question.

— If a chapter seems useful, read its opening and closing paragraphs and skim any headings.

— Consider the author's style and approach. Does the style suggest enough intellectual depth for your purpose? Does the author seem to present ideas in an unbiased way?

PREVIEWING AN ARTICLE

— Consider the publication in which the article is printed. Is the publisher reputable? Who is the target audience of the publication? Might the publication be biased toward the target audience?

— For a magazine or journal article, look for an abstract or a statement of purpose at the beginning; also look for a summary at the end.

— For a newspaper article, focus on the headline and the opening sentences, known as the *lead*.

— Skim any headings and take a look at any charts, graphs, diagrams, or illustrations that might indicate the article's focus and scope.

PREVIEWING A WEB SITE

— Browse the home page. Do its contents and links seem relevant to your research question?

— Consider the reputation, credibility, and motive of the site's author. Is the site reputable enough to consider for further evaluation?

— Check to see if there is a note about when the site was last updated. For a current topic, some sites may be outdated.

When you read with a critical eye, you are not necessarily judging an author's work harshly; you are simply examining its assumptions, assessing its evidence, and weighing its conclusions.

Distinguishing between primary and secondary sources

As you begin assessing the evidence in a text, consider whether you are reading a primary or a secondary source. Primary sources are original documents such as speeches, diaries, novels, legislative bills, laboratory studies, field research reports, and eyewitness accounts. Secondary sources are commentaries on primary sources.

Although a primary source is not necessarily more reliable than a secondary source, it has the advantage of being a firsthand account. Naturally, you can better evaluate what a secondary source says if you have first read any primary sources it discusses.

Being alert for signs of bias

Both in print and online, some publishers and authors are more objective than others. If you were exploring the conspiracy theories surrounding the Kennedy assassination, for example, you wouldn't look to a supermarket tabloid such as the *National Enquirer* for answers. You would rely instead on newspapers and magazines with a national reputation for fair and objective reporting. Even reputable publications, however, can be editorially biased. For example, *USA Today, National Review,* and *Ms.* are likely to interpret certain events quite differently. If you are uncertain of a particular publication's special interests, check *Magazines for Libraries* and *Book Review Digest.*

Like publishers, some authors are more objective than others. No authors are altogether objective, of course, since they are human beings with their own life experiences, values, and beliefs. But if you have reason to believe that an author is particularly biased, you will want to assess his or her arguments with special care. For a list of questions worth asking, see the chart on the next page and the one on page 388.

Evaluating all sources

CHECKING FOR SIGNS OF BIAS

- Do the author and publisher have reputations for accurate and balanced reporting?

- Does the author or publisher have political leanings or religious views that could affect objectivity?

- Is the author or publisher associated with a special-interest group, such as Greenpeace or the National Rifle Association, that might see only one side of an issue?

- How fairly does the author treat opposing views?

- Does the author's language show signs of bias?

ASSESSING AN ARGUMENT

- What is the author's central claim or thesis?

- How does the author support this claim—with relevant and sufficient evidence or with just a few anecdotes or emotional examples?

- Are statistics accurate? Have they been used fairly? (It is possible to "lie" with statistics by using them selectively or by omitting mathematical details.)

- Are any of the author's assumptions questionable?

- Does the author consider opposing arguments and refute them persuasively? (See 46e.)

- Does the author fall prey to any logical fallacies? (See 47c.)

Assessing the author's argument

In nearly all subjects worth writing about, there is some element of argument, so don't be surprised to encounter experts who disagree. When you find areas of disagreement, you will want to read your source's arguments with special care, testing them with your own critical intelligence. Questions such as those in the charts on this and the next page can help you weigh the strengths and weaknesses of each author's argument.

Evaluating Web sources

AUTHORSHIP   Can you determine the author of the site? When you are on an internal page of a site, the author may not be named. To find out who wrote the material or what group sponsored the site, try going to the home page.

CREDIBILITY   Is the author of the site knowledgeable and credible? Does the site offer links to the author's home page, résumé, or e-mail address?

OBJECTIVITY   Who, if anyone, sponsors the site? Note that a site's domain name often specifies the type of group hosting the site: commercial (.com), educational (.edu), nonprofit (.org), governmental (.gov), military (.mil), or network (.net).

AUDIENCE AND PURPOSE   Who is the intended audience of the site? Why is the information available: to argue a position? to sell a product? to inform readers?

DOCUMENTATION   On the Internet, traditional methods of documentation are often replaced with links to original sources. Whenever possible, check out a linked source to confirm its authority.

QUALITY OF PRESENTATION   Consider the design and navigation of the site. Is it well laid out and easy to use? Do its links work, and are they up-to-date and relevant? Is the material well written and relatively free of errors?

50

Managing information

50a   Maintain a working bibliography.

Keep a record of any sources that you decide to consult. You will need this record, called a *working bibliography*, when you compile the list of works cited that will appear at the end of your paper. (See pp. 446–47 for an example.) The working bibliography will contain more sources than you'll actually use and put in your list of works cited.

Traditionally, researchers recorded bibliographic information about sources on 3˝ × 5˝ cards that they sorted alphabetically before typing their list of works cited. Today, however, many researchers save time by printing out bibliographic information from the library's computer catalog and periodical indexes or from the Internet. Although this printed bibliographic information will not appear in the exact form required for entries in the list of works cited, it will usually contain all the information you need to create the list. That information is given in the chart on page 390.

50b As you read, manage information systematically.

With a systematic method for managing information, you will save yourself time. In addition, a systematic method will help you remember later, when you are drafting your paper, just which words and phrases belong to your sources and which are your own. This is a crucial matter, for if any exact language from your sources finds its way into your final draft without quotation marks and proper documentation, you will be guilty of plagiarism, a serious academic offense. (See 50c and 52b.)

Working with photocopies and printouts

Most libraries provide photocopy machines so that you can copy pages from reference books and magazine articles and other sources that can't be removed from the library. In addition, many computer indexes now allow you to print full texts of articles. You can also print out texts from the Internet.

Working with photocopies and other "hard copy" has several advantages. It saves you time spent in the library. It allows you to highlight key passages, perhaps even color-coding the highlighted passages to reflect divisions in your outline. And you can annotate the text with notes in the margins and get a head start on the process of taking notes. (See p. 391 for an example.) Finally, working with hard copy reduces the chances of unintentional plagiarism (see 50c), since you will be able to compare your use of a source in your paper with the actual source, not just with your notes.

Information for a working bibliography

FOR BOOKS

- Call number
- All authors; any editors or translators
- Title and subtitle
- Edition (if not the first)
- Publication information: city, publisher, and date

FOR PERIODICAL ARTICLES

- All authors of the article
- Title and subtitle of the article
- Title of the magazine, journal, or newspaper
- Date and page numbers
- Volume and issue numbers, if relevant

FOR INTERNET SOURCES

- All authors, editors, compilers, or translators of the text
- Title and subtitle of the material you want to use (if available) and title of the longer work (if applicable)
- Publication information for any print version of the source
- Title of the site or discussion list name
- Author, editor, or compiler of the Web site or online database
- Date of publication (or latest update) if available
- Any page or paragraph numbers
- Name of any organization or institution sponsoring or associated with the site
- Date you visited the site
- URL (address of the site) or other information needed to access the site

CAUTION: Punctuation, spelling, and sometimes even capitalization must be exact to access Internet sites. To ensure accuracy, you may wish to cut and paste the address from your browser into a computer file.

NOTE: For the exact bibliographic format to be used in the final papper, see 55b.

SAMPLE ANNOTATED PRINTOUT

California Mountain Lion Page — http://www.sierraclub.org/chapters/ca/mountain-lion/

California Mountain Lion Page
California Wildlife Protection Coalition

Is this site sponsored by the Sierra Club?

Prop. 197 defeated. Thanks everyone!

Note: These web pages were written to help defeat Prop. 197 last March 1996. For up to date information on Mountain Lions, please see the Mountain Lion Foundation's web page at http://www.mtn-lion.org
- DEA 12/96.

Lobbyists from the Gun Owners of California, National Rifle Association (NRA) and Safari Club rammed Senate Bill 28 through the legislature. It appeared on the March ballot as Proposition 197, but was defeated. Without collecting a single voter signature, and hiding behind a disingenuous concern for public safety, trophy hunters convinced the politicians to delete the protections for cougars that were set into law directly by the citizens of California. They are exploiting people's concerns about public safety so they can make mountain lions over their mantelpieces.

very strong language!

→ But not all supporters were gun-toting "trophy Hunters."

If you blow all the smoke away, the bottom line is that Proposition 197 was a special interest trophy hunting measure, NOT a public safety measure.

→ may be true; proposition is difficult to read.

Current law allows the killing of any mountain lion that poses a threat to people. It also incorporates Department of Fish and Game (DFG) regulations that specifically allow trained state personnel to kill (or authorize others to kill) any and all lions that damage livestock, domestic animals, or other private property.

argues that current law is sufficient —but is it?

But DFG won't do their job to provide public safety. Official testimony at legislative hearings and an internal DFG memo reveal that the Department has deliberately ignored the occasions when mountain lions posed a threat. Now, the media stories that have resulted from DFG's inaction are being used to bolster a campaign to restore trophy hunting. DFG's motivation? The Department obtains much of its funding from selling licenses to trophy hunters, and relies heavily on legislative lobbying by special interest groups like NRA for their annual budget.

Mountain Lion Background Information
Trophy Hunting of Mountain Lions: A History of Deception
Mountain Lions and **Public Safety**
Full text of Proposition 197 (defeated)

Is this true? Look for proof in linked pages. Also, look for DFG view. Is there a DFG-Sponsored site?

Other sources say that current law makes it hard for DFG to do their job.

When researching on the Internet, you will probably find it easier to print out pages of text to work from rather than to take notes from a computer screen. In addition, it is useful to keep a hard copy of sources found on the Internet because a source may not be accessible at a future date. Be sure that your printed materials include the site's URL, the date of access, and the full title of the site so you can include them in your list of works cited. (See above for an example of a printout from the Internet.)

NOTE: Libraries and computer labs may have restrictions on downloading and printing files. Check with a librarian or lab director to find out what options are available to you.

Using computer files

Computer files are a useful alternative to traditional note cards, especially if you prefer to type rather than to handwrite your notes. Once you have a sense of the natural subdivisions of your topic, you can create a file for each one.

For a paper on mountain lions, John Garcia created files with these labels: endangered, resurgence, attacks on humans, California propositions, and wildlife management. Working mainly with photocopied articles, Garcia typed notes into each of these files. (Garcia's paper appears in 55e.)

CAUTION: Although you can download information from the Internet into your computer files and patch parts of it into your own work, be extremely careful. Some researchers have plagiarized their sources unintentionally because they lost track of which words came from a source and which were their own. To prevent unintentional plagiarism, put quotation marks around any text that you have patched into your own work, and make sure to introduce the quoted text with a signal phrase naming the author. (See 52b and 53a.)

50c As you take notes, avoid unintentional plagiarism.

You will discover that it is amazingly easy to borrow too much language from a source as you take notes. Do not allow this to happen. You are guilty of the academic offense known as *plagiarism* if you half-copy the author's sentences—either by mixing the author's phrases with your own without using quotation marks or by plugging your synonyms into the author's sentence structure. (For examples of this kind of plagiarism, see 52b.)

To prevent unintentional borrowing, resist the temptation to look at the source as you take notes—except when you are quoting. Keep the source close by so you can check for accuracy, but don't try to put ideas in your own words with the source's sentences in front of you.

There are three kinds of note taking: summarizing, paraphrasing, and quoting. As you take notes, be sure to include exact page references, since you will need the page numbers later if you use the information in your paper.

Summarizing without plagiarizing

A summary condenses information, perhaps reducing a chapter to a short paragraph or a paragraph to a single sentence. A summary should be written in your own words; if you use phrases from the source, put them in quotation marks.

Here is a passage from an original source read by John Garcia in researching a paper on mountain lions. Following the passage is Garcia's summary of the source.

ORIGINAL SOURCE

In some respects, the increasing frequency of mountain lion encounters in California has as much to do with a growing *human* population as it does with rising mountain lion numbers. The scenic solitude of the western ranges is prime cougar habitat, and it is falling swiftly to the developer's spade. Meanwhile, with their ideal habitat already at its carrying capacity, mountain lions are forcing younger cats into less suitable terrain, including residential areas. Add that cougars have generally grown bolder under a lengthy ban on their being hunted, and an unsettling scenario begins to emerge.

—Rychnovsky, "Clawing into Controversy," p. 40

SUMMARY

```
Source: Rychnovsky, "Clawing into Controversy" (40)
Encounters between mountain lions and humans are on the
rise in California because increasing numbers of lions are
competing for a shrinking habitat. As the lions' wild habitat
shrinks, older lions force younger lions into residential
areas. These lions have lost some of their fear of humans
because of a ban on hunting.
```

Paraphrasing without plagiarizing

Like a summary, a paraphrase is written in your own words; but whereas a summary reports significant information in fewer words than the source, a paraphrase retells the information in roughly the same number of words. If you retain occasional choice phrases from the source, use quotation marks so you'll know later which phrases are your own.

As you read the following paraphrase of the original source on page 393, notice that the language is significantly different from that in the original.

PARAPHRASE

> Source: Rychnovsky, "Clawing into Controversy" (40)
> Californians are encountering mountain lions more frequently
> because increasing numbers of humans and a rising population
> of lions are competing for the same territory. Humans have
> moved into mountainous regions once dominated by the lions,
> and the wild habitat that is left cannot sustain the current
> lion population. Therefore, the older lions are forcing
> younger lions out of the wilderness and into residential
> areas. And because of a ban on hunting, these younger lions
> have become bolder--less fearful of encounters with humans.

Using quotation marks to avoid plagiarizing

A quotation consists of the exact words from a source. In your notes, put all quoted material in quotation marks; do not trust yourself to remember later which words, phrases, and passages you have quoted and which are your own. When you quote, be sure to copy the words of your source exactly, including punctuation and capitalization. In the following example, John Garcia quotes from the original source on page 393.

QUOTATION

> Source: Rychnovsky, "Clawing into Controversy" (40)
> Rychnovsky explains that because the mountain lions'
> natural habitat can no longer sustain the population,
> older lions "are forcing younger cats into less suitable
> terrain, including residential areas" (40).

51

Planning and drafting

51a Form a tentative thesis and sketch a rough outline.

Before you begin writing, you should decide on a tentative thesis and construct a preliminary outline. Remain flexible, however, because you may need to revise your approach later. Writing about a subject is a way of learning about it; as you write, your understanding of your subject will almost certainly deepen.

Tentative thesis

Once you have read a variety of sources and considered all sides of your issue, you are ready to form a tentative thesis: a one-sentence (or occasionally a two-sentence) statement of your central idea. (See also 2a and 51b.) The thesis expresses not just your opinion, but your informed, reasoned judgment.

In a research paper, your thesis will answer the central research question that you posed earlier (see 48a). Here, for example, is John Garcia's research question and his tentative thesis statement. (For Garcia's final thesis, see p. 397.)

RESEARCH QUESTION

Because of increasing numbers of mountain lion attacks on humans, should Californians reconsider their laws protecting the lions?

TENTATIVE THESIS

Because the mountain lion is not endangered in California and because attacks on humans are increasing, California should lift its ban on hunting and thinning the lion population.

Rough outline

Before committing yourself to a detailed outline, create a rough outline consisting of your thesis and your key ideas supporting

the thesis. For his outline, John Garcia used phrases similar to the titles of the computer files into which he had typed his notes.

```
Thesis: Because the mountain lion is not endangered
        in California and because attacks on humans
        are increasing, California should lift its
        ban on hunting and thinning the lion popu-
        lation.
        --The once-endangered mountain lion
        --Resurgence of the mountain lion
        --Human attacks on the rise
        --The 1996 California referendum
        --Wildlife management: a reasonable
          solution
```

51b Include your thesis in the introduction.

Readers are accustomed to seeing the thesis statement—the paper's main point—at the end of the first or second paragraph. The advantage of putting it in the first paragraph is that readers can immediately grasp your purpose. The advantage of delaying the thesis until the second paragraph is that you can provide a fuller context for your point.

As you draft your introduction, you may change your preliminary thesis, either because you have refined (or even changed) your main point or because new wording fits more smoothly into the context you have provided for it. For example, John Garcia decided that although he was in favor of wildlife management, he opposed sport hunting. His revised thesis on page 397 reflects this refined view.

TENTATIVE THESIS

```
Because the mountain lion is not endangered in Cal-
ifornia and because attacks on humans are increas-
ing, California should lift its ban on hunting and
thinning the lion population.
```

FINAL THESIS

```
When California politicians revisit the mountain
lion question, they should frame the issue in a new
way. A future proposition should retain the ban on
sport hunting but allow the Department of Fish and
Game to control the population.
```

In addition to stating your thesis and establishing a context for it, an introduction should hook readers. Sometimes you can connect your topic to something recently in the news or bring readers up to date about changing ideas. Other strategies are to pose a puzzling problem or to open with a startling statistic. John Garcia's paper begins like this: "On April 23, 1994, as Barbara Schoener was jogging in the Sierra foothills of California, she was pounced on from behind by a mountain lion."

51c Provide organizational cues.

Even if you are working with a good outline, your paper will appear disorganized unless you provide organizational cues: topic sentences, transitions between major sections of the paper, and perhaps headings. (See pp. 53, 55, 56, and 79–82.)

John Garcia uses headings to help readers follow his organization (see 55e). Some of the annotations in the margins of Garcia's paper call attention to these and other organizational cues.

51d Draft the paper in an appropriate voice.

A chatty, breezy voice is usually not welcome in academic papers, but neither is a stuffy, pretentious style or a timid, unsure one.

TOO CHATTY	The cougar is a lean, mean killing machine.
BETTER	The cougar is so strong, fast, and agile that it can bring down prey five or six times its size.
TOO STUFFY	It has been determined that mountain lion onslaughts on humans are ascending exponentially.

BETTER	Statistics show that mountain lion attacks on humans are increasing at a dramatic rate.
TOO TIMID	Although I am no expert, it seems to me that state laws should treat the mountain lion just like any other species that is not endangered.
BETTER	State laws should treat the mountain lion just like any other species that is not endangered.

52

Citing sources; avoiding plagiarism

52a Use a consistent system for citing sources.

In a research paper, you will be drawing on the work of other writers, and you must document their contributions by citing your sources. You must include a citation when you quote from a source, when you summarize or paraphrase a source, and when you borrow facts and ideas from a source that are not common knowledge. (See also 52b.)

The various academic disciplines use their own editorial styles for citing sources. Most English professors prefer the Modern Language Association's system of in-text citations, the system used in the examples throughout sections 52–55. Here, very briefly, is how an MLA in-text citation usually works:

1. The source is introduced by a signal phrase that names its author.
2. The material being cited is followed by a page number in parentheses.
3. At the end of the paper, a list of works cited (arranged alphabetically according to the authors' last names) gives complete publication information about the source.

IN-TEXT CITATION

As lion authority John Seidensticker remarks, "The boldness displayed by mountain lions just doesn't square with the shy, retiring behavior familiar to those of us who have studied these animals" (117).

ENTRY IN THE LIST OF WORKS CITED

Seidensticker, John. "Mountain Lions Don't Stalk
    People: True or False?" <u>Audubon</u> Feb. 1992:
    113-22.

Handling an MLA citation is not always this simple. For a detailed discussion of possible variations, see 55a.

If your instructor has asked you to use the American Psychological Association (APA) style of in-text citation, consult 56. For a list of style manuals used in a variety of disciplines, see 56e.

52b Avoid plagiarism.

Your research paper is a collaboration between you and your sources. To be fair and ethical, you must acknowledge your debt to the writers of these sources. If you don't, you are guilty of plagiarism, a serious academic offense.

Three different acts are considered plagiarism: (1) failing to cite quotations and borrowed ideas, (2) failing to enclose borrowed language in quotation marks, and (3) failing to put summaries and paraphrases in your own words.

Citing quotations and borrowed ideas

You must of course document all direct quotations. You must also cite any ideas borrowed from a source: paraphrases of sentences, summaries of paragraphs or chapters, statistics and little-known facts, and tables, graphs, or diagrams.

The only exception is common knowledge—information that your readers could find in any number of general sources because it is commonly known. For example, the current population of the United States is common knowledge in such fields as sociology and economics; Freud's theory of the unconscious is common knowledge in the field of psychology.

As a rule, when you have seen certain information repeatedly in your reading, you don't need to cite it. However, when information has appeared in only one or two sources or when it is controversial, you should cite it. If a topic is new to you and you are not sure what is considered common knowledge

or what is controversial, ask someone with expertise. When in doubt, cite the source.

Enclosing borrowed language in quotation marks

To indicate that you are using a source's exact phrases or sentences, you must enclose them in quotation marks unless they have been set off from the text by indenting (see p. 406). To omit the quotation marks is to claim—falsely—that the language is your own. Such an omission is plagiarism even if you have cited the source.

ORIGINAL SOURCE

We see conflicting pictures of the mountain lion through the eyes of hunters, ranchers, scientists, wildlife managers, and preservationists. Each viewpoint, like a piece of glass in a kaleidoscope, is a shard, a fragment until it is combined with the other pieces to create a total image.   —Karen McCall and Jim Dutcher,
Cougar: Ghost of the Rockies, p. 137

PLAGIARISM

McCall and Dutcher observe that we see conflicting pictures of the mountain lion through the eyes of hunters, ranchers, scientists, wildlife managers, and preservationists. Each viewpoint, like a piece of glass in a kaleidoscope, is a shard, a fragment until it is combined with the other pieces to create a total image (137).

BORROWED LANGUAGE IN QUOTATION MARKS

McCall and Dutcher observe that "hunters, ranchers, scientists, wildlife managers, and preservationists" see the mountain lion quite differently: "Each viewpoint, like a piece of glass in a kaleidoscope, is a shard, a fragment until it is combined with the other pieces to create a total image" (137).

Putting summaries and paraphrases in your own words

When you summarize or paraphrase, you must restate the source's meaning using your own language. (See also 50c.) In the following example, the paraphrase is plagiarized—even though the source is cited—because too much of its language is borrowed from the source. The underlined strings of words have been copied word-for-word (without quotation marks). In addition, the writer has closely followed the sentence structure of the original source, merely plugging in some synonyms (*children* for *minors, brutally* for *severely,* and *assault* for *attack*).

ORIGINAL SOURCE

The park [Caspers Wilderness Park] was closed to minors in 1992 after the family of a girl severely mauled there in 1986 won a suit against the county. The award of $2.1 million for the mountain lion attack on Laura Small, who was 5 at the time, was later reduced to $1.5 million.

      —Reyes and Messina, "More Warning Signs," p. B1

PLAGIARISM: UNACCEPTABLE BORROWING

Reyes and Messina report that Caspers Wilderness Park was closed to children in 1992 after the family of a girl brutally mauled there in 1986 sued the county. The family was ultimately awarded $1.5 million for the mountain lion assault on Laura Small, who was 5 at the time (B1).

To avoid plagiarizing an author's language, set the source aside, write from memory, and consult the source later to check for accuracy. This strategy prevents you from being captivated by the words on the page.

TWO ACCEPTABLE PARAPHRASES

Reyes and Messina report that in 1992 Caspers Wilderness Park was placed off-limits to minors because of an incident that had occurred there some years earlier. In 1986, a five-year-old, Laura Small, was mauled by a mountain lion and seriously injured. Her family sued the county and eventually won a settlement of $1.5 million (B1).

In 1992, officials banned minors from Caspers Wilderness Park. Reyes and Messina explain that park officials took this measure after a mountain lion attack on a child led to a lawsuit. The child,

five-year-old Laura Small, had been severely mauled
by a lion in 1986, and her parents sued the county.
Eventually they received an award of $1.5 million
(B1).

53

Integrating information from sources

With practice, you will learn to integrate information from
sources (quotations, summaries, paraphrases, and facts)
smoothly into your own text.

53a Use signal phrases to introduce quotations; limit your use of quotations.

Using signal phrases

Readers need to move from your own words to the words of
a source without feeling a jolt. Avoid dropping quotations into
the text without warning. Instead, provide clear signal phrases,
usually including the author's name, to prepare readers for a
quotation.

DROPPED QUOTATION

California law prevents the killing of mountain
lions except for specific lions that have been
proved to be a threat to humans or livestock. "Fish
and Game is even blocked from keeping mountain
lions from killing the endangered desert bighorn
sheep" (Perry B4).

QUOTATION WITH SIGNAL PHRASE

California law prevents the killing of mountain
lions except for specific lions that have been
proved to be a threat to humans or livestock. Tony

> Perry points out that, ironically, "Fish and Game
> is even blocked from keeping mountain lions from
> killing the endangered desert bighorn sheep" (B4).

To avoid monotony, try to vary both the language and the placement of your signal phrases. The models in the chart below suggest a range of possibilities.

When your signal phrase includes a verb, choose one that is appropriate in the context. Is your source arguing a point, making an observation, reporting a fact, drawing a conclusion, refuting an argument, or stating a belief? By choosing an appropriate verb, you can make your source's stance clear. See the chart below for a list of verbs commonly used in signal phrases.

Varying signal phrases

MODEL SIGNAL PHRASES

In the words of lion researcher Maurice Hornocker, ". . ."
As Kevin Hansen has noted, ". . ."
Karen McCall and Jim Dutcher point out that ". . ."
". . . ," claims CLAW spokesperson Stephani Cruickshank.
". . . ," writes Rychnovsky, ". . ."
California politician Tim Leslie offers an odd argument for this view:
Jerome Robinson answers these objections with the following analysis:

VERBS IN SIGNAL PHRASES

acknowledges	comments	endorses	reasons
adds	compares	grants	refutes
admits	confirms	illustrates	rejects
agrees	contends	implies	reports
argues	declares	insists	responds
asserts	denies	notes	suggests
believes	disputes	observes	thinks
claims	emphasizes	points out	writes

Limiting your use of quotations

Although it is tempting to insert many long quotations in your paper and to use your own words only for connecting passages, do not quote excessively. It is almost impossible to integrate numerous long quotations smoothly into your own text.

Except for the following legitimate uses of quotations, use your own words to summarize and paraphrase your sources and to explain your own ideas.

WHEN TO USE QUOTATIONS

—When language is especially vivid or expressive
—When exact wording is needed for technical accuracy
—When it is important to let the debaters of an issue explain their positions in their own words
—When the words of an important authority lend weight to an argument
—When the language of a source is the topic of your discussion (as in an analysis or interpretation)

It is not always necessary to quote full sentences from a source. To reduce your reliance on the words of others, you can often integrate a phrase from a source into your own sentence structure.

```
Uncommon as lion sightings may be, they are highly
publicized. As George Laycock points out, a lion
sighting in southern California "can push Pope,
President, or the Los Angeles Dodgers off the front
page" (88).

Jeff Rennike points out that Montana had no con-
firmed attacks by lions on humans "in its entire
history prior to 1989" but has since recorded
"as many as twenty-five incidents in a single
year" (30).
```

Using the ellipsis mark and brackets

Two useful marks of punctuation, the ellipsis mark and brackets, allow you to keep quoted material to a minimum and to integrate it smoothly into your text.

THE ELLIPSIS MARK   To condense a quoted passage, you can use the ellipsis mark (three periods, with spaces between) to indicate that you have omitted words. What remains must be grammatically complete.

MLA now recommends putting brackets around ellipsis dots. These brackets make clear that the ellipsis dots do not appear in the original work you are quoting. You may wish to check with your instructor before following this new MLA guideline. If you are using a citation style other than MLA (such as APA), do not use brackets around ellipsis dots.

> The title of John Seidensticker's article poses a
> question: "Mountain lions don't stalk people. True
> or False?" The answer, writes Seidensticker, is
> "False. In the old West, the big cats were nearly
> wiped out, but [. . .] they are back--and going on
> the attack" (113).

On the rare occasions when you want to omit one or more full sentences, use a period before the three ellipsis dots.

> Michael Milstein, a former ranger for the National
> Park Service, reports that the eastern cougar "is
> probably already extinct. [. . .] Though rare re-
> ports of sightings still surface, a recent search
> by the U.S. Fish and Wildlife Service failed to
> turn up any sightings" (20).

Ordinarily, do not use an ellipsis mark at the beginning or at the end of a quotation. Your readers will understand that the quoted material is taken from a longer passage, so such marks are not necessary. The only exception occurs when words at the end of the final quoted sentence have been dropped. In such cases, put bracketed ellipsis dots before the closing quotation mark and parenthetical reference: [. . .]" (103).

Obviously you should not use an ellipsis mark to distort the meaning of your source.

BRACKETS   Brackets (square parentheses) allow you to insert words of your own into quoted material. You can insert words in brackets to clarify matters or to keep a sentence grammatical in your context.

```
According to Tony Perry of the Los Angeles Times,
"The mountain lion [in California] has never been
in danger of extinction, not even during the 56
years (1907-1963) when several rural counties in
California tried to eradicate lions by paying boun-
ties to hunters" (B4).
```

The writer has added "in California" in brackets to make the context of Perry's claim clear: Perry is writing about California lions, not about lions in states (such as Florida) where the lion has faced extinction.

Setting off long quotations

When you quote more than four typed lines of prose or more than three lines of poetry, set off the quotation by indenting it one inch (or ten spaces) from the left margin. Use the normal right margin and do not single-space.

Long quotations should be introduced by an informative sentence, usually followed by a colon. Quotation marks are unnecessary because the indented format tells readers that the words are taken directly from the source.

```
Lion researcher Maurice Hornocker offers some prac-
tical advice to hikers:
          Visitors to lion habitat should carry a
          big stick and make noise as they hike to
          let the animal know they are approaching.
          Lions are intimidated by height, so if a
          cougar is sighted in the area, parents
          should put their children on their shoul-
          ders. If attacked, a person should not
          run, nor should he play dead. Stand firm,
          fight back, and yell--most people who
          have resisted attack have successfully
          fought off the lion. (60)
```

Notice that at the end of an indented quotation the parenthetical citation goes outside the final period. (When a quotation runs in to your text, the opposite is true. See the sample citation at the top of this page.)

53b Use signal phrases to introduce most summaries and paraphrases.

Introduce most summaries and paraphrases with a signal phrase that names the author and places the material in context. Readers will then understand that everything between the signal phrase and the parenthetical citation summarizes or paraphrases the cited source.

Without the signal phrase (underlined) in the following example, readers might think that only the last sentence is being cited, when in fact the whole paragraph is based on the source.

> For much of this century, the U.S. government has encouraged the extermination of mountain lions and other wild animals. <u>Sketching a brief history, Kevin Hansen tells us that</u> in 1915 Congress appropriated funds to wipe out animals that were attacking cattle, and the U.S. Biological Survey hired hunters and trappers to accomplish the mission. Then, in 1931, the government stepped up its efforts with the passage of the Animal Damage Control Act, nicknamed "All Dead Critters" by its critics. Between 1937 and 1970, reports Hansen, over seven thousand mountain lions were killed by Animal Damage Control (57).

53c With statistics and other facts, a signal phrase may not be needed.

When you are citing a statistic or other specific fact, a signal phrase is often not necessary. In most cases, readers will understand that the citation refers to the statistic or fact (not the whole paragraph).

> Even road kill statistics confirm the dramatic increase in California lions. In the 1970s only one or two lions were killed on state highways, but twenty-five to thirty were killed in 1989 alone (Turback 74).

There is nothing wrong, however, with using a signal phrase to introduce a statistic or other fact.

> Gary Turback points out that even road kill statistics confirm the dramatic increase in California lions. In the 1970s, he says, only one or two lions were killed on California highways, but twenty-five to thirty were killed in 1989 alone (74).

54

Revising your draft

When you are revising any paper, it is a good idea to concentrate first on global elements—focus, organization, content, and audience appeal—and then turn to matters of style and correctness. (See 3a.) With a research paper, this strategy is especially important because reviewing your use of quotations and other source material requires considerable attention to detail.

Below is a two-part chart for reviewing the draft of a research paper: one part on global revision, the other on proper handling of sources.

Reviewing a research paper: Global revisions

FOCUS

- Is the thesis stated clearly enough? Is it placed where readers will notice it?
- Does each paragraph support the thesis?

ORGANIZATION

- Can readers follow the organization? Would headings help?
- Do topic sentences signal new ideas? Do transitions help readers move from one major group of paragraphs to another?
- Are ideas presented in a logical order?

Reviewing a research paper: Global revisions *(cont.)*

CONTENT

- Is the supporting material persuasive? Are the arguments strong enough to stand up to arguments of those who disagree with the thesis?
- Are the parts proportioned sensibly? Do the major ideas receive enough attention?
- Is the draft concise—free of irrelevant, unimportant, or repetitious material?

STYLE

- Is the voice appropriate—not too chatty, too stuffy, or too timid?
- Are the sentences clear, emphatic, and varied?

Reviewing a research paper: Use of sources

USE OF QUOTATIONS

- Is quoted material enclosed within quotation marks (unless it has been set off from the text)? (See 52b.)
- Is quoted language word-for-word accurate? If not, do brackets or ellipsis marks indicate the changes or omissions? (See pp. 405–06.)
- Does a clear signal phrase (usually naming the author) prepare readers for each quotation? (See 53a.)
- Does a parenthetical citation follow each quotation? (See 52a.)

USE OF SUMMARIES AND PARAPHRASES

- Are summaries and paraphrases free of plagiarized wording (not copied or half-copied from the source)? (See 52b.)
- Are summaries and paraphrases documented with parenthetical citations? (See 52a.)
- Do readers know where the material being cited begins? In other words, does a signal phrase mark the beginning of the cited material unless the context makes clear exactly what is being cited? (See 53b.)

USE OF STATISTICS AND OTHER FACTS

- Are statistics and facts (other than common knowledge) documented with parenthetical citations? (See 52a.)
- If there is no signal phrase, will readers understand exactly which facts are being cited? (See 53c.)

55

MLA documentation

In academic research papers and in any other writing that borrows information from sources, the borrowed information—quotations, summaries, paraphrases, and any facts or ideas that are not common knowledge—must be clearly documented. (See also 52b.)

The various academic disciplines use their own editorial styles for citing sources and for listing the works that have been cited. The style described in this section is that of the Modern Language Association (MLA), contained in the *MLA Handbook for Writers of Research Papers*, 5th ed. (New York: MLA, 1999), which recommends in-text citations and a list of works cited.

If your instructor prefers the American Psychological Association (APA) style of in-text citation, see section 56. That section also contains a list of style manuals.

Directory to MLA in-text citations (55a)

Directory to MLA works cited entries (55b)

55a MLA in-text citations

MLA in-text citations are made with a combination of signal phrases and parenthetical references. A signal phrase indicates that something taken from a source (such as a quotation, summary, or paraphrase) is about to be used; usually the signal phrase includes the author's name. The parenthetical reference includes at least a page number (unless the work has no page numbers or is organized alphabetically).

Citations in parentheses should be as concise as possible but complete enough so that readers can find the source in the list of works cited at the end of the paper, where works are listed alphabetically by authors' last names. The following models illustrate the form for the MLA style of citation.

1. **AUTHOR NAMED IN A SIGNAL PHRASE** Ordinarily, you should introduce the material being cited with a signal phrase that includes the author's name. In addition to preparing readers for the source, the signal phrase allows you to keep the parenthetical citation brief.

> Turback claims that "regulated sport hunting has
> never driven any wild species into extinction"
> (74).

The signal phrase — "Turback claims that" — provides the name of the author; the parenthetical citation gives the page number where the quoted words may be found. By looking up the author's last name in the list of works cited, readers will find complete information about the work's title, publisher, and place and date of publication.

Notice that the period follows the parenthetical citation. For the MLA technique for handling quotations that end in a question mark or an exclamation point, see pages 306–7.

2. **AUTHOR NOT NAMED IN A SIGNAL PHRASE** If the signal phrase does not include the author's name (or if there is no signal phrase), the author's last name must appear in parentheses along with the page number.

```
Though the number of lion attacks on humans is low,
the rate of increase of attacks since the 1960s is
cause for serious concern (Rychnovsky 43).
```

Use no punctuation between the name and the page number.

3. TWO OR MORE WORKS BY THE SAME AUTHOR If your list of works cited includes two or more works by the same author, include the title of the work either in the signal phrase or in abbreviated form in the parenthetical reference.

```
In his article "California and the West," reporter
T. Christian Miller asserts that from 1990 to 1997,
California spent roughly $26 million on conserva-
tion lands "to provide habitat for exactly 2.6
mountain lions" (A3).
```

```
According to T. Christian Miller, "Mountain lions,
also called pumas or cougars, range vast territo-
ries in search of food, sometimes as large as 100
square miles" ("Cougars" 1).
```

The title of an article from a periodical should be put in quotation marks, as in the examples. The title of a book should be underlined or italicized.

In the rare case when both the author and a short title must be given in parentheses, the citation should appear as follows:

```
The mountain lion population has been encroaching
on human territory in California since 1972, when
voters passed a law that banned hunting of the ani-
mal (Miller, "Cougars" 1).
```

4. TWO OR THREE AUTHORS If your source has two or three authors, name them in the signal phrase or include them in the parenthetical reference.

```
Reyes and Messina report that the adult mountain
lion population in California is now estimated at
four to six thousand (B1).
```

5. FOUR OR MORE AUTHORS   If your source has four or more authors, include only the first author's name followed by "et al." (Latin for "and others") in the signal phrase or in the parenthetical reference.

> The study was extended for two years, and only af-
> ter results were duplicated on both coasts did the
> authors publish their results (Doe et al. 137).

6. CORPORATE AUTHOR   When the author is a corporation or an organization, either name the corporate author in the signal phrase or include a shortened version in the parentheses.

> The Internal Revenue Service warns businesses that
> deductions for "lavish and extravagant entertain-
> ment" are not allowed (43).

7. UNKNOWN AUTHOR   If the author is not given, either use the complete title in a signal phrase or use a short form of the title in the parentheses.

> In California, fish and game officials estimate
> that since 1972 lion numbers have increased from
> 2,400 to at least 6,000 ("Lion" A21).

8. AUTHORS WITH THE SAME LAST NAME   If your list of works cited includes works by two or more authors with the same last name, include the first name of the author you are citing in the signal phrase or parenthetical reference.

> At least 66,665 lions were killed between 1907 and
> 1978 in Canada and the United States (Kevin Hansen
> 58).

9. A MULTIVOLUME WORK   If your paper cites more than one volume of a multivolume work, indicate in the parentheses the volume you are referring to, followed by a colon.

> Terman's studies of gifted children reveal a pat-
> tern of accelerated language acquisition (2: 279).

If your paper cites only one volume of a multivolume work, you will include the volume number in the list of works cited at the end of the paper and will not need to include it in the parentheses.

10. A NOVEL, A PLAY, OR A POEM In citing literary sources, include information that will enable readers to find the passage in various editions of the work. For a novel, put the page number first and then, if possible, indicate the part or chapter in which the passage can be found.

> One of Kingsolver's narrators, teenager Rachel,
> pushes her vocabulary beyond its limits. For ex-
> ample, Rachel complains that being forced to live in
> the Congo with her missionary family is "a sheer ta-
> pestry of justice" because her chances of finding a
> boyfriend are "dull and void" (177; bk. 2, ch. 10).

For a verse play, list the act, scene, and line numbers, separated by periods. Use arabic numerals unless your instructor prefers roman numerals.

> In his famous advice to the players, Shakespeare's
> Hamlet defines the purpose of theater, "whose end,
> both at the first and now, was and is, to hold, as
> 'twere, the mirror up to nature" (3.2.21-23).

For a poem, cite the part (if there are a number of parts) and the line numbers, separated by periods.

> When Homer's Odysseus came to the hall of Circe, he
> found his men "mild / in her soft spell, fed on her
> drug of evil" (10.209-11).

11. THE BIBLE Include the edition of the Bible, the book of the Bible, and the chapter and verse numbers either in the signal phrase or in the parentheses.

> Consider the words of Solomon: "If your enemies are
> hungry, give them bread to eat; and if they are
> thirsty, give them water to drink" (New Revised
> Standard Bible, Prov. 25.21).

12. A WORK IN AN ANTHOLOGY   Put the name of the author of the work (not the editor of the anthology) in the signal phrase or in the parentheses.

> At the end of Kate Chopin's "The Story of an Hour,"
> Mrs. Mallard drops dead upon learning that her hus-
> band is alive. In the final irony of the story,
> doctors report that she has died of a "joy that
> kills" (25).

13. AN INDIRECT SOURCE   When a writer's or speaker's quoted words appear in a source written by someone else, begin the citation with the abbreviation "qtd. in."

> "When lion sightings become common," says Fjelline,
> "trouble often follows" (qtd. in Robinson 30).

14. AN ENTIRE WORK   To cite an entire work, use the author's name in a signal phrase or a parenthetical reference. There is of course no need to use a page number.

> Robinson succinctly describes the status of the
> mountain lion controversy in California.

15. TWO OR MORE WORKS   To cite more than one source to document a particular point, separate the citations with a semicolon.

> The dangers of mountain lions to humans have been
> well documented (Rychnovsky 40; Seidensticker 114;
> Williams 30).

Multiple citations can be distracting to readers, however, so the technique should not be overused. If you want to alert readers to several sources that discuss a particular topic, consider using an information note instead (discussed in 55c).

16. A WORK WITHOUT PAGE NUMBERS   You may omit the page number if a work has no page numbers. Some electronic sources use paragraph numbers instead of page numbers. For such sources, use the abbreviation "par." or "pars." in the parentheses: (Smith, par. 4).

17. AN ELECTRONIC SOURCE   To cite an electronic source in the text of your paper, follow the same rules as for print sources. If the source has an author and there is a page number, provide both.

> Using historical writings about leprosy as an ex-
> ample, Demaitre argues that "the difference between
> curability and treatability is not a modern inven-
> tion" (29).

Electronic sources often lack page numbers. If the source uses some other numbering system, such as paragraphs or sections, specify them, using an abbreviation ("par.," "sec.") or a full word ("screen"). Otherwise, use no number at all.

> According to Routt, a clip of the film Demoliton
> d'un mur demonstrates that "cinema is all about
> transformation, not mere movement" (sec. 1).

> Volti writes, "As with all significant innovations,
> the history of the automobile shows that techno-
> logical advance is fueled by more than economic
> calculation."

If the electronic source has no known author, either use the complete title in a signal phrase or use a short form of the title in parentheses.

> According to a Web page sponsored by the Children's
> Defense Fund, fourteen American children die from
> gunfire each day ("Child").

55b   MLA list of works cited

A list of works cited, which appears at the end of your research paper, gives publication information for each of the sources you have cited in the paper. Start on a new page and title your list "Works Cited." Then list in alphabetical order all the sources that you have cited in the paper. Unless your instructor asks for them, do not include sources not actually cited in the paper, even if you read them.

Alphabetize the list by the last names of the authors (or editors); if a work has no author or editor, alphabetize by the first word of the title other than *A, An,* or *The.*

Do not indent the first line of each works cited entry, but indent any additional lines one-half inch (or five spaces). This technique highlights the names by which the list has been alphabetized (see, for example, the list of works cited at the end of the student paper on pp. 446–47).

The following models illustrate the form that the Modern Language Association (MLA) recommends for works cited entries.

Books

1. **BASIC FORMAT FOR A BOOK** For most books, arrange the information into three units, each followed by a period and one space: (1) the author's name, last name first; (2) the title and subtitle, underlined or italicized; and (3) the place of publication, the publisher, and the date.

Tannen, Deborah. <u>The Argument Culture: Moving from
Debate to Dialogue</u>. New York: Random, 1998.

The information is taken from the title page of the book and from the reverse side of the title page (the copyright page), not from the outside cover. The complete name of the publisher (in this case Random House) need not be given. You may use a short form as long as it is easily identifiable; omit terms such as *Press, Inc.,* and *Co.* except when naming university presses (Harvard UP, for example). The date to use in your works cited entry is the most recent copyright date.

2. **TWO OR THREE AUTHORS** Name the authors in the order in which they are presented on the title page; reverse the name of only the first author.

Short, Kathy Gnagey, and Lois Bridges Bird. <u>Literature
as a Way of Knowing</u>. York, ME: Stenhouse, 1997.

The names of three authors are separated by commas.

Rosenfeld, Louis, Joseph Janes, and Martha Vander
Holk. <u>The Internet Compendium: Subject Guides to
Humanities Resources</u>. New York: Neal, 1995.

3. FOUR OR MORE AUTHORS Cite only the first author, name reversed, followed by "et al." (Latin for "and others").

```
Holloway, Susan D., et al. Through My Own Eyes: Single
    Mothers and the Cultures of Poverty. Cambridge:
    Harvard UP, 1997.
```

4. EDITORS An entry for an editor is similar to that for an author except that the name is followed by a comma and the abbreviation "ed." for "editor." If there is more than one editor, use the abbreviation "eds." for "editors."

```
Kitchen, Judith, and Mary Paumier Jones, eds. In
    Short: A Collection of Brief Creative Nonfiction.
    New York: Norton, 1996.
```

5. AUTHOR WITH AN EDITOR Begin with the author and title, followed by the name of the editor. In this case the abbreviation "Ed." means "Edited by," so it is the same for one or multiple editors.

```
Wells, Ida B. The Memphis Diary. Ed. Miriam DeCosta-
    Willis. Boston: Beacon, 1995.
```

6. TRANSLATION List the entry under the name of the author, not the translator. After the title, write "Trans." (for "Translated by") and the name of the translator.

```
Mahfouz, Naguib. Arabian Nights and Days. Trans. Denys
    Johnson-Davies. New York: Doubleday, 1995.
```

7. CORPORATE AUTHOR List the entry under the name of the corporate author, even if it is also the name of the publisher.

```
Bank of Boston. Bank by Remote Control. Boston: Bank
    of Boston, 1997.
```

8. UNKNOWN AUTHOR Begin with the title. Alphabetize the entry by the first word of the title other than *A, An,* or *The.*

```
Oxford Essential World Atlas. New York: Oxford UP,
    1996.
```

9. TWO OR MORE WORKS BY THE SAME AUTHOR   If your list of works cited includes two or more works by the same author, use the author's name only for the first entry. For subsequent entries use three hyphens followed by a period. The three hyphens must stand for exactly the same name or names as in the preceding entry. List the titles in alphabetical order.

Updike, John. In the Beauty of the Lilies. New York:
    Knopf, 1996.

---. Toward the End of Time. New York: Knopf, 1997.

10. EDITION OTHER THAN THE FIRST   If you are citing an edition other than the first, include the number of the edition after the title: 2nd ed., 3rd ed., and so on.

Boyce, David George. The Irish Question and British
    Politics, 1868-1996. 2nd ed. New York: St.
    Martin's, 1996.

11. MULTIVOLUME WORK   Include the total number of volumes before the city and publisher, using the abbreviation "vols."

Conway, Jill Ker, ed. Written by Herself. 2 vols. New
    York: Random, 1996.

If your paper cites only one of the volumes, give the volume number before the city and publisher and give the total number of volumes in the work after the date.

Conway, Jill Ker, ed. Written by Herself. Vol 2. New
    York: Random, 1996. 2 vols.

12. ENCYCLOPEDIA OR DICTIONARY   Articles in well-known dictionaries and encyclopedias are handled in abbreviated form. Simply list the author of the article (if there is one), the title of the article, the title of the reference work, the edition number, if any, and the date of the edition.

"Sonata." Encyclopaedia Britannica. 15th ed. 1997.

Volume and page numbers are not necessary because the entries are arranged alphabetically and therefore are easy to locate.

If a reference work is not well known, provide full publication information as well.

13. THE BIBLE Give the edition of the Bible, underlined, the editor's name (if any), and publication information.

<u>New American Bible</u>. New York: Catholic Book Publish-

  ing, 1970.

14. WORK IN AN ANTHOLOGY Present the information in this order, with each item followed by a period: author of the selection; title of the selection; title of the anthology; editor of the anthology, preceded by "Ed." (meaning "Edited by"); city, publisher, and date; page numbers on which the selection appears.

Malouf, David. "The Kyogle Line." <u>The Oxford Book of</u>

  <u>Travel Stories</u>. Ed. Patricia Craig. Oxford:

  Oxford UP, 1996. 390-96.

If an anthology gives the original publication information for a selection and if your instructor prefers that you use it, cite that information first. Follow with "Rpt. in" (for "Reprinted in"), the title, editor, and publication information for the anthology, and the page numbers in the anthology on which the selection appears.

Rodriguez, Richard. "Late Victorians." <u>Harper's</u> Oct.

  1990: 57-66. Rpt. in <u>The Best American Essays</u>

  <u>1991</u>. Ed. Joyce Carol Oates. New York: Ticknor,

  1991. 119-34.

15. TWO OR MORE WORKS FROM THE SAME ANTHOLOGY If you wish, you may cross-reference two or more works from the same anthology. Provide a separate entry for the anthology with complete publication information.

Craig, Patricia, ed. <u>The Oxford Book of Travel Stories</u>.

  Oxford: Oxford UP, 1996.

Then list each selection separately, giving the author and title of the selection followed by a cross-reference to the anthology. The cross-reference should include the last name of the editor of the anthology and the page numbers in the anthology on which the selection appears.

```
Desai, Anita. "Scholar and Gypsy." Craig 251-73.

Malouf, David. "The Kyogle Line." Craig 390-96.
```

16. FOREWORD, INTRODUCTION, PREFACE, OR AFTERWORD If in your paper you quote from one of these elements, begin with the name of the writer of that element. Then identify the element being cited, neither underlined nor in quotation marks, followed by the title of the complete book, the book's author, and the book's editor, if any. After the publication information, give the page numbers on which the foreword, introduction, preface, or afterword appears.

```
Kennedy, Edward M. Foreword. Make a Difference. By
    Henry W. Foster, Jr., and Alice Greenwood. New
    York: Scribner, 1997, 9-15.
```

If the foreword, introduction, preface, or afterword has a title, place the title in quotation marks and include it immediately after the writer's name.

```
Ozick, Cynthia. "Portrait of the Essay as a Warm
    Body." Introduction. The Best American Essays
    1998. Ed. Ozick. Boston: Houghton, 1998. xv-xxi.
```

17. BOOK WITH A TITLE WITHIN ITS TITLE If the book title contains a title normally underlined (or italicized), neither underline (or italicize) the internal title nor place it in quotation marks.

```
Vanderham, Paul. James Joyce and Censorship: The
    Trials of Ulysses. New York: New York UP, 1997.
```

If the title within the title is normally enclosed within quotation marks, retain the quotation marks and underline (or italicize) the entire title.

```
Faulkner, Dewey R. Twentieth Century Interpretations
    of "The Pardoner's Tale." Englewood Cliffs:
    Spectrum-Prentice, 1973.
```

18. BOOK IN A SERIES Before the publication information, cite the series name as it appears on the title page followed by the series number, if any.

Malena, Anne. <u>The Dynamics of Identity in Francophone</u>
    <u>Caribbean Narrative</u>. Francophone Cultures and
    Literatures Ser. 24. New York: Lang, 1998.

19. REPUBLISHED BOOK After the title of the book, cite the original publication date followed by the current publication information. If the republished book contains new material, such as an introduction or afterword, include that information after the original date.

McClintock, Walter. <u>Old Indian Trails</u>. 1926. Foreword
    William Least Heat Moon. Boston: Houghton, 1992.

20. PUBLISHER'S IMPRINT If a book was published by an imprint of a publishing company, cite the name of the imprint followed by a hyphen and the publisher's name. The name of the imprint usually precedes the publisher's name on the title page.

Coles, Robert. <u>The Moral Intelligence of Children: How</u>
    <u>to Raise a Moral Child</u>. New York: Plume-Random,
    1997.

Articles in periodicals

21. ARTICLE IN A MONTHLY MAGAZINE In addition to the author, the title of the article, and the title of the magazine, list the month and year and the page numbers on which the article appears. Abbreviate the names of months except May, June, and July.

Kaplan, Robert D. "History Moving North." <u>Atlantic</u>
    <u>Monthly</u> Feb. 1997: 21+.

This example uses "21+" because the article did not appear on consecutive pages. For articles appearing on consecutive pages, provide the range of pages (for example, 50–53).

22. ARTICLE IN A WEEKLY MAGAZINE Handle articles in weekly (or biweekly) magazines as you do those for monthly magazines, but give the exact date of the issue, not just the month and year.

Pierpont, Claudia Roth. "A Society of One: Zora Neale
    Hurston, American Contrarian." <u>New Yorker</u> 17 Feb.
    1997: 80-86.

23. ARTICLE IN A JOURNAL PAGINATED BY VOLUME Many professional journals continue page numbers throughout the year instead of beginning each issue with page 1; at the end of the year, all of the issues are collected in a volume. Interested readers need only the volume number, the year, and the page numbers to find an article.

Cheuse, Alan. "Narrative Painting and Pictorial Fic-
    tion." <u>Antioch Review</u> 55 (1997): 277-91.

24. ARTICLE IN A JOURNAL PAGINATED BY ISSUE If each issue of the journal begins with page 1, you need to indicate the number of the issue. Simply place a period after the volume number and follow it with the issue number.

Dennis, Carl. "What Is Our Poetry to Make of Ancient
    Myths?" <u>New England Review</u> 18.4 (1997): 128-40.

25. ARTICLE IN A DAILY NEWSPAPER Begin with the author, if there is one, followed by the title of the article. Next give the name of the newspaper, the date, and the page number (including the section letter). Use a plus sign (+) after the page number if the article does not appear on consecutive pages.

Knox, Richard A. "Please Don't Dial and Drive, Study
    Suggests." <u>Boston Globe</u> 13 Feb. 1997: A1+.

If the section is marked with a number rather than a letter, handle the entry as follows:

Wilford, John Noble. "In a Golden Age of Discovery,
    Faraway Worlds Beckon." <u>New York Times</u> 9 Feb.
    1997, late ed., sec. 1: 1+.

If an edition of the newspaper is specified on the masthead, name the edition after the date and before the page reference: eastern ed., late ed., natl. ed., and so on.

26. UNSIGNED ARTICLE IN A NEWSPAPER OR MAGAZINE Use the same form you would use for an article in a newspaper or a weekly or monthly magazine, but begin with the title of the article.

"Marines Charged in Assault Case." Houston Chronicle
    14 Feb. 1998: 6A.

27. EDITORIAL IN A NEWSPAPER Cite an editorial as you would an unsigned article, adding the word "Editorial" after the title.

"Health Risk on Tap." Editorial. Los Angeles Times
    11 Feb. 1998: B6.

28. LETTER TO THE EDITOR Cite the writer's name, followed by the word "Letter" and the publication information for the newspaper or magazine in which the letter appears.

Peters, Tom. Letter. New Yorker 16 Feb. 1998: 13.

29. BOOK OR FILM REVIEW Cite first the reviewer's name and the title of the review, if any, followed by the words "Rev. of" and the title and author or director of the work reviewed. Add the publication information for the publication in which the review appears.

France, Peter. "His Own Biggest Hero." Rev. of Victor
    Hugo, by Graham Robb. New York Times Book Review
    15 Jan. 1998: 7.

Taubin, Amy. "Year of the Lady." Rev. of The Portrait
    of a Lady, dir. Jane Campion. Village Voice
    7 Jan. 1997: 64.

Electronic sources

The documentation style for electronic sources presented in this section is consistent with MLA's most recent guidelines, which can be found at < http://www.mla.org > or in the *MLA Handbook for Writers of Research Papers* (5th ed., 1999).

NOTE: When an Internet address in a works cited entry must be divided at the end of a line, break it after a slash. Do not insert a hyphen.

30. ONLINE SCHOLARLY PROJECT OR REFERENCE DATABASE For an on-line source accessed from within a larger scholarly project or reference database, begin with the author (if any) and title of the source, followed by any editors or translators. Use quotation marks for titles of short works such as poems and articles; underline or italicize book and periodical titles. Include publication information for any print version of the source before giving the title of the online project or database (underlined or italicized), followed by the author or editor of the project or database; the date of electronic publication (or latest update); page or paragraph numbers (if any); the name of any institution or organization sponsoring or associated with the site; the date of access; and the electronic address, or URL, of the source (in angle brackets).

Dickinson, Emily. "Hope." <u>Poems by Emily Dickinson</u>.
    3rd ser. Boston, 1896. <u>Project Bartleby Archive</u>.
    Ed. Steven van Leeuwen. 15 Dec. 1995. Columbia U.
    2 Feb. 1998 <http://www.columbia.edu/acis/bartleby/
    dickinson/dickinson1.html#3>.

"Gog and Magog." <u>The Encyclopedia Mythica</u>. Ed. Micha
    F. Lindemans. 2 Jan. 1998. 31 Jan. 1998 <http://
    www.pantheon.org/mythica/articles/g/
    gog_and_magog.html>.

To refer to an entire scholarly project, begin with the title of the project.

<u>The Einstein Papers Project</u>. Ed. Robert Schulmann.
    9 Nov. 1997. Boston U. 29 Jan. 1998 <http://
    albert.bu.edu>.

31. PERSONAL OR PROFESSIONAL WEB SITE For a citation to a personal or professional Web site, begin with the creator of the site (if available) and continue with the title of the site (or a description such as "Home page" if no title is available), the date of publication or of the latest update, the name of any organization associated with the site, the date of access, and the URL.

Spanoudis, Steve, Bob Blair, and Nelson Miller. Poets'
    Corner. 2 Feb. 1998. 4 Feb. 1998 <http://
    www.geocities.com/~spanoudi/poems>.

Blue Note Records. 19 Mar. 1998. Blue Note Records.
    25 Mar. 1998 <http://www.bluenote.com>.

32. ONLINE BOOK For citations to books available online, include
all available information required for printed books (see pp.
418–23), followed by the date of access and the URL.

Brontë, Charlotte. Jane Eyre. 1846. 16 Mar. 1998
    <gopher://gopher.vt.edu:10010/02/50/1>.

If the online book is part of a scholarly project or reference
database, follow any information about the printed book with
information about the project or database (see p. 426).

Brown, William W. Narrative of William W. Brown, an
    American Slave. Written by Himself. London, 1849.
    Documenting the American South: The Southern Ex-
    perience in Nineteenth-Century America. Ed.
    Natalia Smith. 1996. Academic Affairs Lib., U of
    North Carolina, Chapel Hill. 9 Feb. 1998 <http://
    sunsite.unc.edu/docsouth/brown/brown.html>.

Shelley, Mary. Frankenstein. An Online Library of Lit-
    erature. Ed. Peter Galbavy. 22 Apr. 1998. 23 June
    1998 <http://www.literature.org/Works/
    Mary-Shelley/frankenstein>.

33. ARTICLE IN AN ONLINE PERIODICAL When citing online articles,
follow the guidelines for printed articles (see pp. 423–25), giving whatever information is available in the online source. At
the end of the citation, include the date of access and the URL.

Baucom, Ian. "Charting the Black Atlantic." Postmodern
    Culture 8.1 (1997): 28 pars. 3 Feb. 1998
    <http://www.iath.virginia.edu/pmc/current.issue/
    baucom.997.html>.

Romano, Jay. "Computers That Tend the Home." <u>New York
    Times on the Web</u> 14 Mar. 1998 <http://
    www.nytimes.com/library/tech/98/03/biztech/
    articles/15home.html>.

Coontz, Stephanie. "Family Myths, Family Realities."
    <u>Salon</u> 12 Dec. 1997. 3 Feb. 1998 <http://
    www.salonmagazine.com/mwt/feature/1997/12/
    23coontz.html>.

34. WORK FROM AN ONLINE SUBSCRIPTION SERVICE To cite a work from a personal subscription service such as America Online, give the information about the source followed by the name of the service, the date of access, and the keyword used to retrieve the source.

Sleek, Scott. "Blame Your Peers, Not Your Parents,
    Author Says." <u>APA Monitor</u> 29.1 (1998). America
    Online. 1 Mar. 1999. Keyword: The Nurture
    Assumption.

For a source found in an online subscription service accessed at a library, give the information about the source followed by the name of the service, the library, the date of access, and the URL of the service, if known.

Miller, Christian. "Cougars Reported in Tarzana, Wood-
    land Hills." <u>Los Angeles Times</u> 25 Nov. 1997:
    Metro 1. Electric Lib. O'Neill Lib., Boston
    Coll., Chestnut Hill, MA. 12 Mar. 1998 <http://
    www.elibrary.com>.

35. ONLINE POSTING Begin with the author's name, followed by the title or subject line (in quotation marks), the words "Online posting," the posting date, the list or group name, any identifying number of the posting, the date of access, and the URL or the e-mail address of the list.

Crosby, Connie. "Literary Criticism." Online posting.
    2 Feb. 1996. Café Utne. 17 Mar. 1998 <http://

```
www.utne.com/motet/bin/
show?-u4Lsul+it-1a+Literature+12>.
```

36. E-MAIL For correspondence received via electronic mail, include the author, the subject line (if any) in quotation marks, and the word "E-mail" followed by the recipient and the date of the message.

```
Schubert, Josephine. "Re: Culture shock." E-mail to
    the author. 14 Mar. 1998.
```

37. SYNCHRONOUS COMMUNICATION To cite a synchronous communication posted in a MUD or a MOO, include the speaker's name (if relevant), a description and date of the event, the title of the forum, the date of access, and the URL. If an archival version of the communication is unavailable, include the telnet address.

```
Kelley, Heather. Jill's Borderland Tour of DU. 14 Dec.
    1995. Borderlands MOOspace. 16 Mar. 1998 <http://
    www.cyberstation.net/~idd/v2/bordj24.htm>.
```

38. OTHER ONLINE SOURCES For other materials accessed online, cite them as you would otherwise, including identifying labels where necessary. End the citation with the access date and the URL.

```
"No More Kings." Animation. America Rock. Schoolhouse
    Rock. ABC. 1975. 16 Mar. 1998 <http://
    genxtvland.simplenet.com/SchoolHouseRock/
    song.hts?hi+kings>.
```

```
"City of New Orleans, LA." Map. Yahoo! Maps. Yahoo!
    1998. 4 Feb. 1998 <http://maps.yahoo.com/yahoo>.
```

39. CD-ROM ISSUED IN A SINGLE EDITION Some works on CD-ROM, such as dictionaries and encyclopedias, are released in single editions that are not updated periodically. Treat such sources as you would a book, but give the medium ("CD-ROM") before the publication information.

Sheehy, Donald, ed. <u>Robert Frost: Poems, Life, Legacy</u>.
    CD-ROM. New York: Holt, 1997.

"Picasso, Pablo." <u>The 1997 Grolier Multimedia Encyclo-
    pedia</u>. CD-ROM. Danbury: Grolier, 1997.

40. CD-ROM ISSUED PERIODICALLY CD-ROM databases that are produced periodically (monthly or quarterly, for example) may contain previously published material, such as journal or newspaper articles, or material that has not been previously published, such as reports. In either case, cite such material as you would a printed source, followed by the title of the database (underlined or italicized), the medium ("CD-ROM"), the name of the company producing the CD-ROM, and the date of electronic publication.

Bohlen, Celestine. "Albania Struggles to Contain Dis-
    sent over Lost Investments." <u>New York Times</u>
    11 Feb. 1997, late ed.: A9. <u>InfoTrac: General
    Periodicals ASAP</u>. CD-ROM. Information Access.
    13 Feb. 1997.

Wattenberg, Ruth. "Helping Students in the Middle."
    <u>American Educator</u> 19.4 (1996): 2-18. <u>ERIC</u>. CD-ROM.
    SilverPlatter. Sept. 1996.

Other sources

41. GOVERNMENT PUBLICATION Treat the government agency as the author, giving the name of the government followed by the name of the agency.

United States. Bureau of the Census. <u>Statistical Ab-
    stract of the United States</u>. 117th ed. Washington:
    GPO, 1997.

42. PAMPHLET Cite a pamphlet as you would a book.

United States. Dept. of the Interior. Natl. Park Ser-
    vice. <u>National Design Competition for an Indian
    Memorial: Little Bighorn Battlefield National Mon-
    ument</u>. Washington: GPO, 1996.

43. PUBLISHED DISSERTATION Cite a published dissertation as you would a book, underlining (or italicizing) the title and giving the place of publication, the publisher, and the year of publication. After the title, add the word "Diss.," the name of the institution, and the year the dissertation was written.

```
Damberg, Cheryl L. Healthcare Reform: Distributional
     Consequences of an Employer Mandate for Workers in
     Small Firms. Diss. Rand Graduate School, 1995.
     Santa Monica: Rand, 1996.
```

44. UNPUBLISHED DISSERTATION Begin with the author's name, followed by the dissertation title in quotation marks, the word "Diss.," the name of the institution, and the year the dissertation was written.

```
Healey, Catherine. "Joseph Conrad's Impressionism."
     Diss. U of Massachusetts, 1997.
```

45. ABSTRACT OF A DISSERTATION Cite as you would an unpublished dissertation. After the dissertation date, give the abbreviation *DA* or *DAI* (for *Dissertation Abstracts* or *Dissertation Abstracts International*), followed by the volume number, the date of publication, and the page number.

```
Chun, Maria Bow Jun. "A Study of Multicultural Activi-
     ties in Hawaii's Public Schools." Diss. U of
     Hawaii, 1996. DAI 57 (1997): 2813A.
```

46. PUBLISHED PROCEEDINGS OF A CONFERENCE Cite published conference proceedings as you would a book, adding information about the conference after the title.

```
Chattel, Servant, or Citizen: Women's Status in
     Church, State, and Society. Proc. of Irish Conf.
     of Historians, 1993, Belfast. Belfast: Inst. of
     Irish Studies, 1995.
```

47. WORK OF ART Cite the artist's name, followed by the title of the artwork, usually underlined, and the institution and city in which the artwork can be found.

```
Constable, John. Dedham Vale. Victoria and Albert Mu-
    seum, London.
```

48. MUSICAL COMPOSITION   Cite the composer's name, followed by the title of the work. Underline the title of an opera, a ballet, or a composition identified by name, but do not underline or use quotation marks around a composition identified by number or form.

```
Copland, Aaron. Appalachian Spring.
```

```
Shostakovich, Dmitri. Quartet no. 1 in C, op. 49.
```

49. PERSONAL LETTER   To cite a letter you have received, begin with the writer's name and add the phrase "Letter to the author," followed by the date.

```
Cipriani, Karen. Letter to the author. 25 Apr. 1998.
```

50. LECTURE OR PUBLIC ADDRESS   Cite the speaker's name, followed by the title of the lecture (if any) in quotation marks, the organization sponsoring the lecture, the location, and the date.

```
Middleton, Frank. "Louis Hayden and the Role of the
    Underground Railroad in Boston." Boston Public
    Lib. Boston. 6 Feb. 1998.
```

51. PERSONAL INTERVIEW   To cite an interview that you conducted, begin with the name of the person interviewed. Then write "Personal interview," followed by the date of the interview.

```
Meeker, Dolores. Personal interview. 21 Apr. 1998.
```

52. PUBLISHED INTERVIEW   Name the person interviewed, followed by the title of the interview, if there is one, in quotation marks and the publication in which the interview was printed. If the interview does not have a title, include the word "Interview" after the interviewee's name.

```
Renoir, Jean. "Renoir at Home: Interview with Jean
    Renoir." Film Quarterly 50.1 (1996): 2-8.
```

53. RADIO OR TELEVISION INTERVIEW   Name the person interviewed, followed by the word "Interview." Then give the title of the program, underlined (or italicized), and identifying information about the broadcast.

```
Gates, Henry Louis, Jr. Interview. Charlie Rose. PBS.
     WNET, New York. 13 Feb. 1997.
```

54. FILM OR VIDEOTAPE   Begin with the title. For a film, cite the director and the lead actors or narrator ("Perf." or "Narr."), followed by the distributor and year. For a videotape, add the word "Videocassette" before the distributor.

```
The English Patient. Dir. Anthony Minghella. Perf.
     Ralph Fiennes, Juliette Binoche, Willem Dafoe, and
     Kristin Scott Thomas. Miramax, 1996.

Jane Eyre. Dir. Robert Young. Perf. Samantha Morton
     and Ciaran Hinds. Videocassette. New Video Group.
     1997.
```

55. RADIO OR TELEVISION PROGRAM   List the relevant information about the program in this order: the title of the program, underlined or italicized; the writer ("By"), director ("Dir."), narrator ("Narr."), producer ("Prod."), or main actors ("Perf."), if relevant; the series, neither underlined nor in quotation marks; the network; the local station (if any) on which you heard or saw the program and the city; and the date the program was broadcast. If a television episode or radio segment has a title, place the title, in quotation marks, before the program title.

```
"The New Face of Africa." The Connection. Host
     Christopher Lydon. Natl. Public Radio. WBUR,
     Boston. 27 Mar. 1998.

Primates. Wild Discovery. Discovery Channel. 23 Mar.
     1998.
```

56. LIVE PERFORMANCE OF A PLAY   Begin with the title of the play, followed by the author ("By"). Then include specific information about the live performance: the director ("Dir."), the major actors ("Perf."), the theater company, the theater and its location, and the date of the performance.

Six Characters in Search of an Author. By Luigi
        Pirandello. Dir. Robert Brustein. Perf. Jeremy
        Geidt, David Ackroyd, Monica Koskey, and Marianne
        Owen. American Repertory Theatre, Cambridge.
        14 Jan. 1997.

57. SOUND RECORDING Begin with the composer (or author, if the recording is spoken), followed by the title of the piece. Next list pertinent artists (such as performers, readers, or musicians) and the orchestra and conductor. End with the manufacturer and the date. If the recording is not on a CD, indicate the medium (such as "Audiocassette") before the manufacturer's name, followed by a period. Do not underline or italicize the name of the medium or enclose it in quotation marks.

Bizet, Georges. Carmen. Perf. Jennifer Larmore, Thomas
        Moser, Angela Gheorghiu, and Samuel Ramey. Bavar-
        ian State Orch. and Chorus. Cond. Giuseppe Sino-
        poli. Warner, 1996.

58. CARTOON Begin with the cartoonist's name, the title of the cartoon (if it has one) in quotation marks, the word "Cartoon," and the publication information for the publication in which the cartoon appears.

Adams, Scott. "Dilbert." Cartoon. Editorial Humor
        3 Mar. 1998: 9.

59. MAP OR CHART Cite a map or chart as you would a book with an unknown author. Underline the title of the map or chart and add the word "Map" or "Chart" following the title.

Winery Guide to Northern and Central California. Map.
        Modesto: Compass Maps, 1996.

55c MLA information notes

Researchers who use the MLA system of parenthetical documentation (see 55a) may also use information notes for one of two purposes:

1. to provide additional material that might interrupt the flow of the paper yet is important enough to include;
2. to refer readers to any sources not discussed in the paper.

Information notes may be either footnotes or endnotes. Footnotes appear at the foot of the page; endnotes appear on a separate page at the end of the paper, just before the list of works cited. For either style, the notes are numbered consecutively throughout the paper. The text of the paper contains a raised arabic numeral that corresponds to the number of the note.

TEXT

```
California is not alone in its concern about moun-
tain lion attacks.¹
```

NOTE

```
     ¹For a discussion of lion attacks in other
western states, see Turback 34.
```

55d MLA manuscript format

In most English and humanities classes, you will be asked to use the MLA (Modern Language Association) manuscript format. The following guidelines are consistent with advice in the *MLA Handbook for Writers of Research Papers,* 5th ed. (New York: MLA, 1999). For a sample MLA research paper, see 55e.

MATERIALS Use good-quality 8½″ × 11″ white paper. If the paper emerges from the printer in a continuous sheet, separate the pages, remove the feeder strips from the sides of the paper, and assemble the pages in order. Secure the pages with a paper clip. Unless your instructor suggests otherwise, do not staple the pages together or use any sort of binder.

TITLE AND IDENTIFICATION MLA does not require a title page. On the first page of your paper, place your name, your instructor's name, the course title, and the date on separate lines against the left margin. Then center your title. (See page 438 for a sample first page.)

MARGINS, SPACING, AND INDENTATION Leave margins of at least one inch but no more than an inch and a half on all sides of the page. Do not justify the right margin.

Double-space lines and indent the first line of each paragraph one-half inch (or five spaces) from the left margin.

For a quotation longer than four typed lines of prose or three lines of verse, indent each line one inch (or ten spaces) from the left margin. Double-space between the body of the paper and the quotation, and double-space between the lines of the quotation. Quotation marks are not needed when a quotation is set off from the text by indenting. See page 442 for an example of an indented quotation; see also 37b.

PAGINATION Put your last name followed by the page number in the upper right corner of each page, one-half inch below the top edge. (If you have a separate title page, the title page is uncounted and unnumbered.) Use arabic numerals (1, 2, 3, and so on). Do not put a period after the number and do not enclose the number in parentheses.

PUNCTUATION AND TYPING In typing the paper, leave one space after words, commas, semicolons, and colons and between dots in ellipsis marks. MLA allows either one or two spaces after periods, question marks, and exclamation points. To form a dash, type two hyphens with no space between them; do not put a space on either side of the dash.

When an Internet address mentioned in the text of your paper must be divided at the end of a line, do not insert a hyphen (a hyphen could appear to be part of the address). For advice on dividing Internet addresses in your list of works cited, see page 425.

HEADINGS MLA neither encourages nor discourages use of headings and currently provides no guidelines for their use. If you would like to use headings in a long essay or research paper, check first with your instructor. Although headings are not used as frequently in English and the humanities as in other disciplines, the trend seems to be changing.

For a full discussion of headings, including their phrasing and placement, see 5b. For a sample research paper that uses headings see pages 438–47.

VISUALS MLA classifies visuals as tables and figures (figures include graphs, charts, maps, photographs, and drawings). Label each table with an arabic numeral (Table 1, Table 2, and so on) and provide a clear caption that identifies the subject; the label and caption should appear on separate lines above the table. For each figure, a label and a caption are usually placed below the figure, and they need not appear on separate lines. The word "Figure" may be abbreviated to "Fig."

Visuals should be placed in the text, as close as possible to the sentences that relate to them, unless your instructor prefers them in an appendix. See page 440 for a visual included in the text of a paper.

NOTE: See 55a for guidelines on using MLA in-text citations and 55b for preparing an MLA list of works cited.

55e Sample research paper: MLA style

On the following pages is a research paper written by John Garcia, a student in a composition class. Garcia's paper is documented with the MLA style of in-text citations and list of works cited. Annotations in the margins of the paper draw your attention to features of special interest.

Research Guide

John Garcia

Professor Hacker

English 101

7 April 1999

The Mountain Lion:

Once Endangered, Now a Danger

On April 23, 1994, as Barbara Schoener was jogging in the Sierra foothills of California, she was pounced on from behind by a mountain lion. After an apparent struggle with her attacker, Schoener was killed by bites to her neck and head (Rychnovsky 39). In 1996, because of Schoener's death and other highly publicized attacks, California politicians presented voters with Proposition 197, which contained provisions repealing much of a 1990 law enacted to protect the lions. The 1990 law outlawed sport hunting of mountain lions and even prevented the Department of Fish and Game from thinning the lion population.

Proposition 197 was rejected by a large margin, probably because the debate turned into a struggle between hunting and antihunting factions. When California politicians revisit the mountain lion question, they should frame the issue in a new way. A future proposition should retain the ban on sport hunting but allow the Department of Fish and Game to control the population. Wildlife management would reduce the number of lion attacks on humans and in the long run would also protect the lions.

The once-endangered mountain lion

To early Native Americans, mountain lions--also known as cougars, pumas, and panthers--were objects of reverence. The European colonists, however, did not share the Native American view. They conducted what Ted

---

Annotations (left margin):

Double-spacing used throughout.

Title is centered.

Summary: citation with author's name and page number in parentheses.

Thesis asserts writer's main point.

Headings help readers follow the organization.

Garcia 2

Williams calls an "all-out war on the species" (29). The lions were eliminated from the eastern United States except for a small population that remains in the Florida Everglades.

The lions lingered on in the West, but in smaller and smaller numbers. At least 66,665 lions were killed between 1907 and 1978 in Canada and the United States (Hansen 58). As late as 1969, the country's leading authority on the big cat, Maurice Hornocker, estimated the United States population as fewer than 6,500 and probably dropping (Williams 30).

Resurgence of the mountain lion

In western states today, the mountain lion is no longer in danger of extinction. In fact, over the past thirty years, the population has rebounded dramatically. In California, fish and game officials estimate that since 1972 lion numbers have increased from 2,400 to at least 6,000 ("Lion" A21).

Similar increases are occurring outside of California. For instance, for nearly fifty years mountain lions had virtually disappeared from Yellowstone National Park, but today lion sightings are increasingly common. In 1992, Hornocker estimated that at least eighteen adults were living in the park (59). In the United States as a whole, some biologists estimate that there are as many as 50,000 mountain lions, a dramatic increase over the 1969 estimate of 6,500 (Williams 30). For the millions of Americans interested in the preservation of animal species, this is good news, but unfortunately the increase has led to a number of violent encounters between human and lion.

Marginal annotations:

Quotation: author named in signal phrase; page number in parentheses.

Statistics documented with citations.

Hornocker introduced as an expert.

Short title given in parentheses because the work has no author.

A clear transition prepares readers for the next section.

Increasing attacks on humans

There is no doubt that more and more humans are being attacked. A glance at figure 1, a graph of statistics compiled by mountain lion researcher Paul Beier, confirms just how dramatically the attacks have increased since the beginning of the century.

Ray Rychnovsky reports that thirteen people have been killed and another fifty-seven have been mauled by lions since 1890. "What's most startling," writes Rychnovsky, "is that nearly three-quarters of the attacks [. . .] have taken place in the last twenty-five years" (41).

Particularly frightening are the attacks on children. Kevin Hansen points out that children have been "more vulnerable than adults, making up 64 percent of the victims" (69). This is not surprising, since chil-

The writer explains what the graph shows.

Ellipsis dots in brackets indicate words omitted from the original source (see p. 405).

Quotation introduced with a signal phrase.

The graph displays evidence of increased attacks.

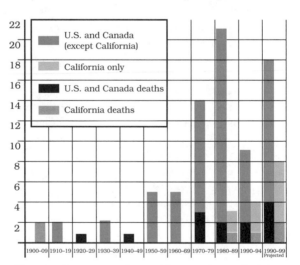

Fig. 1. Cougar attacks--a history, by Paul Beier, Northern Arizona University; rpt. in Rychnovsky (42).

Garcia 4

dren, being small and active, resemble the lion's natural prey. Lion authority John Seidensticker reports
that when he worked for the National Zoo in Washington,
DC, he regularly observed cats stalking children who
passed by the lion cages (120).

Since 1986, four children have been attacked in
California ("Mountain" 7). One of these attacks was se-
rious enough to prompt officials to place Caspers
Wilderness Park off-limits to children (Tran B8). In
July 1997 alone, two attacks on children, one fatal,
occurred in different national parks in Colorado
(McPhee A1).

In California, the state where the lion is most
fully protected, 1994 was a particularly bad year. Los
Angeles Times writer Tony Perry reports that two women
were killed by lions in 1994 and that the year brought
a dramatic increase in mountain lion sightings, "many
in suburban and urban areas where the animal had previously not been spotted" (B4). With two killings in one
year and an increasing number of sightings, it is not
surprising that California politicians responded with
Proposition 197, aimed at repealing the ban on hunting
the lions.

The 1996 California referendum

The debate over Proposition 197 was inflamed by
campaigns of misinformation on both sides of the issue.
The pro faction included the National Rifle Association
(NRA), the Safari Club, and Gun Owners of California.
On the other side were animal rights groups such as the
Sierra Club, the Fund for Animals, and the Mountain
Lion Foundation.

The proposition itself, introduced by Republican
Tim Leslie, is laced with legalese and deceptive phras

Summary intro-
duced with a
signal phrase.

Clear topic sen-
tences, like this
one, used
throughout the
paper.

ing. For example, in a provision aimed at amending section 4801 of the Fish and Game Code, the word
<u>hunters</u> does not appear, though the legalistic term
<u>designee</u> clearly includes hunters:

> The department may remove or take, or autho-
> rize its designee, including, but not limited
> to, an appropriate governmental agency with
> public safety responsibility, an appropriate
> governmental agency with wildlife management
> responsibility, or an owner of land, to re-
> move or take, one or more mountain lions that
> are perceived to be an imminent threat to
> public health or safety or livestock anywhere
> in the state except within the state park
> system. ("Proposition" sec. 5)

The proposition's euphemistic language, such as <u>remove</u>
<u>or take</u>, was echoed by the hunting factions, who spoke
much about "controlling" the lion population, avoiding
such words as <u>hunt</u> and <u>shoot</u>.

   Supporters of Proposition 197 were not above exag-
gerating the dangers posed by mountain lions, preferring lurid accounts of maulings and killings to solid
statistics. For example, writing on the Internet in an
attempt to sway voters, Terrence M. Eagan, Wayne Long,
and Steven Arroyo appeal to human fears of being eaten:
"Two small children woke up one morning without a
mother because a lion ate her." To underscore the
point, they describe a grisly discovery: "A lion prey-
ing upon neighborhood pets was found with parts of five
different puppies in its stomach."

   Whereas the pro-hunting groups used deceptive language and exaggerated the dangers posed by lions, the
pro-lion groups invoked inflammatory language and ignored the dangers. A Web page written by a coalition of

---

Margin annotations:

Quotation set off from text is clearly introduced.

Quotation longer than four lines is indented 1″ (or ten spaces); quotation marks are omitted; no period is used after citation.

Short title given in parentheses because the work has no author.

No parenthetical citation necessary for unpaginated Internet source when author is named in signal phrase.

Transition helps readers move from one topic to another.

wildlife preservationists is typical. Calling Proposition 197 "a special interest trophy hunting measure,"
the coalition claims that the Gun Owners of California,
the NRA, and the Safari Club "rammed" the proposition
onto the ballot while "hiding behind a disingenuous
concern for public safety." Asserting that the mountain
lion poses a minimal threat to humans, the coalition
accuses the Department of Fish and Game of "creating a
climate of fear" so that the public will choose to re-
instate lion hunting (California Wildlife Protection
Coalition). While it is true that human encounters with
mountain lions are rare, some pro-lion publications
come close to ridiculing Californians who fear that
lion attacks on humans and pets will continue to accel-
erate unless something is done.

Internet source
with no page
number.

Population control: A reasonable solution

Without population control, the number of attacks
on Californians will almost certainly continue to rise,
and the lions may become even bolder. As lion authority
John Seidensticker remarks, "The boldness displayed by
mountain lions just doesn't square with the shy, retiring behavior familiar to those of us who have studied
these animals" (177). He surmises that the lions have
become emboldened because they no longer have to contend with wolves and grizzly bears, which dominated
them in the past. The only conceivable predator to re-
instill that fear is the human.

Credentials of
author men-
tioned in signal
phrase.

Sadly, the only sure way to reduce lion attacks on
humans is to thin the population. One basic approach to
thinning is sport hunting, which is still legal, though
restricted in various ways, in every western state except California. A second approach involves state-

directed wildlife management, usually the hiring of professional hunters to shoot or trap the lions.

Sport hunting is a poor option--and not just because it is unpopular with Californians. First, it is difficult to control sport hunting. For instance, a number of western states have restrictions on killing a female lion with kittens, but sport hunters are rarely knowledgeable enough to tell whether a lion has kittens. Second, because some sport hunters are poor shots, they wound but don't kill the lions, causing needless suffering. Finally, certain hunting practices are anything but sport. There is a growing business in professionally led cougar hunts, as a number of ads on the World Wide Web attest. One practice is to tree a lion with radio-equipped dogs and then place a phone call to the client to come and shoot the lion. In some cases, the lion may be treed for two or more days before the client arrives to bag his trophy. Such practices are so offensive that even the California Park Rangers Association opposed Proposition 197. As a spokesperson explained, "We support managing the lions. But they shouldn't be stuck on the wall in a den" (qtd. in Perry B4).

We should entrust the thinning of the lion population to wildlife specialists guided by science, not to hunters seeking adventure or to safari clubs looking for profits. Unlike hunters, scientific wildlife managers have the long-term interests of the mountain lion at heart. An uncontrolled population leads to an ecological imbalance, with more and more lions competing for territory and a diminishing food supply. The highly territorial lions will fight to the death to defend their hunting grounds; and because the mother lion ultimately ejects her offspring from her own territory,

---

Citation of indirect source: words quoted in another source.

No citation needed for "common knowledge" available in many sources.

Garcia 8

young lions face an uncertain future. Stephani Cruickshank, a spokesperson for California Lion Awareness
(CLAW), explains, "The overrun of lions is biologically
unsound and unfair to the lions, especially those
forced to survive in marginal or clearly unnatural urban settings" (qtd. in Robinson 35).

   In conclusion, wildlife management would benefit
both Californians and the California lions. Although
some have argued that California needs fewer people,
not fewer lions, humans do have an obligation to protect themselves and their children, and the fears of
people in lion country are real. As for the lions, they
need to thrive in a natural habitat with an adequate
food supply. "We simply cannot let nature take its
course," writes Terry Mansfield of the Department of
Fish and Game (qtd. in Perry B4). In fact, not to take
action in California is as illogical as reintroducing
the lions to Central Park and Boston Common, places
they once also roamed.

The writer con-
cludes with his
own stand on
the controversy.

The paper ends
with the writer's
own words.

Works Cited

California Wildlife Protection Coalition. California
  Mountain Lion Page. 27 Mar. 1996. Sierra Club.
  24 Mar. 1999 <http://www.sierraclub.org/chapters/
  ca/mountain-lion>.

Eagan, Terrence M., Wayne Long, and Steven Arroyo. "Re-
  buttal to Argument against Proposition 197." 1996
  California Primary Election Server. 1996. California Secretary of State. 24 Mar. 1999 <http://
  primary96.ss.ca.gov/e/ballot/197again2.html>.

Hansen, Kevin. Cougar: The American Lion. Flagstaff:
  Northland, 1992.

Hornocker, Maurice G. "Learning to Live with Lions."
  National Geographic July 1992: 37-65.

"Lion Attacks Prompt State to Respond." New York Times
  18 Oct. 1995, late ed.: A21.

McPhee, Mike. "Danger Grows as Lions Lose Fear." Denver
  Post 19 July 1997. 2nd ed.: A1.

"Mountain Lion Attacks on Humans." Outdoor California.
  21 Mar. 1996. State of California. Dept. of Fish
  and Game. 24 Mar. 1999 <http://www.dfg.ca.gov/
  lion/outdoor.lion.html>.

Perry, Tony. "Big Cat Fight." Los Angeles Times 8 Mar.
  1996, home ed.: B1+.

"Proposition 197: Text of Proposed Law." 1996 California Primary Election Server. 1996. California Secretary of State. 24 Mar. 1999 <http://
  primary96.ss.ca.gov/e/ballot/197txt.html>.

Robinson, Jerome B. "Cat in the Ballot Box." Field and
  Stream Mar. 1996: 30-35.

Rychnovsky, Ray. "Clawing into Controversy." Outdoor
  Life Jan. 1995: 38-42.

Seidensticker, John. "Mountain Lions Don't Stalk
  People: True or False?" Audubon Feb. 1992: 113-22.

Heading centered 1″ from top of page.

List is alphabetized by authors' last names.

First line of each entry is at left margin; subsequent lines are indented ½″ (or five spaces).

Double-spacing used throughout.

Tran, Trini. "Near-Attack by Cougar Reported." <u>Los An-
    geles Times</u> 2 Jan. 1998: B8.

Williams, Ted. "The Lion's Silent Return." <u>Audubon</u> Nov.
    1994: 28-35.

56

APA and other styles

In most social sciences classes, such as psychology, sociology, anthropology, and business, you will be asked to use the APA style of in-text citations and references. The guidelines in this section are consistent with those of the *Publication Manual of the American Psychological Association,* 4th ed. (Washington: APA, 1994).

56a APA in-text citations

The American Psychological Association recommends an author/date style of in-text citations. These citations refer readers to a list of references at the end of the paper.

APA in-text citations provide at least the author's last name and the date of publication. For direct quotations, a page number is given as well.

1. BASIC FORMAT FOR A QUOTATION   Ordinarily, introduce the quotation with a signal phrase that includes the author's last name followed by the date of publication in parentheses. Put the page number (preceded by "p.") in parentheses at the end of the quotation.

> According to Hart (1996), some primatologists "won-
> dered if apes had learned Language, with a capital
> <u>L</u>" (p. 109).

When the author's name does not appear in the signal phrase, place the author's name, the date, and the page number in parentheses at the end of the quotation. Use commas between items in the parentheses: (Hart, 1996, p. 109).

2. BASIC FORMAT FOR A SUMMARY OR A PARAPHRASE   For a summary or a paraphrase, include the author's last name and the date either in a signal phrase or in parentheses at the end.

Directory to APA in-text citations (56a)

Directory to APA references (bibliographic entries) (56b)

> According to Hart (1996), researchers took Ter-
> race's conclusions seriously, and funding for lan-
> guage experiments soon declined.

> Researchers took Terrace's conclusions seriously,
> and funding for language experiments soon declined
> (Hart, 1996).

NOTE: A page number is not required, but provide one if it would help your readers find a specific page in a long work.

3. A WORK WITH TWO AUTHORS   Name both authors in the signal phrase or parentheses each time you cite the work. In the parentheses, use "&" between the authors' names; in the signal phrase, use "and."

> Patterson and Linden (1981) agreed that the gorilla
> Koko acquired language more slowly than a normal
> speaking child.

> Koko acquired language more slowly than a normal
> speaking child (Patterson & Linden, 1981).

4. A WORK WITH THREE TO FIVE AUTHORS   Identify all authors in the signal phrase or the parentheses the first time you cite the source.

> Researchers found a marked improvement in the com-
> puter skills of students who took part in the pro-
> gram (Levy, Bertrand, Muller, Vining, & Majors,
> 1997).

In subsequent citations, use the first author's name followed by "et al." in either the signal phrase or the parentheses.

> Though school board members were skeptical at
> first, the program has now won the board's full
> support (Levy et al., 1997).

5. A WORK WITH SIX OR MORE AUTHORS   Use only the first author's name followed by "et al." in the signal phrase or the parentheses.

> Better measurements of sophistication in computer
> use could be obtained through more thorough testing
> (Blili et al., 2000).

6. UNKNOWN AUTHOR If the author is not given, use the first word or two of the title in the signal phrase or the parenthetical citation.

> Massachusetts state and municipal governments have
> initiated several programs to improve public
> safety, including community policing and after-
> school activities ("Innovations," 1999).

If "Anonymous" is specified as the author, treat it as if it were a real name: (Anonymous, 1999). In the bibliographic references, also use the name Anonymous as author.

7. CORPORATE AUTHOR If the author is a government agency or other corporate organization with a long and cumbersome name, spell out the name the first time you use it in a citation followed by an abbreviation in brackets. In later citations, simply use the abbreviation.

> **FIRST CITATION**   (National Institute of Mental Health
>   [NIMH], 2000)
>
> **LATER CITATIONS** (NIMH, 2000)

8. TWO OR MORE WORKS IN THE SAME PARENTHESES When your parenthetical citation names two or more works, put them in the same order that they appear in the bibliography, separated by semicolons.

> Researchers have investigated the degree to which
> gender affects the distribution of welfare
> (Gilbert, 1995; Leira, 1994).

9. AUTHORS WITH THE SAME LAST NAME To avoid confusion, use initials with the last names if your bibliography lists two or more authors with the same last name.

> Research by D. L. Johnson (1999) revealed that . . .

10. PERSONAL COMMUNICATION Conversations, memos, letters, e-mail, and similar unpublished person-to-person communications should by cited by initials, last name, and precise date.

```
F. Moore (personal communication, January 4, 2000)
has said that funding for the program will continue
for at least another year.
```

It is not necessary to include personal communications in the bibliographic references at the end of your paper.

11. WEB SITE Cite material from a Web site by giving the Web address in parentheses: (http://pgweb.pg.cc.md.us). If you are referring to the entire site, you do not need a bibliographic entry; if you are referring to a specific document from the site, provide a bibliographic entry in the list of references (see p. 457).

56b APA references (bibliographic list)

In APA style, the alphabetical list of works cited is called "References." This section presents specific models to follow while preparing each entry in your list, along with the following general advice.

TITLE AND PLACEMENT OF LIST The list of references begins on a new page at the end of your paper. Center the title "References" (without quotation marks) in the width of the page. See pages 468–69 for an example.

INDENTING Unless your instructor suggests otherwise, do not indent the first line of an entry, but indent any additional lines one-half inch (or five spaces), as follows:

```
Stoessinger, J. G. (1998). Why nations go to war
       (7th ed.). New York: St. Martin's Press.
```

This technique, known as a "hanging indent," is used for final copy: student papers and actual journal articles. For manuscripts submitted to journals, APA requires paragraph-style indents, as follows:

> Stoessinger, J. G. (1998). <u>Why nations go to
> war</u> (7th ed.). New York: St. Martin's Press.

Throughout this section, documentation models are shown as final copy, with hanging indents. Use the format that your instructor prefers.

ALPHABETIZING THE LIST Alphabetize your list by the last names of the authors (or editors); if there is no author or editor, alphabetize by the first word of the title other than *A, An,* or *The*.

AUTHORS' NAMES Invert *all* authors' names, and use initials instead of first names. With two or more authors, use an ampersand (&) rather than the word "and." Separate the names with commas. Use all authors' names; do not use "et al."

DATE Place the date of publication in parentheses immediately after the last author's name.

TITLES OF BOOKS Underline titles and subtitles of books; capitalize only the first word of the title and subtitle (as well as all proper nouns).

TITLES OF ARTICLES Do not place titles of periodical articles in quotation marks, and capitalize only the first word of the title and subtitle (and all proper nouns).

TITLES OF PERIODICALS Capitalize titles of periodicals as you would capitalize them ordinarily (see 45c). Underline the volume number of periodicals.

PAGE NUMBERS Use the abbreviation "p." (or "pp.") before page numbers of newspaper articles and works in anthologies, but do not use it before page numbers of articles appearing in magazines and scholarly journals.
Provide inclusive page numbers such as "pp. 203–214." If the page numbers of an article are discontinuous, provide all of them, separated by commas (for example, "A1, A5, A7").

PUBLISHERS' NAMES You may use a short form of a publisher's name as long as it is easily recognizable.

Books

1. BASIC FORMAT FOR A BOOK

Tapscott, D. (1998). Growing up digital. New York:
    McGraw-Hill.

2. TWO OR MORE AUTHORS

Hamer, D., & Copeland, P. (1998). Living with our
    genes: Why they matter more than you think. New
    York: Doubleday.

Winncott, D. W., Shepherd, R., Johns, J., & Robinson,
    H. T. (1996). Thinking about children. Reading,
    MA: Addison-Wesley.

3. CORPORATE AUTHOR   When the author is an organization, the publisher is often the same organization. In such a case, give the publisher's name as "Author."

Bank of Boston. (1997). Banking by remote control.
    Boston: Author.

4. UNKNOWN AUTHOR

Oxford essential world atlas. (1996). New York: Oxford
    University Press.

5. EDITORS

Duncan, G. J., & Brooks-Gunn, J. (Eds.). (1997).
    Consequences of growing up poor. New York:
    Russell Sage Foundation.

6. TRANSLATION

Singer, I. B. (1998). Shadows on the Hudson (J. Sher-
    man, Trans.). New York: Farrar, Straus and
    Giroux. (Original work published 1957)

7. EDITION OTHER THAN THE FIRST

Helfer, M. E., Kempe, R. S., & Krugman, R. D. (1997).
    The battered child (5th ed.). Chicago: University
    of Chicago Press.

8. WORK IN AN ANTHOLOGY

Fesmire, S. (1997). The social basis of character: An
    ecological humanist approach. In H. LaFollette
    (Ed.), Ethics in practice (pp. 282-292). Cam-
    bridge, MA: Blackwell.

9. MULTIVOLUME WORK

Wiener, P. (Ed.). (1973). Dictionary of the history of
    ideas (Vols. 1-4). New York: Scribner's.

10. TWO OR MORE WORKS BY THE SAME AUTHOR Use the author's
name for all entries. Arrange each of the entries by date, the
earliest first.

Jones, J. M. (1988). Why should black undergraduate
    students major in psychology? In P. J. Woods
    (Ed.), Is psychology for them? A guide to under-
    graduate advising (pp. 178-181). Washington, DC:
    American Psychological Association.

Jones, J. M. (1996). Racism and white racial identity:
    Merging realities. In B. P. Bowser and R. G. Hunt
    (Eds.), Impacts of racism on white Americans (pp.
    1-23). Thousand Oaks, CA: Sage.

Articles in periodicals

11. ARTICLE IN A JOURNAL PAGINATED BY VOLUME

McLoyd, V. C. (1998). Socioeconomic disadvantage and
    child development. American Psychologist, 53,
    185-204.

12. ARTICLE IN A JOURNAL PAGINATED BY ISSUE

Roberts, P. (1998). The new food anxiety. Psychology
    Today. 31(2), 30-38, 74.

13. ARTICLE IN A MAGAZINE

Kadrey, R. (1998, March). Carbon copy: Meet the first
    human clone. Wired, 6, 146-150, 180, 220.

14. ARTICLE IN A NEWSPAPER

Haney, D. Q. (1998, February 20). Finding eats at mys-
    tery of appetite. The Oregonian, pp. A1, A17.

15. LETTER TO THE EDITOR

Westberg, L. (1997). South Bronx, New York [Letter to
    the editor]. Orion, 16(1), 4.

16. REVIEW

Ehrenhalt, A. (1997, February 10). [Review of the book
    Virtuous reality]. The Weekly Standard, pp. 31-34.

17. TWO OR MORE WORKS BY THE SAME AUTHOR IN THE SAME YEAR   Cite
the works according to the usual style, and arrange them alphabetically by title. Add lowercase letters beginning with "a,"
"b," and so on, within the parentheses immediately following
the year.

Chapin, W. D. (1997a). Ausländer raus? The empirical
    relationship between immigration and crime in
    Germany. Social Science Quarterly, 78, 543-558.

Chapin, W. D. (1997b). Explaining the electoral suc-
    cess of the new right: The German case. Western
    European Politics, 20, 53-72.

Electronic sources

The following guidelines for electronic sources are based
on APA's June 1, 1999, update posted on its Web site, < http://
www.apa.org/journals/webref.html >. You may wish to check
this Web site for future updates.

18. MATERIAL FROM AN ONLINE DATABASE

Fletcher, M. (1998, January). Ohio law sets managed
    care standards. <u>Business Insurance,</u> 32(1), 27.
    Retrieved June 17, 1999 from DIALOG@SITE online
    database (Business & Industry, 02035266)

19. MATERIAL FROM A CD-ROM DATABASE

Cummings, A. (1995). Test review made easy [Abstract].
    <u>Learning.</u> 23(5), 68. Retrieved from ERIC database
    (ERIC Reproduction Service, CD-ROM, Fall 1998
    release, No. ED 316 784)

20. MATERIAL FROM A DATABASE ACCESSED VIA THE WEB

Caruba, A. (1998, January 1). The plague of boredom.
    <u>The World & I,</u> 13. Retrieved June 17, 1999 from
    Electric Library database (Magazines) on the
    World Wide Web: http://www.elibrary.com

21. DOCUMENT FROM A WEB SITE

Coram, J. (1999, June 4). Commencement grads show
    richness, diversity. <u>Community College Times.</u>
    Retrieved June 17, 1999 from the World Wide Web:
    http://www.aacc.nche.edu/headline/060499head2.htm

22. E-MAIL E-mail messages are personal communications and
are not included in the list of references.

23. COMPUTER PROGRAM

Kaufmann, W. J., III, & Comins, N. F. (1998). Discov-
    ering the Universe 4.1 [Computer software]. New
    York: W. H. Freeman.

Other sources

24. DISSERTATION ABSTRACT

Hu, X. (1996). Consumption and social inequality in
    urban Guangdong, China (Doctoral dissertation,
    University of Hawaii, 1996). <u>Dissertation Ab-</u>
    <u>stracts International, 57,</u> 3280A.

25. GOVERNMENT DOCUMENT

U.S. Bureau of the Census. (1996). <u>Statistical ab-</u>
    <u>stract of the United States</u> (116th ed.). Washing-
    ton, DC: U.S. Government Printing Office.

26. PROCEEDINGS OF A CONFERENCE

Schnase, J. L., & Cunnius, E. L. (Eds.). (1995). <u>Pro-</u>
    <u>ceedings of CSCL '95: The First International</u>
    <u>Conference on Computer Support for Collaborative</u>
    <u>Learning.</u> Mahwah, NJ: Erlbaum.

27. VIDEOTAPE

Public Broadcasting System (Producer). (1997). <u>The new</u>
    <u>urban renewal: Reclaiming our neighborhoods</u>
    [Videotape]. Alexandria, VA: PBS Video.

56c APA manuscript format

This section presents guidelines for formatting a manuscript according to APA style. Also see the sample research paper formatted in APA style (pp. 461–69) and guidelines for preparing
the reference list (pp. 452–53).

MATERIALS AND TYPEFACE Use good-quality 8½″ × 11″ white paper. For a paper typed on a computer, make sure that the print quality meets your instructor's standards. Avoid a typeface that is unusual or hard to read.

TITLE PAGE Begin a college paper with a title page. Type the page number, flush right (against the right margin), about one-half inch from the top of the page. Before the page number type a short title, consisting of the first two or three words of your title.

The APA manual does not provide guidelines for the placement of certain information necessary for college papers, but most instructors will want you to supply a title page similar to the one on page 461.

MARGINS, SPACING, AND INDENTATION Use margins of at least one inch on all sides of the page. If you are working on a computer, do not justify the right margin.

Double-space throughout the paper, and indent the first line of each paragraph one-half inch (or five spaces).

For quotations longer than forty words, indent each line one-half inch (or five spaces) from the left margin. Double-space between the body of the paper and the quotation, and double-space between lines of the quotation. Quotation marks are not needed when a quotation is indented. (See 37b).

PAGE NUMBERS AND SHORT TITLE In the upper right-hand corner of each page, about one-half inch from the top of the page, type the page number, preceded by the short title that you typed on the title page. Number all pages, including the title page.

PUNCTUATION AND TYPING Although the APA guidelines call for one space after all punctuation, many college professors allow two spaces at the end of a sentence. Use one space after all other punctuation.

To form a dash, type two hyphens with no space between them. Do not put a space on either side of the dash.

ABSTRACT   If your instructor requires one, include an abstract right after the title page. Center the word "Abstract" about one inch from the top of the page; double-space the text of the abstract as you do the body of your paper.

An abstract is a 75-to-100-word paragraph that provides readers with a quick overview of your essay. It should express your thesis (or central idea) and your key points; it should also briefly suggest any implications or applications of the research you discuss in the paper.

HEADINGS   Although headings are not necessary, their use is encouraged in the social sciences. For most undergraduate papers, use no more than one or two levels of headings. Major headings should be centered, with the first letter of important words capitalized; minor words — articles, short prepositions, and coordinating conjunctions — are not capitalized unless they are the first word. Subheadings should be typed flush left (against the left margin) and underlined; the rules on capitalization are the same as for major headings. See pages 461–69 for an APA paper with headings.

VISUALS   The APA classifies visuals as tables and figures (figures include graphs, charts, drawings, and photographs). Keep visuals as simple as possible. Label each clearly — Table 1, Figure 3, and so on — and include a caption that concisely describes its subject. In the text of your paper, discuss the most significant features of each visual. Ask your instructor for guidelines on placement of visuals in the paper.

56d Sample research paper: APA style

On the following pages is a research paper written by Karen Shaw, a student in a psychology class. Shaw's assignment was to write a "review of the literature" documented with APA-style citations and references.

In preparing her final manuscript, Shaw followed APA guidelines. She did not include an abstract because her instructor did not require one.

Apes and Language   1

Short title and page number for student papers.

Apes and Language:
A Review of the Literature

Full title, writer's name, name and section number of course, instructor's name, and date all centered.

Karen Shaw

Psychology 110, Section 2
Professor Verdi
March 4, 1999

Apes and Language:

A Review of the Literature

Over the past thirty years, researchers have demonstrated that the great apes (chimpanzees, gorillas, and orangutans) resemble humans in language abilities more than had been thought possible. Just how far that resemblance extends, however, has been a matter of some controversy. Researchers agree that the apes have acquired fairly large vocabularies in American Sign Language and in artificial languages, but they have drawn quite different conclusions in addressing the following questions:

1. How spontaneously have apes used language?
2. How creatively have apes used language?
3. Can apes create sentences?
4. What are the implications of the ape language studies?

This review of the literature on apes and language focuses on these four questions.

How Spontaneously Have
Apes Used Language?

In an influential article, Terrace, Petitto, Sanders, and Bever (1979) argued that the apes in language experiments were not using language spontaneously but were merely imitating their trainers, responding to conscious or unconscious cues. Terrace and his colleagues at Columbia University had trained a chimpanzee, Nim, in American Sign Language, so their skepticism about the apes' abilities received much attention. In fact, funding for ape language research was sharply reduced following publication of their 1979 article "Can an Ape Create a Sentence?"

In retrospect, the conclusions of Terrace et al. seem to have been premature. Although some early

---

Full title, centered.

The writer sets up her organization in the introduction.

Headings, centered, help readers follow the organization.

A signal phrase names all four authors and gives date in parentheses.

ape language studies had not been rigorously controlled
to eliminate cuing, even as early as the 1970s R. A.
Gardner and B. T. Gardner were conducting double-blind
experiments that prevented any possibility of cuing
(Fouts, 1997, p. 99). Since 1979, researchers have
diligently guarded against cuing. For example, Lewin
(1991) reported that instructions for bonobo (pygmy
chimpanzee) Kanzi were "delivered by someone out of his
sight," with other team members wearing earphones so
that they "could not hear the instructions and so could
not cue Kanzi, even unconsciously" (p. 51). More recently, philosopher Stuart Shanker of York University
has questioned the emphasis placed on cuing, pointing
out that since human communication relies on the ability to understand cues and gestures in a social setting, it is not surprising that apes might rely on similar signals (Johnson, 1995).

There is considerable evidence that apes have
signed to one another spontaneously, without trainers
present. Like many of the apes studied, gorillas Koko
and Michael have been observed signing to one another
(Patterson & Linden, 1981). At Central Washington University the baby chimpanzee Loulis, placed in the care
of the signing chimpanzee Washoe, mastered nearly fifty
signs in American Sign Language without help from humans. "Interestingly," wrote researcher Fouts (1997),
"Loulis did not pick up any of the seven signs that we
[humans] used around him. He learned only from Washoe
and [another chimp] Ally" (p. 244).

The extent to which chimpanzees spontaneously use
language may depend on their training. Terrace trained
Nim using the behaviorist technique of operant condi-
tioning, so it is not surprising that many of Nim's
signs were cued. Many other researchers have used a

Because the au-
thor of the work
is not named in
the signal
phrase, his name
appears in
parentheses,
along with the
date. Citation
from a long
work has page
number pre-
ceded by "p."

For a quotation,
a page number
preceded by "p."
appears in
parentheses.

An ampersand
links the names
of two authors
in parentheses.

Brackets are
used to indicate
words not in
original source.

conversational approach that parallels the process by
which human children acquire language. In an experimental study, O'Sullivan and Yeager (1989) contrasted the
two techniques, using Terrace's Nim as their subject.
They found that Nim's use of language was significantly
more spontaneous under conversational conditions.

The word "and"
links the names
of two authors
in the signal
phrase.

How Creatively Have
Apes Used Language?

There is considerable evidence that apes have invented creative names. One of the earliest and most
controversial examples involved the Gardners' chimpanzee Washoe. Washoe, who knew signs for "water" and
"bird," once signed "water bird" when in the presence
of a swan. Terrace et al. (1979) suggested that there
was "no basis for concluding that Washoe was character-
izing the swan as a 'bird that inhabits water.'" Washoe
may simply have been "identifying correctly a body of
water and a bird, in that order" (p. 895).

When this ar-
ticle was first
cited, all four
authors were
named. In sub-
sequent citations
of a work with
three to five au-
thors, "et al." is
used after the
first author's
name.

Other examples are not so easily explained away.
The bonobo Kanzi has requested particular films by combining symbols in a creative way. For instance, to ask
for Quest for Fire, a film about early primates discovering fire, Kanzi began to use symbols for "campfire"
and "TV" (Eckholm, 1985). And the gorilla Koko has a
long list of creative names to her credit: "elephant
baby" to describe a Pinocchio doll, "finger bracelet"
to describe a ring, "bottle match" to describe a cigarette lighter, and so on (Patterson & Linden, 1981, p.
146). If Terrace's analysis of the "water bird" example
is applied to the examples just mentioned, it does not
hold. Surely Koko did not first see an elephant and
then a baby before signing "elephant baby"--or a bottle
and a match before signing "bottle match."

The writer
interprets the
evidence; she
doesn't just
report it.

Apes and Language   5

Can Apes Create Sentences?

The early ape language studies offered little
proof that apes could combine symbols into grammatically ordered sentences. Apes strung together various
signs, but the sequences were often random and repetitious. Nim's series of 16 signs is a case in point:
"give orange me give eat orange me eat orange give me
eat orange give me you" (Terrace et al., 1979, p. 895).

More recent studies with bonobos at the Yerkes
Primate Research Center in Atlanta have broken new
ground. Kanzi, a bonobo trained by Savage-Rumbaugh,
seems to understand simple grammatical rules about lexigram order. For instance, Kanzi learned that in two-
word utterances action precedes object, an ordering
also used by human children at the two-word stage. In a
major article reporting on their research, Greenfield
and Savage-Rumbaugh (1990) wrote that Kanzi rarely "repeated himself or formed combinations that were seman-
tically unrelated" (p. 556).

> The writer draws attention to an important article.

More important, Kanzi began on his own to create
certain patterns that may not exist in English but can
be found among deaf children and in other human languages. For example, Kanzi used his own rules when combining action symbols. Lexigrams that involved an invitation to play, such as "chase," would appear first;
lexigrams that indicated what was to be done during
play ("hide") would appear second. Kanzi also created
his own rules when combining gestures and lexigrams. He
would use the lexigram first and then gesture, a practice often followed by young deaf children (Greenfield &
Savage-Rumbaugh, 1990, p. 560).

> The writer gives a page number for this summary because the article is long.

In a recent study, Kanzi's abilities were shown to
be similar to those of a 2-1/2-year-old human, Alia.
Rumbaugh (1995) reported that "Kanzi's comprehension of

over 600 novel sentences of request was very comparable
to Alia's; both complied with the requests without assistance on approximately 70% of the sentences"
(p. 722).

For quotations, a
page number is
required.

What Are the Implications of the
Ape Language Studies?

Kanzi's linguistic abilities are so impressive
that they may help us understand how humans came to acquire language. Pointing out that 99% of our genetic
material is held in common with the chimpanzees, Greenfield and Savage-Rumbaugh (1990) have suggested that
something of the "evolutionary root of human language"
can be found in the "linguistic abilities of the great
apes" (p. 540). Noting that apes' brains are similar to
those of our human ancestors, Leakey and Lewin (1992)
argued that in ape brains "the cognitive foundations
on which human language could be built are already
present" (p. 244).

The suggestion that there is a continuity in the
linguistic abilities of apes and humans has created
much controversy. Linguist Noam Chomsky has strongly
asserted that language is a unique human characteristic
(Booth, 1990). Terrace has continued to be skeptical of
the claims made for the apes, as have Petitto and
Bever, coauthors of the 1979 article that caused such
skepticism earlier (Gibbons, 1991).

The writer pre-
sents a balanced
view of the
philosophical
controversy.

Recently, neurobiologists have made discoveries
that may cause even the skeptics to take notice. Ongoing studies at the Yerkes Primate Research Center have
revealed remarkable similarities in the brains of chimpanzees and humans. Through brain scans of live chimpanzees, researchers have found that, as with humans,
"the language-controlling PT [planum temporale] is
larger on the left side of the chimps' brain than on

the right. But it is not lateralized in monkeys, which are less closely related to humans than apes are" (Begley, 1998, p. 57).

Although the ape language studies continue to generate controversy, researchers have shown over the past thirty years that the gap between the linguistic abilities of apes and humans is far less dramatic than was once believed.

The tone of the conclusion is objective.

Apes and Language   8

References

Begley, S. (1998, January 19). Aping language. <u>Newsweek</u> <u>131</u>, 56-58.

Booth, W. (1990, October 29). Monkeying with language: Is chimp using words or merely aping handlers? <u>The Washington Post</u>, p. A3.

Eckholm, E. (1985, June 25). Kanzi the chimp: A life in science. <u>The New York Times</u>, pp. C1, C3.

Fouts, R. (1997). <u>Next of kin: What chimpanzees taught me about who we are</u>. New York: William Morrow.

Gibbons, A. (1991). Déjà vu all over again: Chimp-language wars. <u>Science, 251</u>, 1561-1562.

Greenfield, P. M., & Savage-Rumbaugh, E. S. (1990). Grammatical combination in <u>Pan paniscus</u>: Processes of learning and invention in the evolution and development of language. In S. T. Parker & K. R. Gibson (Eds.), <u>"Language" and intelligence in monkeys and apes: Comparative developmental perspectives</u> (pp. 540-578). Cambridge: Cambridge University Press.

Johnson, G. (1995, June 6). Chimp talk debate: Is it really language? <u>The New York Times</u> [Online], pp. C1, C10. Available: http://www.santafe.edu/ ~johnson/articles.chimp.html [2 February 1998].

Leakey, R., & Lewin, R. (1992). <u>Origins reconsidered: In search of what makes us human</u>. New York: Doubleday.

Lewin, R. (1991, April 29). Look who's talking now. <u>New Scientist, 130</u>, 49-52.

O'Sullivan, C., & Yeager, C. P. (1989). Communicative context and linguistic competence: The effect of social setting on a chimpanzee's conversational skill. In R. A. Gardner, B. T. Gardner, & T. E. Van Cantfort (Eds.). <u>Teaching sign language to chimpanzees</u> (pp. 269-279). Albany: SUNY Press.

Marginal notes:

List of references begins on a new page. Heading is centered.

List is alphabetized by authors' names.

In student papers the first line of an entry is at left margin; subsequent lines indent ½" (or five spaces). (See p. 452.)

Double-spacing used throughout.

Patterson, F., & Linden, E. (1981). The education of
    Koko. New York: Holt, Rinehart & Winston.
Rumbaugh, D. (1995). Primate language and cognition:
    Common ground. Social Research, 62, 711-730.
Terrace, H. S., Petitto, L. A., Sanders, R. J., &
    Bever, T. G. (1979). Can an ape create a sentence?
    Science, 206, 891-902.

56e List of style manuals

A useful list of sources (both print and online) and documentation models for many disciplines can be found on a Web site that accompanies this text: *Research and Documentation in the Electronic Age* < http://www.bedfordstmartins.com/hacker/resdoc > .

Rules for Writers describes two commonly used systems of documentation: MLA, used in English and the humanities (see 55), and APA, used in psychology and the social sciences (see 56a–d). Following is a list of style manuals used in a variety of disciplines.

BIOLOGY
Council of Biology Editors. *Scientific Style and Format: The CBE Manual for Authors, Editors, and Publishers.* 6th ed. New York: Cambridge UP, 1994.

BUSINESS
American Management Association. *The AMA Style Guide for Business Writing.* New York: AMACOM, 1996.

CHEMISTRY
Dodd, Janet S., ed. *The ACS Style Guide: A Manual for Authors and Editors.* Washington: Amer. Chemical Soc., 1986.

ENGLISH AND THE HUMANITIES (SEE 55.)
Gibaldi, Joseph. *MLA Handbook for Writers of Research Papers.* 5th ed. New York: MLA, 1999.

GEOLOGY
Bates, Robert L., Rex Buchanan, and Marla Adkins-Heljeson, eds. *Geowriting: A Guide to Writing, Editing, and Printing in Earth Science.* 5th ed. Alexandria: Amer. Geological Inst., 1992.

GOVERNMENT DOCUMENTS
Garner, Diane L. *The Complete Guide to Citing Government Information Resources: A Manual for Writers and Librarians.* Rev. ed. Bethesda: Congressional Information Service, 1993.

United States Government Printing Office. *Manual of Style.* Washington: GPO, 1988.

HISTORY

The Chicago Manual of Style. 14th ed. Chicago: U of Chicago P, 1993.

JOURNALISM

Goldstein, Norm, ed. *Associated Press Stylebook and Libel Manual.* 32nd ed. New York: Associated Press, 1997.

LAW

Columbia Law Review. *A Uniform System of Citation.* 16th ed. Cambridge: Harvard Law Rev. Assn., 1996.

LINGUISTICS

Linguistic Society of America. "LSA Style Sheet." Published annually in the December issue of the *LSA Bulletin.*

MATHEMATICS

American Mathematical Society. *The AMS Author Handbook: General Instructions for Preparing Manuscripts.* Providence: AMS, 1994.

MEDICINE

Iverson, Cheryl, et al. *American Medical Association Manual of Style: A Guide for Authors and Editors.* 9th ed. Baltimore: Williams, 1998.

MUSIC

Holoman, D. Kern, ed. *Writing about Music: A Style Sheet from the Editors of* 19th-Century Music. Berkeley: U of California P, 1988.

PHYSICS

American Institute of Physics. *Style Manual: Instructions to Authors and Volume Editors for the Preparation of AIP Book Manuscripts.* 5th ed. New York: AIP, 1995.

POLITICAL SCIENCE

American Political Science Association. *Style Manual for Political Science.* Rev. ed. Washington: Amer. Political Science Assn., 1993.

PSYCHOLOGY AND THE SOCIAL SCIENCES (SEE 56a–d.)

American Psychological Association. *Publication Manual of the American Psychological Association.* 4th ed. Washington: APA, 1994.

SCIENCE AND TECHNICAL WRITING

American National Standard for the Preparation of Scientific Papers for Written or Oral Presentation. New York: Amer. Natl. Standards Inst., 1979.

Microsoft Corporation. *Microsoft Manual of Style for Technical Publications.* Redmond, WA: Microsoft, 1998.

Rubens, Philip, ed. *Science and Technical Writing: A Manual of Style.* New York: Holt, 1992.

SOCIAL WORK

National Association of Social Workers. *Writing for NASW.* 2nd ed. Silver Springs: Natl. Assn. of Social Workers, 1994.

The Basics

57

Parts of speech

Traditional grammar recognizes eight parts of speech: noun, pronoun, verb, adjective, adverb, preposition, conjunction, and interjection. Many words can function as more than one part of speech. For example, depending on its use in a sentence, the word *paint* can be a noun (*The paint is wet*) or a verb (*Please paint the ceiling next*).

57a Nouns

A noun is the name of a person, place, or thing, or an idea. Nouns are often but not always signaled by an article (*a, an, the*).

> N   N   N
> The cat in gloves catches no mice.

> N   N   N
> Repetition does not transform a lie into truth.

Nouns sometimes function as adjectives modifying other nouns.

> N/ADJ   N/ADJ
> You can't make a silk purse out of a sow's ear.

Nouns are classified for a variety of purposes. When capitalization is the issue, we speak of *proper* versus *common nouns* (see 45a). If the problem is one of word choice, we may speak of *concrete* versus *abstract nouns* (see 18b). The distinction between *count nouns* and *noncount nouns* is useful primarily for nonnative speakers of English (see 30a and 30b). The term *collective noun* refers to a set of nouns that may cause problems with subject-verb or pronoun-antecedent agreement (see 21f and 22b).

EXERCISE 57–1

Underline the nouns (and noun/adjectives) in the following sentences. Answers to lettered sentences appear in the back of the book. Example:

Idle hands are the devil's workshop.

a. The sun will set without your assistance.　　—Hebrew proverb
b. Pride is at the bottom of all great mistakes.　　　—John Ruskin
c. The trouble with being in the rat race is that even if you win, you're still a rat.　　　　　　　　　　　　　　　—Lily Tomlin
d. The ultimate censorship is the flick of the dial.
　　　　　　　　　　　　　　　　　　　　　　　—Tom Smothers
e. Figures won't lie, but liars will figure.　　　　　—Anonymous

1. Truthfulness so often goes with ruthlessness.　　—Dodie Smith
2. Luck is a matter of preparation meeting opportunity.
　　　　　　　　　　　　　　　　　　　　　　—Oprah Winfrey
3. Problems are only opportunities in work clothes.
　　　　　　　　　　　　　　　　　　　　　　—Henry Kaiser
4. A woman must have money and a room of her own.
　　　　　　　　　　　　　　　　　　　　　　—Virginia Woolf
5. The devil often cites Scripture for his purpose.　—Shakespeare

57b Pronouns

A pronoun is a word used in place of a noun. Usually the pronoun substitutes for a specific noun, known as its *antecedent*.

When the *wheel* squeaks, *it* is greased.

Although most pronouns function as substitutes for nouns, some can function as adjectives modifying nouns.

This hanging will surely be a lesson to me.

Because they have the form of a pronoun and the function of an adjective, such pronouns may be called *pronoun/ adjectives*.

Pronouns are classified as personal, possessive, intensive and reflexive, relative, interrogative, demonstrative, indefinite, and reciprocal.

PERSONAL PRONOUNS　Personal pronouns refer to specific persons or things. They always function as noun equivalents.

Singular: I, me, you, she, her, he, him, it

Plural: we, us, you, they, them

POSSESSIVE PRONOUNS   Possessive pronouns indicate ownership.

Singular: my, mine, your, yours, her, hers, his, its

Plural: our, ours, your, yours, their, theirs

Some of these possessive pronouns function as adjectives modifying nouns: *my, your, her, his, its, our, their.*

INTENSIVE AND REFLEXIVE PRONOUNS   Intensive pronouns emphasize a noun or another pronoun (The senator *herself* met us at the door). Reflexive pronouns, which have the same form as intensive pronouns, name a receiver of an action identical with the doer of the action (Paula cut *herself*).

Singular: myself, yourself, himself, herself, itself

Plural: ourselves, yourselves, themselves

RELATIVE PRONOUNS   Relative pronouns introduce subordinate clauses functioning as adjectives (The man *who robbed us* was never caught). In addition to introducing the clause, the relative pronoun, in this case *who,* points back to a noun or pronoun that the clause modifies (*man*). (See 59b.)

who, whom, whose, which, that

Some grammarians also treat *whichever, whoever, whomever, what,* and *whatever* as relative pronouns. These words introduce noun clauses; they do not point back to a noun or pronoun. (See 59b.)

INTERROGATIVE PRONOUNS   Interrogative pronouns introduce questions (*Who* is expected to win the election?).

who, whom, whose, which, what

DEMONSTRATIVE PRONOUNS   Demonstrative pronouns identify or point to nouns. Frequently they function as adjectives (*This* chair is my favorite), but they may also function as noun equivalents (*This* is my favorite chair).

this, that, these, those

INDEFINITE PRONOUNS   Indefinite pronouns refer to nonspecific persons or things. Most are always singular (*everyone, each*);

some are always plural (*both, many*); a few may be singular or plural (see 21e).

all	anything	everyone	nobody	several
another	both	everything	none	some
any	each	few	no one	somebody
anybody	either	many	nothing	someone
anyone	everybody	neither	one	something

RECIPROCAL PRONOUNS Reciprocal pronouns refer to individual parts of a plural antecedent (By turns, we helped *each other* through college).

each other, one another

NOTE: Pronouns cause a variety of problems for writers. See pronoun-antecedent agreement (22), pronoun reference (23), distinguishing between pronouns such as *I* and *me* (24), and distinguishing between *who* and *whom* (25).

EXERCISE 57–2

Underline the pronouns (and pronoun/adjectives) in the following sentences. Answers to lettered sentences appear in the back of the book. Example:

Beware of persons <u>who</u> are praised by <u>everyone</u>.

a. He has every attribute of a dog except loyalty.
   —Thomas Gore
b. A fall does not hurt those who fly low.   —Chinese proverb
c. I have written some poetry that I myself don't understand.
   —Carl Sandburg
d. I am firm. You are obstinate. He is a pig-headed fool.
   —Katherine Whitehorn
e. She never lets ideas interrupt the easy flow of her conversation.
   —Jean Webster

1. Doctors can bury their mistakes, but architects can only advise their clients to plant vines.   —Frank Lloyd Wright
2. Nothing is interesting if you are not interested.
   —Helen MacInness
3. We will never have friends if we expect to find them without fault.
   —Thomas Fuller
4. The gods help those who help themselves.   —Aesop
5. You never find yourself until you face the truth.
   —Pearl Bailey

The Basics

57c Verbs

The verb of a sentence usually expresses action (*jump, think*) or being (*is, become*). It is composed of a main verb possibly preceded by one or more helping verbs:

> MV
> The best fish *swim* near the bottom.

> HV   MV
> A marriage *is* not *built* in a day.

> HV   HV   MV
> Even God *has been defended* with nonsense.

Notice that words can intervene between the helping and the main verb (*is* not *built*).

Helping verbs

Helping verbs in English include forms of *have, do,* and *be,* which may also function as main verbs, and verbs known as modals, which function only as helping verbs. The forms of *have, do,* and *be* change form to indicate tense; the modals do not.

FORMS OF *HAVE, DO,* AND *BE*
have, has, had

do, does, did

be, am, is, are, was, were, being, been

MODALS
can, could, may, might, must, shall, should, will, would

The phrase *ought to* is often classified as a modal as well.

Main verbs

A main verb changes form if put into the following test sentences. When both the past-tense and past-participle forms end in *-ed,* the verb is regular; otherwise, the verb is irregular (see 27a).

BASE FORM	Usually I (*walk, ride*).
PAST TENSE	Yesterday I (*walked, rode*).

PAST PARTICIPLE	I have (*walked, ridden*) many times before.
PRESENT PARTICIPLE	I am (*walking, riding*) right now.
-S FORM	Usually he/she/it (*walks, rides*).

If a word doesn't change form when slipped into these test sentences, you can be certain that it is not a main verb. For example, the noun *revolution,* though it may seem to suggest an action, can never function as a main verb. Just try to make it behave like one (*Today I revolution . . . Yesterday I revolutioned . . .*) and you'll see why.

The verb *be* is highly irregular, having eight forms instead of the usual five: the base form *be;* the present-tense forms *am, is,* and *are;* the past-tense forms *was* and *were;* the present participle *being;* and the past participle *been.*

NOTE: Some verbs are followed by words that look like prepositions but are so closely associated with the verb that they are a part of its meaning. These words are known as *particles.* Common verb-particle combinations include *bring up, call off, drop off, give in, look up, run into,* and *take off.*

> A lot of parents *pack up* their troubles and *send* them *off* to camp. —Raymond Duncan

NOTE: Verbs cause many problems for writers. See subject-verb agreement (21), standard English verb forms (27), verb tense, mood, and voice (28), and ESL problems with verbs (29).

EXERCISE 57–3

Underline the verbs in the following sentences, including helping verbs and particles. If a verb is part of a contraction (such as *is* in *isn't* or *would* in *I'd*), underline only the letters that represent the verb. Answers to lettered sentences appear in the back of the book. Example:

A full cup must be carried steadily.

a. Great persons have not commonly been great scholars.
   —Oliver Wendell Holmes, Sr.
b. There are no atheists on turbulent airplanes. —Erica Jong
c. One arrow does not bring down two birds. —Turkish proverb
d. If love is the answer, could you please rephrase the question?
   —Lily Tomlin

e. Throw a lucky man into the sea, and he will emerge with a fish in his mouth.   —Arab proverb

1. Do not needlessly endanger your lives until I give you the signal.
                                          —Dwight D. Eisenhower
2. Wrong must not win by technicalities.   —Aeschylus
3. Love your neighbor, but don't pull down the hedge.
                                          —Swiss proverb
4. I'd rather have roses on my table than diamonds around my neck.
                                          —Emma Goldman
5. He is a fine friend. He stabs you in the front.
                                          —Leonard Louis Levinson

57d Adjectives

An adjective is a word used to modify, or describe, a noun or pronoun. An adjective usually answers one of these questions: Which one? What kind of? How many?

> ADJ
> the lame elephant [Which elephant?]

> ADJ   ADJ
> valuable old stamps [What kind of stamps?]

> ADJ
> sixteen candles [How many candles?]

Adjectives usually precede the words they modify. However, they may also follow linking verbs, in which case they describe the subject (see 58b).

> ADJ
> Good medicine always tastes bitter.

Articles, sometimes classified as adjectives, are used to mark nouns. There are only three: the definite article *the* and the indefinite articles *a* and *an*.

> ART   ART
> A country can be judged by the quality of its proverbs.

NOTE: Writers sometimes misuse adjectives (see 26b). Speakers of English as a second language often encounter problems with the articles *a, an,* and *the* and occasionally have trouble placing adjectives correctly (see 30 and 31d).

57e Adverbs

An adverb is a word used to modify, or qualify, a verb (or verbal), an adjective, or another adverb. It usually answers one of these questions: When? Where? How? Why? Under what conditions? To what degree?

Pull *gently* at a weak rope. [Pull how?]

Read the best books *first*. [Read when?]

Adverbs modifying adjectives or other adverbs usually intensify or limit the intensity of the word they modify.

ADV   ADV
Be *extremely* good, and you will be *very* lonesome.

The negators *not* and *never* are classified as adverbs. A word such as *cannot* contains the helping verb *can* and the adverb *not*. A contraction such as *can't* contains the helping verb *can* and a contracted form of the adverb *not*.

NOTE: Writers sometimes misuse adverbs (see 26a). Speakers of English as a second language may have trouble placing adverbs correctly (see 31d).

EXERCISE 57–4

Underline the adjectives and circle the adverbs in the following sentences. If a word is a pronoun in form but an adjective in function, treat it as an adjective. Also treat the articles *a, an,* and *the* as adjectives. Answers to lettered sentences appear in the back of the book. Example:

A wild goose (never) laid a tame egg.

a. General notions are generally wrong.
                                   —Lady Mary Wortley Montagu
b. The American public is wonderfully tolerant.   —Anonymous
c. Gardening is not a rational act.   —Margaret Atwood
d. A clean glove often hides a dirty hand.   —English proverb
e. Sleep faster. We need the pillows.   —Yiddish proverb

1. Success is a public affair; failure is a private funeral.
                                          —Rosalind Russell
2. Their civil discussions were not interesting, and their interesting discussions were not civil.   —Lisa Alther

3. Money will buy a pretty good dog, but it will not buy the wag of
   its tail. —Josh Billings
4. A little sincerity is a dangerous thing, and a great deal of it is ab-
   solutely fatal. —Oscar Wilde
5. Feelings are untidy. —Esther Hautzig

57f Prepositions

A preposition is a word placed before a noun or pronoun to
form a phrase modifying another word in the sentence. The
prepositional phrase nearly always functions as an adjective or
as an adverb. (See 59a.)

The road *to hell* is usually paved *with good intentions.*

To hell functions as an adjective, modifying the noun *road; with
good intentions* functions as an adverb, modifying the verb *is
paved.*

There are a limited number of prepositions in English. The
most common ones are included in the following list.

about	beside	from	outside	toward
above	besides	in	over	under
across	between	inside	past	underneath
after	beyond	into	plus	unlike
against	but	like	regarding	until
along	by	near	respecting	unto
among	concerning	next	round	up
around	considering	of	since	upon
as	despite	off	than	with
at	down	on	through	within
before	during	onto	throughout	without
behind	except	opposite	till	
below	for	out	to	

Some prepositions are more than one word long. *Along with,
as well as, in addition to,* and *next to* are common examples.

NOTE: Except for certain idiomatic uses (see 18d), prepositions
cause few problems for native speakers of English. For second-
language speakers, however, prepositions can cause considerable difficulty (see 29d and 31f).

57g Conjunctions

Conjunctions join words, phrases, or clauses, and they indicate the relation between the elements joined.

COORDINATING CONJUNCTIONS   A coordinating conjunction is used to connect grammatically equal elements. The coordinating conjunctions are *and, but, or, nor, for, so,* and *yet.*

Poverty is the parent of revolution *and* crime.

Admire a little ship, *but* put your cargo in a big one.

In the first sentence, *and* connects two nouns; in the second, *but* connects two independent clauses.

CORRELATIVE CONJUNCTIONS   Correlative conjunctions come in pairs: *either . . . or; neither . . . nor; not only . . . but also; whether . . . or; both . . . and.* Like coordinating conjunctions, they connect grammatically equal elements.

Either Jack Sprat *or* his wife could eat no fat.

SUBORDINATING CONJUNCTIONS   A subordinating conjunction introduces a subordinate clause and indicates its relation to the rest of the sentence (see 59b). The most common subordinating conjunctions are *after, although, as, as if, because, before, even though, how, if, in order that, once, rather than, since, so that, than, that, though, unless, until, when, where, whether, while,* and *why.*

If you want service, serve yourself.

CONJUNCTIVE ADVERBS   A conjunctive adverb may be used with a semicolon to connect independent clauses; it usually serves as a transition between the clauses. The most common conjunctive adverbs are *consequently, finally, furthermore, however, moreover, nevertheless, similarly, then, therefore,* and *thus.* (See p. 293 for a more complete list.)

When we want to murder a tiger, we call it sport; *however,* when the tiger wants to murder us, we call it ferocity.

NOTE: The ability to distinguish between conjunctive adverbs and coordinating conjunctions will help you avoid run-on sentences and make punctuation decisions (see 20, 32a, and 32b). The ability to recognize subordinating conjunctions will help you avoid sentence fragments (see 19).

57h Interjections

An interjection is a word used to express surprise or emotion (*Oh! Hey! Wow!*).

58

Sentence patterns

Most English sentences flow from subject to verb to any objects or complements. The vast majority of sentences conform to one of these five patterns:

> subject / verb / subject complement
> subject / verb / direct object
> subject / verb / indirect object / direct object
> subject / verb / direct object / object complement
> subject / verb

Adverbial modifiers (single words, phrases, or clauses) may be added to any of these patterns, and they may appear nearly anywhere—at the beginning, the middle, or the end.

Predicate is the grammatical term given to the verb plus its objects, complements, and adverbial modifiers.

58a Subjects

The subject of a sentence names who or what the sentence is about. The simple subject is always a noun or a pronoun; the complete subject consists of the simple subject (ss) and all of its modifiers.

⌐SS⌐
The purity of a revolution usually lasts about two weeks.

⌐SS⌐
Historical books that contain no lies are extremely tedious.

⌐SS⌐
In every country *the sun* rises in the morning.

To find the complete subject, ask Who? or What?, insert the verb, and finish the question. What usually lasts about two weeks? *The purity of a revolution.* What are extremely tedious? *Historical books that contain no lies.* What rises in the morning? *The sun* [not *In every country, the sun*].

To find the simple subject, strip away all modifiers in the complete subject. This includes single-word modifiers such as *the* and *historical,* phrases such as *of a revolution,* and subordinate clauses such as *that contain no lies.*

A sentence may have a compound subject containing two or more simple subjects joined with a coordinating conjunction such as *and, but,* or *or.*

⌐SS⌐   ⌐SS⌐
Much industry and little conscience make us rich.

In imperative sentences, which give advice or issue commands, the verb's subject is understood but not actually present in the sentence. The subject of an imperative sentence is understood to be *you,* as in the following example.

[*You*] Hitch your wagon to a star.

Although the subject ordinarily comes before the verb, occasionally it does not. When a sentence begins with *There is* or *There are* (or *There was* or *There were*), the subject follows the verb. The word *There* is an expletive in such constructions, an empty word serving merely to get the sentence started.

⌐SS⌐
There is *no substitute for victory.*

Occasionally a writer will invert a sentence for effect.

⌐SS⌐
Happy is *the nation that has no history.*

Happy is an adjective, so it cannot be the subject. Turn this sentence around and its structure becomes obvious: *The nation that has no history is happy.*

In questions, the subject frequently appears in an unusual position, sandwiched between parts of the verb.

⌐SS⌐
Do *married men* make the best husbands?

Turn the question into a statement, and the words will appear in their usual order: *Married men do make the best husbands.* (*Do make* is the verb.) For more about possible positions of subjects in questions, see 58c.

NOTE: The ability to recognize the subject of a sentence will help you edit for a variety of problems such as sentence fragments (19), subject-verb agreement (21), and choice of pronouns such as *I* and *me* (24). If English is not your native language, see also 31a and 31b.

EXERCISE 58–1

In the following sentences, underline the complete subject and write *SS* above the simple subject(s). If the subject is an understood *you,* insert it in parentheses. Answers to lettered sentences appear in the back of the book. Example:

> SS   SS
> **Fools and their money are soon parted.**

a. Sticks and stones may break my bones, and words can sting like anything. —Anonymous
b. To some lawyers, all facts are created equal.
 — Felix Frankfurter
c. Speak softly and carry a big stick. —Theodore Roosevelt
d. There is nothing permanent except change. —Heraclitus
e. The only difference between a rut and a grave is their dimensions.
 —Ellen Glasgow

1. The secret of being a bore is to tell everything. —Voltaire
2. Don't be humble. You're not that great. —Golda Meir
3. In the eyes of its mother, every beetle is a gazelle.
 —Moorish proverb
4. The price of hating other human beings is loving oneself less.
 —Eldridge Cleaver
5. There are no signposts in the sea. —Vita Sackville-West

58b Verbs, objects, and complements

Section 57c explains how to find the verb of a sentence, which consists of a main verb possibly preceded by one or more helping verbs. A sentence's verb is classified as linking, transitive, or intransitive, depending on the kinds of objects or complements the verb can (or cannot) take.

Linking verbs and subject complements

Linking verbs (*v*) take subject complements (*sc*), words or word groups that complete the meaning of the subject (*s*) by either renaming it or describing it.

```
┌──────────── S ─────────────┐ ┌─V─┐ ┌─SC─┐
The handwriting on the wall may be a forgery.

┌─S─┐ V ┌─SC─┐
Love is blind.
```

When the simple subject complement renames the subject, it is a noun or pronoun, such as *forgery;* when it decribes the subject, it is an adjective, such as *blind.*

Linking verbs are usually a form of *be: be, am, is, are, was, were, being, been.* Verbs such as *appear, become, feel, grow, look, make, prove, remain, seem, smell, sound,* and *taste* are linking when they are followed by a word group that names or describes the subject.

Transitive verbs and direct objects

A transitive verb takes a direct object, a word or word group that names a receiver of the action.

```
┌────── S ──────┐ ┌─V─┐ ┌──────── DO ────────┐
The little snake studies the ways of the big serpent.
```

The simple direct object is always a noun or pronoun, in this case *ways.*

Transitive verbs usually appear in the active voice, with the subject doing the action and a direct object receiving the action. Active-voice sentences can be transformed into the passive voice, with the subject receiving the action instead (see 58c).

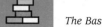

Transitive verbs, indirect objects, and direct objects

The direct object of a transitive verb is sometimes preceded by an indirect object, a noun or pronoun telling to whom or for whom the action of the sentence is done.

> S   V   IO ┌─DO─┐   S ┌──V──┐ IO ┌──DO──┐
> You show me a hero, and I will write you a tragedy.

The simple indirect object is always a noun or pronoun. To test for an indirect object, insert the word *to* or *for* before the word or word group in question. If the sentence makes sense, the word or word group is an indirect object.

> You show [to] me a hero, and I will write [for] you a tragedy.

An indirect object may be turned into a prepositional phrase using *to* or *for: You show a hero to me, and I will write a tragedy for you.*

Transitive verbs, direct objects, and object complements

The direct object of a transitive verb is sometimes followed by an object complement, a word or word group that completes the direct object's meaning by renaming or describing it.

> ┌─S─┐   ┌V┐┌─DO─┐ ┌──────── OC────────┐
> People now call a spade an agricultural implement.

> ┌S┐ ┌─V─┐ ┌───DO───┐ ┌─OC─┐
> Love makes all hard hearts gentle.

When the object complement renames the direct object, it is a noun or pronoun (such as *implement*). When it describes the direct object, it is an adjective (such as *gentle*).

Intransitive verbs

Intransitive verbs take no objects or complements. Their pattern is always subject/verb.

> S   V
> Money talks.

> ┌────S────┐   ┌V┐
> Revolutions never go backward.

Nothing receives the actions of talking and going in these sentences, so the verbs are intransitive. Notice that such verbs may or may not be followed by adverbial modifiers. In the second sentence, *backward* is an adverb modifying *go*.

NOTE: The dictionary will tell you whether a verb is transitive or intransitive. Some verbs have both transitive and intransitive functions.

> **TRANSITIVE** Sandra flew her Cessna over the canyon.
>
> **INTRANSITIVE** A bald eagle flew overhead.

In the first example, *flew* has a direct object that receives the action: *her Cessna*. In the second example, the verb is followed by an adverb (*overhead*), not by a direct object.

EXERCISE 58–2

Label the subject complements, direct objects, indirect objects, and object complements in the following sentences. If an object or complement consists of more than one word, bracket and label all of it. Answers to lettered sentences appear in the back of the book. Example:

> $\quad\quad\quad\quad DO \quad \ulcorner\!\!-OC-\!\!\urcorner$
> **All work and no play make Jack a dull boy.**

a. The best mind-altering drug is truth. —Lily Tomlin
b. No one tests the depth of a river with both feet.
　　　　　　　　　　　　　　　　　　　—West African proverb
c. All looks yellow to a jaundiced eye　　　—Alexander Pope
d. Luck never made a man [or a woman] wise.
　　　　　　　　　　　　　　　　　　　—Seneca the Younger
e. You show me a capitalist and I will show you a bloodsucker.
　　　　　　　　　　　　　　　　　　　—Malcolm X

1. Accomplishments have no color.　　　—Leontyne Price
2. Victory has a hundred fathers, but defeat is an orphan.
　　　　　　　　　　　　　　　　　　—Count Galeazzo Ciano
3. Acting is a form of confession.　　　—Tallulah Bankhead
4. I never promised you a rose garden.　　　—Hannah Green
5. Some folk want their luck buttered.　　　—Anonymous

58c Pattern variations

Although most sentences follow one of the five patterns listed on page 484, variations of these patterns commonly occur in questions, commands, sentences with delayed subjects, and passive transformations.

Questions and commands

Questions are sometimes patterned in normal word order, with the subject preceding the verb.

```
S   ┌─V─┐
```
Who will take the first step?

Just as frequently, however, the pattern of a question is inverted, with the subject appearing between the helping and main verbs or after the verb.

```
HV   S   MV
```
Will you take the first step?

```
V ┌──── S ────┐
```
Why is the first step so difficult?

In commands, the subject of the sentence is an understood *you.*

[You] Keep your mouth shut and your eyes open.

Sentences with delayed subjects

Writers sometimes choose to delay the subject of a sentence to achieve a special effect such as suspense or humor.

```
V ┌────S────┐
```
Behind the phony tinsel of Hollywood lies the real tinsel.

The subject of the sentence is also delayed in sentences opening with the expletive *There* or *It.* When used as expletives, the words *There* and *It* have no strict grammatical function; they serve merely to get the sentence started.

```
V ┌──────────S──────────┐
```
There are many paths to the top of the mountain.

```
V        ┌──────S──────┐
```
It is not good to wake a sleeping lion.

The subject in the second example is an infinitive phrase (see 59c).

Passive transformations

Transitive verbs, those that can take direct objects, usually appear in the active voice. In the active voice, the subject does the action and a direct object receives the action.

ACTIVE The early bird sometimes catches the early worm.

Sentences in the active voice may be transformed into the passive voice, with the subject receiving the action instead.

PASSIVE The early worm is sometimes caught by the early bird.

What was once the direct object (*the early worm*) has become the subject in the passive-voice transformation, and the original subject appears in a prepositional phrase beginning with *by.* The *by* phrase is frequently omitted in passive-voice constructions.

PASSIVE The early worm is sometimes caught.

Verbs in the passive voice can be identified by their form alone. The main verb is always a past participle, such as *caught* (see 57c), preceded by a form of *be (be, am, is, are, was, were, being, been)*: *is caught.* Sometimes adverbs intervene (*is sometimes caught*).

NOTE: Writers sometimes use the passive voice when the active voice would be more appropriate (see 14a).

59

Subordinate word groups

Subordinate word groups cannot stand alone. They function only within sentences, usually as adjectives, adverbs, or nouns.

59a Prepositional phrases

A prepositional phrase begins with a preposition such as *at, by, for, from, in, of, on, to,* or *with* (see 57f) and ends with a noun or a noun equivalent called its *object.*

Prepositional phrases function as adjectives or adverbs. When functioning as an adjective, a prepositional phrase usually appears right after the noun or pronoun it modifies.

Variety is the spice *of life.*

Adjective phrases answer one or both of the questions Which one? and What kind of? If we ask Which spice? or What kind of spice? we get a sensible answer: *the spice of life.*

Adverbial prepositional phrases modifying the verb can appear nearly anywhere in a sentence.

Do not judge a tree *by its bark.*

Tyranny will *in time* lead to revolution.

To the ant, a few drops of rain are a flood.

Adverb phrases usually answer one of these questions: When? Where? How? Why? Under what conditions? To what degree?

Do not judge a tree *how? By its bark?*

Tyranny will lead to revolution *when? In time.*

A few drops of rain are a flood *under what conditions? To the ant.*

NOTE: The ability to recognize the object of a preposition will help you distinguish between pronouns such as *I* and *me* (see 24b).

EXERCISE 59–1

Underline the prepositional phrases in the following sentences. Be prepared to explain the function of each phrase. Answers to lettered sentences appear in the back of the book. Example:

You can stroke people <u>with words</u>. *(Adverb phrase modifying*

can stroke)

   a. A résumé is a balance sheet without any liabilities.
                                        —Robert Half
   b. Any mother could perform the job of several air traffic controllers
      with ease.   —Lisa Alther
   c. She wears her morals like a loose garment.
                                     —Langston Hughes
   d. You can tell the ideals of a nation by its advertising.
                                   —Norman Douglas
   e. In France, cooking is a serious art form and a national sport.
                                   —Julia Child

   1. We know that the road to freedom has always been stalked by
      death.   —Angela Davis
   2. The quarrels of friends are the opportunities of foes.   —Aesop
   3. Some people feel with their heads and think with their hearts.
                              —G. C. Lichtenberg
   4. By a small sample, we may know the whole piece.
                                  —Cervantes
   5. You and I come by road or rail, but economists travel on infra-
      structure.   —Margaret Thatcher

59b Subordinate clauses

Subordinate clauses are patterned like sentences, having subjects and verbs and sometimes objects or complements. But they function within sentences as adjectives, adverbs, or nouns. They cannot stand alone as complete sentences.

    A subordinate clause usually begins with a subordinating conjunction or a relative pronoun.

SUBORDINATING CONJUNCTIONS

after	before	rather than	though	where
although	even though	since	unless	whether
as	how	so that	until	while
as if	if	than	when	why
because	in order that	that		

RELATIVE PRONOUNS

that	who	whom	whose	which

Adjective clauses

Adjective clauses modify nouns or pronouns, usually answering the question Which one? or What kind of? They begin with a relative pronoun (*who, whom, whose, which,* or *that*) or a relative adverb (*when* or *where*).

The arrow *that has left the bow* never returns.

Relatives are persons *who live too near and visit too often.*

In addition to introducing the clause, the relative pronoun points back to the noun that the clause modifies.

The fur *that warms a monarch* once warmed a bear.

Relative pronouns are sometimes "understood."

The things [*that*] *we know best* are the things [*that*] *we haven't been taught.*

Occasionally an adjective clause is introduced by a relative adverb, usually *when, where,* or *why.*

Home is the place *where you slip in the tub and break your neck.*

The parts of an adjective clause are often arranged as in sentences (subject/verb/object or complement).

                      S   V   DO
We often forgive the people *who bore us.*

Frequently, however, the object or complement appears first, violating the normal order of subject/verb/object.

                          DO   S   V
We rarely forgive those *whom we bore.*

NOTE: For punctuation of adjective clauses, see 32e and 33e. If English is not your native language, see 31c for a common problem with adjective clauses.

Adverb clauses

Adverb clauses modify verbs, adjectives, or other adverbs, usually answering one of these questions: When? Where? Why? How? Under what conditions? To what degree? They begin with a subordinating conjunction (*after, although, as, as if, because, before, even though, if, in order that, rather than, since, so that, than, that, though, unless, until, when, where, whether, while*).

When the well is dry, we know the worth of water.

Venice would be a fine city *if it were only drained.*

Adverb clauses are sometimes elliptical, with some of their words being "understood."

When [it is] painted, the room will look larger.

Noun clauses

Noun clauses function as subjects, objects, or complements. They usually begin with one of the following words: *how, that, which, who, whoever, whom, whomever, what, whatever, when, where, whether, whose, why.*

———— S ————
Whoever gossips to you will gossip of you.

———— DO ————
We never forget *that we buried the hatchet.*

The word introducing the clause may or may not play a significant role in the clause. In the preceding example sentences, *whoever* is the subject of its clause, but *that* does not perform a function in its clause.

As with adjective clauses, the parts of a noun clause may appear out of their normal order (subject/verb/object).

DO S V
Talent is *what you possess.*

The parts of a noun clause may also appear in their normal order.

S V DO
Genius is *what possesses you.*

EXERCISE 59–2

Underline the subordinate clauses in the following sentences. Be prepared to explain the function of each clause. Answers to lettered sentences appear in the back of the book. Example:

> **Dig a well before you are thirsty.** *(Adverb clause modifying Dig)*

a. It is hard to fight an enemy who has outposts in your head.
> —Sally Kempton

b. A rattlesnake that doesn't bite teaches you nothing.
> —Jessamyn West

c. When I am an old woman, I shall wear purple.   —Jenny Joseph

d. Dreams say what they mean, but they don't say it in daytime language.   —Gail Godwin

e. A fraud is not perfect unless it is practiced on clever persons.
> —Arab proverb

1. What history teaches us is that we have never learned anything from it.   —Georg Wilhelm Hegel

2. When the insects take over the world, we hope that they will remember our picnics with gratitude.   —Anonymous

3. A woman who will tell her age will tell anything.
> —Rita Mae Brown

4. Science commits suicide when it adopts a creed.
> —T. H. Huxley

5. He gave her a look that you could have poured on a waffle.
> —Ring Lardner

59c Verbal phrases

A verbal is a verb form that does not function as the verb of a clause. Verbals include infinitives (the word *to* plus the base form of the verb), present participles (the *-ing* form of the verb), and past participles (the verb form usually ending in *-d, -ed, -n, -en,* or *-t*). (See 27a and 57c.)

Verbals can take objects, complements, and modifiers to form verbal phrases. These phrases are classified as participial, gerund, and infinitive.

Participial phrases

Participial phrases always function as adjectives. Their verbals are either present participles, always ending in *-ing,* or past participles, frequently ending in *-d, -ed, -n, -en,* or *-t* (see 27a).

Participial phrases frequently appear right after the noun or pronoun they modify.

Congress shall make no law *abridging the freedom of speech or of the press.*

Truth *kept in the dark* will never save the world.

They can also precede the word they modify or appear at some distance from the word they modify.

Being weak, foxes are distinguished by superior tact.

History is something that never happened, *written by someone who wasn't there.*

Gerund phrases

Gerund phrases are built around present participles (verb forms ending in *-ing*), and they always function as nouns: usually as subjects, subject complements, direct objects, or objects of a preposition.

Justifying a fault doubles it.

The secret of education is *respecting the pupil.*

Kleptomaniacs can't help *helping themselves.*

The hen is an egg's way of *producing another egg.*

Infinitive phrases

Infinitive phrases, usually constructed around *to* plus the base form of the verb (*to call, to drink*), can function as adjectives, adverbs, or nouns. When functioning as a noun, an infinitive phrase usually plays the role of subject, subject complement, or direct object.

We do not have the right *to abandon the poor.*

He cut off his nose *to spite his face.*

To side with truth is noble.

NOTE: In some constructions, the infinitive is unmarked; in other words, the *to* does not appear: *No one can make you [to] feel inferior without your consent.* (See 29c.)

EXERCISE 59–3

Underline the verbal phrases in the following sentences. Be prepared to explain the function of each phrase. Answers to lettered sentences appear in the back of the book. Example:

Do you want <u>to be a writer</u>? Then write. *(Infinitive phrase used as direct object of <u>Do want</u>)*

a. The best substitute for experience is being sixteen.
　　　　　　　　　　　　　　　　　　　—Raymond Duncan
b. The trouble with being punctual is that nobody is there to appreciate it.　　　　　　　　　　　　　　—Franklin P. Jones
c. Poetry is the impish attempt to paint the color of the wind.
　　　　　　　　　　　　　　　　　　—Maxwell Bodenheim
d. Being a philosopher, I have a problem for every solution.
　　　　　　　　　　　　　　　　　　　　—Robert Zend
e. For years I wanted to be older, and now I am.
　　　　　　　　　　　　　　　　　　—Margaret Atwood

1. The thing generally raised on city land is taxes.
　　　　　　　　　　　　　　　　　　　　—C. D. Warner
2. Do not use a hatchet to remove a fly from your friend's forehead.
　　　　　　　　　　　　　　　　　　—Chinese proverb
3. He has the gall of a shoplifter returning an item for a refund.
　　　　　　　　　　　　　　　　　　　—W. I. E. Gates
4. Tact is the ability to describe others as they see themselves.
　　　　　　　　　　　　　　　　　　—Mary Pettibone Poole
5. He could never see a belt without hitting below it.
　　　　　　　　　　　　　　　　　　　—Harriet Braiker

59d Appositive phrases

Though strictly speaking they are not subordinate word groups, appositive phrases function somewhat as adjectives do, to describe nouns or pronouns. Instead of modifying nouns or pronouns, however, appositive phrases rename them. In form they are nouns or noun equivalents.

Appositives are said to be "in apposition" to the nouns or pronouns they rename.

> Politicians, *acrobats at heart,* can sit on a fence and yet keep both ears to the ground.

Acrobats at heart is in apposition to the noun *politicians.*

59e Absolute phrases

An absolute phrase modifies a whole clause or sentence, not just one word, and it may appear nearly anywhere in the sentence. It consists of a noun or noun equivalent usually followed by a participial phrase.

> *His words dipped in honey*, the senator mesmerized the crowd.

> The senator mesmerized the crowd, *his words dipped in honey.*

60

Sentence types

Sentences are classified in two ways: according to their structure (simple, compound, complex, and compound-complex) and according to their purpose (declarative, imperative, interrogative, and exclamatory).

60a Sentence structures

Depending on the number and types of clauses they contain, sentences are classified as simple, compound, complex, or compound-complex.

Clauses come in two varieties: independent and subordinate. An independent clause is a full sentence pattern that does not function within another sentence pattern: It contains a subject and verb plus any objects, complements, and modifiers of that verb, and it either stands alone or could stand alone. A subordinate clause is a full sentence pattern that functions within a sentence as an adjective, an adverb, or a noun but that cannot stand alone as a complete sentence (see 59b).

Simple sentences

A simple sentence is one independent clause with no subordinate clauses.

> ┌──────── INDEPENDENT CLAUSE ────────┐
> Without music, life would be a mistake.

This sentence contains a subject (*life*), a verb (*would be*), a complement (*a mistake*), and an adverbial modifier (*Without music*).

A simple sentence may contain compound elements—a compound subject, verb, or object, for example—but it does not contain more than one full sentence pattern. The following sentence is simple because its two verbs (*enters* and *spreads*) share a subject (*Evil*).

> ┌──────── INDEPENDENT CLAUSE ────────┐
> Evil enters like a needle and spreads like an oak.

Compound sentences

A compound sentence is composed of two or more independent clauses with no subordinate clauses. The independent clauses are usually joined with a comma and a coordinating conjunction (*and, but, or, nor, for, so, yet*) or with a semicolon. (See 8.)

> ┌─INDEPENDENT CLAUSE ─┐   ┌──── INDEPENDENT CLAUSE ────┐
> One arrow is easily broken, but you can't break a bundle of ten.

> ┌──────── INDEPENDENT CLAUSE ────────┐ ┌INDEPENDENT ─
> We are born brave, trusting, and greedy; most of us have
>
> ──── CLAUSE───┐
> remained greedy.

Complex sentences

A complex sentence is composed of one independent clause with one or more subordinate clauses (see 59b).

ADJECTIVE
SUBORDINATE
┌──── CLAUSE────┐
They that sow in tears shall reap in joy.

ADVERB
SUBORDINATE
┌──── CLAUSE────┐
If you scatter thorns, don't go barefoot.

NOUN
┌──────── SUBORDINATE CLAUSE────────┐
What the scientists have in their briefcases is terrifying.

Compound-complex sentences

A compound-complex sentence contains at least two independent clauses and at least one subordinate clause. The following sentence contains two full sentence patterns that can stand alone.

┌INDEPENDENT CLAUSE┐   ┌────INDEPENDENT CLAUSE────┐
Tell me what you eat, and I will tell you what you are.

And each independent clause contains a subordinate clause, making the sentence both compound and complex.

┌──── IND CL────┐   ┌──── IND CL────┐
      ┌──SUB CL──┐   ┌──SUB CL──┐
Tell me what you eat, and I will tell you what you are.

60b Sentence purposes

Writers use declarative sentences to make statements, imperative sentences to issue requests or commands, interrogative sentences to ask questions, and exclamatory sentences to make exclamations.

DECLARATIVE   The echo always has the last word.

IMPERATIVE   Love your neighbor.

INTERROGATIVE   Are second thoughts always wisest?

EXCLAMATORY   I want to wash the flag, not burn it!

EXERCISE 60–1

Identify the following sentences as simple, compound, complex, or compound-complex. Be prepared to identify the subordinate clauses and classify them according to their function: adjective, adverb, or noun. (See 59b.) Answers to lettered sentences appear in the back of the book. Example:

The frog in the well knows nothing of the ocean. *(Simple)*

a. People who sleep like a baby usually don't have one.
—Leo Burke

b. My folks didn't come over on the *Mayflower*; they were there to meet the boat. —Will Rogers

c. The impersonal hand of the government can never replace the helping hand of a neighbor. —Hubert Humphrey

d. If you don't go to other people's funerals, they won't go to yours.
—Clarence Day

e. Tell us your phobias, and we will tell you what you are afraid of.
—Robert Benchley

1. The tragedy of life is that people don't change.
—Agatha Christie

2. Those who write clearly have readers; those who write obscurely have commentators. —Albert Camus

3. The children are always the chief victims of social chaos.
—Agnes Meyer

4. Morality cannot be legislated, but behavior can be regulated.
—Martin Luther King, Jr.

5. When an elephant is in trouble, even a frog will kick him.
—Hindu proverb

Glossary of Usage

This glossary includes words commonly confused (such as *accept* and *except*), words commonly misused (such as *hopefully*), and words that are nonstandard (such as *hisself*). It also lists colloquialisms and jargon. Colloquialisms are expressions that may be appropriate in informal speech but are inappropriate in formal writing. Jargon is needlessly technical or pretentious language that is inappropriate in most contexts. If an item is not listed here, consult the index. For irregular verbs (such as *sing, sang, sung*), see 27a. For idiomatic use of prepositions, see 18d.

a, an   Use *an* before a vowel sound, *a* before a consonant sound: *an apple, a peach*. Problems sometimes arise with words beginning with *h*. If the *h* is silent, the word begins with a vowel sound, so use *an: an hour, an heir, an honest senator, an honorable deed*. If the *h* is pronounced, the word begins with a consonant sound, so use *a: a hospital, a hymn, a historian, a hotel*. When an abbreviation or acronym begins with a vowel sound, use *an: an EKG, an MRI, an AIDS* patient.

accept, except   *Accept* is a verb meaning "to receive." *Except* is usually a preposition meaning "excluding." *I will accept all the packages except that one. Except* is also a verb meaning "to exclude." *Please except that item from the list.*

adapt, adopt   *Adapt* means "to adjust or become accustomed"; it is usually followed by *to. Adopt* means "to take as one's own." *Our family adopted a Vietnamese orphan, who quickly adapted to his new surroundings.*

adverse, averse   *Adverse* means "unfavorable." *Averse* means "opposed" or "reluctant"; it is usually followed by *to. I am averse to your proposal because it could have an adverse impact on the economy.*

advice, advise   *Advice* is a noun, *advise* a verb. *We advise you to follow John's advice.*

affect, effect   *Affect* is usually a verb meaning "to influence." *Effect* is usually a noun meaning "result." *The drug did not affect the disease, and it had adverse side effects. Effect* can also be a verb meaning "to bring about." *Only the president can effect such a change.*

aggravate   *Aggravate* means "to make worse or more troublesome." *Overgrazing aggravated the soil erosion.* In formal writing, avoid the colloquial use of *aggravate* meaning "to annoy or irritate." *Her babbling annoyed* (not *aggravated*) *me.*

agree to, agree with   *Agree to* means "to give consent." *Agree with* means "to be in accord" or "to come to an understanding." *He agrees with me about the need for change, but he won't agree to my plan.*

ain't   *Ain't* is nonstandard. Use *am not, are not* (*aren't*), or *is not* (*isn't*). *I am not* (not *ain't*) *going home for spring break.*

all ready, already   *All ready* means "completely prepared." *Already* means "previously." *Susan was all ready for the concert, but her friends had already left.*

all right   *All right* is written as two words. *Alright* is nonstandard.

all together, altogether   *All together* means "everyone gathered." *Altogether* means "entirely." *We were not altogether certain that we could bring the family all together for the reunion.*

allude   To *allude* to something is to make an indirect reference to it. Do not use *allude* to mean "to refer directly." *In his lecture the professor referred* (not *alluded*) *to several pre-Socratic philosophers.*

allusion, illusion   An *allusion* is an indirect reference. An *illusion* is a misconception or false impression. *Did you catch my allusion to Shakespeare? Mirrors give the room an illusion of depth.*

a lot   *A lot* is two words. Do not write *alot*. *We have had a lot of rain this spring.* See also *lots, lots of.*

among, between   See *between, among.*

amongst   In American English, *among* is preferred.

amoral, immoral   *Amoral* means "neither moral nor immoral"; it also means "not caring about moral judgments." *Immoral* means "morally wrong." *Until recently, most business courses were taught from an amoral perspective. Murder is immoral.*

amount, number   Use *amount* with quantities that cannot be counted; use *number* with those that can. *This recipe calls for a large amount of sugar. We have a large number of toads in our garden.*

an   See *a, an.*

and etc.   *Et cetera* (*etc.*) means "and so forth"; therefore, *and etc.* is redundant. See also *etc.*

and/or   Avoid the awkward construction *and/or* except in technical or legal documents.

angry at, angry with To write that one is *angry at* another person is nonstandard. Use *angry with* instead.

ante-, anti- The prefix *ante-* means "earlier" or "in front of"; the prefix *anti-* means "against" or "opposed to." *William Lloyd Garrison was one of the leaders of the antislavery movement during the antebellum period. Anti-* should be used with a hyphen when it is followed by a capital letter or a word beginning with *i*.

anxious *Anxious* means "worried" or "apprehensive." In formal writing, avoid using *anxious* to mean "eager." *We are eager* (not *anxious*) *to see your new house.*

anybody, anyone *Anybody* and *anyone* are singular. (See 21e and 22a.)

anymore Reserve the adverb *anymore* for negative contexts, where it means "any longer." *Moviegoers are rarely shocked anymore by profanity.* Do not use *anymore* in positive contexts. Use *now* or *nowadays* instead. *Interest rates are so low nowadays* (not *anymore*) *that more people can afford to buy homes.*

anyone See *anybody, anyone.*

anyone, any one *Anyone,* an indefinite pronoun, means "any person at all." *Any one,* the pronoun *one* preceded by the adjective *any,* refers to a particular person or thing in a group. *Anyone from Chicago may choose any one of the games on display.*

anyplace *Anyplace* is informal for *anywhere.* Avoid *anyplace* in formal writing.

anyways, anywheres *Anyways* and *anywheres* are nonstandard. Use *anyway* and *anywhere.*

as *As* is sometimes used to mean "because." But do not use it if there is any chance of ambiguity. *We canceled the picnic because* (not *as*) *it began raining. As* here could mean "because" or "when."

as, like See *like, as.*

as to *As to* is jargon for *about. He inquired about* (not *as to*) *the job.*

averse See *adverse, averse.*

awful The adjective *awful* means "awe-inspiring." Colloquially it is used to mean "terrible" or "bad." The adverb *awfully* is sometimes used in conversation as an intensifier meaning "very." In formal writing, avoid these colloquial uses. *I was very* (not *awfully*) *upset last night. Susan had a terrible* (not *an awful*) *time calming her nerves.*

awhile, a while *Awhile* is an adverb; it can modify a verb, but it cannot be the object of a preposition such as *for.* The two-word form *a while* is a noun preceded by an article and therefore can be the object of a preposition. *Stay awhile. Stay for a while.*

back up, backup *Back up* is a verb phrase. *Back up the car carefully. Be sure to back up your hard drive.* A *backup* is a duplicate of electronically stored data. *Keep your backup in a safe place. Backup* can also be used as an adjective. *I regularly create backup disks.*

bad, badly   *Bad* is an adjective, *badly* an adverb. (See 26a and 26b.) *They felt bad about being early and ruining the surprise. Her arm hurt badly after she slid headfirst into second base.*

being as, being that   *Being as* and *being that* are nonstandard expressions. Write *because* or *since* instead. *Because* (not *Being as*) *I slept late, I had to skip breakfast.*

beside, besides   *Beside* is a preposition meaning "at the side of" or "next to." *Annie Oakley slept with her gun beside her bed. Besides* is a preposition meaning "except" or "in addition to." *No one besides Terrie can have that ice cream. Besides* is also an adverb meaning "in addition." *I'm not hungry; besides, I don't like ice cream.*

between, among   Ordinarily, use *among* with three or more entities, *between* with two. *The prize was divided among several contestants. You have a choice between carrots and beans.*

bring, take   Use *bring* when an object is being transported toward you, *take* when it is being moved away. *Please bring me a glass of water. Please take these flowers to Mr. Scott.*

burst, bursted; bust, busted   *Burst* is an irregular verb meaning "to come open or fly apart suddenly or violently." Its principal parts are *burst, burst, burst*. The past-tense form *bursted* is nonstandard. *Bust* and *busted* are slang for *burst* and, along with *bursted,* should not be used in formal writing.

can, may   The distinction between *can* and *may* is fading, but many careful writers still observe it in formal writing. *Can* is traditionally reserved for ability, *may* for permission. *Can you ski down the advanced slope without falling? May I help you?*

capital, capitol   *Capital* refers to a city, *capitol* to a building where lawmakers meet. *Capital* also refers to wealth or resources. *The capitol has undergone extensive renovations. The residents of the state capital protested the development plans.*

censor, censure   *Censor* means "to remove or suppress material considered objectionable." *Censure* means "to criticize severely." *The library's new policy of censoring controversial books has been censured by the media.*

cite, site   *Cite* means "to quote as an authority or example." *Site* is usually a noun meaning "a particular place." *He cited the zoning law in his argument against the proposed site of the gas station.* Locations on the Internet are usually referred to as *sites. The library's Web site improves every week.*

climactic, climatic   *Climactic* is derived from *climax,* the point of greatest intensity in a series or progression of events. *Climatic* is derived from *climate* and refers to meteorological conditions. *The climac-*

tic period in the dinosaurs' reign was reached just before severe climatic conditions brought on an ice age.

coarse, course *Coarse* means "crude" or "rough in texture." *The coarse weave of the wall hanging gave it a three-dimensional quality. Course* usually refers to a path, a playing field, or a unit of study; the expression *of course* means "certainly." *I plan to take a course in car repair this summer. Of course, you are welcome to join me.*

compare to, compare with *Compare to* means "to represent as similar." *She compared him to a wild stallion. Compare with* means "to examine the ways in which two things are similar." *The study compared the language ability of apes with that of dolphins.*

complement, compliment *Complement* is a verb meaning "to go with or complete" or a noun meaning "something that completes." *Compliment* as a verb means "to flatter"; as a noun it means "flattering remark." *Her skill at rushing the net complements his skill at volleying. Mother's flower arrangements receive many compliments.*

conscience, conscious *Conscience* is a noun meaning "moral principles." *Conscious* is an adjective meaning "aware or alert." *Let your conscience be your guide. Were you conscious of his love for you?*

continual, continuous *Continual* means "repeated regularly and frequently." *She grew weary of the continual telephone calls. Continuous* means "extended or prolonged without interruption." *The broken siren made a continuous wail.*

could care less *Could care less* is a nonstandard expression. Write *couldn't care less* instead. *He couldn't* (not *could*) *care less about his psychology final.*

could of *Could of* is nonstandard for *could have. We could have* (not *could of*) *had steak for dinner if we had been hungry.*

council, counsel A *council* is a deliberative body, and a *councilor* is a member of such a body. *Counsel* usually means "advice" and can also mean "lawyer"; *counselor* is one who gives advice or guidance. *The councilors met to draft the council's position paper. The pastor offered wise counsel to the troubled teenager.*

criteria *Criteria* is the plural of *criterion,* which means "a standard or rule or test on which a judgment or decision can be based." *The only criterion for the scholarship is ability.*

data *Data* is a plural noun technically meaning "facts or propositions." But *data* is increasingly being accepted as a singular noun. *The new data suggest* (or *suggests*) *that our theory is correct.* (The singular *datum* is rarely used.)

different from, different than Ordinarily, write *different from. Your sense of style is different from Jim's.* However, *different than* is acceptable to avoid an awkward construction. *Please let me know if your plans are different than* (to avoid *from what*) *they were six weeks ago.*

differ from, differ with   *Differ from* means "to be unlike"; *differ with* means "to disagree." *She differed with me about the wording of the agreement. My approach to the problem differed from hers.*

disinterested, uninterested   *Disinterested* means "impartial, objective"; *uninterested* means "not interested." *We sought the advice of a disinterested counselor to help us solve our problem. He was uninterested in anyone's opinion but his own.*

don't   *Don't* is the contraction for *do not. I don't want any. Don't* should not be used as the contraction for *does not,* which is *doesn't. He doesn't* (not *don't*) *want any.* (See 27c.)

due to   *Due to* is an adjective phrase and should not be used as a preposition meaning "because of." *The trip was canceled because of* (not *due to*) *lack of interest. Due to* is acceptable as a subject complement and usually follows a form of the verb *be. His success was due to hard work.*

each   *Each* is singular. (See 21e and 22a.)

effect   See *affect, effect.*

e.g.   In formal writing, replace the Latin abbreviation *e.g.* with its English equivalent: *for example* or *for instance.*

either   *Either* is singular. (See 21e and 22a.) (For *either . . . or* constructions, see 21d and 22d.)

elicit, illicit   *Elicit* is a verb meaning "to bring out" or "to evoke." *Illicit* is an adjective meaning "unlawful." *The reporter was unable to elicit any information from the police about illicit drug traffic.*

emigrate from, immigrate to   *Emigrate* means "to leave one country or region to settle in another." *In 1900, my grandfather emigrated from Russia to escape the religious pogroms. Immigrate* means "to enter another country and reside there." *Many Mexicans immigrate to the United States to find work.*

eminent, imminent   *Eminent* means "outstanding" or "distinguished." *We met an eminent professor of Greek history. Imminent* means "about to happen." *The announcement is imminent.*

enthused   Many people object to the use of *enthused* as an adjective. Use *enthusiastic* instead. *The children were enthusiastic* (not *enthused*) *about going to the circus.*

etc.   Avoid ending a list with *etc.* It is more emphatic to end with an example, and in most contexts readers will understand that the list is not exhaustive. When you don't wish to end with an example, *and so on* is more graceful than *etc.* See also *and etc.*

eventually, ultimately   Often used interchangeably, *eventually* is the better choice to mean "at an unspecified time in the future" and *ultimately* is better to mean "the furthest possible extent or greatest extreme." *He knew that eventually he would complete his degree. The existentialist considered suicide the ultimately rational act.*

everybody, everyone *Everybody* and *everyone* are singular. (See 21e and 22a.)

everyone, every one *Everyone* is an indefinite pronoun. *Every one,* the pronoun *one* preceded by the adjective *every,* means "each individual or thing in a particular group." *Every one* is usually followed by *of. Everyone wanted to go. Every one of the missing books was found.*

except See *accept, except.*

expect Avoid the colloquial use of *expect* meaning "to believe, think, or suppose." *I think* (not *expect*) *it will rain tonight.*

explicit, implicit *Explicit* means "expressed directly" or "clearly defined"; *implicit* means "implied, unstated." *I gave him explicit instructions not to go swimming. My mother's silence indicated her implicit approval.*

farther, further *Farther* usually describes distances. *Further* usually suggests quantity or degree. *Chicago is farther from Miami than I thought. You extended the curfew further than you should have.*

female, male The terms *female* and *male* are jargon when used to refer to specific people. *Two women* (not *females*) *and one man* (not *male*) *applied for the position.*

fewer, less *Fewer* refers to items that can be counted; *less* refers to general amounts. *Fewer people are living in the city. Please put less sugar in my tea.*

finalize *Finalize* is jargon meaning "to make final or complete." Use ordinary English instead. *The architect prepared final drawings* (not *finalized the drawings*).

firstly *Firstly* sounds pretentious, and it leads to the ungainly series *firstly, secondly, thirdly, fourthly,* and so on. Write *first, second, third* instead.

further See *farther, further.*

get *Get* has many colloquial uses. In writing, avoid using *get* to mean the following: "to evoke an emotional response" (*That music always gets to me*); "to annoy" (*After a while his sulking got to me*); "to take revenge on" (*I got back at him by leaving the room*); "to become" (*He got sick*); "to start or begin" (*Let's get going*). Avoid using *have got to* in place of *must. I must* (not *have got to*) *finish this paper tonight.*

good, well *Good* is an adjective, *well* an adverb. (See section 26.) *He hasn't felt good about his game since he sprained his wrist last season. She performed well on the uneven parallel bars.*

hanged, hung *Hanged* is the past-tense and past-participle form of the verb *hang* meaning "to execute." *The prisoner was hanged at dawn. Hung* is the past-tense and past-participle form of the verb *hang* meaning "to fasten or suspend." *The stockings were hung by the chimney with care.*

hardly   Avoid expressions such as *can't hardly* and *not hardly,* which are considered double negatives. *I can* (not *can't*) *hardly describe my elation at getting the job.* (See 26d.)

has got, have got   *Got* is unnecessary and awkward in such constructions. It should be dropped. *We have* (not *have got*) *three days to prepare for the opening.*

he   At one time *he* was commonly used to mean "he or she." Today such usage is inappropriate. (See 17f and 22a.)

he/she, his/her   In formal writing, use *he or she* or *his or her.* For alternatives to these wordy constructions, see 17f and 22a.

hisself   *Hisself* is nonstandard. Use *himself.*

hopefully   *Hopefully* means "in a hopeful manner." *We looked hopefully to the future.* Some usage experts object to the use of *hopefully* as a sentence adverb, apparently on grounds of clarity. To be safe, avoid using *hopefully* in sentences such as the following: *Hopefully, your son will recover soon.* At least some educated readers will want you to indicate who is doing the hoping: *I hope that your son will recover soon.*

hung   See *hanged, hung.*

i.e.   In formal writing, replace the Latin abbreviation *i.e.* with its English equivalent: *that is.*

if, whether   Use *if* to express a condition and *whether* to express alternatives. *If you go on a trip, whether it be to Nebraska or New Jersey, remember to bring traveler's checks.*

illusion   See *allusion, illusion.*

immigrate, emigrate   See *emigrate from, immigrate to.*

imminent   See *eminent, imminent.*

immoral   See *amoral, immoral.*

implement   *Implement* is a pretentious way of saying "do," "carry out," or "accomplish." Use ordinary language instead. *We carried out* (not *implemented*) *the director's orders with some reluctance.*

imply, infer   *Imply* means "to suggest or state indirectly"; *infer* means "to draw a conclusion." *John implied that he knew all about computers, but the interviewer inferred that John was inexperienced.*

in, into   *In* indicates location or condition; *into* indicates movement or a change in condition. *They found the lost letters in a box after moving into the house.*

individual   *Individual* is a pretentious substitute for *person. We invited several persons* (not *individuals*) *from the audience to participate in the experiment.*

ingenious, ingenuous   *Ingenious* means "clever." *Sarah's solution to the problem was ingenious. Ingenuous* means "naive" or "frank." *For a successful manager, Ed is surprisingly ingenuous.*

in regards to   *In regards to* confuses two different phrases: *in regard to* and *as regards*. Use one or the other. *In regard to* (or *As regards*) *the contract, ignore the first clause.*

irregardless   *Irregardless* is nonstandard. Use *regardless*.

is when, is where   These mixed constructions are often incorrectly used in definitions. *A run-off election is a second election held to break a tie* (not *is when a second election breaks a tie*). (See 11c.)

it is   *It is* is nonstandard when used to mean "there is." *There is* (not *It is*) *a fly in my soup.*

its, it's   *Its* is a possessive pronoun; *it's* is a contraction for *it is*. (See 36c and 36e.) *The dog licked its wound whenever its owner walked into the room. It's a perfect day to walk the twenty-mile trail.*

kind(s)   *Kind* is singular and should be treated as such. Don't write *These kind of chairs are rare*. Write instead *This kind of chair is rare*. *Kinds* is plural and should be used only when you mean more than one kind. *These kinds of chairs are rare.*

kind of, sort of   Avoid using *kind of* or *sort of* to mean "somewhat." *The movie was somewhat* (not *kind of*) *boring*. Do not put *a* after either phrase. *That kind of* (not *kind of a*) *salesclerk annoys me.*

lead, led   *Lead* is a noun referring to a metal. *Led* is the past tense of the verb *lead*. *He led me to the treasure.*

learn, teach   *Learn* means "to gain knowledge"; *teach* means "to impart knowledge." *I must teach* (not *learn*) *my sister to read.*

leave, let   *Leave* means "to exit." Avoid using it with the nonstandard meaning "to permit." *Let* (not *Leave*) *me help you with the dishes.*

less   See *fewer, less.*

let, leave   See *leave, let.*

liable   *Liable* means "obligated" or "responsible." Do not use it to mean "likely." *You're likely* (not *liable*) *to trip if you don't tie your shoelaces.*

lie, lay   *Lie* is an intransitive verb meaning "to recline or rest on a surface." Its principal parts are *lie, lay, lain. Lay* is a transitive verb meaning "to put or place." Its principal parts are *lay, laid, laid*. (See 27b.)

like, as   *Like* is a preposition, not a subordinating conjunction. It can be followed only by a noun or a noun phrase. *As* is a subordinating conjunction that introduces a subordinate clause. In casual speech you may say *She looks like she hasn't slept* or *You don't know her like I do*. But in formal writing, use *as*. *She looks as if she hasn't slept. You don't know her as I do.* (See prepositions and subordinating conjunctions, 57f and 57g.)

loose, lose   *Loose* is an adjective meaning "not securely fastened." *Lose* is a verb meaning "to misplace" or "to not win." *Did you lose your only loose pair of work pants?*

lots, lots of   *Lots* and *lots of* are colloquial substitutes for *many, much,* or *a lot*. Avoid using them in formal writing.

male, female   See *female, male*.

mankind   Avoid *mankind* whenever possible. It offends many readers because it excludes women. Use *humanity, humans, the human race,* or *humankind* instead.

may   See *can, may*.

maybe, may be   *Maybe* is an adverb meaning "possibly." *May be* is a verb phrase. *Maybe the sun will shine tomorrow. Tomorrow may be a brighter day.*

may of, might of   *May of* and *might of* are nonstandard for *may have* and *might have*. *We may have* (not *may of*) *had too many cookies.*

media, medium   *Media* is the plural of *medium*. *Of all the media that cover the Olympics, television is the medium that best captures the spectacle of the events.*

most   *Most* is colloquial when used to mean "almost" and should be avoided. *Almost* (not *Most*) *everyone went to the parade.*

must of   See *may of*.

myself   *Myself* is a reflexive or intensive pronoun. Reflexive: *I cut myself*. Intensive: *I will drive you myself*. Do not use *myself* in place of *I* or *me*. *He gave the flowers to Melinda and me* (not *myself*). (See also 24.)

neither   *Neither* is singular. (See 21e and 22a.) For *neither . . . nor* constructions, see 21d and 22d.

none   *None* is usually singular. (See 21e.)

nowheres   *Nowheres* is nonstandard for *nowhere*.

number   See *amount, number*.

of   Use the verb *have*, not the preposition *of*, after the verbs *could, should, would, may, might,* and *must*. *They must have* (not *of*) *left early.*

off of   *Off* is sufficient. Omit *of*. *The ball rolled off* (not *off of*) *the table.*

OK, O.K., okay   All three spellings are acceptable, but in formal speech and writing avoid these colloquial expressions for consent or approval.

parameters   *Parameter* is a mathematical term that has become jargon for "fixed limit," "boundary," or "guideline." Use ordinary English instead. *The task force was asked to work within certain guidelines* (not *parameters*).

passed, past   *Passed* is the past tense of the verb *pass*. *Mother passed me another slice of cake.* *Past* usually means "belonging to a former time" or "beyond a time or place." *Our past president spoke until past midnight. The hotel is just past the next intersection.*

percent, per cent, percentage   *Percent* (also spelled *per cent*) is always used with a specific number. *Percentage* is used with a descriptive term such as *large* or *small,* not with a specific number. *The candidate won 80 percent of the primary vote. Only a small percentage of registered voters turned out for the election.*

phenomena *Phenomena* is the plural of *phenomenon,* which means "an observable occurrence or fact." *Strange phenomena occur at all hours of the night in that house, but last night's phenomenon was the strangest of all.*

plus *Plus* should not be used to join independent clauses. *This raincoat is dirty; moreover* (not *plus*)*, it has a hole in it.*

precede, proceed *Precede* means "to come before." *Proceed* means "to go forward." *As we proceeded up the mountain path, we noticed fresh tracks in the mud, evidence that a group of hikers had preceded us.*

principal, principle *Principal* is a noun meaning "the head of a school or organization" or "a sum of money." It is also an adjective meaning "most important." *Principle* is a noun meaning "a basic truth or law." *The principal expelled her for three principal reasons. We believe in the principle of equal justice for all.*

proceed, precede See *precede, proceed.*

quote, quotation *Quote* is a verb; *quotation* is a noun. Avoid using *quote* as a shortened form of *quotation. Her quotations* (not *quotes*) *from Shakespeare intrigued us.*

raise, rise *Raise* is a transitive verb meaning "to move or cause to move upward." It takes a direct object. *I raised the shades. Rise* is an intransitive verb meaning "to go up." It does not take a direct object. *Heat rises.*

real, really *Real* is an adjective; *really* is an adverb. *Real* is sometimes used informally as an adverb, but avoid this use in formal writing. *She was really* (not *real*) *angry.* (See 26a.)

reason is because Use *that* instead of *because. The reason I'm late is that* (not *because*) *my car broke down.* (See 11c.)

reason why The expression *reason why* is redundant. *The reason* (not *The reason why*) *Jones lost the election is clear.*

relation, relationship *Relation* describes a connection between things. *Relationship* describes a connection between people. *There is a relation between poverty and infant mortality. Our business relationship has cooled over the years.*

respectfully, respectively *Respectfully* means "showing or marked by respect." *Respectively* means "each in the order given." *He respectfully submitted his opinion to the judge. John, Tom, and Larry were a butcher, a baker, and a lawyer, respectively.*

sensual, sensuous *Sensual* means "gratifying the physical senses," especially those associated with sexual pleasure. *Sensuous* means "pleasing to the senses," especially those involved in the experience of art, music, and nature. *The sensuous music and balmy air led the dancers to more sensual movements.*

set, sit   *Set* is a transitive verb meaning "to put" or "to place." Its principal parts are *set, set, set. Sit* is an intransitive verb meaning "to be seated." Its principal parts are *sit, sat, sat. She set the dough in a warm corner of the kitchen. The cat sat in the warmest part of the room.*

shall, will   *Shall* was once used as the helping verb with *I* or *we: I shall, we shall, you will, he/she/it will, they will.* Today, however, *will* is generally accepted even when the subject is *I* or *we.* The word *shall* occurs primarily in polite questions (*Shall I find you a pillow?*) and in legalistic sentences suggesting duty or obligation (*The applicant shall file form 1080 by December 31*).

should of   *Should of* is nonstandard for *should have. They should have* (not *should of*) *been home an hour ago.*

since   Do not use *since* to mean "because" if there is any chance of ambiguity. *Since we won the game, we have been celebrating with a pitcher of beer. Since* here could mean "because" or "from the time that."

sit   See *set, sit.*

site, cite   See *cite, site.*

somebody, someone   *Somebody* and *someone* are singular. (See 21e and 22a.)

something   *Something* is singular. (See 21e.)

sometime, some time, sometimes   *Sometime* is an adverb meaning "at an indefinite or unstated time." *Some time* is the adjective *some* modifying the noun *time* and is spelled as two words to mean "a period of time." *Sometimes* is an adverb meaning "at times, now and then." *I'll see you sometime soon. I haven't lived there for some time. Sometimes I run into him at the library.*

suppose to   Write *supposed to.*

sure and   *Sure and* is nonstandard for *sure to. We were all taught to be sure to* (not *and*) *look both ways before crossing a street.*

take   See *bring, take.*

than, then   *Than* is a conjunction used in comparisons; *then* is an adverb denoting time. *That pizza is more than I can eat. Tom laughed, and then we recognized him.*

that   See *who, which, that.*

that, which   Many writers reserve *that* for restrictive clauses, *which* for nonrestrictive clauses. (See 32e.)

theirselves   *Theirselves* is nonstandard for *themselves. The two people were able to push the Volkswagen out of the way themselves* (not *theirselves*).

them   The use of *them* in place of *those* is nonstandard. *Please send those* (not *them*) *flowers to the patient in room 220.*

there, their, they're   *There* is an adverb specifying place; it is also an expletive. Adverb: *Sylvia is lying there unconscious.* Expletive: *There are two plums left.* *Their* is a possessive pronoun. *Fred and Jane finally washed their car. They're* is a contraction of *they are. They're later than usual today.*

they   The use of *they* to indicate possession is nonstandard. Use *their* instead. *Cindy and Sam decided to sell their* (not *they*) *1975 Corvette.*

this kind   See *kind(s).*

to, too, two   *To* is a preposition; *too* is an adverb; *two* is a number. *Too many of your shots slice to the left, but the last two were right on the mark.*

toward, towards   *Toward* and *towards* are generally interchangeable, although *toward* is preferred in American English.

try and   *Try and* is nonstandard for *try to. The teacher asked us all to try to* (not *and*) *write an original haiku.*

ultimately, eventually   See *eventually, ultimately.*

unique   Avoid expressions such as *most unique, more straight, less perfect, very round.* Either something is unique or it isn't. It is illogical to suggest degrees of uniqueness. (See 26c.)

usage   The noun *usage* should not be substituted for *use* when the meaning intended is "employment of." *The use* (not *usage*) *of computers dramatically increased the company's profits.*

use to   Write *used to.*

utilize   *Utilize* means "to make use of." It often sounds pretentious; in most cases, *use* is sufficient. *I used* (not *utilized*) *the best workers to get the job done fast.*

wait for, wait on   *Wait for* means "to be in readiness for" or "await." *Wait on* means "to serve." *We're only waiting for* (not *waiting on*) *Ruth to take us to the game.*

ways   *Ways* is colloquial when used to mean "distance." *The city is a long way* (not *ways*) *from here.*

weather, whether   The noun *weather* refers to the state of the atmosphere. *Whether* is a conjunction referring to a choice between alternatives. *We wondered whether the weather would clear up in time for our picnic.*

well, good   See *good, well.*

where   Do not use *where* in place of *that. I heard that* (not *where*) *the crime rate is increasing.*

which   See *that, which* and *who, which, that.*

while   Avoid using *while* to mean "although" or "whereas" if there is any chance of ambiguity. *Although* (not *While*) *Gloria lost money in the slot machine, Tom won it at roulette.* Here *While* could mean either "although" or "at the same time that."

who, which, that   Do not use *which* to refer to persons. Use *who* instead. *That,* though generally used to refer to things, may be used to refer to a group or class of people. *Fans wondered how an old man who* (not *that* or *which*) *walked with a limp could play football. The team that scores the most points in this game will win the tournament.* (See 23e.)

who, whom   *Who* is used for subjects and subject complements; *whom* is used for objects. (See section 25.)

who's, whose   *Who's* is a contraction of *who is; whose* is a possessive pronoun. *Who's ready for more popcorn? Whose coat is this?* (See 36c and 36e.)

will   See *shall, will.*

would of   *Would of* is nonstandard for *would have. She would have* (not *would of*) *had a chance to play if she had arrived on time.*

you   In formal writing, avoid *you* in an indefinite sense meaning "anyone." (See 23d.) *Any spectator* (not *You*) *could tell by the way John caught the ball that his throw would be too late.*

your, you're   *Your* is a possessive pronoun; *you're* is a contraction of *you are. Is that your new motorcycle? You're on the list of finalists.* (See 36c and 36e.)

Answers to Tutorials and Lettered Exercises

Answers to Tutorial 1, page xvii

1. A verb has to agree with its subject. (21)
2. Each pronoun should agree with its antecedent. (22)
3. Avoid sentence fragments. (19)
4. It's important to use apostrophes correctly. (36)
5. Check for *-ed* verb endings that have been dropped. (27d)
6. Discriminate carefully between adjectives and adverbs. (26)
7. If your sentence begins with a long introductory word group, use a comma to separate the word group from the rest of the sentence. (32b)
8. Don't write a run-on sentence; you must connect independent clauses with a comma and a coordinating conjunction or with a semicolon. (20)
9. For clarity, a writer must be careful not to shift his or her [*not* their] point of view. *Or* For clarity, writers should be careful not to shift their point of view. (13a)
10. Do not capitalize a word just to make it look important. (45)

Answers to Tutorial 2, page xviii

1. The index entry "each" mentions that the word is singular, so you might not need to look further to realize that the verb should be *has,* not *have.* The first page reference takes you to section 21, which explains in more detail why *has* is correct. The index entry "*has* versus *have*" also leads you to section 21.
2. The index entry "*lay, lie*" takes you to section 27b and to the Glossary of Usage, where you will learn that *lying* (meaning "reclining or resting on a surface") is correct.
3. Look up "*only*" and you will be directed to section 12a, which explains that limiting modifiers such as *only* should be placed before the words they modify. The sentence should read *We looked at only two houses before buying the house of our dreams.*
4. Looking up "*you,* inappropriate use of" leads you to section 23d and the Glossary of Usage, which explain that *you* should not be used to mean "anyone in general." You can revise the sentence by using *a person* or *one* instead of *you,* or you can restructure the sentence completely: *In Saudi Arabia, accepting a gift is considered ill mannered.*
5. The index entries "*I* versus *me*" and "*me* versus *I*" take you to section 24, which explains why *me* is correct.

Answers to Tutorial 3, page xviii

1. Section 32c states that although usage varies, most experts advise using a comma between all items in a series—to prevent possible misreadings or ambiguities. To find this section, Ray Farley would probably use the menu system.
2. Maria Sanchez and Mike Lee would consult section 30, on articles. This section is easy to locate on the main menu.

3. Section 24 explains why "Jane and me" is correct. To find section 24, John Pell could use the menu system if he knew to look under "Problems with pronouns." Otherwise, he could look up "*I* versus *me*" in the index. Pell could also look up "*myself*" in the index or he could consult the Glossary of Usage, where a cross-reference would direct him to section 24b.

4. Selena Young's employees could turn to sections 21 and 27c for help. Young could use the menu system to find these sections if she knew to look under "Subject-verb agreement" or "Standard English verb forms." If she wasn't sure about the grammatical terminology, she could look up "-*s*, as verb ending" or "Verbs, -*s* forms of" in the index.

5. Section 26b explains why "I felt bad about her death" is correct. To find section 26b, Joe Thompson could use the menu system if he knew that *bad* versus *badly* is a choice between an adjective and an adverb. Otherwise he could look up "*bad, badly*" in the index or the Glossary of Usage.

Answers to Tutorial 4, page xix

1. Changing attitudes toward alcohol have *affected* the beer industry.
2. It is *human* nature to think wisely and act foolishly.
3. Correct.
4. Everyone in our office is *enthusiastic* about this project.
5. Most sleds are pulled by no *fewer* than two dogs and no more than ten.

Answers to Tutorial 5, page xx

Codoga, Helen. "Gambling on Reservations." E-mail to the author. 10 Apr. 1999.

Cooper, Mary H. "Native Americans' Future: Do U.S. Policies Block Opportunities for Progress?" CQ Researcher 6 (1996): 603-19.

Dao, James. "Gambling Proponents See Indian Casinos as Alternative." New York Times 30 Jan. 1997, late ed.: B2.

Johansen, Bruce E. Life and Death in Mohawk Country. Golden. CO: North American, 1993.

Pollack, Kenan. "Mashantucket Pequots: A Tribe That's Raking It In." U.S. News Online 17 Feb. 1998. 1 May 1999 <http://www.usnews.com/ usnews/issue/gambleb8.htm>.

Ridgebear, Sam. "Guilty Hands: Traditionalism and the Indian Gaming Industry." Many Voices: American Indian Students Journal 1.1 (1995). 2 Apr. 1999 <http://thecity.sfsu.edu/users/ BANN/journal/guiltyhands.html>.

Schine, Eric. "First Gambling, Then a Bank: California Has Reservations." <u>Business Week</u> 9 Sept. 1996: 47.

EXERCISE 8-1, page 107

Possible revisions:

a. A user-friendly instruction manual is enclosed with your computer.
b. Part of my earnings went toward the purchase of a ten-speed bicycle, which I hoped would serve as my primary form of transportation.
c. There are five fishing piers on the island, each with a bait and tackle shop.
d. Student volunteers from Baltimore City Community College help the younger children with their weakest subjects, reading and math.
e. Because the home study course seemed to have everything I was looking for, I thought my troubles were over, but in reality they were just beginning.

EXERCISE 8-2, page 109

Possible revisions:

a. During a routine morning at the clinic, an infant in cardiac arrest arrived by ambulance.
b. My 1969 Camaro, an original SS396, is no longer street legal.
c. This highly specialized medical training, called a "residency," usually takes four years to complete.
d. Although outsiders have forced changes on them, native Hawaiians try to preserve their ancestors' sacred customs.
e. Ash Lawn, located only two miles from Monticello, is the restored home of our fifth president, James Monroe.

EXERCISE 9-1, page 114

Possible revisions:

a. The system has capabilities such as communicating with other computers, processing records, and performing mathematical functions.
b. The personnel officer told me that I would answer the phone, welcome visitors, distribute mail, and do some typing.
c. The African elephants are endangered primarily because poachers kill them and because they have less and less space to live in.
d. How ideal it seems to raise a family here in Winnebago instead of in the air-polluted suburbs.
e. In combat the soldiers were brave but sometimes foolish — because of poor training, lack of confidence, and inexperience.

EXERCISE 10-1, page 118

Possible revisions:

a. Dip the paintbrush into the paint remover and spread a thick coat on a small section of the door.
b. Christopher had an attention span longer than that of the other students.
c. SETI (the Search for Extraterrestrial Intelligence) has excited and will continue to excite interest among space buffs.
d. Samantha got along better with the chimpanzees than with Albert. [*or* . . . than Albert did.]
e. We were glad to see that Yellowstone National Park was recovering from the devastating forest fire.

EXERCISE 11–1, page 122

Possible revisions:

a. The name of the song is "Words Unspoken."
b. A cloverleaf allows traffic on limited-access freeways to change direction.
c. Bowman established the format that future football card companies would emulate for years to come.
d. When prostate cancer is diagnosed early, it is often curable.
e. The number and strength of drinks, the amount of time that has passed since the last drink, and one's body weight determine the concentration of alcohol in the blood.

EXERCISE 12–1, page 127

Possible revisions:

a. At our warehouse sale, only cash, MasterCard, or Visa will be accepted.
b. Not all thin people are anorexic or bulimic.
c. Celia received a flyer from a Japanese nun about a workshop on making a kimono.
d. Jurors are encouraged to sift through the evidence thoroughly.
e. As the train reached the border, all passengers were asked to have their passports ready.

EXERCISE 12–2, page 130

Possible revisions:

a. Reaching the heart, the surgeon performed a bypass on the severely blocked arteries.
b. To enter college early, students need more than good grades.
c. While we dined at night, the lights along the Baja coastline created a romantic atmosphere perfect for our first anniversary.
d. While my sister was still a beginner at tennis, the coaches recruited her to train for the Olympics.
e. After Marcus Garvey returned to Jamaica, his Back to Africa movement slowly died.

EXERCISE 13–1, page 134

Possible revisions:

a. My hopes rose and fell as Joseph's heart started and stopped. The doctors inserted a large tube into his chest, and blood flowed from the incision onto the floor.
b. Ministers often have a hard time because they have to please so many different people.
c. We drove for eight hours until we reached the South Dakota Badlands. We could hardly believe the eeriness of the landscape at dusk.
d. The question is whether ferrets bred in captivity have the instinct to prey on prairie dogs or whether this is a learned skill.
e. You should protect yourself from the sun, especially on the first day of extensive exposure.

EXERCISE 14–1, page 139

Possible revisions:

a. The Prussians defeated the Saxons in 1745.
b. Ahmed, the producer, manages the entire operation.
c. Emphatic and active; no change.

   d. Players fought on both sides of the rink.
   e. Emphatic and active; no change.

Possible revisions:

a. The drawing room in the west wing is said to be haunted.
b. Ten terry cloth towels stuffed under the door did nothing to stop the flow.
c. Bloom's race for the governorship is futile.
d. In the heart of Beijing lies the Forbidden City, an imperial palace built during the Ming dynasty.
e. Seeing the barrels, the driver slammed on his brakes.

Possible revisions:

a. Ignore those who try to dissuade you from reaching your goals.
b. This conference will help me serve my clients better.
c. Have you ever been accused of beating a dead horse?
d. When Sal was laid off from his high-paying factory job, he learned what it was like to be poor.
e. Passengers should try to complete the customs declaration form before leaving the plane.

Possible revisions:

a. Dr. Geralyn Farmer is the chief surgeon at University Hospital. Dr. Paul Green is her assistant.
b. A young graduate who is careful about investments can accumulate a significant sum in a relatively short period.
c. An elementary school teacher should understand the concept of nurturing if he or she intends to be a success.
d. The vice president for community affairs asked Elizabeth and Joseph to serve as cochairs of the Red Cross blood drive.
e. If we do not stop polluting our environment, we will perish.

Possible revisions:

a. We regret this delay; thank you for your patience.
b. Those who believe that books written for children are all sweetness and light are suffering from an illusion.
c. Liu Kwan began his career as a lawyer, but now he is a real estate mogul.
d. When Robert Frost died at age eighty-eight, he left a legacy of poems that will make him immortal.
e. In general, the Internet has had a positive effect on our society.

Possible revisions:

a. Queen Anne was so angry with Sarah Churchill that she dismissed her once faithful servant.
b. Correct
c. Dad told us to be sure to visit the ghost towns of Nevada.

d. For the frightened refugees, the dangerous trek across the mountains was preferable to life in a war zone.

e. The baby fell off the couch and landed on the soft cushion of the dog's bed.

EXERCISE 18–4, page 166

Possible revisions:

a. John stormed into the room like a hurricane.

b. The president thought that the scientists were using science as a means to further their political goals.

c. The Cubs easily beat the Mets, who were in trouble early in the game today at Wrigley Field.

d. We ironed out the wrinkles in our relationship.

e. Sasha told us that he wasn't willing to take a chance.

EXERCISE 19–1, page 174

Possible revisions:

a. As I stood in front of the microwave, I recalled my grandmother bending over her old black stove and remembered what she taught me: that any food can have soul if you love the people you are cooking for.

b. The resort was full of attractions: three swimming pools, four restaurants, five bars, and every game imaginable, including a life-sized chess set.

c. Correct

d. We need to stop believing myths about drinking—that strong black coffee will sober you up, for example, or that a cold shower will straighten you out.

e. On Sundays, James scrupulously read the newspaper's employment listings, scrutinizing every position that held even the remotest possibility.

EXERCISE 20–1, page 182

Possible revisions:

a. The city had one public swimming pool that stayed packed with children all summer long.

b. The building is being renovated, so at times we have no heat, water, or electricity.

c. Why shouldn't a divorced wife receive half of her husband's pension and retirement benefits? She was her husband's partner for many years.

d. Suddenly there was a loud silence; the shelling had stopped.

e. The experience taught Juanita a lesson: She could not always rely on her parents to bail her out of trouble.

EXERCISE 20–2, page 183

Possible revisions:

a. Although Ted never drove the vintage cars that he had inherited, he could not bring himself to sell them.

b. Correct

c. In the Middle Ages, when the streets of London were dangerous places, it was safer to travel by boat along the Thames.

d. Researchers studying the fertility of Texas land tortoises X-rayed all the female tortoises to see how many eggs they had.

e. We had planned to spend the last few days of our vacation at the beach; the hurricane, however, brought us home in a hurry.

EXERCISE 21–1, page 195

a. Subject: history and life; verb: have. b. Subject: shelters; verb: offer. c. Subject: Each; verb: was. d. Subject: chances; verb: are. e. Subject: signs or traces; verb: were

EXERCISE 21–2, page 196

a. High concentrations of carbon monoxide result in headaches, dizziness, unconsciousness, and even death.
b. Correct
c. Correct
d. Crystal chandeliers, polished floors, and a new oil painting have transformed Sandra's apartment.
e. Correct

EXERCISE 22–1, page 200

Possible revisions:

a. Correct
b. The instructor has asked students to bring their own tools to carpentry class.
c. An eighteenth-century architect was also a classical scholar who was often at the forefront of archaeological research.
d. Anyone caught smoking on the premises will be severely reprimanded.
e. Why should we care about the timber wolf? One answer is that it has proven beneficial to humans by killing off weakened prey.

EXERCISE 23–1, page 205

Possible revisions:

a. The detective removed the bloodstained shawl from the body and then photographed the body.
b. In Professor Jamal's class, students are lucky to earn a C.
c. The Comanche braves lived violent lives; they gained respect for their skill as warriors.
d. All students can secure parking permits from the campus police office, which is open from 8 A.M. until 8 P.M.
e. Our German conversation group is made up of six people, three of whom I had never met before.

EXERCISE 24–1, page 211

Possible revisions:

a. My Ethiopian neighbor was puzzled by the dedication of us joggers.
b. Correct
c. Sue's husband is ten years older than she.
d. Everyone laughed whenever Sandra described how her brother and she had seen the Loch Ness monster and fed it sandwiches.
e. We appreciate your bringing this problem to our attention.

EXERCISE 25–1, page 215

a. In his first production of *Hamlet,* whom did Laurence Olivier replace?
b. Correct
c. Correct
d. The bank doors were locked, and whoever was inside remained there until the police officers arrived.
e. One of the women whom Martinez hired became the most successful lawyer in the agency.

EXERCISE 26–1, page 220

Possible revisions:

a. When Tina began breathing normally, we could relax.
b. All of us on the team felt bad about our performance.

c. This incident could have been handled more professionally if lines of communication had been kept open.
d. Correct
e. Fiona has developed the most unusual Web site I've ever seen.

EXERCISE 27–1, page 226

a. Noticing that my roommate was shivering and looking pale, I rang for the nurse.
b. When I get the urge to exercise, I lie down until it passes.
c. Grandmother had driven our new jeep to the sunrise church service on Savage Mountain, so we were left with the station wagon.
d. Last June my cousin Lucia swam the length of the lake in forty minutes.
e. Correct

EXERCISE 27–2, page 233

a. The cops were after my hot rod Lincoln. We were passing cars like they were standing still.
b. The museum visitors were not supposed to touch the exhibits.
c. Our church has all the latest technology, even a closed-circuit television.
d. We often don't know whether he is angry or just joking.
e. Has there ever been a time in your life when you were too depressed to get out of bed?

EXERCISE 28–1, page 240

a. Watson and Crick discovered the mechanism that controls inheritance in all life: the workings of the DNA molecule.
b. Correct
c. In the feminist rewriting of "Sleeping Beauty," the girl is not awakened by a prince.
d. Correct
e. They had planned to adopt a girl, but they got twin boys.

EXERCISE 28–2, page 242

Possible revisions:

a. Fra Angelico painted each cell in the monastery.
b. Scientists use carbon dating to determine the approximate age of an object.
c. As the patient undressed, we saw scars on his back, stomach, and thighs. We suspected child abuse.
d. We noted right away that the taxi driver had been exposed to Americans because he knew all the latest slang.
e. Researchers have discovered diseases more often than cures.

EXERCISE 29–1, page 247

a. We will make this a better country.
b. There is nothing in the world that TV has not touched on.
c. Did the landlord tell you that he's going to raise the rent?
d. A hard wind was blowing while we were climbing the mountain.
e. The child's innocent world has been taken away from him.

EXERCISE 29–2, page 249

Possible revisions:

a. He would have won the election if he had gone to the port cities to campaign.

b. If Martin Luther King, Jr., were alive today, he would be appalled by the violence in our inner cities.
c. Whenever there is a fire in our neighborhood, everybody comes out to watch.
d. We will lose our largest client unless we update our computer system.
e. If I lived in southern California, I wouldn't need to buy a winter coat.

EXERCISE 29-3, page 253

Possible revisions:

a. I enjoy riding my motorcycle.
b. Will you encourage Samantha to enter the writing contest?
c. The team hopes to work hard and win the championship.
d. Ricardo and his brothers miss surfing during the winter.
e. The babysitter let Roger stay up until midnight.

EXERCISE 31-1, page 263

a. There are some cartons of ice cream in the freezer.
b. There are several emergency telephone numbers listed next to the phones at the hotel.
c. The prime minister is the most popular leader in my country.
d. Juana wants to travel to many countries that she has read about.
e. The king, who had served since the age of sixteen, was an old man when he died.

EXERCISE 31-2, page 266

a. an attractive young Vietnamese woman
b. a dedicated Catholic priest
c. her old blue wool sweater
d. Joe's delicious Scandinavian bread
e. many ornate wooden bird feeders

EXERCISE 31-3, page 268

a. Listening to everyone's complaints all day was irritating.
b. During the long lecture, many students appeared tired.
c. Correct
d. The violence in recent movies is often disgusting.
e. Correct

EXERCISE 31-4, page 270

a. Whenever we eat at the Centerville Diner, we sit at a small table in the corner of the room.
b. Correct
c. Usually she met with her patients in the afternoon, but on that day she stayed at home to take care of her son.
d. The clock is hanging on the wall in the dining room.
e. Our rabbi moved to the Northwest in 1994 and has been with our temple in Seattle since 1996.

EXERCISE 32-1, page 274

a. Correct
b. The man at the next table complained loudly, and the waiter stomped off in disgust.
c. If you complete the enclosed card and return it within two weeks, you will receive a free breakfast during your stay.
d. Nursing is physically and mentally demanding, yet the pay is low.

e. Uncle Swen's dulcimers disappeared as soon as he put them up for sale, but he always kept one for himself.

EXERCISE 32–2, page 276

a. She wore a black silk cape, a rhinestone collar, satin gloves, and high-tops.
b. An ambulance threaded its way through police cars, fire trucks, and irate citizens.
c. City Café is noted for its spicy vegetarian dishes and its friendly, efficient service.
d. When air-conditioning arrived in the workplace, it had a large, measurable impact on productivity.
e. Correct

EXERCISE 32–3, page 279

a. B. B. King and Lucille, his customized black Gibson, have electrified audiences all over the world.
b. The United States Coast Survey, which was established in 1807, was the first scientific agency in this country.
c. Correct
d. Shakespeare's tragedy *King Lear* was given a splendid performance by the actor Laurence Olivier.
e. Correct

EXERCISE 32–4, page 284

a. April 16, 1999, is the final deadline for all applications.
b. The coach having bawled us out thoroughly, we left the locker room with his last, harsh words ringing in our ears.
c. Good technique does not guarantee, however, that the power you develop will be sufficient for Kyok Pa competition.
d. We all piled into Sadiq's car, which we affectionately referred to as the "Blue Goose."
e. As a matter of fact, sales have far exceeded initial projections.

EXERCISE 33–1, page 290

a. We'd rather spend our money on blue-chip stocks than speculate on porkbellies.
b. Being prepared for the worst is one way to cope.
c. Please telephone me if you cannot send the information promptly or if you have any questions.
d. The Marx Brothers made delightful, hilarious movies.
e. I quickly accepted the fact that I was literally in third-class quarters.

EXERCISE 34–1, page 295

a. When a woman behaves like a man, why doesn't she behave like a nice man?
b. Do not ask me to be kind; just ask me to act as though I were.
c. Don't talk about yourself; it will be done when you leave.
d. The only sensible ends of literature are first, the pleasurable toil of writing; second, the gratification of one's family and friends; and lastly, the solid cash.
e. I do not rule Russia; ten thousand clerks do.

EXERCISE 34–2, page 295

a. At the outbreak of the American Civil War, many believed that the conflict would be over in a month; others had a dreadful premonition of the future.

b. America has been called a country of pragmatists, although the American devotion to ideals is legendary.
c. The first requirement is honesty; everything else follows.
d. I am not fond of opera; I must admit, however, that I was greatly moved by *Les Misérables.*
e. The Theban plays by Sophocles consist of *Antigone,* which deals with the conscience and the state; *King Oedipus,* which explores the question of fate and circumstance; and *Oedipus at Colonus,* which presents themes of suffering and redemption.

EXERCISE 35–1, page 298

a. The Greeks were right: Character is fate.
b. Some examples of reptiles are lizards, snakes, crocodiles, and turtles.
c. Correct
d. For example, Teddy Roosevelt once referred to the wolf as "the beast of waste and desolation."
e. Correct

EXERCISE 36–1, page 302

a. In a democracy, anyone's vote counts as much as mine.
b. Correct
c. The puppy's favorite activity was chasing its tail.
d. After we bought J. J. the latest style pants and shirts, he decided that last year's faded, ragged jeans were perfect for all occasions.
e. The snow doesn't rise any higher than the horses' fetlocks.

EXERCISE 37–1, page 309

a. Correct
b. As Emerson wrote in 1849, "I hate quotations. Tell me what you know."
c. Andrew Marvell's most famous poem, "To His Coy Mistress," is a tightly structured argument.
d. "Ladies and gentlemen," said the emcee, "I am happy to present our guest speaker."
e. Historians Segal and Stineback note that the English settlers considered these epidemics "the hand of God making room for His followers in the 'New World.' "

EXERCISE 39–1, page 317

a. I was born in Davenport, Iowa.
b. Pat helped Jeff put the tail on his kite, which was made of scraps from old dresses, and off they went to the park.
c. Correct
d. Every person there—from the youngest toddler to the oldest great-grandparent—was expected to sit through the three-hour sermon in respectful silence.
e. The class stood, faced the flag, placed hands over hearts, and raced through "I pledge allegiance . . . liberty and justice for all" in less than sixty seconds.

EXERCISE 40–1, page 323

a. Correct
b. A number of government officials have been reviewing the records of some small brokerage firms in the area.
c. Correct

d. The first discovery of America was definitely not in A.D. 1492.
e. Denzil spent all night studying for his psychology exam.

EXERCISE 41–1, page 325

a. We have ordered four azaleas, three rhododendrons, and two mountain laurels for the back area of the garden.
b. Correct
c. Correct
d. We ordered three 4-door sedans for the company executives.
e. The Vietnam Veterans Memorial in Washington, D.C., had 58,132 names inscribed on it when it was dedicated in 1982.

EXERCISE 42–1, page 328

a. Howard Hughes commissioned the *Spruce Goose,* a beautifully built but thoroughly impractical wooden aircraft.
b. The old man screamed his anger, shouting to all of us, "I will not leave my money to you worthless layabouts!"
c. Even though it is almost always hot in Mexico in the summer, you can usually find a cool spot on one of the park benches in the town's *zócalo.*
d. Correct
e. *The City and the Pillar* was an early novel by Gore Vidal.

EXERCISE 44–1, page 340

a. Correct
b. The swiftly moving tugboat pulled up alongside the barge and directed it away from the oil spill in the harbor.
c. Correct
d. Your dog is well known in our neighborhood.
e. Roadblocks were set up along all the major highways leading out of the city.

EXERCISE 45–1, page 345

a. District Attorney Bax was disgusted when the jurors turned in a verdict of not guilty after only one hour of deliberation.
b. My mother has begun to research the history of her Cherokee ancestors in Georgia.
c. Correct
d. Refugees from Central America are finding it more and more difficult to cross the Rio Grande into the United States.
e. I obtained profiles of both candidates from a useful Web site called *Vote Smart Web.*

EXERCISE 47–1, page 360

a. hasty generalization; b. false analogy; c. emotional appeal; d. faulty cause-and-effect reasoning; e. *either . . . or* fallacy

EXERCISE 57–1, page 474

a. sun, assistance; b. Pride, bottom, mistakes; c. trouble, rat (noun/adjective), race, rat; d. censorship, flick, dial; e. Figures, liars

EXERCISE 57–2, page 477

a. He, every (pronoun/adjective); b. those, who; c. I, some (pronoun/adjective), that, I, myself; d. I, You, He; e. She, her (pronoun/adjective)

EXERCISE 57-3, page 479

a. have been; b. are; c. does bring down; d. is, could rephrase; e. Throw, will emerge

EXERCISE 57-4, page 481

a. Adjectives: General, wrong; adverb: generally; b. Adjectives: The (article), American, tolerant; adverb: wonderfully; c. Adjectives: a (article), rational; adverb: not; d. Adjectives: A (article), clean, a (article), dirty; adverb: often; e. Adjective: the (article); adverb: faster

EXERCISE 58-1, page 486

a. Complete subjects: Sticks and stones, words; simple subjects: Sticks, stones, words; b. Complete subject: all facts; simple subject: facts; c. Complete subject: (You); d. Complete subject: nothing except change; simple subject: nothing; e. Complete subject: The only difference between a rut and a grave; simple subject: difference

EXERCISE 58-2, page 489

a. Subject complement: truth; b. Direct object: the depth of a river; c. Subject complement: yellow; d. Direct object: a man [or a woman]; object complement: wise; e. Indirect objects: me, you; direct objects: a capitalist, a bloodsucker

EXERCISE 59-1, page 492

a. without any liabilities (adjective phrase modifying *sheet*); b. of several air traffic controllers (adjective phrase modifying *job*), with ease (adverb phrase modifying *could perform*); c. like a loose garment (adverb phrase modifying *wears*); d. of a nation (adjective phrase modifying *ideals*), by its advertising (adverb phrase modifying *can tell*); e. In France (adverb phrase modifying *is*)

EXERCISE 59-2, page 496

a. who has outposts in your head (adjective clause modifying *enemy*); b. that doesn't bite (adjective clause modifying *rattlesnake*); c. When I am an old woman (adverb clause modifying *shall wear*); d. what they mean (noun clause used as direct object of *say*); e. unless it is practiced on clever persons (adverb clause modifying *is*)

EXERCISE 59-3, page 498

a. being sixteen (gerund phrase used as subject complement); b. being punctual (gerund phrase used as object of the preposition *with*), to appreciate it (infinitive phrase modifying *is*); c. to paint the color of the wind (infinitive phrase modifying *attempt*); d. Being a philosopher (participial phrase modifying *I*); e. to be older (infinitive phrase used as direct object of *wanted*)

EXERCISE 60-1, page 502

a. Complex; who sleep like a baby (adjective clause); b. Compound; c. Simple; d. Complex; If you don't go to other people's funerals (adverb clause); e. Compound-complex; what you are afraid of (noun clause)

(continued from page vi)

The American Heritage Dictionary of the English Language, Third Edition, from the entry "regard." Copyright © 1992 by Houghton Mifflin Company. Reprinted by permission from *The American Heritage Dictionary of the English Language,* Third Edition.

Eugene Boe, from "Pioneers to Eternity: Norwegians on the Prairie," from *The Immigrant Experience*, edited by Thomas C. Wheeler. Copyright © 1971 by Thomas C. Wheeler. Reprinted by permission of Doubleday, a division of Bantam Doubleday Dell Publishing.

Jane Brody, from *Jane Brody's Nutrition Book*. Copyright © 1981 by Jane E. Brody. Reprinted by permission of W. W. Norton & Company, Inc. and Wendy Weil Agency, Inc.

California Mountain Lion Page from the Sierra Club Web site (< http://www .sierraclub.org/chapters/ca/mountain-lion >). Copyright © 1996 by the Sierra Club.

Roger Caras, from "What's a Koala?" Copyright © 1983 by Roger Caras. First appeared in *Geo* magazine, May 1983. Reprinted by permission of Curtis Brown, Ltd.

Bruce Catton, from "Grant and Lee: A Study in Contrasts," from *The American Story*, edited by Earl Schenck Miers. Copyright © 1956 by U.S. Capitol Historical Society, all rights reserved.

Barnaby Conrad III, from " 'Train of Kings, the King of Trains' Is Back on Track," *Smithsonian*, December 1983. Reprinted by permission of *Smithsonian*.

Earl Conrad, from *Harriet Tubman*. Copyright © 1943, 1969 by Earl Conrad. Reprinted by permission of Paul S. Eriksson, Publisher.

James Underwood Crockett, Oliver E. Allen, and the Editors of Time-Life Books, from *The Time-Life Encyclopedia of Gardening: Wildflower Gardening*. Copyright © 1977 Time-Life Books, Inc.

Emily Dickinson, from "The Snake." Reprinted by permission of the publishers and the Trustees of Amherst College from *The Poems of Emily Dickinson*. Thomas H. Johnson, Ed. Cambridge, Mass.: The Belknap Press of Harvard University Press. Copyright © 1951, 1955, 1979, 1983 by the President and Fellows of Harvard College.

Excerpt from *The Dorling Kindersley Encyclopedia of Fishing*. Copyright © 1994 Dorling Kindersley. Reprinted with permission.

Stephen Jay Gould, from "Were Dinosaurs Dumb?" from *The Panda's Thumb: More Reflections on Natural History*. Copyright © 1978 by Stephen Jay Gould. Reprinted by permission of W. W. Norton & Company, Inc.

Dan Gutman, from *The Way Baseball Works*. Reprinted with permission of Simon & Schuster. Copyright © 1996 by Byron Preiss and Richard Ballantine, Inc.

Hillary Hauser, from "Exploring a Sunken Realm in Australia." *National Geographic*, January 1984. Reprinted by permission of the National Geographic Society.

Richard Hofstadter, from *America at 1750: A Social Portrait*. Copyright © 1971 by Beatrice Hofstadter, executrix of the estate of Richard Hofstadter. Reprinted by permission of Alfred A. Knopf, Inc.

William Least Heat Moon, from *Blue Highways*. Copyright © 1982 by William Least Heat Moon. Reprinted by permission of Little, Brown and Company.

Xia Li and Nancy Crane, "Electronic Sources: APA Style of Citation," from *Electronic Styles: A Handbook of Citing Electronic Information,* by Xia Li and Nancy Crane. Copyright © 1996 by Information Today, Inc., Medford, NJ. Reprinted by permission of Information Today, Inc.

Margaret Mead, from "New Superstitions for Old," *A Way of Seeing*. Reprinted by permission of William Morrow & Company, Inc.

Gloria Naylor, from *Linden Hills*. Copyright © 1985 by Gloria Naylor. Used by permission of Viking Penguin, a division of Penguin Books USA, Inc.

Portland Community College home page and Netscape browser frame. Copyright © 1998 by Portland Community College. Reprinted with permission of Russell Banks, Division of Publications, Portland Community College. Copyright © 1998 Netscape Communications Corp. All Rights Reserved. This electronic file or page may not be reprinted or copied without the express written permission of Netscape. Netscape Communications Corporation has not authorized, sponsored, endorsed, or approved this publication and is not responsible for its contents. Netscape and Netscape Communications Corporate Logos are trademarks and trade names of Netscape Communications Corporation. All product names and/or logos are trademarks of their respective owners.

Purdue University Libraries Web Site Home Page. All contents Copyright © 1998 Purdue University. All Rights Reserved. This is the official World Wide Web page of Purdue University.

Chet Raymo, from "Curious Stuff, Water and Ice." *The Boston Globe*, January 27, 1986. Reprinted by permission of the author.

Paul Reps, from "The Moon Cannot Be Stolen," from *Zen Flesh, Zen Bones*. Reprinted by permission of Charles E. Tuttle Co., Inc., of North Clarendon, Vermont, and Tokyo, Japan. First printing © 1957.

Anne Rudloe and Jack Rudloe, from "Electric Warfare: The Fish That Kill with Thunderbolts," *Smithsonian,* August 1993. Copyright © Anne Rudloe and Jack Rudloe.

Lewis Thomas, from "On Societies as Organisms." Copyright © 1971 by the Massachusetts Medical Society, from *The Lives of a Cell* by Lewis Thomas. Reprinted by permission of Viking Penguin, a division of Penguin Putnam Inc.

Olivia Vlahos, from *Human Beginnings*. Published by Viking Penguin, Inc. Reprinted by permission of the author.

Index

A Writer's Online Resources

Thomas: Legislative Information on the Internet	< http://thomas.loc.gov >
U.S. State & Local Gateway	< http://www.statelocal.gov >
U.S. Government Printing Office	< http://www.access.gpo.gov >
United Nations	< http://www.un.org >

NEWS SITES

The New York Times on the Web	< http://www.nytimes.com >
The Washington Post	< http://www.washingtonpost.com >
U.S. News Online	< http://www.usnews.com/usnews/home.htm >
nationalgeographic.com	< http://www.nationalgeographic.com/main.html >
CNN Interactive	< http://www.cnn.com >

NEWSGROUPS AND LISTSERVS

Tile.Net	< http://www.tile.net >
Liszt	< http://www.liszt.com >
Deja News	< http://www.dejanews.com >

BEDFORD/ST. MARTIN'S SITES

Hacker Handbook Home Page	< http://www.bedfordstmartins.com/hacker >
Research and Documentation Online (links to sites in a variety of disciplines)	< http://www.bedfordstmartins.com/hacker/resdoc >
Bedford Links to Resources in Literature	< http://www.bedfordstmartins.com/litlinks >
Bedford/St. Martin's Links to History Resources	< http://www.bedfordstmartins.com/history/historylinks.html >

SITES FOR EVALUATING SOURCES

"Checklist for Evaluating Web Sites," *Canisius College Library & Internet*	< http://www.canisius.edu/canhp/canlib/webcrit.htm >
"Evaluating Web Sites: Criteria and Tools," *Olin Kroch Uris Libraries*	< http://www.library.cornell.edu/okuref/research/webeval.html >
"Evaluating Internet Information," *Internet Navigator*	< http://sol.slcc.edu/lr/navigator/discovery/eval.html >

ESL Menu

Boldface numbers refer to sections of the handbook.

Revision Symbols

abbr	faulty abbreviation	**40**
ad	adverb or adjective	**26**
add	Add needed word	**10**
agr	agreement	**21, 22**
appr	inappropriate language **17**	
art	article	**30**
awk	awkward	
cap	capital letter	**45**
case	case	**24, 25**
cliché	cliché	**18e**
coh	coherence	**4e**
coord	coordination	**8b**
cs	comma splice	**20**
dev	inadequate development	**4b**
dm	dangling modifier	**12e**
-ed	*-ed* ending	**27d**
emph	emphasis	**14**
ESL	English as a second language	**29–31**
exact	inexact language	**18**
frag	sentence fragment	**19**
fs	fused sentence	**20**
gl/us	see Glossary of Usage	
hyph	hyphen	**44**
idiom	idiom	**18d**
inc	incomplete construction **10**	
irreg	irregular verb	**27a**
ital	italics (underlining)	**42**
jarg	jargon	**17a**
lc	use lowercase letter	**45**
mix	mixed construction	**11**
mm	misplaced modifier	**12a–d**
mood	mood	**28b**
nonst	nonstandard usage	**17d, 27**
num	numbers	**41**
om	omitted word	**10, 30, 31a**

p	punctuation	
⌃	comma	**32**
no ,	no comma	**33**
;	semicolon	**34**
:	colon	**35**
⌄	apostrophe	**36**
" "	quotation marks	**37**
. ? !	period, question mark, exclamation point	**38**
— ( )	dash, parentheses,	
[ ] …	brackets, ellipses marks,	
/	slash	**39**
¶	paragraph	**4**
pass	ineffective passive	**14a, 28c**
pn agr	pronoun agreement	**22**
proof	proofreading problem	**3c**
ref	pronoun reference	**23**
run-on	run-on sentence	**20**
-s	*-s* ending on verb	**21, 27c**
sexist	sexist language	**17f, 22a**
shift	distracting shift	**13**
sl	slang	**17d**
sp	misspelled word	**43**
sub	subordination	**8**
sv agr	subject-verb agreement	**21, 27c**
t	error in verb tense	**28a**
trans	transition needed	**4e**
usage	see Glossary of Usage	
v	voice	**14a, 28c**
var	sentence variety	**8, 15**
vb	problem with verb	**27–29**
w	wordy	**16**
//	faulty parallelism	
∧	insert	
x	obvious error	
#	insert space	
⌒	close up space	

Detailed Menu